STUDIES IN LINGUISTICS

Edited by
Laurence Horn
Yale University

A ROUTLEDGE SERIES

Studies in Linguistics

Laurence Horn, *General Editor*

Syllable Weight

Phonetics, Phonology, Typology

Matthew Kelly Gordon

Routledge
New York & London

Routledge
Taylor & Francis Group
270 Madison Avenue
New York, NY 10016

Routledge
Taylor & Francis Group
2 Park Square
Milton Park, Abingdon
Oxon OX14 4RN

© 2006 by Taylor & Francis Group, LLC
Routledge is an imprint of Taylor & Francis Group, an Informa business

Printed in the United States of America on acid-free paper
10 9 8 7 6 5 4 3 2 1

International Standard Book Number-10: 0-415-97609-X (Hardcover)
International Standard Book Number-13: 978-0-415-97609-1 (Hardcover)

Library of Congress Cataloging-in-Publication Data

Gordon, Matthew Kelly.
    Syllable weight : phonetics, phonology, typology / Matthew Kelly Gordon.
       p. cm. -- (Studies in linguistics)
    Includes bibliographical references and index.
    ISBN 0-415-97609-X (alk. paper)
    1. Grammar, Comparative and general--Syllable. 2. Phonetics. 3. Language and languages--Variation. 4. Typology (Linguistics) I. Title.

P236.G67 2006
414'.6--dc22
                                                           2006025492

Visit the Taylor & Francis Web site at
http://www.taylorandfrancis.com

and the Routledge Web site at
http://www.routledge-ny.com

Contents

Preface

Phonologists have long known that many prosodic phenomena are sensitive to the inherent "weight" of syllables. For example, Latin preferentially stresses closed syllables and syllables containing long vowels over open syllables containing a short vowel (Allen 1973). Closed syllables and syllables containing long vowels are thus heavy in the Latin stress system. In addition to stress, many other prosodic phenomena have been argued to instantiate weight: poetic metrics, tone, compensatory lengthening, etc.

This thesis explores the idea that syllable weight is driven by phonetic considerations. As a starting point in the investigation, results of an extensive typological survey of syllable weight in approximately 400 languages are presented. This survey suggests that weight is not a property of languages, as predicted by most contemporary theories, but rather is more closely linked to the particular phonological phenomenon involved. It is argued that the primarily process-specific nature of weight is attributed to differences in the phonetic demands imposed by different processes. To illustrate the process-driven nature of syllable weight, focus is on phonetic studies of two weight-sensitive phenomena with divergent phonetic underpinnings: weight-sensitive tone and weight-sensitive stress. Weight-sensitive tone is shown to be guided by the requirement that tonal contrasts be realized on a sufficiently sonorous backdrop to allow for auditory recovery of tonal information. Weight-sensitive stress, on the other hand, is argued to be sensitive to a syllable's auditory loudness, which captures the auditory system's net response to an acoustic stimulus over time. Phonetic considerations are demonstrated to both constrain the range of cross-linguistic variation in weight criteria and also to predict the language specific choice of weight criteria for a given phenomenon.

In addition to being phonetically motivated, it is also shown that the phonology of weight is guided by the requirement that the phonological processes manipulate structurally simple classes of segments. Weight distinctions that are too complex phonologically are avoided, even if they provide a better fit to the phonetic map than other simpler criteria. The result is a compromise between phonetic sensibility and phonological simplicity.

This book is a slightly revised version of a UCLA dissertation completed in 1999. Portions of the material have been reproduced with permission from Cambridge University Press from a chapter "Syllable weight" in the book *Phonetically Based Phonology* (edited by Bruce Hayes, Robert Kirchner, and Donca Steriade, 2004, Cambridge University Press). Material has also been reproduced with permission from the Linguistic Society of America from an article "A phonetically-driven account of syllable weight" appearing in the journal *Language* (vol. 78, 2002, pp. 51–80).

Acknowledgments

There are many people to whom I owe a great debt of gratitude for the inspiration, ideas, time, and support that made completion of this dissertation possible. Although their contributions have greatly improved this work, they should in no way be held responsible for the shortcomings that certainly remain.

First of all, I am deeply indebted to my committee members, Bruce Hayes, Ian Maddieson, Pam Munro, Ralph Sonnenschein, and Donca Steriade, for their abundant intellectual and moral support as I've thought and re-thought the data, the analysis, and the views presented here.

My advisor, Bruce Hayes, has contributed to this dissertation and, more generally, my development as a linguist in more ways than could possibly be apparent in reading what follows. He has always been there for me, contributing crucial insights and encouraging me to approach my work with renewed rigor during moments of mental fatigue or uncertainty. Beyond the actual ideas and advice that he has so generously contributed, Bruce has taught me that being a good linguist involves taking risks. For this valuable lesson and many others, I thank him.

Ian Maddieson also contributed greatly to this work through his meticulous comments and thoughtful advice, particularly in matters phonetic. He has taught me the important skill of looking at data closely and extracting the meaningful patterns.

Pam Munro has been a constant source of encouragement and technical advice in all matters linguistic, always steering me toward new and interesting data (as well as speakers). Thanks to her support, I never lost confidence even in moment of doubts and uncertainty.

Ralph Sonnenschein has always been a welcome and reassuring face in the audience; his comments and questions have helped me to keep in mind the place of linguistics in the broader scientific context.

I have benefited enormously from my discussions with Donca Steriade, who has provided me with clever ideas and insights I could not have possibly had on my own. Although she may not agree with everything contained in this book, her comments and suggestions have made this a far stronger work than it would otherwise have been.

Beyond my committee members, there are numerous other people whose data, comments, and ideas appear in the pages that follow. Thanks to the UCLA faculty members who contributed their time and advice. Thanks to Sun-Ah Jun, Pat Keating, and Peter Ladefoged for their helpful input in phonetic and presentational matters. Also, thanks to Russ Schuh for assistance with the Hausa data and discussion. Other people whom I thank for their contributions include the following (I offer my humble apologies in advance to anyone whom I might have unwittingly overlooked here): Adam Albright, Arto Anttila, Diana Archangeli, Marco Baroni, Taehong Cho, Abby Cohn, Katherine Crosswhite, Susanna Cumming, Jack Dubois, Gorka Elordieta, Edward Flemming, Cecile Fougeron, Ed Garrett, Carol Genetti, Steve Greenberg, Mike Hammond, Larry Hyman, Chai-Shune Hsu, Kathleen Hubbard, Larry Hyman, Sun-Ah Jun, Michael Kenstowicz, Pat Keating, Paul Kiparsky, Robert Kirchner, Jody Kreiman, Paul De Lacy, Peter Ladefoged, Margaret MacEachern, Ian Maddieson, Armin Mester, Pamela Munro, David Perlmutter, Janet Pierrehumbert, Doug Pulleyblank, Sharon Rose, Barry Schein, Dan Silverman, Sumiko Takayanagi, Kim Thomas, Motoko Ueyama, Draga Zec, Jie Zhang, Cheryl Zoll, and audiences at the 19th GLOW Colloquium in Athens, the 23rd meeting of the Berkeley Linguistics Society, the 3rd annual SWOT meeting at UCLA in 1996, and at UCLA, Cornell, MIT, USC, Northwestern, University of Hawaii, UCSB, and UCSD for their helpful feedback and suggestions. A warm thank you is also owed to the speakers who so graciously and patiently contributed the phonetic data contained in this book.

Finally, I wish to thank family members who provided me with much needed emotional support and helped me to never get too lost in my linguistic books. Thanks to my mother and father who have always offered me their unconditional support in matters academic and otherwise and who have always encouraged me to pursue my interests and aspirations and to not let fear of failure stand in my way.

And last but certainly not least, a special debt of gratitude is owed to my wife, Rhonda, for always believing in me, bringing me happiness, and showing me that there's more to life than linguistics.

Chapter One
Introduction

1.0 BACKGROUND

Linguists have long observed that certain phonological phenomena in many languages distinguish between "heavy" and "light" syllables (e.g. Jakobson 1931, Trubetzkoy 1939, Allen 1973, Newman 1972, Hyman 1977, McCarthy 1979a,b, etc.). For example, Latin preferentially stressed closed syllables and syllables containing long vowels over open syllables containing a short vowel (Allen 1973). Closed syllables and syllables containing long vowels were thus heavier in weight than open syllables containing a short vowel in Latin.

While the exact definition of syllable weight is elusive, it may be defined very broadly as that property which differentiates syllables with respect to their prosodic behavior. The difficulty in explicitly defining syllable weight lies in determining which prosodic aspects of language fall under the rubric of weight. As indicated by the Latin stress example above, stress figures prominently among those phenomena considered to involve syllable weight. The domain of weight, however, is not limited to stress. Other phenomena that are potentially sensitive to the weight of syllables include poetic metrics, compensatory lengthening, tone assignment, quantitative aspects of syllable structure, and reduplication. We consider here how these weight sensitive processes instantiate weight. In many languages, only certain types of syllables, the heavier ones, may carry contour tones (Hyman 1985, Duanmu 1994a,b). Weight distinctions are also relevant in many poetic traditions, in which the placement of syllables within the meter is governed by their weight (Hayes 1988). Similarly, many languages have constraints on the minimal size of many classes of words, typically content words. In such languages, words that are subminimal, or not heavy enough, are either disallowed or strongly restricted in their distribution (McCarthy and Prince 1986, 1990, 1995a). Many processes that lengthen or shorten syllables or segments also have been argued to fall under the rubric of weight-based phenomena. For example, long vowels do not occur in closed syllables in many languages, a restriction that has been argued to result from constraints on the maximum weight of the syllable (Steriade 1991, Hayes 1995). Reduplication has also been argued to be a weight sensitive process, because the reduplicant in many languages assumes a certain prosodic shape that appears to conform to some weight standard (McCarthy and Prince 1986, 1990, 1995a). All of these processes superficially have in common that they are sensitive to the phonological weight of syllables.

1.1. FORMAL REPRESENTATIONS OF WEIGHT

As the number of prosodic phenomena argued to instantiate syllable weight has grown, the notion of weight has played an increasingly larger role in phonological theory. In response to the burgeoning role of syllable weight in linguistic theory, phonologists have developed simple yet compelling representations of weight grounded in fundamental concepts such as phonemic length, segment count and sonority.

Of these theories of weight, the two that have gained widest acceptance are skeletal slot models, including CV and X slot models (McCarthy 1979a,b, Steriade 1982, Clements and Keyser 1983, Levin 1985), and moraic models (Hyman 1985, Hayes 1989). The appeal of both of these models is that they assume representations that are projected from independently contrastive properties such as segmental and length distinctions. Units of weight, either skeletal slots (in CV and X slot models) or moras, are assigned to segments. Syllables with a greater number of segments logically receive a greater number of weight units. Similarly, contrasts in segmental length are represented by assigning long segments two weight units, while short segments are associated with one unit of weight. Weight distinctions are thus reducible to differences in the number of units of weight in the syllable. Syllables with a greater number of weight units are "heavier" than syllables with fewer weight units.

The link between syllable weight and the representations designed to model it becomes clearer if we consider the case of Latin, using both moraic and skeletal slot models of weight. Recall from above that Latin preferentially stresses closed syllables and syllables containing long vowels over open syllables containing short vowels. The Latin primary stress rule that demonstrates this weight distinction is as follows: primary stress falls on a heavy penultimate syllable, equivalent to a closed syllable (1a) or one containing a long vowel or diphthong (1b). If the penult is not heavy, stress retracts onto the antepenult (1c) (Allen 1973).

(1) Latin stress
    a. kar'pentum 'carriage'
    b. a'miːkuːs 'friend'
    c. 'simile 'similar' nom., acc.sg. neuter

1.1.1. Skeletal slot models of weight

First let us consider the representation of Latin weight in a skeletal slot model (McCarthy 1979a,b, Clements and Keyser 1983, Levin 1985); the one presented here is that of Levin (1985). In skeletal slot models, the syllable is divided into constituents. Syllables consist of a nucleus, typically a vowel, which may be preceded by one or more consonants (the syllable onset) and also (in many languages) may be followed by one or more consonants (the coda). Together the nucleus and the coda form a constituent termed the rime (or rhyme). Short segments each project a timing position while long segments project two. In Latin, as in virtually all languages, the onset is ignored for purposes of calculating weight (but see Chapter Four). Only segments (and their associated skeletal slots) that belong to the rime contribute to the weight of a syllable.

The Latin weight distinction has a fairly straightforward representation in this model, as shown in Figure 1.1. (A syllable with both a long vowel and a coda consonant is also heavy, of course, since it contains three timing positions in the rime.)

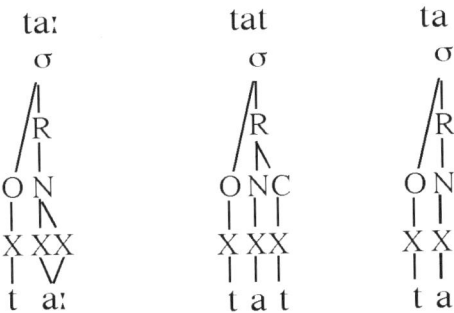

Figure 1.1. Skeletal slot representations of three syllable types

1.1.2. Moraic models of weight

Now let us consider the representation of Latin weight in moraic theory (Hyman 1985, Hayes, 1989). The units of weight in moraic theory are moras.

The weightless nature of onsets is directly captured by assuming that onsets are non-moraic. Contrasts in duration between short and long segments are represented as differences in mora count, parallel to the representation of duration contrasts as differences in the number of timing positions in skeletal slot models. Short segments receive one mora and long segments receive two, as shown in Figure 1.2. In Latin, consonants following a tautosyllabic vowel, i.e. those corresponding to coda consonants in skeletal slot models, are also moraic. The heavy vs. light distinction is thus captured succinctly in terms of mora count; syllables with at least two moras are heavy.

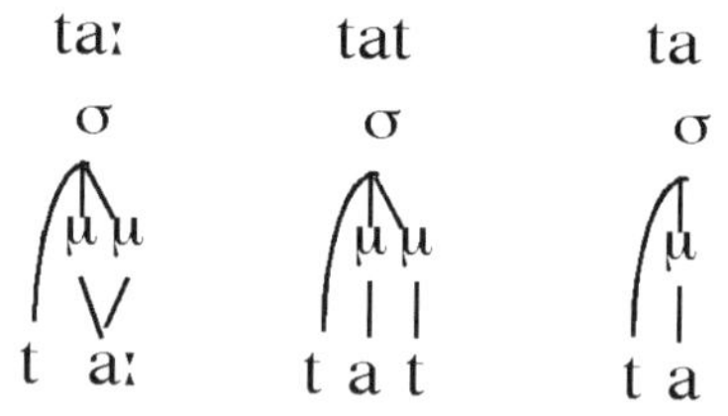

Figure 1.2. Moraic representations of three syllable types

1.1.3. Representations of Weight and Cross-Linguistic Variation in Weight Criteria

Clearly both skeletal slot and moraic models are well equipped to handle weight distinctions of the Latin type according to which closed syllables and syllables containing long vowels are heavy. The Latin weight distinction, however, is not the only weight criterion observed cross-linguistically. Another quite common weight distinction is one that treats only syllables containing long vowels as heavy. For example, in Khalkha Mongolian (Bosson 1964, Walker 1995, 1996), syllables with long vowels, including diphthongs, are heavy, while those containing short vowels are light, whether they are open or not.

The Khalkha weight distinction requires a slight expansion of the principles underlying the representations presented in Figures 1.1 and 1.2. Skeletal slot models must assume that the domain over which weight is calculated may differ between languages. Weight may be calculated over either the entire rime, as in Latin, or over just the nucleus, as in Khalkha. The moraic model must assume that the weight of coda consonants is subject to language specific parameterization, Hayes' (1989) Weight by Position parameter. In languages like Latin, coda consonants are moraic, whereas in languages like Khalkha, they are not.

Interestingly, the Khalkha and Latin type weight distinctions do not exhaust the range of cross-linguistic variation in weight systems. As the database on weight sensitive phenomena available to theoretical phonologists has expanded to include information on a larger cross-section of languages, a diverse array of weight systems has been unearthed, necessitating expansions of the formal apparatus available to theories of weight.

Several languages, e.g. Komi Jaz'va (Itkonen 1955), Chukchi (Skorik 1961, Kenstowicz 1997), Kobon (Davies 1980, Kenstowicz 1997), Yimas (Foley 1991), which base their weight distinctions on neither segment count nor phonemic length contrasts, but rather on vowel quality, have attracted attention in the literature (see Chapter Two). Representing weight contrasts based on vowel quality in terms of differences in the number of weight units is problematic, since moras and skeletal slots are assumed to be projected from contrasts in segment length, not contrasts in segment quality.

Phonologists have also relatively recently noted the existence of languages with greater than binary weight distinctions (see Chapter Two). For example, stress systems in several languages, e.g. Klamath (Barker 1964), Chickasaw (Munro and Willmond 1994), Mam (England 1983, 1986), draw a ternary weight distinction with long vowels and diphthongs (CVV) at the top of the weight hierarchy, closed syllables containing a short vowel (CVC) in the middle, and open syllables containing a short vowel (CV) at the bottom. The representation of a ternary weight distinction of this type as a contrast in numbers of weight units requires that the heaviest syllable in the hierarchy, CVV, receive three moras. This practical necessity, however, violates the principle that representations of weight are projected from contrasts in length. This principle dictates that long vowels should receive two and not three moras. Recent work has even documented the existence of languages with greater than three levels of weight for stress assignment (see Chapter Two), e.g. Kobon (Davies 1980, Kenstowicz 1997), Kara (de Lacy 1997).

1.2. INCONSISTENCY OF WEIGHT CRITERIA

Another standard notion of weight which recent research has shown to be problematic is the view that weight is consistent across phenomena within the same language (Hyman 1985, McCarthy and Prince 1986, 1995b, Zec 1988, Hayes 1989). According to this hypothesis, which I will term the "moraic uniformity hypothesis," all weight sensitive phenomena within a single language observe the same weight criterion and thus employ the same weight representations. Standard representations of weight have captured the assumption that weight is a property of languages by parameterizing weight criteria. For example, Hayes' (1989) moraic theory assumes that coda weight is parameterized; some languages assign a mora to syllable-final (coda) consonants by the Weight by Position parameter, while others do not. Similarly, in skeletal slot models (e.g. Levin 1985), the syllabic affiliation of sonorant consonants is parameterized on a language specific basis: some languages syllabify postvocalic sonorant consonants in the nucleus, while others syllabify them as codas.

Several exceptions to the moraic uniformity hypothesis have surfaced in recent literature, e.g. Steriade (1991), Crowhurst (1991), Hyman (1992), Hayes (1995). For example, Steriade (1991) shows that the stress system, the system of poetic metrics, and the minimal root requirement of Early and Classical Greek are sensitive to different weight criteria from the pitch accent system. At both historical stages of Greek, the stress and metrical systems as well as the minimal root requirement treat both CVV and CVC as heavy. Pitch accent weight criteria are more stringent, however, at both stages. In Early Greek only CVV and syllables closed by a sonorant consonant (CVR) are heavy, while in Ancient Greek only CVV is heavy for purposes of pitch accent placement. A process of vowel shortening in syllables closed by a sonorant also points to the greater weight of CVR relative to syllables closed by an obstruent (CVO) in Early Greek. Crowhurst (1991), Hyman (1992), and Hayes (1995) present additional cases of non-uniformity of weight criteria within a single language.

Cases of conflicted weight criteria are problematic for two reasons. First, they necessarily require reference to at least three levels of weight in a single language. To see this, consider the case of Classical Greek (Steriade 1991). In Classical Greek, CVV is heavy for pitch accent assignment, minimal root requirements, and poetic metrics. CVC is heavy only in the metrical system and for the minimal word requirement but not for pitch accent placement. CV is light for all phenomena. Thus, collapsing all phenomena, CVV is heaviest, followed by CVC, followed by CV. For reasons discussed above, representing this ternary weight distinction is problematic in theories like moraic theory that encode weight distinctions as differences in number of timing positions. A ternary weight distinction requires that the heaviest syllable types, those containing long vowels, carry three moras, but long vowels should only be bimoraic. In fact, the potential for complex weight hierarchies involving more than three levels of weight grows as the number of weight-sensitive phenomena considered increases.

A second challenge presented by cases of conflicted weight criteria concerns the fundamental conception of weight as a language-driven rather than a process-driven phenomenon. Given the increasing number of cases of conflicted weight criteria reported in the literature, it seems worthwhile to explore systematically the alternative and equally plausible hypothesis that weight is more a function of process rather than language. Under this view, variation in weight criteria would be attributed principally to differences between weight-based *phenomena* in the weight distinctions they characteristically employ, rather than to differences between *languages*. For example, it could turn out that weight-sensitive tone tends to observe different weight criteria than weight-sensitive stress and that this process specificity accounts for many cases of conflicted weight criteria. If this scenario turned out to be true, the focus of the theory of weight should shift from explaining how and why languages differ in terms of their weight criteria to addressing how and why weight criteria differ between weight-sensitive phenomena. Exploring weight as not only a language-driven but also a process-driven property also has the potential to provide insight into cases of weight uniformity. To see how examination of the process specific nature of weight is potentially useful, consider the following hypothetical scenario. Let us suppose that coda consonants did not count in determining minimal word requirements in the majority of languages. Similarly, suppose that coda consonants also did not count in determining weight for tone in most languages of the world. This would raise two questions. First, we might ask why codas are characteristically weightless for computing minimal word requirements. Second, we would also want to know why codas are also weightless for purposes of tone in most languages. Crucially, in this hypothetical scenario in which codas are characteristically weightless for both tone and minimal word requirements, even if we were to find a language (in fact, even if we found many such languages) in which coda consonants were weightless for both tone and minimal word requirements, this would not provide support for the view that weight is uniform as a function of language. Rather, assuming that other weight-sensitive phenomena did not display the same cross-linguistic distribution of weight criteria as tone and minimal word requirements, the convergence of weight criteria for tone and minimal words within the same language would be an artifact of the process specificity of weight criteria for these two phenomena: both processes exploit substantially the same weight criterion cross-linguistically. The moral of this story is that, when considering the evidence for uniformity of weight, it is as important to pay attention to the cross-linguistic weight patterns displayed by a single process as to any convergences or divergences of weight criteria within the same language.

Steriade (1991) and Hayes (1995) represent preliminary attempts to introduce process specificity into the theory of weight. These works propose representations designed to account for languages in which one phenomenon or set of phenomena treats both CVV and CVC as heavy while another treats only a subset of these syllable types (usually CVV) as heavy. They also offer tentative observations about which phenomena tend to observe one criterion and which characteristically observe a different criterion. Neither account, however, systematically tests these observations against a large set of data. Furthermore, while both theories attempt to accommodate cases of conflicted weight criteria, neither explicitly addresses the question of whether weight should be modeled as a primarily language-driven or process-driven property.

One of the principal goals of this work is to explore the hypothesis that weight is primarily a property of languages and compare it to the alternative view that weight is mainly a feature of individual processes. To the extent that weight is a property of languages and not of processes, we are justified in parameterizing representations of weight on a language specific basis. If, however, examination of a large set of data demonstrated that weight is more a function of the particular process under consideration than the language involved, we must seek explanations and representations unique to each phenomenon or set of phenomena. Only by examining multiple weight sensitive phenomena in a large number of languages are we able to determine the extent to which weight is determined on a language or process specific basis.

The language- versus process specific nature of weight criteria may be considered from two different angles. First, we may look at languages with more than one weight sensitive process and see whether different phenomena respect the same weight criterion. This is the method that has formed the basis for the discussion up to now. Another possibility is to look at all languages displaying a particular weight sensitive process to determine which criteria are most common for that process cross-linguistically. This can be done for several different weight sensitive processes. Both procedures potentially provide important information about the nature of syllable weight. Weight uniformity will be considered from both of these angles in this work.

Another major goal of this book is to explain the nature and reasons for variation in weight criteria, both variation attributed to process specificity and variation due to language specific properties. We will also propose formal representations of weight and explore how these representations are couched within a formal analysis of weight. The paradigm adopted here for the analyses is that of Optimality Theory (Prince and Smolensky 2004) which is well-suited to capturing the scalar nature of weight and the role of both process specificity and language specificity in the theory of weight.

1.3. THE STRUCTURE OF THE BOOK

The structure of the book is as follows. Chapter Two lays out the basic proposals developed in this work. First, weight will be shown to be more process-specific than language specific. This point will be made based on a typology of weight in approximately 400 languages, focusing on weight-sensitive tone and weight-sensitive stress but also briefly surveying four other weight-sensitive phenomena. Second, Chapter Two advances a proposal that is developed more explicitly in later chapters: that weight criteria are chosen on the basis of a combination of phonetic effectiveness and phonological simplicity. Chapter Two also discusses other assumptions adopted in this book, including the representations of weight employed throughout the work.

Chapters Three and Four present detailed case studies of weight-sensitive tone and stress, respectively, the two phenomena that are the focus of this book. It is in Chapters Three and Four that the grounding of syllable weight in considerations of phonetic effectiveness and phonological simplicity is explored in detail, using phonetic data from several languages. Chapters Three and Four present formal analyses of representative weight-sensitive tone and stress systems, respectively. Chapter Five presents results of the typology of the weight-sensitive phenomena not discussed in detail in Chapter Two, i.e. phenomena other than weight-sensitive tone and stress. Chapter Six provides a summary of the principal findings of the book and directions for future research.

Chapter Two
The Typology of Weight

2.0 A SURVEY OF WEIGHT

This chapter examines the strength of the evidence for weight uniformity both as a function of process and as a function of language. As a starting point in the assessment of the evidence for weight uniformity, a cross-linguistic survey of six phonological phenomena commonly assumed to instantiate weight was conducted. These phenomena are listed in Table 2.1.

Table 2.1. Six weight-sensitive phenomena examined in the survey
- weight-sensitive stress
- weight-sensitive tone
- minimal word requirements
- metrics
- compensatory lengthening
- syllable template phenomena, i.e. closed syllable vowel shortening

Of these six phenomena, the two that serve as the focus of this chapter, and indeed, the focus of the entire book, are weight-sensitive stress and weight-sensitive tone, comparison of which provides crucial insight into the nature of weight as a primarily process-driven phenomenon. Discussion of the other phenomena, which also provides evidence for the process-specific nature of weight, will be limited in this chapter, but will be considered in greater depth in Chapter Five.

2.1. PRELIMINARY TO THE RESULTS: THE SYLLABLE AS A PHONOLOGICAL CONSTITUENT

Implicit in the discussion of weight is the notion that the syllable constitutes a real phonological constituent. If there were no syllables, it would be difficult to characterize the Latin stress rule, since it is the combination of the vowel and the immediately following coda consonant that makes the penultimate syllable heavy, and hence stress-attracting, in Latin (see section 1.1).

Many diagnostics, phonological, phonetic, and psycholinguistic, have been invoked in the literature to determine syllable affiliations, with weight-sensitive processes figuring prominently among the diagnostics. Phonotactic patterns have also been used to decompose words into syllables. For example, if a language does not allow any consonant clusters initially in the word, it is often assumed that a syllable boundary divides clusters of consonants word-internally, the logic being that the language has a uniform constraint against syllable-initial clusters in *all* positions of the word. Similarly, if all words in a language begin with a consonant, the standard conclusion is that any single intervocalic consonant belongs to the same syllable as the following vowel, under the assumption that all syllables must begin with a consonant. Language games have also been used to determine syllable breaks (see Bagemihl 1995 for a survey of the literature on language games). For example, certain languages allow groups of segments to be transposed to another position in the word; thus, the string /pakta/ may become /tapak/ in a hypothetical language game. Segments that move as a single unit, such as /ta/ and /pak/ in the preceding example, are often considered members of the same syllable.

Syllables also appear to have phonetic correlates in many languages. For example, vowels in closed syllables are in most languages phonetically shorter than their counterparts in open syllables (Maddieson 1985). Thus, if a vowel is shortened before a cluster of consonants but not before a single intervocalic consonant, this might provide evidence that at least the first consonant in the cluster belongs to the same syllable as the immediately preceding vowel. Segments may even have different realizations depending on their position in the syllable (e.g. /l/ in many dialects of English); in many cases, these diagnostics accord with other diagnostics of syllable structure. Furthermore, speakers may have strong intuitions about syllable boundaries.

The goal of this book is not to examine the evidence for the syllable as a valid constituent in phonology, an immense topic in and of itself. However, a working definition of the syllable is necessary to discuss phonological weight. For most of the data discussed in this paper, different diagnostics for syllable structure do not conflict with one another. Where there is some question about syllable affiliation, such as occasionally arises in the interpretation of tone bearing units, this will be mentioned in the appropriate places. Unless there is evidence to the contrary in a particular language, I will assume standard syllabification conventions: i.e. a single intervocalic consonant belongs to the same syllable as the immediately following vowel, and a syllable boundary divides sequences of two or more adjacent consonants.

2.2. METHODOLOGY OF THE SURVEY

The primary goal of the weight survey was to examine whether weight tends to be a property of languages or a property of individual phenomena, or a combination of both. As discussed in Chapter One, a large survey of weight can tackle this question from multiple angles. First, we can examine different weight-sensitive processes within the same language to determine the extent to which these processes converge on the same conclusions about weight in a single language. Second, we can look at a particular process in many languages to ascertain whether the same process tends to show the same weight distinctions in many languages. Ultimately, an examination of these issues will enable us to determine the significance of conflicts and convergences in weight criteria.

In order to meet these goals, the survey from which generalizations about weight are drawn must be diverse, both genetically and also, to the extent possible, geographically. Devising a diverse and representative survey is a difficult task for both methodological and practical reasons (see Maddieson 1984 for discussion of many of the issues involved in constructing a typology). The availability of materials on diverse languages is a particularly problematic issue given the type of data sought in a typology of weight. In many cases, consideration of certain weight-sensitive phenomena fell outside the scope of the grammar(s) consulted, through no fault of the authors, since it is quite difficult and time consuming to collect data on weight. In this regard, data on minimal word requirements, metrics, syllable template restrictions, and compensatory lengthening were particularly difficult to locate for most languages. Data on tone and stress, the focus of this work, were easier to access, though descriptions of these prosodic features were often incomplete in the grammars consulted. Generally, the set of grammars that were explicit and thorough enough to enable collection of weight data was only a subset of grammars useful in examining other more transparent phonological properties such as segment inventories.

Given these limitations, the survey must thus include only a subset of languages from each large genetic grouping (termed phyla), in order not to bias the survey in favor of better-documented language phyla. Despite the difficulties inherent in constructing a representative survey of weight, construction of such a survey seems a necessary and worthwhile step in enhancing our understanding of the nature of the weight. Although there will inevitably be gaps or deficiencies in any large-scale typology, I believe that the survey used in this work provides a reasonable gauge for assessing syllable weight on a cross-linguistic basis.

We will now outline the method employed in constructing the typology of syllable weight used in this book. The relatively conservative genetic groupings appearing in the Language Family Index of the twelfth edition of the Ethnologue (Grimes and Grimes 1993) served as the basis for the survey. At least two languages from each of the highest level grouping of languages, which I will term the phylum (i.e. the highest branch in each genetic grouping), were targeted for inclusion in the study. In order to construct a diverse survey, an attempt was made to include no more than two languages from any single language family, the level of classification above the individual languages themselves. As many language isolates and unclassified languages were included as data allowed, since their inclusion did not threaten to bias the data unfairly in favor of certain phyla. Nine language isolates were included in the survey. Only two (Movima and Warembori) of 136 languages that Grimes and Grimes list as unclassified were sufficiently documented to meet criteria for inclusion. (The extreme paucity of data on unclassified languages is perhaps not surprising assuming that languages remain unclassified, as opposed to being classified as language isolates, precisely because they are insufficiently documented to allow for classification.)

The fact that a maximum of two languages per family was targeted as opposed to some other number is the result of a compromise between the goals of achieving as large a survey as possible, but also one that did not unfairly skew the data in favor of better-documented language phyla. For certain language phyla, the target number of languages could either barely be achieved or could not be reached due to a paucity of data. Increasing the number of target languages would thus unfairly bias the survey in favor of better-documented phyla by including more data from better-documented phyla to the exclusion of other less studied phyla. Within each phylum, an attempt was made, as far as resources allowed, to choose diverse languages.

All told 408 languages were included in the survey of weight. Of the 408 languages, 238 are drawn from 19 phyla (each with at least 8 languages represented), with the remaining 159 languages coming from the other 52 phyla (including language isolates and unclassified languages) in Grimes and Grimes. There were 16 small phyla located in either South America or Papua New Guinea that could not be represented in the survey due to a lack of relevant data.

Languages included in the survey of weight appear below in Table 2.2 listed by phylum. Sources consulted for each language appear at the end of the book in Appendix One.

Table 2.2. The genetic classification of languages included in the survey of weight

Phylum	No.	Languages
1. Afro-Asiatic	16	Tamazight, Siwa, Musey, Lamang, Mulwi, Hausa, Somali, Oromo, Iraqw, Dizi, Mocha, Aramaic, Arabic, Tigre, Gurage, Amharic
2. Algic	6	Ojibwa, Menomini, Malecite-Passamaquoddy, Munsee, Blackfoot, Yurok
3. Altaic	10	Buriat, Khalkha, Moghol, Evenki, Even, Turkish, Chuvash, Tatar, Uzbek, Bashkir
4. Andamanese	2	Andamanese, Onge
5. Araucanian	1	Araucanian
6. Arawakan	6	Banawá, Guahibo, Paraujano, Asheninca Campa, Achagua, Arawak
7. Arutani-Sape	0	
8. Australian	6	Maung, Alawa, Djingili, Tiwi, Wardaman, Nyawaygi
9. Austro-Asiatic	13	Khmer, Khmu, Muong, Vietnamese, Sre, Khasi, Pacoh, Brao, Halang, Stieng, Mundari, Santali, Sapuan
10. Austronesian	26	Atayal, Paiwan, Tsou, Kavalan, Larike, Kisar, Kedang, Tetun, Sumbanese, West Tarangan, Loniu, Fijian, Ndumbea, Kara, Patep, Kilivila, Sawai, Murut, Malagasy, Chamorro, Cebuano, Manobo, Karao, Javanese, Malay, Yapese
11. Aymara	2	Aymara, Jaqaru
12. Caddoan	4	Wichita, Pawnee, Kitsai, Caddo
13. Cahuapanan	0	
14. Carib	8	Carib, Hixkaryana, Kashuyana, Pemon, Tiriyo, Waiwai, Machushi, Apalaí
15. Chapacura-Wanham	1	Wari'
16. Chibchan	2	Cuna, Cofán

(continued)

Table 2.2. The genetic classification of languages included in the survey of weight (*continued*)

Phylum	No.	Languages
17. Chimakuan	1	Quileute
18. Chon	1	Selknam
19. Chukotko-Kamchatkan	4	Chukchi, Alutor, Koryak, Kamchadal
20. Coahuiltecan	1	Tonkawa
21. Creole	10	Nubi, Naga, Belizean Creole, Berbice, Krio, Haitian Creole, Korlai, Sango, Torres Strait, Ndyuka
22. Daic	8	Boyao Ai-Cham, Ching (Mak), Khamti, Lao, Shan, Lung Ming Tai, Thai, Saek
23. Dravidian	10	Malto, Koya, Telugu, Malayalam, Tamil, Brahui, Kolami, Kui, Toda, Gonda
24. East Bird's Head	0	
25. East Papuan	2	Anem, Yele
26. Eskimo-Aleut	6	Aleut, Greenlandic, North Alaskan Inupiaq, Central Yupik, Pacific Gulf Yupik, Sirenik
27. Geelvink Bay	0	
28. Gulf	3	Atakapa, Chitimacha, Tunica[1]
29. Hokan	11	Diegueño, Karok, Kashaya Pomo, Eastern Pomo, Mojave, Paipai, Salinan, Yana, Hualapai, Maricopa, Kiliwa
30. Huavean	1	Huave (de San Mateo del Mar)
31. Indo-European	14	Albanian, Gaelic, Icelandic (Old), English, Hindi, Gujarati, Farsi, Maithili, Latin, French, Russian, Czech, Lithuanian, Greek
32. Iroquoian	6	Mohawk, Oneida, Onondaga, Cayuga, Seneca, Cherokee
33. Japanese	3	Japanese, Yonaguni, Amami (Shodon)
34. Jivaroan	1	Jivaro
35. Katukinan	0	

(continued)

Table 2.2.—*(continued)*

Phylum	No.	Languages
36. Keres	1	Acoma (Western Keres)
37. Khoisan	6	Nama, Kung (Zu|'Hóasi), Sandawe, Gana-Khwe (||Ani), Naro, !Xóõ
38. Kiowa Tanoan	4	Kiowa, Tiwa, Taos, Jemez
39. Kwontari-Baibai	0	
40. language isolates	11	Ainu, Andoke, Basque, Burushaski, Cayubaba, Gilyak, Korean, Tol (Jicaque), Warao, Yuchi, Zuni
41. Left May	0	
42. Macro-Ge	5	Apinayé, Kaingang, Xavánte, Kayapó, Canela-Krahô
43. Maku	0	
44. Mascoian	0	
45. Mataco-Guaicuru	0	
46. Mayan	8	Aguacatec, Cakchiquel, Chontal, Huasteco, Mam, Tolojolabal, Yucateco, Tsotsil
47. Miao-Yao	1	Green Hmong
48. Misumalpan	0	
49. Mixe-Zoque	4	Sierra Popoluca, Zoque, Totontepec Mixe, Coatlán Mixe
50. Mosetenan	0	
51. Mura	1	Mura-Pirahã
52. Muskogean	2	Chickasaw, Koasati
53. Na Dene	8	Haida, Navajo, Chiricahua Apache, Slavey, Hupa, Tolowa, Sarsi, Tlingit
54. Nambiquaran	2	S. Nambiquara, N. Nambiquara (Mamaindé)
55. Niger-Congo	24	Fula, Wolof, Kisi, Ijo, Jukun, Bushong, Diola, Tunen, Ganda, Bete, Kru, Fong, Anufo, Senoufo, Kabiye, Luganda, Mumuye, Krongo, Moro, Tura, Bobo, Vai, Mende, Kpelle

(continued)

Table 2.2. The genetic classification of languages included in the survey of weight (*continued*)

Phylum	No.	Languages
56. Nilo-Saharan	14	Didinga, Turkana, Shilluk, Nandi, Lango, Fur, Kunama, Runga, Tubu, Songai, Mbai, Mangbetu, Bagirmi, Yulu
57. North Caucasian	4	Kabardian, Lak, Abkhaz, Ubyx
58. Oto-Manguean	6	Mixtec, Otomi, Mazatec, Mitla Zapotec, Trique, Comaltepec Chinantec
59. Paezan	2	Cayapa, Paez
60. Panoan	5	Amahuaca, Capanahua, Cashinahua, Chacobo, Marubu
61. Peba-Yaguan	1	Yagua
62. Penutian	8	Klamath, Sierra Miwok, Nez Perce, Tsimshian, Tzutujil, Wintu, Yawelmani Yokuts, Maidu
63. Quechan	4	Huallaga Quechua, Inga Quechua, Junin-Huanca Quechua, Quicha
64. Salishan	5	Kalispel, Lushootsheed, Comox, Lillooet, Halkomelem
65. Salivan	0	
66. Sepik-Ramu	6	Abau, Alamblak, Boiken, Hewa, Mayo, Yimas
67. Sino-Tibetan	14	Mandarin, Cantonese, Nocte, Tangsa, Tang-khul, Gurung, Dzongkha, Tibetan, Dumi, Burmese, Maru, Lahu, Karen, Nung
68. Siouan	6	Winnebago, Crow, Stoney, Lakota, Mandan, Assiniboine
69. Sko	0	
70. South Caucasian	2	Georgian, Laz
71. Subtiaba-Tlapanec	0	
72. Tacanan	2	Cavineña, Tacana
73. Torricelli	4	Arapesh, Au, Urim, Yil
74. Totonacan	1	Totonac (Misantla)
75. Trans New Guinea	14	Amele, Tauya, Usan, Biangai, Sentani, Abelam, Kobon, Dani, Telefol, Eipomek, Orya, Orokolo, Nankina, Murik

(continued)

Table 2.2.—*(continued)*

Phylum	No.	Languages
76. Tucanoan	4	Barasano, Siona, Siriano, Coreguaje
77. Tupi	5	Guarani, Kamayurá, Júma, Kayabí, Émérillon
78. Unclassified	2	Movima, Warembori
79. Uralic	14	Selkup, Nganasan, Nenets, Hungarian, Ostyak, Komi, Mari, Mordvin, Eastern Sámi, Northern Sámi, Finnish, Estonian, Veps, Votic
80. Uto-Aztecan	8	Hopi, Kawaiisu, Nahuatl, Cora, Tepehuan, Tubatulabal, Luiseño, Comanche
81. Wakashan	2	Kwakw'ala, Nuuchahnulth
82. West Papuan	6	Tidore, Mai Brat, Ternate, Sahu, Tehit, Pagu
83. Witotoan	2	Ocaina, Huitoto
84. Yonamam	1	Sanuma
85. Yenisei	1	Ket
86. Yukaghir	1	Yukaghir
87. Yuki	1	Wappo
88. Zamucoan	0	
89. Zaparoan	1	Arabela

2.3. RESULTS OF THE SURVEY OF WEIGHT-SENSITIVE STRESS AND TONE

In sections 2.3.1–2.3.2, I discuss the results of the typology of weight, focusing on two aspects of weight: the consistency (or lack of consistency, as it turns out) of weight criteria for different phenomena within a single language, and the consistency (or lack thereof) of weight criteria for a single phenomenon in different languages. Examination of these two aspects of weight will provide an answer to the fundamental question of whether weight is primarily a property of languages or of individual processes. We will now turn to discussion of stress and tone. A complete list of all languages in the survey and their weight criteria for all processes examined appears in Appendix Two.

2.3.1. Weight-Sensitive Stress

One of the most commonly invoked diagnostics for syllable weight is weight-sensitive stress (Allen 1973, Hyman 1977, McCarthy 1979a, b). In languages with weight-sensitive stress systems, there are certain syllable types that tend to attract stress based on their relatively greater weight. This differs from weight-*insensitive* languages, which assign stress to a fixed syllable, e.g. the final or penultimate syllable or the stem, regardless of the internal makeup of syllables in the word. In section 1.1, we saw an example of weight-sensitive stress in Latin, in which a CVC(C) or a CVV(C) penult attracts stress. If the penult is neither CVC(C) nor CVV(C), stress retracts to the antepenult.

2.3.1.1. Weight-Sensitive Stress: Results of the Survey

Of the 408 languages in the survey, 314 (or 77.0%) are described as having either stress or pitch accent systems. (This figure does not include languages for which sources did not discuss stress.) Of these 314 documented accent languages, 4 possess pitch accents systems in which words contrast in terms of the presence or absence of a pitch accent. These languages will be excluded from the discussion of stress that follows. Languages that may be characterized as pitch accent languages in sources, e.g. Ainu, Kashaya Pomo, and Koasati, but in which each content word carries at least one accented syllable will, however, be included in the survey figures. Although a pitch peak may be the most salient cue to accent, perhaps the only one, in these languages, their accentual system resembles a traditional stress one in that the accent is culminative, meaning every content word possesses a syllable that is more prominent than others (see Beckman 1986 for discussion of differences between stress and pitch accent systems).

Of the 310 languages with culminative accent systems in the survey, 136 (or 43.9%) have stress systems that are at least partially sensitive to syllable weight.[2] For most of these languages, it is primary stress that is weight-sensitive, although there are several (most of them, Uralic) languages in which weight is involved only in the determination of secondary stress (e.g. Finnish, Hungarian, Veps, Votic, Cayapa, and Yapese). The Turkish weight distinction is employed in only a section of the vocabulary consisting of loan words and proper names (Kaisse 1985, Barker 1989, Kornfilt 1990).

In nine languages in the survey, stress is determined by tone. Six of these languages (Barasano, Bobo, Crow, Haida, Kpelle, and Nubi) are reported to be sensitive only to tone in determining stress placement. These languages are thus not included in the figure of 136 languages with weight-sensitive stress. However, three languages (Ijo, Iraqw, and Krongo) have stress systems that are sensitive to both tone and segmental weight; they are thus treated as weight-sensitive languages. In all languages in which tone is a factor in stress assignment, it is always a high or a contour tone containing a high tone that attracts stress. Bobo makes a three-way weight distinction, with high tones heaviest, followed in turn by mid tones and low tones (Le Bris 1981). A reason for the affinity of stress and high tone will be proposed in Chapter Four.

Of the 136 weight-sensitive languages, 118 employ binary weight distinctions, while 18 are sensitive to complex weight hierarchies involving more than a binary distinction. If we first confine discussion to the binary weight distinctions, certain weight distinctions are far more common than others. If we consider only languages which are diagnostic for differentiating between weight criteria, i.e. languages that both allow coda consonants and have either long vowels or diphthongs, the CVV(C) heavy distinction, which is found in 35 languages, and the CVV(C), CVC heavy distinction, which is found in 42 languages, predominate. This latter figure includes Stoney Dakota, in which CVCC and CVVC are heavy; this distinction has in common with the CVV(C), CVC heavy criterion its treatment of coda consonants as weight-bearing. An additional 5 languages were not assigned to either the CVV(C), CVC heavy or the CVV(C) heavy criteria since they lack coda consonants, thus preventing comparison of the weight of CVV(C) and CVC. Two Yupik languages treat closed syllables as heavy in word-initial syllables, but treat only CVV(C) syllables as heavy elsewhere in the word. Three languages in the survey, Seneca, Oneida, and Kashaya Pomo, treat CVC as heavier than CVV for pitch accent placement. This distinction is unattested in stress systems in the survey.[3]

After the Latin and Khalkha type distinctions, there is a sharp drop-off in the frequency of other weight distinctions for stress. The full vs. reduced vowel distinction is the next most common criterion, but is found in only 12 languages. Note crucially that the term "reduced vowels" in the context of weight refers to *underlying* short central vowels and not to vowels that have undergone post-stress reduction, as for example occurs in English. A variant of this criterion, according to which only reduced vowels in open syllables are light (i.e. all closed syllables and open syllables containing a full vowel are heavy), is found in five languages. Three languages (Kwakw'ala, Nuuchahnulth, and Inga Quechua) treat both long vowels and syllables closed by a sonorant as heavy. Another language, Orya, treats syllables closed by a sonorant preceding another sonorant as heavy. Two languages (Mayo and Yimas) treat low vowels as heavy, while one language (Komi Jaz'va) treats non-high vowels as heavy. In Lamang, full vowels and all syllables closed by a sonorant are heavy, while reduced vowels in open syllables and in syllables closed by an obstruent are light. Kamchadal and Mundari treat syllables containing a glottal stop as heavy. The weight of syllables closed by a glottal stop will be discussed in Chapter Four.

Of the 18 languages with ternary weight distinctions, the most popular type of hierarchy treats long vowels as heaviest, followed by closed syllables containing a short vowel, followed by open syllables containing a short vowel: i.e. CVV(C) > CVC > CV. This weight hierarchy is found in six languages; in one of these languages (Mam) syllables closed by a glottal stop are equivalent in weight to long voweled syllables. The relative frequency of the CVV(C) > CVC > CV hierarchy relative to other ternary weight distinctions is perhaps not surprising, given that it is a conflation of the two most common binary distinctions.

The only other complex weight criterion found in more than one language is the CVVC, (CVCC) > CVV, CVC > CV distinction, which occurs in three languages in the survey. In two of these languages (Pulaar Fula and Eipomek), CVCC syllables do not occur. The only language that has CVCC syllables and employs this three-way distinction, Hindi, has a stress system that is the subject of controversy (see M. Ohala 1977 for discussion).[4] The remaining complex weight distinctions for stress are quite diverse, capitalizing either on differences in vowel quality, vowel length or the presence or absence of coda consonants, or on a combination of these factors.

A list of languages and their weight distinctions for stress appears in Table 2.3. Except where otherwise indicated, the indicated syllable types are those that are heavy. Note the following conventions adopted in Table 2.3 and subsequent tables displaying the distribution of weight criteria. A superscripted [a] indicates that the language does not have codas in any position that is relevant for diagnosing weight for stress. A superscripted [b] indicates an absence of phonemic long vowels. A superscripted [d] indicates an absence of obstruent codas. A superscripted [e] indicates an absence of phonemic long vowels and diphthongs. VV stands for both long vowels, if found in a language, and diphthongs unless otherwise noted. Onset consonants are irrelevant for the processes examined unless indicated otherwise, but are merely included following standard convention. R stands for a sonorant coda, K for a voiceless consonant, G for a voiced consonant. Shaded languages do not contain coda consonants and are thus not useful for diagnosing at least certain weight distinctions.

Certain important generalizations emerge from discussion of these stress systems. First, there are no languages with clear stress accent systems in which consonants are heavier than vowels. The only three languages in Table 2.3 that superficially appear to violate this generalization are Oneida, Seneca, and Kashaya Pomo, all of which possess prominence systems based on pitch accent. In the languages with stress accent systems, if closed syllables containing a short vowel are heavy in a language, then by implication, long vowels (and diphthongs unless phonetically short) will also necessarily be heavy. Crucially,

Table 2.3. Languages with weight-sensitive stress

Language	Phylum	Stress
Aguacatec	Mayan	CVV(C)
Aleut	Eskimo-Aleut	CVV(C)
Aymara	Aymara	CVV(C)
Buriat	Altaic	CVV(C)
Cayuga	Iroquoian	CVV(C)
Cherokee	Iroquoian	CVV(C)
Comanche	Uto-Aztecan	CVV(C)
Fijian[a]	Austronesian	CVV(C)
Huasteco	Mayan	CVV(C)
Hupa	Na Dene	CVV(C)
Ijo[a]	Niger-Congo	CVV(C), H or contour tone
Iraqw	Afro-Asiatic	CVV(C), H tone[5]
Karok	Hokan	CVV(C)
Kawaiisu[a][6]	Uto-Aztecan	CVV(C)
Khalkha	Altaic	CVV(C)
Koasati	Muskogean	CVV(C)
Krongo	Niger-Congo	CVV(C), H tone[7]
Kunama	Nilo-Saharan	CVV(C)
Luiseño	Uto-Aztecan	CVV(C)
Malagasy[a]	Austronesian	CVV(C)
Malayalam	Dravidian	CVV(C)
Malecite Passamaquoddy	Algic	CVV(C)
Malto	Dravidian	CVV(C)
Menomini	Algic	CVV(C)
Mojave	Hokan	CVV(C)
Murik	Trans New Guinea	CVV(C)

(continued)

Table 2.3. Languages with weight-sensitive stress *(continued)*

Language	Phylum	Stress
Nganasan	Uralic	CVV(C)
Nyawaygi	Australian	CVV(C)
Ojibwa	Algic	CVV(C)
Quechua, Huallaga	Quechan	CVV(C)
Quechua, Junin-Huanca	Quechan	CVV(C)
Selkup	Uralic	CVV(C)
Telugu	Dravidian	CVV(C)
Tibetan (Lhasa)	Sino-Tibetan	CVV(C)
Tidore[b]	West Papuan	CVV(C)
Tsou[a8]	Austronesian	CVV(C)
Tubatulabal	Uto-Aztecan	CVV(C)
Winnebago	Siouan	CVV(C)
Wintu	Penutian	CVV(C)
Wolof	Niger-Congo	CVV(C)
Ainu[9]	isolate	CVV(C), CVC
Amele	Trans New Guinea	CVV(C), CVC
Apalaí	Carib	CVV(C), CVC[10]
Arabic	Afro-Asiatic	CVV(C), CVC
Boiken[b]	Sepik-Ramu	CVV(C), CVC[11]
Brahui	Dravidian	CVV(C), CVC
Carib	Carib	CVV(C), CVC
Cayapa	Paezan	CVV(C), CVC except CV?[12]
Cebuano	Austronesian	CVV(C), CVC
Cuna	Chibchan	CVV(C), CVC[13]
English	Indo-European	CVV(C), CVC
Estonian	Uralic	CVV(C), CVC[14]

(continued)

Table 2.3.—*(continued)*

Language	Phylum	Stress
Evenki	Altaic	CVV(C), CVC
Finnish	Uralic	CVV(C), CVC[15]
Greek (Classical)	Indo-European	CVV(C), CVC
Hixkaryana[e]	Carib	CVV(C), CVC
Hopi	Uto-Aztecan	CVV(C), CVC
Huave (de San Mateo del Mar)	Huavean	CVV(C), CVC
Hungarian	Uralic	CVV(C), CVC[16]
Kabardian[e]	North Caucasian	CVV(C), CVC
Kashuyana[e]	Carib	CVV(C), CVC
Khmer	Austro-Asiatic	CVV(C),CVC
Kiriwina[d]	Austronesian	CVV(C), CVC
Korlai[b]	Creole	CVV(C), CVC
Koya	Dravidian	CVV(C), CVC
Latin	Indo-European	CVV(C), CVC
Macushi	Carib	CVV(C), CVC
Maidu	Penutian	CVV(C), CVC
Maung[e]	Australian	CVV(C), CVC
Miwok, Sierra	Penutian	CVV(C), CVC
Mixe, Coatlán	Mixe-Zoque	CVV(C), CVC[17]
Munsee	Algic	CVV(C), CVC
Nambiquara, N.	Nambiquaran	CVV(C), CVC
Ndyuka[d]	Creole	CVV(C), CVC
Nez Perce	Penutian	CVV(C), CVC
Stoney Dakota[e][18]	Siouan	CVVC, CVC
Tepehuan	Uto-Aztecan	CVV(C), CVC
Tol (Jicaque)[e]	isolate	CVV(C), CVC

(continued)

Table 2.3. Languages with weight-sensitive stress *(continued)*

Language	Phylum	Stress
Totonac (Misantla)	Totonacan	CVV(C), CVC[19]
Turkish	Altaic	CVV(C), CVC[20]
Veps[b][21]	Uralic	CVV(C), CVC
Votic	Uralic	CVV(C), CVC
West Tarangan[c]	Austronesian	CVV(C), CVC
Yana	Hokan	CVV(C), CVC
Yupik, Central	Eskimo-Aleut	CVV(C); initial CVC
Yupik, Pacific Gulf	Eskimo-Aleut	CVV(C); initial CVC
Kwakw'ala	Wakashan	CVV(C), CVR
Nootka	Wakashan	CVV(C), CVR
Quechua, Inga[c]	Quechan	CVV(C), CVR
Komi (Jaz'va)[c]	Uralic	Non-high V
Mayo[b]	Sepik-Ramu	Low V
Yimas[b]	Sepik-Ramu	Low V
Mundari[b]	Austro-Asiatic	CVʔ(C)
Orya	Trans New Guinea	CVV(C), CVR.R[22]
Kamchadal[c]	Chukotko-Kamchatkan	ʔV, Vʔ
Au	Torricelli	Full V
Chuvash[c]	Altaic	Full V
Javanese[c]	Austronesian	Full V
Lillooet[c]	Salish	FullV[23]
Lushootseed[c]	Salishan	Full V
Mordvin[c]	Uralic	Full V
Nankina[c]	Trans New Guinea	Full V, onset[24]
Ostyak (Vach)[c]	Uralic	Full V
Patep[b]	Austronesian	Full V
Sawai[c]	Austronesian	Full V[25]

(continued)

Table 2.3.—*(continued)*

Language	Phylum	Stress
Urim[b 26]	Torricelli	Full V
Yil[b 27]	Torricelli	Full V
Aljutor[e]	Chukotko-Kamchatkan	Red V in open syll light
Malay[e]	Austronesian	Red V in open syll light
Mari[b] (literary)	Uralic	Red V in open syll light
Sarangani Manobo[e]	Austronesian	Red V in open syll light
Sentani[e]	Trans New Guinea	Red V in open syll light
Lamang[b 28]	Afro-Asiatic	Full V, CVR
Abelam[b]	Trans New Guinea	CaV > CʌV > Cij, Cuw > CV
Asheninca Campa	Arawakan	CVV > Ca(C), Ce(C), Co(C), CiC > Ci > Cɨ[29 30]
Chickasaw	Muskogean	CVV(C) > CVC > CV
Chukchi[e]	Chukotko-Kamchatkan	Low V, Mid V > High V > Red V
Eipomek[b]	Trans New Guinea	CVVC > CVV, CVC > CV
Fula(Pulaar)	Niger-Congo	CVVC > CVV, CVC > CV
Gujarati	Indo-European	LowV >CəC > Non-low V >Cə
Hindi	Indo-European	CVCC, CVVC > CVV, CVC > CV[31]
Irish (Munster)	Indo-European	CVV(C) > Cax > CV[32]
Júma[e]	Tupi	final syll unless onsetless
Kara	Austronesian	CV: > CaV, CaC > Ca > CV_iV_k, CVC > CNon-low V[33]
Klamath	Penutian	CVV(C) > CVC > CV

(continued)

Table 2.3. Languages with weight-sensitive stress *(continued)*

Language	Phylum	Stress
Kobon[ab34]	Trans New Guinea	Low V> MidV > High V > Red V
Maithili	Indo-European	CVV(C) > CVC > CV
Mam	Mayan	CVV, CV? > CVC > CV
Moro[b]	Niger-Congo	CVC > Full V> Red V
Mura-Pirahã[a]	Mura	KVV > GVV > VV > KV > GV
Tamil	Dravidian	CVV(C) > CVC > CV
Yapese	Austronesian	CVV(C) > CVC > CV

the converse is not true; there are many languages such as Khalkha, in which long vowels are heavy but closed syllables containing a short vowel are light. A few languages make a distinction between sonorant and obstruent codas. This distinction also respects an implicational relationship: If obstruent codas are heavy, then sonorant codas will also be heavy. If we conflate the distinction between sonorant and obstruent codas with the distinction between long vowels and closed syllables, an implicational hierarchy emerges with long vowels and diphthongs at the top of the weight hierarchy, followed in turn by syllables closed by a sonorant, syllables closed by an obstruent, and open syllables containing a short vowel, i.e. CVV(C) > CVR > CVO > CV.

There is a second implicational hierarchy for weight in stress systems. Lower vowels are universally at least as heavy as higher vowels. Thus, in languages that make a weight distinction between vowels of different heights, it is always the lower vowels that are heavier than the higher ones. An exception to this generalization is provided by reduced vowels, which although articulatorily lower than high vowels, are nevertheless treated as lighter than high vowels in several languages, notably those in which they are phonetically quite short (see section 4.1.1). In fact, reduced vowels are never heavier than full vowels in any language, suggesting that reduced vowels can be incorporated into the hierarchy of weight based on vowel quality, at the bottom of the scale. The resulting scale is thus Low Vowels > Mid Vowels > High Vowels > Reduced Vowels, where the full vowels are the low, mid, and high vowels. As this hierarchy predicts, although there are no languages which treat reduced vowels as heavier than any of the full vowels, there are languages which treat reduced vowels as lighter than the full vowels.

A second important generalization is that, in virtually all languages in the survey with four[35] exceptions (Júma, Pirahã, Banawá, which are spoken in South America but which are genetically unrelated, and Nankina, a language belonging to the Trans New Guinea phylum), syllable onsets do not play any role in the calculation of weight for weight-sensitive stress. The weightless status of onsets is not a property unique to weight-sensitive stress systems; onsets are characteristically weightless for all weight-sensitive phenomena (Hyman 1985, Hayes 1989). Reasons for this weight asymmetry between onsets and the rest of the syllable will not be explored here. Hopefully further research, perhaps along similar lines to the approach developed here for rime-sensitive syllable weight, will shed more light on the question of why onsets are weightless.[36] Chapter Four contains some discussion of the motivations behind onset sensitivity in stress systems.

2.3.2. Weight-Sensitive Tone

Weight has also been linked in the literature to tonal phenomena (e.g. Woo 1969, Hyman 1985, Zec 1988, Hyman and Ngunga 1994, Duanmu 1994a,b), most commonly to account for languages in which only a subset of syllable types may carry contour tones or rising or falling pitch accents. Henceforth, I will frequently use the term "tone" as a blanket term for both tone and pitch accent phenomena. To take an example of a language with weight-sensitive tone, consider the case of Navajo (Sapir and Hoijer 1967), which tolerates contour tones only on long vowels (CVV)(2a). Syllables containing short vowels may not carry a contour tone, whether they are open or closed (2b).

(2) Navajo tone
     a. **kâːkǐː** 'crow', sǐzěːtí 'my cousin'
     b. (hypothetical) *kânkǐː or *kâkǐː

Depending on the language, the asymmetrical ability of some but not other syllable types to carry contour tones may manifest itself in a few different ways, including for example, tone sandhi or spreading phenomena and lexical restrictions against contour tones or pitch accents on certain syllables.

It is typically assumed that contour tones result from the combination of two level tones (e.g. Woo 1969, Hyman 1985, Duanmu 1994a,b). Thus, a rising tone reflects the combination of a low tone followed by a high tone, while a falling tone is represented as a combination of a high tone followed by a low tone. Given the compositionality of contour tones, restrictions against contour tones are often assumed to arise from a prohibition against associations between more than one tone and a single timing position (either a skeletal slot or mora). Thus, because a contour tone consists of two tones, it requires two timing positions on which to be realized, one for each element of the contour, in languages with weight-sensitive tone. For example, the Navajo restriction against contour tones on CVO and CV follows if we assume that only vowels are associated with weight bearing timing positions in Navajo. In moraic representations, this is captured by assuming that only vocoids are moraic in Navajo. Sample representations of a long vowel carrying a level tone and a long vowel carrying a contour tone appear in Figure 2.1.

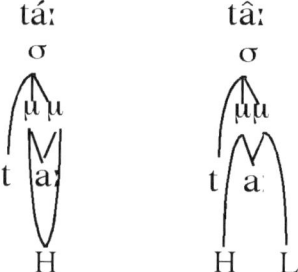

Figure 2.1. Moraic representations of weight-sensitive tone

In a skeletal slot model, we may assume that the relevant weight-bearing constituent for Navajo tone is the nucleus. Branching nuclei, those with two skeletal slots, may support contour tones, as shown in Figure 2.2; each element of the contour links to a timing position associated with a vowel. Syllables that do not contain branching nuclei may not support a contour tone, since tone units cannot be associated with coda consonants and more than one tone may not link to a single timing position.

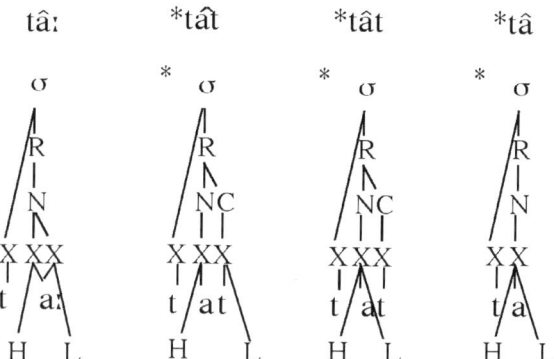

Figure 2.2. Skeletal slot representations of weight-sensitive tone

There are certain complicating issues that arise in the discussion of tonal restrictions of this sort. First, many languages have independent restrictions on syllable structure that preclude evaluation of the weight status of certain syllable types. For example, there are several languages in the survey (e.g. Ijo, Jukun), in which only long vowels may bear contour tones, but coda consonants are not permitted. Though such languages are weight-sensitive, they do not shed light on the question of whether codas are weighted or not. Furthermore and along similar lines, there are many languages in the survey (e.g. Mbai, Tura, Kabiye) that only tolerate sonorant codas. While these languages provide insight into the overall weight status of codas relative to vowels, they offer no evidence, either confirming or disconfirming, for a weight distinction between sonorant and obstruent consonants.

There is another more subtle confounding issue that is relevant to the study of weight. Many authors treat tone as a property of the syllable rather than as a property of segments. For example, if a language only allows contour tones on long vowels or sequences of vowels, one possible interpretation, in fact one commonly adopted, is that all syllables consist maximally of a single short vowel and that the domain of tone is the syllable. Under these assumptions, no syllable may carry a contour tone.

In many cases, this is in fact the correct diachronic analysis: long vowels or sequences of vowels have arisen from disyllabic sequences through loss of the intervocalic consonant. However, this analysis rests on the crucial assumption that a phonetically long vowel on the surface is actually interrupted by a syllable boundary. In most cases, the most compelling synchronic evidence for this interpretation comes from tonal assignment itself, a circular argument; works typically describe long vowels as phonetically single vowels which are neither rearticulated in the middle of their production nor are characterized by changes in amplitude or phonation type, all potential phonetic cues to syllable boundaries. In such cases, I assume for purposes of the survey that long vowels are tautosyllabic, unless there is independent distributional evidence that a syllable boundary divides the long vowel in half.

A related but somewhat less problematic issue concerns the syllabic status of tone bearing nasal consonants in many languages, most notably Niger-Congo languages. In many languages, the only segments other than vowels that may carry tone are nasals. In languages with this characteristic, there is typically independent distributional evidence that nasals are syllabic and pattern with vowels. Some distributional respects in which syllabic nasals may pattern with vowels are as follows. They may head a syllable or they may immediately follow or precede a consonant even if consonant clusters are otherwise prohibited. Furthermore, syllabic nasals may have greater energy and be longer than their non-syllabic nasal counterparts (see Price 1980 on phonetic correlates of syllabic consonants in English). The upshot of this discussion is that the ability of syllabic nasals to carry tone to the exclusion of other consonants often cannot be reliably treated as a property of the nasal as opposed to a property related to their status as syllabic consonants.

2.3.2.1. Weight-Sensitive Tone: Results of the Survey

Of the 408 languages in the survey, 110 (or 27.0%) are described as using tone contrastively at the lexical level or for morphological purposes. Of these 111 languages, 61 have contour tone restrictions that are relevant to the issue of syllable weight. In most of the languages surveyed with weight related restrictions on contour tones, the restrictions operate on the surface. However, in at least one language (Shilluk), the restriction on contour tones holds only at the lexical level and may be violated on the surface.

The remaining 50 tone languages that do not have weight-sensitive tone restrictions either allow contour tones on short vowels in open syllables in addition to other syllable types or do not tolerate tautosyllabic contours at all. Thirteen languages appear to lack contour tones completely. An additional language, Khmu, lacks contour tones, but nevertheless makes a tonal weight distinction: the only syllables preceding the root that may carry tones are those containing a sonorant. Khmu is thus included among those with weight-sensitive tone. This leaves 37 languages that allow contour tones on all syllable types. A large number of these languages (17) have an impoverished syllable structure, either lacking coda consonants completely or limiting them to sonorants or to glottal stop. In fact, languages which possess a rich inventory of syllable types, including open and closed syllables and a wide variety of coda types, all of which can support contour tones, appear to be a rarity cross-linguistically, though they are attested, for example, in languages such as Mangbetu, Mocha, Kunama, and Mulwi. Tolerance of contour tones on all syllable types seems to be most prevalent in Afro-Asiatic and Nilo-Saharan languages.

The two types of syllables that cross-linguistically are most likely to tolerate contour tones are long vowels and syllables closed by a sonorant. A total of 28 languages allow contour tones only on long vowels. Of these 28, four lack coda consonants, and are thus not probative for diagnosing coda weight. A large number of languages, 30, allow contour tones only on long vowels and syllables closed by a sonorant. Of these 30, five have only sonorant codas and are thus not instructive for diagnosing the relative weight of obstruents and sonorants. This leaves 25 that display the CVV(C), CVR heavy criterion for tone. In one of these, Acoma, the sonorant consonant that contributes weight belongs to the following onset.[37] In three other languages (Cantonese, Vietnamese and Maru), phonemic short vowels may carry a contour tone in open syllables. It is plausible to assume that short vowels are phonetically long in open syllables in these languages, since they all lack phonemic long vowels either in all environments (Vietnamese, Maru) or in open syllables (Cantonese); there is thus no threat of a length neutralization if vowels were lengthened in open syllables. In fact, in support of this hypothesis, phonetic data from one of these languages, Cantonese (see Kao 1971 and Chapter Three), show that vowels are phonetically long in open syllables.

Seven languages with the CVV(C), CVR heavy criterion for tone allow a limited set of tonal contrasts but allow certain contour tones on syllables closed by an obstruent. These languages are relevant to the issue of the weight, since lighter syllables have a reduced ability to carry tonal information. Crucially, light syllables in these languages can carry tones ending at both low and high levels, demonstrating that the limited tone inventory is not the result of a segmental effect, such as phonetic high tone triggered by voiceless obstruents.

The final weight distinction found in the survey, according to which contour tones can fall on long vowels and all closed syllables, is attested in only three languages (Hausa, Luganda, and Musey). This distinction is discussed further in Chapter Three.

A list of languages and their weight-sensitive tone restrictions appears in Table 2.4. The indicated syllable types are those that are heavy.

Weight-sensitive tone follows an implicational hierarchy identical to one of the hierarchies observed in weight-sensitive stress systems. If a language allows contour tones on open syllables containing a short vowel, then that language also permits contour tones on closed syllables. If a language allows short voweled syllables closed by an obstruent (CVO) to carry a contour tone, it also allows short voweled syllables closed by a sonorant (CVR) to carry a contour tone. If a language allows syllables closed by a sonorant to carry contour tones, then it also allows syllables with a long vowel (CVV) to have contour tones. Thus, we have the hierarchy CVV(C) > CVR > CVO > CV. Certain languages that draw a weight distinction between light CVO and heavy CV and CVR provide an apparent exception to this hierarchy. In Chapter Three, we will see evidence from Cantonese, which draws a similar distinction, that the light status of obstruent-closed syllables in these languages is plausibly related to the short duration of vowels before obstruents relative to vowels in other environments. Another exceptional aspect of Cantonese, its allowance of contours on CVR but not CVVO, will also be linked in Chapter Three to phonetic duration.

Table 2.4. Languages with weight-sensitive tone

A superscripted ᵃ indicates that the language does not have codas. A superscripted ᵇ indicates an absence of phonemic long vowels. A superscripted ᵈ indicates an absence of nonsonorant codas. A superscripted ᶠ indicates syllabic nasals, which bear tone unless indicated in a footnote. A superscripted ⁿ indicates that heavy syllables carry a fuller range of tones than light syllables, though light syllables may carry certain phonetic contour tones. R stands for a sonorant coda. Shaded languages do not contain coda consonants and are thus not diagnostic for weight.

Language	Macro-Phylum	Tone
Abau	Sepik-Ramu	CVV(C)
Andoke	isolate	CVV(C)[38]
Anufo[d][f]	Niger-Congo	CVV(C)[39]
Apache, Chiracahua[f]	Na Dene	CVV(C)
Bete[a]	Niger-Congo	CVV(C)
Bushong	Niger-Congo	CVV(C)
Cherokee	Iroquoian	CVV(C)
Crow	Siouan	CVV(C)
Didinga	Nilo-Saharan	CVV(C)
Duala[f]	Niger-Congo	CVV(C)
Greek (Classical)	Indo-European	CVV(C)
Ijo[a]	Niger-Congo	CVV(C)
Jukun[a][f]	Niger-Congo	CVV(C)
Kiliwa	Hokan	CVV(C)
Krongo	Niger-Congo	CVV(C)
Kru	Niger-Congo	CVV(C)[40]
Kung (Zu|'Hóasĩ)[d][f]	Khoisan	CVV(C)
Mumuye[f]	Niger-Congo	CVV(C)
Mura-Pirahã[a]	Mura	CVV(C)
Navajo[f]	Na Dene	CVV(C)
Ndyuka[d]	Creole	CVV(C)
Ocaina	Witotoan	CVV(C)[41]

(continued)

Table 2.4.—*(continued)*

Language	Macro-Phylum	Tone
Sarsi	Na Dene	CVV(C)
Selknam	Chon	CVV(C)
Shilluk	Nilo-Saharan	CVV(C)[42]
Somali	Afro-Asiatic	CVV(C)
Telefol	Trans New Guinea	CVV(C)
Tubu	Nilo-Saharan	CVV(C)
Acoma[a]	Keres	CVV(C), CVR[43]
Ai-Cham	Daic	CVV(C), CVR[n]
Caddo	Caddoan	CVV(C), CVR
Cantonese[b f]	Sino-Tibetan	CVV(C), CVR[44]
Ching	Daic	CVV(C), CVR[n]
Dzongkha	Sino-Tibetan	CVV(C), CVR
Gana-Khwe (‖ Ani)[d]	Khoisan	CVV(C), CVR
Kabiye[d]	Niger-Congo	CVV(C), CVR
Khamti	Daic	CVV(C), CVR
Kiowa	Kiowa-Tanoan	CVV(C), CVR
Kissi	Niger-Congo	CVV(C), CVR[45]
Khmu	Austro-Asiatic	CVV(C), CVR[46]
Kitsai	Caddoan	CVV(C), CVR
Lao	Daic	CVV(C), CVR
Lithuanian	Indo-European	CVV(C), CVR
Maru[b]	Sino-Tibetan	CVV(C), CVR
Mbai[d]	Nilo-Saharan	CVV(C), CVR
Muong[b]	Austro-Asiatic	CVV(C), CVR[n]
Nama	Khoisan	CVV(C), CVR
Naro[d]	Khoisan	CVV(C), CVR
Nung	Sino-Tibetan	CVV(C), CVR[n]

(continued)

Table 2.4. Languages with weight-sensitive tone *(continued)*

Language	Macro-Phylum	Tone
Saek	Daic	CVV(C), CVR^n
Shan	Daic	CVV(C), CVR^n
Tai, Lung Ming	Daic	CVV(C), CVR^n
Tewa	Kiowa-Tanoan	CVV(C), CVR
Thai	Daic	CVV(C), CVR
Tibetan (Lhasa)	Sino-Tibetan	CVV(C), CVR[47]
Tura[d]	Niger-Congo	CVV(C), CVR
Turkana	Nilo-Saharan	CVV(C), CVR[48]
Vietnamese[b]	Austro-Asiatic	CVV(C), CVR[49]
Hausa	Afro-Asiatic	CVV(C), CVC
Luganda	Niger-Congo	CVV(C), CVC
Musey	Afro-Asiatic	CVV(C), CVC

2.4. A COMPARISON OF WEIGHT CRITERIA FOR TONE AND STRESS

It is striking to compare weight criteria for tone with weight criteria for other processes. Among the weight-sensitive phenomena, only tone displays such a strong tendency to make a weight distinction between CVR and CVO. Conversely, for no other process is the weight discrepancy between CVC and CV so rarely exploited. The asymmetry between weight criteria for tone and other weight-sensitive phenomena can be illustrated by comparing tone and weight-sensitive stress. This is done in Table 2.5, which shows the number of tone and stress systems displaying the three criteria: CVV heavy, CVV, CVR heavy, and CVV, CVC heavy.

Table 2.5. Comparison of weight criteria for tone and stress

	Tone	Stress
CVV(C) heavy	24	35
CVV(C), CVR heavy	25	4
CVV(C), CVC heavy	3	42

It is clear from Table 2.5 that the CVV(C) heavy criterion is quite common for both tone and stress. Most striking is the great discrepancy between the two phenomena in the frequency with which the CVV(C), CVR heavy and CVV(C), CVC heavy criteria are attested. The CVV(C), CVR criterion is quite common for tone but vanishingly rare for stress, whereas the CVV(C), CVC heavy criterion is strikingly rare for tone, but is very common for stress. Only 4 languages with weight-sensitive stress systems make a weight distinction between sonorant and obstruent consonants. In comparison, 25 languages make this weight distinction for tone. Conversely, only 3 languages make the CVV(C), CVC heavy distinction for tone, whereas 42 make it for stress.

2.5. CONFLICTED WEIGHT CRITERIA: TWO CASE STUDIES

The divergence in weight criteria between stress and tone can be seen not only on a broad typological level but also in individual languages that display both a weight-sensitive stress system and weight-sensitive tone restrictions. Of the four languages in the survey which allow coda consonants and which have both weight-sensitive tone and stress, in two of them, Krongo (Reh 1985) and Cherokee (Munro 1996a, Wright 1996), weight criteria for tone and stress agree (CVV(C) heavy in both languages), while in another two languages, Lhasa Tibetan (Odden 1979, Dawson 1980) and Classical Greek (Steriade 1991), weight criteria disagree. It is these cases of conflicted weight criteria that we focus on here. Let us first consider the Lhasa Tibetan case.

2.5.1. Lhasa Tibetan

In Lhasa Tibetan, stress preferentially falls on long vowels. Stress falls on the leftmost long vowel (3a); otherwise, in words without any long vowels, stress falls on the leftmost syllable (3b) (examples from Dawson 1980). Bold-faced syllables are stressed.

(3)   Lhasa Tibetan stress
       a. ám'tôː 'person from Amdo,' 'týːtũ̀ː 'shirt,' láp'téː 'of the school,' kʰá'páː 'telephone'
       b. 'lápʈá 'school,' 'ɲúgú 'pen,' 'wòmá 'milk'

The tone system, in contrast, allows contour tones (high falling and low falling)[50] on both CVV and CVR syllables (4a), but not on CVO or CV syllables. Level tones (high and low) occur on all syllable types (4b) (examples from Dawson 1980).

(4)   Lhasa Tibetan tone
       a. khâm (high falling) 'Kham,' lɔ̂ː 'electricity,' kâ: 'stop,' kà: (low fall-
       ing) 'to be stuck'
       b. ʈɔ̀kpá 'nomad,' kúkpə́ 'dumb,' tèpá 'district officer,' ʃópá 'dice
       player,' rỳːpə́ 'rotten,' sø̀ːsǿ: 'freshest,' ɲíŋpə́ 'old,' nàŋpá 'Buddhist'

Thus, weight criteria for tone and stress conflict with one another in Lhasa
Tibetan; the result is a three-way weight hierarchy with CVV (heavy for both
stress and tone) at the top, followed by CVR (heavy for tone, but light for
stress), followed by CVO and CV (light for both stress and tone) at the bottom, i.e. CVV(C) > CVR > CV(O).

The representation of this weight hierarchy is problematic for reasons
enumerated earlier. In moraic theory, CVV would be expected to be only
bimoraic. Yet, if we are to represent the three-way weight hierarchy in terms
of mora count, CVV(C) would need to be trimoraic to be heavier than
CVR, which would be bimoraic, and CV, which would be monomoraic. In
skeletal slot models, there is no straightforward way to represent the weight
distinction between CVV(C) and CVR. The difference between CVV(C)
and CVR cannot be captured by assuming that weight for stress is calculated over the nucleus and weight for tone is determined over the rime,
since CVO also contains a branching rime but is nevertheless light for both
tone and stress.

In reality, the weight distinction is even more problematic than the
conflict between weight for tone and weight for stress would suggest.
Tibetan displays a compensatory lengthening process, both historically
and synchronically, which lengthens vowels due to the loss of an obstruent
(see Chapter Five). Synchronically, there are alternations between short
vowel plus syllable-final /r, p, k/ and a long vowel (Dawson 1980:13–14):
tsík ~ tsîː 'one,' kə̀pkí ~ kàːkí 'will do, make,' tʃúrkú ~ tʃúːkú 'nineteen.'

This compensatory lengthening process indicates that obstruents carry
weight in Tibetan; the hierarchy is thus sensitive to four degrees of weight:
CVV > CVR > CVO > CV. Needless to say, the complexity of this hierarchy
creates further representational problems for moraic theory.[51]

2.5.2. Conflicted Weight Criteria: The Case of Classical Greek

Another case of a weight conflict between stress and tone is found in Classical Greek (Steriade 1991), which allowed contour tones on only CVV(C) but
treated both CVV(C) and CVC as heavy for purposes of stress assignment.
The minimal word requirement and system of poetic metrics also treated

both CVV(C) and CVC as heavy. The result is a three-way weight hierarchy of the CVV(C) > CVC > CV type. As Steriade (1991) points out, these facts are problematic if we assume that weight distinctions are represented only in terms of mora count without reference to segmental information. Although CVV(C) could in principle be represented as trimoraic in order to differentiate it from CVC, this would run afoul of the principle that moras are projected from phonemic contrasts. Furthermore, the assumption that tones link to weight-bearing units in one-to-one fashion in languages with weight-sensitive tone would be violated if CVV(C) were trimoraic.

Steriade (1991) also discusses a mismatch in weight criteria of a different sort for an even earlier stage of Greek, which following Steriade, we may term "Early Greek." In Early Greek, contour tones could fall on CVV(C) and CVR, but CVV(C) and *all* CVC syllables were heavy in the metrical and stress systems, as well for purposes of minimal word assessment.

The upshot of this discussion is that comparison of weight requirements for stress and tone reveals asymmetries both on a cross-linguistic level and also on the level of individual languages. Cross-linguistically, the distribution of weight criteria for stress and tone are quite divergent from one another. Comparison of the distribution of the CVV(C), CVR heavy criterion for the two phenomena provides a striking example of the difference between tone and stress. The CVV(C), CVR heavy criterion is very common for tone, but exceedingly rare for stress. Given the different cross-linguistic distribution of weight criteria for the two phenomena, it is not surprising that we also find conflicted weight criteria for stress and tone in individual languages, as in Lhasa Tibetan and in Classical and Early Greek. Based on the cross-linguistic figures in Table 2.5, it is also not surprising that either the CVV(C) heavy (Tibetan) or the CVV(C), CVC heavy (Greek) criterion is employed by the stress system in these languages, while the tone system exploits either the CVV(C) heavy (Classical Greek) or the CVV(C), CVR heavy (Tibetan, Early Greek) criterion.

The number of these cases of conflicted weight criteria between stress and tone is at least equivalent (more if we treat Classical and Early Greek or Standard Refugee and Lhasa Tibetan as separate languages) to the number of languages in the survey employing the same weight criterion for the two phenomena, two (Krongo and Cherokee). Thus, consideration of weight criteria for weight-sensitive stress and weight-sensitive tone in languages with both phenomena provides evidence against the hypothesis that weight is uniform within languages.

2.6. A PHONETIC EXPLANATION FOR THE STRESS VS. TONE ASYMMETRY IN WEIGHT CRITERIA

In Chapters Three and Four, a detailed phonetic explanation for the divergent distributions of weight criteria between stress and tone systems will be offered. The different distribution of weight for the two phenomena will be attributed to differences in the phonetic dimensions to which stress and tone are sensitive. Chapter Three focuses on weight-sensitive tone and Chapter Four addresses the driving forces behind weight-sensitive stress. As a prelude to the more explicit discussion in these later chapters, let us consider here the basic phonetic motivations behind the two phenomena that account for their different phonological distribution of weight criteria.

In Chapter Three, weight-sensitive tone will be argued to be sensitive to the total sonority of the portion of the syllable rime occupied by sonorant segments. Languages will be shown to treat rimes with greater overall sonority as calculated over the sonorant portion of the rime as heavier than those with lesser overall sonority. This sensitivity to sonority is responsible for the predominance of weight distinctions such as CVV(C) heavy and CVV(C), CVR heavy. CVV(C) has the greatest overall sonorant energy; hence, the large number of languages which observe the CVV(C) heavy criterion (e.g. Navajo). CVR has slightly less sonorant energy than CVV(C), but nevertheless substantially more than either CVO or CV; hence, the popularity of the CVV(C), CVR heavy criterion (e.g. Kiowa). CVO and CV share very similar profiles in terms of sonorant energy; for this reason, the number of languages observing the CVV(C), CVC heavy criterion (e.g. Hausa) is vanishingly small. In fact, the existence of any tonal systems that allow contours on CVO but not CV on the surface will be called into question in Chapter Three.

Chapter Four will explore the phonetic underpinnings of weight-sensitive stress, which will be shown to be sensitive to a measure of auditory energy encompassing both sonorant and non-sonorant energy. Because the relevant measure of energy for stress is not limited only to sonorant energy, obstruents, in particular voiced obstruents and fricatives, have the potential to contribute substantially to the overall energy profile of a syllable for purposes of stress. For this reason, the CVV(C), CVC criterion is much more likely to be exploited by stress systems than by tone systems. This prediction is corroborated by comparison of the typological surveys of stress and tone systems in this chapter. The CVV(C), CVC heavy criterion is frequently exploited in stress systems, whereas it is rarely observed in tone systems.

In summary, Chapters Three and Four will show that phonetic considerations constrain the range of variation in weight criteria for different phenomena. Because obstruents universally have very little sonorant energy relative to both vowels and sonorant consonants, the potential for obstruents to play a role in weight-sensitive tone systems is minimal. Because obstruents have greater potential to contribute to the overall energy profile of the syllable, including both sonorant and non-sonorant energy, there is a greater likelihood for obstruents to add to the weight of a syllable in stress systems.

2.7. LANGUAGE SPECIFICITY IN WEIGHT CRITERIA

The phonetic motivation behind weight will also be shown in Chapters Three and Four to have a language specific component in addition to the universal component that constrains the range of variation in weight criteria for individual processes. Language specific differences in the phonetic properties responsible for weight lead to variation in weight criteria within individual phenomena. Thus, for instance, if the class of CVC syllables as a whole has greater energy in a language, it is also more likely to be treated as heavy for stress in that language than in a language in which CVC has less energy (see Chapter Four). Many, but not all of these phonetic differences between languages are ultimately linked to differences in segment inventories and syllable structure between languages. Thus, the overall picture that emerges is as follows. Certain aspects of the phonological system, e.g. segmental and syllable structure, contribute to phonetic differences between languages along the dimension(s) responsible for weight for a given phenomena. These phonetic differences, in turn, lead to differences in the choice of weight criteria adopted by individual languages.

The strongest evidence for the view that one aspect of the phonological system can influence phonetics, which in turn can guide the choice of weight criteria, will be advanced in the discussion of weight-sensitive stress in Chapter Four. In this chapter, it will be shown that the parameterization of coda weight in stress systems is linked to differences in syllable structure between languages and that the choice of weight distinctions based on vowel quality is ultimately constrained by the structure of the vowel system. Chapter Three provides evidence for the phonetic basis for interlanguage variation in weight criteria for tone.

2.8. THE ROLE OF PHONOLOGICAL SIMPLICITY IN SYLLABLE WEIGHT

One final crucial ingredient in the analysis of weight offered in this book is phonological simplicity. Recent work by Hayes (1999) has argued that certain phonological processes result from a combination of phonetic and structural factors. Specifically, languages display phonological patterns that simultaneously are phonetically optimal but at the same time are structurally simple in terms of the number of predicates necessary to express the relevant distinction(s). Hayes shows that many languages voice obstruents after nasals but not after other consonants, because obstruents are phonetically more prone to voice after nasals than other consonants. However, languages characteristically do not display place-dependent voicing patterns following nasals (e.g. voicing only of /p/), even though some place-dependent combinations of nasals and obstruents are phonetically more prone to voicing than others. Languages thus display patterns of postnasal voicing which are not only phonetically sensible but also are structurally symmetrical, even if this means having a grammar which is slightly less than ideal from a phonetic standpoint.

The notion of phonological simplicity also appears to be relevant for syllable weight. Weight distinctions attested in the world almost exclusively manipulate symmetrical classes of syllables. For example, many stress systems draw weight distinctions based on the phonological duration of the rime, where syllables with long (branching) rimes, i.e. CVV and CVC, are heavy and syllables with short (non-branching) rimes, i.e. CV, are light. Other languages observe weight distinctions based on vowel length, where syllables containing long vowels, i.e. CVV, are heavy. Many tone systems, and a few stress systems, make weight distinctions based on the duration of the sonorant part of the rime, where rimes containing a phonologically long sonorant phase (i.e. two sonorant timing positions—CVV or CVR) are heavy. Some stress systems are sensitive to distinctions based on vowel height.

Strikingly, languages appear not to make weight distinctions that are simultaneously sensitive to both vowel length and vowel height, e.g. long, low vowels heavy. Nor do languages exploit weight distinctions based simultaneously on vowel height and the sonority of the coda consonant, e.g. CVV, CLowVR heavy.

What sets apart the actually attested weight distinctions from those that are logically possible but nevertheless do not occur is the phonological simplicity of the occurring weight distinctions. A precise account of phonological simplicity will be offered in Chapter Four, where simplicity will be defined in terms of the number of phonological dimensions and the number of phonological predicates needed to differentiate heavy and light syllables.

2.9. SUMMARY OF THE PROPOSED MODEL OF WEIGHT

The model of syllable weight that will be developed in this work is summarized graphically in Figure 2.3.

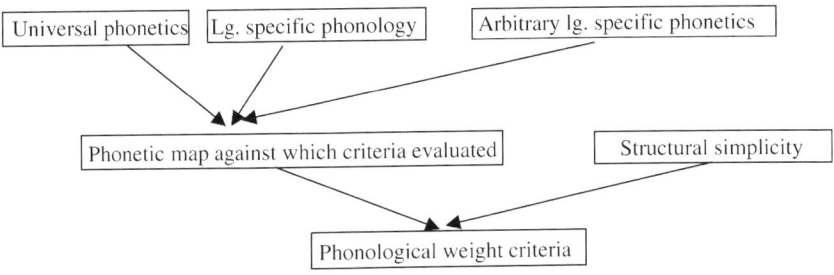

Figure 2.3. A model of syllable weight

At the top of the figure, a combination of universal and language specific phonetic properties together with language specific phonological features shape the phonetic map upon which potential weight criteria are evaluated. Universal phonetic properties are those that do not vary across languages, e.g. the fact that low vowels have greater energy than high vowels, the fact that sonorants have a richer harmonic structure than obstruents, etc. Language specific phonetic properties are those that vary arbitrarily from language to language, e.g. nasals are longer than fricatives in language *x*, nasals have greater intensity than laterals in language *y*, etc. Language specific phonological properties consist of aspects of the phonology that vary from language to language, such as syllable structure and segmental inventories.[52] These phonological properties can influence the phonetic map in several ways, as will be shown in Chapters Three and Four. For example, CVC as a class of syllables has greater energy in languages with a relatively large proportion of sonorant codas relative to obstruent codas. The phonetic evaluation of potential weight criteria mediated by considerations of structural simplicity yields the phonological weight system employed by a given language.

Although the basic relationship between phonetics and phonology and the evaluation of simplicity is the same for all weight-sensitive phenomena, the phonology of weight will necessarily differ between phenomena that are sensitive to different phonetic dimensions.

2.10. REPRESENTATIONS OF WEIGHT

The representations employed in this book are based on a modified version of a skeletal slot model of the syllable much like that proposed by Levin (1985). Unlike Levin's model, however, I will not assume that the rime is divided into coda and nucleus constituents. Rather, I will assume that nuclear segments, which most commonly are vowels, are characterized

by the feature [+syllabic], following early generative treatments. As used
here, a segment is [+syllabic] by virtue of its possessing acoustic properties, such as increased intensity, which make it the syllable nucleus, not by
virtue of its merely being the syllable nucleus. In this work, the [syllabic]
feature could, in most cases, be substituted by a feature that differentiates
between vocalic and non-vocalic segments, since its primary function is to
distinguish between syllables containing long vowels and those containing
short vowels.[53]

Furthermore, differences in weight conditioned by sonority, such as
between CVV and CVC or between CVR and CVO, will be represented
not in terms of differences in the affiliation of timing positions, but rather
in terms of differences in featural associations, following work by Steriade
(1991). For example, heavy CVV can be distinguished from light CVC
because CVV contains two rimal timing positions linked to the feature [+syl-
labic], not because the two timing positions associated with the long vowel
in CVV belong to the nucleus. Likewise, heavy CVR can be distinguished
from light CVO because CVR contains two rimal timing positions linked to
the feature [+sonorant], not because all sonorants belong to the nucleus in
languages in which CVV and CVR are both heavy. Similar feature-sensitive
representations of weight distinctions will be proposed for weight distinctions based on vowel quality in Chapter Four. Representations of weight will
be discussed more in Chapters Three and Four.

An advantage of the proposed model of the syllable over both moraic
models and standard skeletal slot models is that it assumes that weight representations do not vary across languages. The same segments receive the
same number of timing positions and the same syllabic affiliations across
languages. A by-product of this approach is that the proposed model of the
syllable upholds the basic principle that representations of weight are projected from phonemic contrasts. It does not require one to stipulate parameterization of which segments receive a mora or which segments belong to
the nucleus. There is thus one less parameter for the learner to acquire than
in a model that stipulates parameterization of syllable affiliation. For example, in the model adopted here, one need not, indeed one cannot, stipulate
that sonorant codas belong to the nucleus in languages or for processes that
observe the CVV(C), CVR heavy criterion, but not in languages or for processes displaying the CVV(C) heavy criterion. Similarly, under the approach
followed here, one would not assume that sonorant codas are moraic in languages observing the CVV(C), CVR heavy criterion, but not in languages
with the CVV(C) heavy criterion. Furthermore, weight distinctions based on
vowel height do not require stipulation that heavy vowels have two timing

positions and light vowels one. Rather, the CVV(C) heavy and the CVV(C), CVR heavy weight criteria, as well as criteria based on vowel height will be assumed to result from featural differences between the heavy and light syllables and not from differences in either the number of timing positions or their affiliation with a particular constituent.

Having said this, a few words are in order regarding the representation of full and reduced vowels in languages in which they differ in weight. The representation of full and reduced vowels is a difficult issue, and one which is closely tied to the matter of how central vowels should be represented, as reduced vowels are centralized relative to their full counterparts in languages in which the two differ in weight. What is thus necessary is a representation that distinguishes central vowels from both front and back vowels. One possibility is that the difference between central and non-central vowels is encoded using features that are either auditory (Flemming 1995) or articulatory in nature (Clements 1991). For example, under Clements' approach, reduced vowels would be [-coronal, -dorsal] while full vowels would have positive values for one of these features. Alternatively, using auditory features as in Flemming's model, central vowels would be [-low F2] and [-high F2], reflecting the fact that values for the second formant of central vowels are neither as high as for front vowels nor as low as for back vowels.

The approach to reduced vowels adopted here is one followed by Kager (1990) in a moraic framework, according to which reduced vowels lack a timing position. This assumption seems justified if one assumes that segments must be associated with some minimal duration in order to receive a timing position. In languages in which centralized vowels are light, they are characteristically quite short (see discussion in Chapter Four), and thus can plausibly be assumed to lack a timing position. Given this approach, the only cross-linguistic variation in the number of timing positions assigned to segments is between languages in which central vowels are very short in duration and those in which they are not. In languages in which central vowels are extremely short, they do not carry a timing position. In languages in which central vowels are not particularly short, they are associated with a timing position. In this way, the representation of central vowels is predictable based on duration. As an extension of the view that segments must have a minimal duration to receive a timing position, it is also plausible that certain non-schwa-like vowels could also a lack timing position in a language in which they were phonetically quite short. This idea will be pursued in the context of the discussion of Asheninca high vowels in Chapter Four.

2.11. WEIGHT FOR STRESS AND TONE AS COMPARED TO WEIGHT FOR OTHER PHENOMENA

Before concluding this chapter, we will briefly consider the distribution of weight criteria for phenomena other than stress and tone. More complete discussion of these other phenomena is postponed until Chapter Five. The purpose of this section is to demonstrate that stress and tone differ not only from each other but also from other phenomena in terms of weight criteria. This section will also serve to point out certain exceptional cases of different phenomena non-accidentally sharing the same weight criterion in a single language. These non-accidental cases of convergence of weight criteria will be explored briefly in this section and, as appropriate, in the discussion of weight-sensitive tone and stress in Chapters Three and Four, respectively.

The procedure for presenting data in the rest of this chapter is as follows. First, the relation of the four other processes considered in this book (compensatory lengthening, metrics, syllable template restrictions, and minimal word requirements) to the general issue of syllable weight will be briefly discussed. Then, weight criteria observed by these other phenomena will be compared to those observed by tone and stress systems. In performing this comparison, the cross-linguistic distribution of these weight criteria will be considered first to gain an understanding of the overall distribution of weight. Then, weight criteria for stress and tone will be compared to weight criteria for the other phenomena in individual languages to determine the degree of language-internal uniformity of weight criteria.

2.11.1. Compensatory Lengthening

Compensatory lengthening may be defined as the lengthening of a segment to compensate for the loss of another segment in the word. Compensatory lengthening preserves the overall prosodic profile of a word or syllable in the face of the loss of a segment. In moraic terms, compensatory lengthening preserves the underlying mora count (Hock 1986, Hayes 1989). Translated into skeletal slot terms, compensatory lengthening preserves the underlying number of skeletal positions.

There are several subtypes of compensatory lengthening; examples of each are discussed in DeChene and Anderson (1979), Hock (1986) and Hayes (1989). Virtually all cases of compensatory lengthening have in common that they stem from loss of a potentially weight bearing segment, i.e. loss of either a coda consonant or a vowel (Hayes 1989). Thus, as in weight-sensitive stress and tone systems, onsets appear to be largely irrelevant in compensatory lengthening processes.[54]

Compensatory lengthening may be triggered in a number of ways. I focus here on cases of compensatory lengthening triggered by loss of a coda consonant; thus, CVC.CV → CV:.CV. This type of compensatory lengthening is relevant due to the cross-linguistic variation in the weight status of coda consonants.[55]

One of the difficulties involved in assessing the relationship between weight criteria for compensatory lengthening and weight criteria for other weight-sensitive processes is the fact that many compensatory lengthening cases are diachronic rather than synchronic. For many languages in which compensatory lengthening predated historical records, we cannot be certain about weight criteria for other processes at the time at which compensatory lengthening took place. However, if both the language in which compensatory lengthening applied and also its genetically nearest relatives (including those that have not undergone compensatory lengthening) behave uniformly with respect to a given weight-sensitive phenomenon, we can be reasonably confident that the weight criterion displayed by that phenomenon was the same at the time compensatory lengthening took place. Similarly, if compensatory lengthening can be dated through written records to a certain time period, we can potentially assess agreement in weight criteria with other phenomena that can also be dated. In the discussion that follows, only in cases where convergences and/or disagreements in weight criteria can be reliably established are diachronic cases of compensatory lengthening brought to bear on the issue of weight uniformity.

There is a further matter to consider. The survey of compensatory lengthening considered here did not systematically examine cases of coda loss that did *not* trigger compensatory lengthening. For this reason, the data here can only diagnose cases in which codas contribute weight to the syllable, not cases in which codas do not contribute weight. Thus, the occurrence of compensatory lengthening is diagnostic for the CVV(C), CVC heavy criterion, but the absence of compensatory lengthening in the survey does not demonstrate observance of the CVV(C) heavy criterion. Similarly, if compensatory lengthening is triggered by a certain type of coda consonant, e.g. sonorants, we cannot conclusively determine that sonorants are heavier than obstruents, since the survey does not consider cases of consonant loss which did not trigger compensatory lengthening.[56] The upshot of this discussion is that compensatory lengthening, as evaluated here, can only be diagnostic for the CVV(C), CVC heavy criterion.

Despite its deficiency in diagnosing certain weight criteria, compensatory lengthening nevertheless provides insight into the issue of weight uniformity, since it is possible for a language which treats codas as weightless for one or more other phenomena to display compensatory lengthening triggered by coda loss. Such a scenario would be indicative of a weight conflict between compensatory lengthening and the other phenomena. Alternatively, it is possible for a language which treats codas as weight-bearing for one or more other phenomena to also undergo compensatory lengthening, a case of weight uniformity.[57] In summary, compensatory lengthening potentially provides a testing ground for examining the nature of weight as a process-driven or language-driven phenomenon.

2.11.2. Minimal Word Requirements

Another phonological phenomenon that has been linked to syllable weight in the literature are minimal word requirements (McCarthy and Prince 1986, 1990, 1995a, Hayes 1995, Garrett 1999). Many languages have restrictions against words of subminimal size. Typically, this restriction applies only to content words. Function words such as adpositions, pronouns, conjunctions, and also numerals in certain languages are often exempt from these restrictions. Thus for example, the minimal size for content words in the native vocabulary of Finnish is CVV; the only subminimal words that are tolerated are either pronouns or clitics. In some languages, e.g. Sámi and Bengali, minimal word requirements of the CVV type are enforced by lengthening the vowel in a monosyllable whether it is closed or open. A language without a minimal word requirement allows content words with a rime consisting only of a short vowel.

Like other weight-sensitive phenomena, minimal word requirements display cross-linguistic variation in the weight of coda consonants. In some languages, coda consonants contribute to the calculation of minimal word requirements (e.g. Khalkha), while in other languages, they do not (e.g. Bengali, Sámi). As in other weight-sensitive phenomena, onset consonants are characteristically weightless (with a few scattered exceptions discussed in Chapter Five due to vowel loss) for purposes of calculating minimal word requirements.

In formal terms, minimal word requirements are typically attributed to a bimoraic minimum per word, or in skeletal slot terms, to a minimum of timing units in the relevant constituent over which the minimum word is calculated (the nucleus or rime). For example, the minimal word in Khalkha is CVC; thus, the smallest word consists of two skeletal slots in the rime. In Finnish, which observes a CVV minimal word requirement, the minimal word is defined over the nucleus: the smallest word has two skeletal slots in the nucleus.

Comparison of weight criteria for stress and minimal word requirements is particularly relevant, since theoretical literature has assumed a close link between the two phenomena (e.g. McCarthy and Prince 1986, 1995a, Hayes 1995). Syllables that are heavy for stress assignment in a given language are predicted to be those that form the smallest content words allowed in that language. For example, if only CVV(C) is heavy for stress, we would expect the minimal word to also be CVV(C) and not to find any CVC content words. The logic behind this argument is driven by assumptions about metrical foot structure attributed to McCarthy and Prince (1986). The smallest foot in a language consists of a single heavy syllable. Because a word is assumed to consist of minimally one canonical foot, we thus expect a word to consist minimally of a heavy syllable. A single light syllable does not constitute a well-formed foot and therefore may not form a prosodic word.

Evaluation of the role of onset consonants in minimal word requirements is subject to a few pitfalls. First, many languages (e.g. Hupa, German) do not allow onsetless words (all words beginning with a vowel in the orthography have an initial glottal stop) *regardless of the length of the word*, in which case, the requirement that words have an onset is not related to a minimal word requirement. Second, certain languages have restrictions on the shape of roots. For example, some require all roots to end in a consonant (e.g. Yapese, Lillooet). Crucially, these requirements hold of roots regardless of how many syllables they contain. Thus, they are not directly the result of either a minimal word or a minimal root requirement. Yet another more obvious confound in assessing minimal word requirements is that certain languages do not allow any words to end in consonants, in which case no conclusions about the weight of consonants relative to vowels can be drawn.

Another subtler problem in evaluating minimal word requirements is that there are languages in which content words consisting of a single vowel with neither an onset nor coda (i.e. simply V) do not occur. However, this may not be directly attributed to a minimal word requirement, since the number of possible words consisting only of a vowel is quite small: it is equivalent to the number of vowels in the language. Cross-linguistically, function words tend to be shorter than content words. Thus, it is natural for the smallest word templates, those consisting only of a short vowel, to be reserved for function words regardless of minimal word requirements.

As Garrett (1999) points out, much like other weight-sensitive phenomena, minimal word requirements obey a universal implicational hierarchy of the following sort: σσ > CVV > CVC > CV. The existence of a given word type in this hierarchy implies the existence of content word types to its left, provided, of course, that there are no independent restrictions against long vowels or final consonants in the language (or, of course, against words longer than one syllable). Thus, a language with CV words will also have CVC, CVV, and disyllabic words. A language with CVC words will also have CVV and disyllabic words. A language with CVV words will also allow disyllabic words. The rightmost word tolerated in this hierarchy in a given language is the minimal word for that language.

Given the difficulties involved in determining word requirements[58], it was necessary to set up some procedural guidelines for the survey of minimal word requirements. These are as follows. If I was able to locate any CV (or V) content words in a grammar, word list or dictionary that could not be identified as recent borrowings, I assumed the language has no minimal word requirement for purposes of the survey. Otherwise, I took as the minimal word to be the smallest content word (along the hierarchy given above) that I could find. Minimal word requirements, and not minimal root requirements, are considered here. Words identifiable as recent loans that violate minimal word requirements are not counted.

2.11.3. Metrics

Yet another area in which syllable weight has been argued to play an important role is in metrics. Certain languages have poetic traditions, either recited or sung, that are sensitive to syllable weight (Hayes 1988). Languages with weight-based meters place restrictions on where heavy or where light syllables may occur in the verse. To take an example of a weight-sensitive metrical system, consider the Finnish epic poem, *Kalevala*. In the *Kalevala*, syllables appearing in strong metrical positions show a strong tendency to be heavy, where heavy is equivalent to CVV(C) or CVC(C) (Sadeniemi 1949, Kiparsky 1968). In Finnish, this tendency increases in force as a line progresses. Thus the requirement is weakest in the first foot of a line and gradually increases in strictness through the final foot of the line.

Similar tendencies for heavy syllables to be preferred in strong metrical positions, and conversely for weak syllables to be preferred in weak metrical positions are found in other languages. Unfortunately, there is a dearth of data on metrical traditions in many parts of the world. It is thus difficult to draw firm conclusions about the cross-linguistic distribution of weight criteria for metrics. Most (but not all) of the data is gleaned from Indo-European or Afro-Asiatic languages, or from languages that have borrowed metrical traditions from these language families. Despite the overall dearth of data, however, there are a sufficient number of cases in the literature to enable us to speculate, albeit tentatively, on the nature of metrical systems and their relationship to other weight-based phenomena.

2.11.4. Syllable Template Phenomena

Yet another area in which syllable weight has been argued to play a role is in restrictions against long vowels in closed syllables or in syllables closed by a certain type of consonant. Restrictions of this sort have been argued to result from an upper limit of weight allowed per syllable. In formal terms, such restrictions result from a bimoraic maximum per syllable or, in terms of skeletal slots, a limit of two skeletal slots per rime. Under these assumptions, a CVVC syllable is considered too heavy because it contains three units of weight, either moras or skeletal slots, two for the long vowel or diphthong and one for the coda.

Many languages with restrictions against long vowels in closed syllables have active processes that shorten underlying long vowels when morphological processes place them in closed syllables, e.g. Hausa, Kiowa, Sierra Miwok. In other languages, the weight of coda consonants is evident because lengthening of stressed vowels is blocked in closed syllables: e.g. Chickasaw, Vogul, Lake Iroquoian languages, and Yupik languages. The failure of lengthening to apply in closed syllables may be viewed as a weaker ban on CVVC syllables and does not preclude the existence of underlying CVVC syllables that have been preserved on the surface. Indeed, in all of the above-mentioned languages in which stressed vowel lengthening is blocked in closed syllables, CVVC syllables are tolerated elsewhere in the language.[59]

Like compensatory lengthening as diagnosed in this book, syllable template restrictions by their very nature are never sensitive to the CVV(C) heavy criterion, since a restriction against long vowels in closed syllables necessarily implies that long vowels and also at least certain coda consonants are heavy; if they were not, there would be no restriction against long vowels in closed syllables. In the case of syllable template restrictions, unlike compensatory lengthening, there is the possibility, however, of distinguishing between sonorant and obstruent codas, as a language could in principle (as in fact some do in practice, see Chapter Five) disallow long vowels in syllables closed by a sonorant but tolerate long vowels in syllables closed by an obstruent.

2.12. CROSS-LINGUISTIC UNIFORMITY OF WEIGHT-CRITERIA: AN OVERVIEW

In Table 2.6, the number of languages displaying various weight criteria for different processes is presented. Hypens appear where a given process, at least as evaluated here, cannot diagnose the given weight criteria. Thus, neither syllable template restrictions nor compensatory lengthening can diagnose the CVV(C) heavy criteria, as discussed earlier. Nor can compensatory lengthening diagnose the CVV(C), CVR heavy criterion or criteria based on vowel quality for reasons enumerated in section 2.11.1. Note that only languages with binary distinctions are included in the figures in Table 2.6.

One of the more striking distributional asymmetries between different phenomena is one discussed earlier: the difference in weight criteria found in stress systems compared to those found in tone systems. In particular, the CVV(C), CVR heavy criterion is quite common in tonal systems, but extremely rare in stress systems. Conversely, the CVV(C), CVC heavy criterion is vanishingly uncommon for tonal weight, but well attested in stress systems.

Let us now consider some of the other more notable features of weight criteria for the different phenomena in Table 2.6. Compensatory lengthening is not particularly useful in this regard due to the inherent deficiency (at least as surveyed in this book) in the criteria that it has the potential to

Table 2.6. Weight criteria for different processes

		Process					
		Stress	Tone	Compens. Length.	Metrics	Minimal Word	Syllable Template Restriction
Criterion	CVV(C) heavy	35	24	—	0	17	—
	CVV(C), CVC heavy	42	3	27	16	80[60]	53
	CVV(C), CVR heavy	4	25	—	0	0	2
	Full V heavy	12	0	—	0	2	1
	Non-high V heavy	1	0	—	0	0	0
	Low V heavy	2	0	—	0	0	0
	CVC, Full V heavy	5	0	—	0	0	0
	Full V CVR heavy	1	0	—	0	0	0

diagnose. Turning to metrics, minimal word requirement, and syllable template restrictions, we see that the CVV(C), CVC heavy criterion statistically predominates for all three phenomena. There is, however, a large minority of languages displaying the CVV(C) heavy criterion for the minimal word requirement. The symmetry between the three phenomena is further diminished when one considers two other factors. First, syllable template restrictions do not have the potential to observe the CVV(C) heavy criterion. Secondly, the set of weight-sensitive metrical systems found in the survey is fairly small, 17. (One of these, Fijian, lacks closed syllables and thus is not included in the figures in Table 2.6.) Of these 17, only a small handful have independent origins (see Chapter Five); most are either borrowed or found in genetically related languages.

When all these factors are considered, the cross-linguistic evidence for uniformity of weight criteria across processes is not robust at all. This lack of convergence in weight criteria is confirmed statistically by a χ^2 analysis testing the proportion of languages displaying each criterion for different processes. Factoring in all processes in Table 2.6 (except compensatory lengthening and syllable template restrictions which are impoverished in the criteria they can diagnose), there is a highly significant difference in the relative proportion of different weight criteria for different processes (χ^2=137.979, p<.0001). This result indicates that the distribution of weight criteria differs between phenomena.

We can statistically compare the proportion of languages displaying various weight criteria for various weight-sensitive processes in order to see which processes have the most divergent weight criteria.[61] This is done in pairwise fashion in Table 2.7 for all processes except compensatory lengthening and syllable templates for reasons discussed above.

Table 2.7. Statistical difference between weight criteria for pairs of processes

	Stress	Metrics	Minimal Word	Tone
Stress				
Metrics	χ^2=14.560, p=.0007			
Minimal Word	χ^2=24.507, p<.0001	χ^2=3.301, p=.0693		
Tone	χ^2=44.330, p<.0001	χ^2=52.244, p<.0001	χ^2=92.259, p<.0001	

If one considers tone, stress, and minimal word requirements, the three phenomena with the largest set of data on which to base conclusions and the greatest potential to display a diversity of weight criteria, we find an important result. There is no evidence for distributional symmetry in weight criteria. Tone, stress, and minimal word requirements all differ from one another in terms of their weight criteria. As discussed earlier, this is an unexpected result in most theories of weight that model weight as a property that is uniform across phenomena within individual languages. The only two phenomena for which the cross-linguistic distribution in weight criteria does not differ significantly are minimal word requirements and metrics. Both phenomena observe predominantly the CVV(C), CVC heavy criterion; in the case of metrics, this is in fact the only criterion observed in the surveyed languages. This result should be regarded with caution, however, given the paucity of data on weight-sensitive metrics and the fact that the difference in criteria between the two phenomena nearly reaches statistical significance at the $p<.05$ level. The overall picture that thus emerges from cross-linguistic comparison of weight criteria is one of process specificity.

2.13. LANGUAGE INTERNAL UNIFORMITY OF WEIGHT CRITERIA

We now turn to the issue of weight uniformity from a different angle, looking at individual languages displaying more than one weight-sensitive phenomenon. Unlike in sections 2.4 and 2.5, which compared only stress and tone, here we examine languages that combine either weight-sensitive tone or stress systems (or both) with at least one other weight-sensitive phenomenon. First, in section 2.13.1, weight-sensitive stress is compared with phenomena other than tone. Then in section 2.13.2, we compare weight criteria for tone with weight criteria for other phenomena.

2.13.1. Weight-Sensitive Stress Compared to Other Phenomena

Uniformity between weight criteria for stress and weight criteria for other processes is examined in tabular form in Table 2.8. Processes for which the number of matches with weight criteria for stress exceeds the number of mismatches appear in bold. A list that contains weight criteria for individual languages with weight-sensitive stress systems and compares these weight criteria with those observed by other phenomena appears in Table 2.9. Hearts indicate matches in weight criteria, whereas diamonds indicate mismatches in criteria. Hearts and diamonds in shaded rows (indicating

Table 2.8. Weight uniformity between stress and other phenomena

	Agree	Disagree
Tone	2	2
Metrics	7	**2**
Compensatory Lengthening	4	5
Syllable Templates	9	9
Minimal Word	16	26

an absence of coda consonants), in parentheses (indicating either a distinction between geminates and non-geminates or between initial and non-initial CVC), in brackets (for complex weight hierarchies in which weight criteria between two processes potentially both agree and conflict) and next to question marks (indicating uncertainty) in Table 2.9 are not counted in the figures in Table 2.8. For processes marked by a diamond in Table 2.9, the weight criterion observed by the conflicting process appears after the diamond.

Interestingly, the number of weight mismatches is at least as great as, if not greater than, the number of weight matches for all processes with the exception of metrics. Thus, with the exception of the data comparing stress with metrics, Table 3.8 provides evidence *against* the hypothesis that weight is a property of individual languages as opposed to individual processes. If weight were a property of languages, we would expect many more matches than mismatches in weight criteria between stress and other processes.

It is also potentially useful to examine the nature of weight conflicts between stress and other phenomena to determine whether there are any tendencies for mismatches of a certain type to predominate. For example, one might ask, whether, in languages with both weight-sensitive stress and a minimal word requirement, it is often the case that weight criteria for the minimal word are more stringent than weight criteria for stress, or vice versa. Such a comparison was made for stress and tone in sections 2.4 and 2.5. We will now consider the nature of weight conflicts (and convergences) between stress and other phenomena.

2.13.1.1. Stress vs. Metrics

First, let us compare stress with metrics. In all languages in the survey with both weight-sensitive stress and metrics, weight criteria for stress are at least as stringent, if not more stringent, than weight criteria for metrics.

Table 2.9. Languages with weight-sensitive stress

Notes: A superscripted [a] indicates that the language does not have codas in any position that is relevant for stress rules. A superscripted [b] indicates an absence of phonemic long vowels. A superscripted [d] indicates an absence of non-sonorant codas. A superscripted [c] indicates an absence of phonemic long vowels and diphthongs. VV stands for both long vowels and diphthongs unless otherwise noted. Onset consonants are irrelevant for the processes examined unless indicated, but are merely included following standard convention. R stands for a sonorant coda, K for a voiceless consonant, G for a voiced consonant. Shaded languages do not contain coda consonants and are thus not useful for diagnosing the weight.

Language	Phylum	Stress	Metrics	Comp Length	Syll. Templ.	Tone	Minim. Word
Aguacatec	Mayan	CVV(C)					◆ CVV(C), CVC
Aleut	Eskimo-Aleut	CVV(C)					◆ CVV(C), CVC
Aymara	Aymara	CVV(C)			◆ CVV(C), CVC		
Buriat	Altaic	CVV(C)					◆ CVV(C), CVC
Cayuga	Iroquoian	CVV(C)					
Cherokee	Iroquoian	CVV(C)				♥	♥ ??
Comanche	Uto-Aztecan	CVV(C)					♥

Language	Family						
Fijian[a]	Austronesian	CVV(C)	♥			♥	
Huasteco	Mayan	CVV(C)				◆	CVV(C), CVC
Hupa	Na Dene	CVV(C)				◆	CVV(C), CVC
Ijo[a]	Niger-Congo	CVV(C), H or contour tone			♥		
Iraqw	Afro-Asiatic	CVV(C), H tone[62]				◆	CVV(C), CVC
Karok	Hokan	CVV(C)				◆	CVV(C), CVC
Kawaiisu[a][63]	Uto-Aztecan	CVV(C)				♥	
Khalkha	Altaic	CVV(C)				◆	CVV(C), CVC

(continued)

Table 2.9. Languages with weight-sensitive stress (*continued*)

Language	Phylum	Stress	Metrics	Comp Length	Syll. Templ.	Tone	Minim. Word
Koasati	Muskogean	CVV(C)			◆ CVV(C), CVC		◆ CVV(C), CVC
Krongo	Niger-Congo	CVV(C), H tone[64]			◆ CVV(C), CVC	❤	
Kunama	Nilo-Saharan	CVV(C)			◆ CVV(C), CVC		
Luiseño	Uto-Aztecan	CVV(C)			◆ CVV(C), CVC		◆ CVV(C), CVC
Malagasy[a]	Austronesian	CVV(C)					❤
Malayalam	Dravidian	CVV(C)	◆ CVV(C), CVC				◆ CVV(C), CVC
Malecite Passamaquoddy	Algic	CVV(C)					
Malto	Dravidian	CVV(C)					

Language	Family	CVV(C)					
Menomini	Algic	CVV(C)					◆ CVV(C), CVC
Mojave	Hokan	CVV(C)					
Murik	Trans New Guinea	CVV(C)					◆ CVV(C), CVC
Nganasan	Uralic	CVV(C)					
Nyawaygi	Australian	CVV(C)		◆ CVV(C), CVC			
Ojibwa	Algic	CVV(C)					◆ ??
Quechua, Huallaga	Quechan	CVV(C)		◆ CVV(C), CVC	◆ CVV(C), CVC		
Quechua, Junin-Huanca	Quechan	CVV(C)			◆ CVV(C), CVC		
Selkup	Uralic	CVV(C)			◆ CVV(C), CVC		

(continued)

Table 2.9. Languages with weight-sensitive stress *(continued)*

Language	Phylum	Stress	Metrics	Comp Length	Syll. Templ.	Tone	Minim. Word
Telugu	Dravidian	CVV(C)	◆ CVV(C), CVC	◆ CVV(C), CVC			◆ CVV(C), CVC
Tibetan (Lhasa)	Sino-Tibetan	CVV(C)		◆ CVV(C), CVC		◆ CVV(C), CVR	
Tidore[b]	West Papuan	CVV(C)					♥ ??
Tsou[65]	Austronesian	CVV(C)					♥
Tubatulabal	Uto-Aztecan	CVV(C)					◆ CVV(C), CVC
Winnebago	Siouan	CVV(C)					♥
Wintu	Penutian	CVV(C)					◆ CVV(C), CVC
Wolof	Niger-Congo	CVV(C)					◆ CVV(C), CVC

Language	Family	Weight					
Ainu [66]	isolate	CVV(C), CVC			♥		
Amele	Trans New Guinea	CVV(C), CVC					
Apalaí	Carib	CVV(C), CVC[67]					
Arabic	Afro-Asiatic	CVV(C), CVC	♥				♥
Boiken[b]	Sepik-Ramu	CVV(C), CVC[68]					
Brahui	Dravidian	CVV(C), CVC					♥ ??
Carib	Carib	CVV(C), CVC			♥		
Cayapa	Paezan	CVV(C), CVC[69]					
Cebuano	Austronesian	CVV(C), CVC					◆ CVV(C)
Cuna	Chibchan	CVV(C), CVC[70]			♥		
English	Indo-European	CVV(C), CVC	♥	♥			♥

(continued)

Table 2.9. Languages with weight-sensitive stress *(continued)*

Language	Phylum	Stress	Metrics	Comp Length	Syll. Templ.	Tone	Minim. Word
Estonian	Uralic	CVV(C), CVC	♥				♥
Evenki	Altaic	CVV(C), CVC					♥
Finnish	Uralic	CVV(C), CVC[71]	♥		♥		♦ CVV(C)
Greek (Classical)	Indo-European	CVV(C), CVC	♥			♦ CVV(C)	♥
Hixkaryana[e]	Carib	CVV(C), CVC					
Hopi	Uto-Aztecan	CVV(C), CVC					
Hungarian	Uralic	CVV(C), CVC[72]					
Kashuyana[e]	Carib	CVV(C), CVC					
Khmer	Austro-Asiatic	CVV(C), CVC					♥
Kiriwina[d]	Austronesian	CVV(C), CVC					

Language	Family	Weight	C1	C2	C3	C4	C5
Korlai[b]	Creole	CVV(C), CVC					
Koya	Dravidian	CVV(C), CVC	♥		(♦)		
Latin	Indo-European	CVV(C), CVC	♥			♥	♥
Macushi	Carib	CVV(C), CVC			♥		
Maidu (Northeast)	Penutian	CVV(C), CVC			♥		
Maung[c]	Australian	CVV(C), CVC					
Miwok, Sierra	Penutian	CVV(C), CVC	♥		♥		
Mixe, Coatlán	Mixe-Zoque	CVV(C), CVC[73]					
Munsee	Algic	CVV(C), CVC					
Nez Perce	Penutian	CVV(C), CVC					
Stoney Dakota[c][74]	Siouan	CVVC, CVC					

(continued)

Table 2.9. Languages with weight-sensitive stress *(continued)*

Language	Phylum	Stress	Metrics	Comp Length	Syll. Templ.	Tone	Minim. Word
Tepehuan	Uto-Aztecan	CVV(C), CVC					♥
Turkish	Altaic	CVV(C), CVC[75]		♥			♥
Veps[b][76]	Uralic	CVV(C), CVC		♥			
Votic	Uralic	CVV(C), CVC					◆ CVV(C)
West Tarangan[e]	Austronesian	CVV(C), CVC					
Yana	Hokan	CVV(C), CVC			♥		
Yupik, Central	Eskimo-Aleut	CVV(C); initial CVC			(◆)		(♥)
Yupik, Pacific Gulf	Eskimo-Aleut	CVV(C); initial CVC			(◆)		(♥)
Kwakw'ala	Wakashan	CVV(C), CVR					◆ CLowV
Nootka	Wakashan	CVV(C), CVR			♥		

Quechua, Inga[c]	Quechan	CVV(C), CVR					
Komi (Jaz'va)[c]	Uralic	Non-high V					
Mayo[b]	Sepik-Ramu	Low V					
Yimas[b]	Sepik-Ramu	Low V					
Mundari[b]	Austro-Asiatic	Vʔ(C)	◆ (CVV(C), CVC)				
Orya	Trans New Guinea	CVV(C), CVR.R[77]					
Kamchadal[c]	Chukotko-Kamchatkan	ʔV, Vʔ					
Au	Torricelli	Full V				❤	
Chuvash[c]	Altaic	Full V					
Javanese[c]	Austronesian	Full V					◆ CVV(C), CVC
Lillooet[c]	Salish	FullV[78]		◆ CVV(C), CVC			

(continued)

Table 2.9. Languages with weight-sensitive stress (*continued*)

Language	Phylum	Stress	Metrics	Comp Length	Syll. Templ.	Tone	Minim. Word
Lushootseed[e]	Salishan	Full V					
Mordvin[e]	Uralic	Full V					
Nankina[e]	Trans New Guinea	Full V, onset[79]					
Ostyak (Vach)[e]	Uralic	Full V					
Patep[b]	Austronesian	Full V					
Sawai[e]	Austronesian	Full V[80]					
Urim[b 81]	Torricelli	Full V					◆ CVV(C)
Yil[b 82]	Torricelli	Full V					
Aljutor[e]	Chukotko-Kamchatkan	Red V in open syll light					
Malay[e]	Austronesian	Red V in open syll light					◆ CVV(C), CVC
Mari[b] (literary)	Uralic	Red V in open syll light					

							♦ CVV(C), CVC
Sarangani Manobo[e]	Austronesian	Red V in open syll light					♦
Sentani[e]	Trans New Guinea	Red V in open syll lightt					
Lamang[b 83]	Afro-Asiatic	Full V, CVR					
Abelam[b]	Trans New Guinea	CaV > CøV > Cij, Cuw > CV					
Asheninca Campa	Arawakan	CVV > Ca(C), Ce(C), Co(C), CiC > Ci > Ci [84 85]					
Chickasaw	Muskogean	CVV(C) > CVC > CV				[♥, ♦]	[♥, ♦]
Chukchi[c]	Chukotko-Kamchatkan	Low V, Mid V > HighV > Red V					
Eipomek[b]	Trans New Guinea	CVVC > CVV, CVC > CV					

(continued)

Table 2.9. Languages with weight-sensitive stress (*continued*)

Language	Phylum	Stress	Metrics	Comp Length	Syll. Templ.	Tone	Minim. Word
Fula (Pulaar)	Niger-Congo	CVVC > CVV, CVC > CV					♥
Gujarati	Indo-European	LowV > CRedVC > Non-low V > Cə					
Hindi	Indo-European	CVCC, CVVC > CVV, CVC > CV[86]	♥	(♦)	(♦)		♥
Irish (Munster)	Indo-European	CVV(C) > Cax > CV[87]		♦			♦
Júma[e]	Tupi	final syll unless onsetless					
Kara	Austronesian	CV: > CaV, CaC > Ca > CV_ik, CVC > CNon-low V[88]					CVV(C), CVC

Language	Family	Hierarchy					
Klamath	Penutian	CVV(C) > CVC > CV					
Kobon[a b 89]	Trans New Guinea	Low V > MidV > High V > Red V					
Maithili	Indo-European	CVV(C) > CVC > CV	[♥, ◆]				
Mam	Mayan	CVV, CV? > CVC>CV	[♥, ◆]				
Moro[b]	Niger-Congo	CVC > Full V > Red V					
Mura-Pirahã[a]	Mura	KVV > GVV > VV>KV > GV	♥	♥			
Tamil	Dravidian	CVV(C) > CVC > CV	[♥, ◆]				
Yapese	Austronesian	CVV(C)> CVC > CV				(♥, ◆)	

Thus, in seven languages (Latin, Classical Greek, Hindi,[90] Arabic, Hungarian, Estonian, and Finnish), CVV(C) and CVC are heavy for both stress and metrics. In two languages (Telugu and Malayalam), CVC is heavy for metrics but not for stress. In total, seven of nine languages have identical weight criteria for metrics and stress, whereas in two languages, there is a mismatch in weight criteria between metrics and stress. Another language, Fijian, is not diagnostic since it lacks coda consonants.

Due to the relatively small number of languages with both weight-sensitive stress and metrics it is difficult to draw reliable conclusions about uniformity of weight criteria between the two phenomena. Caution is particularly warranted when one considers that the nine languages in the survey which provide data for comparing weight criteria for stress and metrics are drawn from only four linguistic phyla: Indo-European (Latin, Classical Greek, Hindi), Afro-Asiatic (Arabic), Uralic (Finnish, Estonian, Hungarian), and Dravidian (Telugu, Malayalam). Furthermore, the Dravidian languages with weight-sensitive metrical traditions borrowed theirs from Indo-European.

Despite the obvious limitations of the survey, it is perhaps noteworthy that the number of cases of convergence in weight criteria greatly exceeds the number of weight conflicts. In fact, if we put aside the two Dravidian weight-sensitive metrical systems that are borrowed from Indo-Aryan, there are no cases of weight divergences between stress and metrics. This is probably not a surprising result given the fact that many poetic meters either restrict stressed syllables to strong positions in the meter or require that strong positions contain stressed syllables (see Halle and Keyser 1971, Kiparsky 1968, 1975, 1977, Hanson and Kiparsky 1996, Hayes 1988 for discussion). It is thus not surprising that weight criteria as diagnosed by stress and weight as diagnosed by metrical scansion should tend to agree within languages. In fact, we will see in Chapter Four that the same phonetic dimension which serves as the best predictor of weight for stress, energy, also acts as a superior predictor of weight criteria for metrical systems. The convergence of weight between stress and metrical systems is the only cross-linguistically consistent example of uniformity in weight criteria between two processes.[91] This discussion should not suggest that a stress system is a prerequisite for a weight-sensitive metrical system; indeed, a few languages in the survey have weight-sensitive metrical traditions but are said to lack stress: Hausa, Japanese, and Luganda.

This still leaves unanswered an important question concerning the nature of weight criteria in metrical systems. All the languages in the survey of metrics employ the CVV(C), CVC heavy criterion. This differs from stress systems in which the CVV(C), CVC heavy criterion is only slightly more common than the CVV(C) heavy criterion. One might ask whether this asymmetry in weight criteria is symptomatic of stress and metrics operating on distinct phonetic dimensions. Clearly, one would want to examine a larger database to draw any firm conclusions about the phonetic or other factors underlying metrical weight.

It is worth noting that I am aware of at least one language *not included in the survey*, the Australian language Kayardild (Evans 1995), which treats CVV(C) but not CVC as heavy in its metrical tradition which consists of sung verse. This weight criterion is also employed by the stress system of Kayardild. Although I do not have phonetic data from Kayardild, it is most plausible, based on data from other languages in Chapter Four, that this weight distinction is based on energy rather than duration. It is also interesting to note that the Yuman language Havasupai (Hinton 1984) lowers high vowels to mid vowels in strong positions in their chanted verse. This phenomenon has the effect of increasing the duration and, perhaps more importantly, the energy profile of a syllable in strong position. That vowel lowering in strong positions is not exclusively duration-driven is suggested by the fact that it applies even in closed syllables, which cross-linguistically are long enough to occupy heavy positions in other languages.

In summary, despite the limited scope of the survey of weight-sensitive metrics, there is a fair amount of evidence that the tendency for weight criteria for stress and weight criteria for metrics to agree is not mere coincidence, but rather reflects a sensitivity of both phenomena to a common phonetic dimension.

2.13.1.2. Stress vs. Compensatory Lengthening

Of the 9 languages in the survey displaying weight-sensitivity for both phenomena, 5 observe different weight criteria and 4 observe the same weight criterion. Of the languages in which weight criteria for stress and compensatory lengthening conflict, stress always observes the CVV(C) heavy criterion and compensatory lengthening (of course) the CVV(C), CVC heavy criterion. For example, as discussed earlier, Lhasa Tibetan has compensatory lengthening but does not treat CVC as heavy in its stress systems. Mismatches of this type (coda loss triggers compensatory lengthening but CVC is light for stress) occur in Telugu, Nyawaygi, and Huallaga Quechua. In Lillooet, loss of certain codas triggers compensatory lengthening, but the weight system treats full vowels as heavier than reduced vowels. In summary, comparison of weight criteria for compensatory lengthening with those employed by stress systems does not provide any evidence for the view that weight is consistent within languages.

2.13.1.3 Stress vs. Syllable Template Restrictions

We now consider the relationship between stress and syllable template restrictions. Because of the relatively large number of languages with both weight-sensitive stress and syllable template restrictions, the comparison between these two phenomena is more enlightening than the comparisons between stress and the other processes already considered. As indicated in Table 2.8, the number of languages in which weight criteria for the two phenomena conflict is identical to the number of languages in which the two phenomena display the same weight criterion. Let us now consider the nature of weight mismatches between weight criteria for stress and weight criteria for syllable templates in individual languages. Visually, the easiest way to do this is by looking at a matrix with the weight criteria for stress on the one axis and the weight criteria for syllable templates on the another axis, as in Table 2.10. The number of languages in shaded cells represent convergences of weight criteria; numbers in non-shaded cells are cases of conflicted weight criteria.

There are 9 languages with the same weight criterion for both stress and syllable template restrictions. However, 8 of these cases of identical weight criteria occur in languages in which the criterion for both processes is CVV(C), CVC heavy. It is not surprising that this is the weight

Table 2.10. Weight criteria for stress and syllable templates in languages with both phenomena

	Heavy Syllables	Stress		
		CVV(C)	CVV(C) CVC	CVV(C) CVR
Syllable Templates	CVV(C)	0	0	0
	CVV(C), CVC	8	8	0
	CVV(C), CVR	0	0	1

criterion displaying the greatest uniformity between stress and syllable templates, since virtually all languages with restrictions on long vowels in closed syllables treat all codas as equally heavy for purposes of those restrictions (see Chapter Five). Thus, 8 of the 9 cases of converging weight criteria probably are artifacts of the process internal uniformity of weight criteria for syllable template restrictions, rather than reflecting any tendency for uniformity across different processes in the same language. Furthermore, there are many languages (9) in which weight criteria for stress and syllable templates conflict. In all of these languages with conflicting weight criteria, the stress system does not treat codas as heavy, whereas syllable template restrictions do. This type of weight conflict is found in 8 languages. Mundari (not included in Table 2.10 but included in Tables 2.8 and 2.9) has a different type of conflict: CV? is heavy for stress and there is a restriction against CVVC. In summary, we can conclude that there is no tendency for wieght uniformity between stress and syllable template restrictions.

2.12.1.4. Stress vs. Minimal Word Requirements

Next, in Table 2.11, we compare weight criteria for stress with weight criteria for minimal word requirements.

There are a relatively large number of languages with both weight-sensitive stress and a minimal word requirement. Interestingly, there are many more languages with conflicted weight criteria between minimal

Table 2.11. Weight criteria for stress and minimal word requirements in languages with both phenomena

	Heavy Syllables	**Stress**					
		CVV(C)	CVV(C), CVC	CVV(C), CVR	Low V	Full V	Full V, CVC
Minimal Word	CVV(C)	2	3	0	0	1	0
	CVV(C), CVC	18	13	0	0	1	2
	CVV(C), CVR	0	0	0	0	0	0
	Low V	0	0	1	0	0	0
	Full V	0	0	0	0	1	0

word requirements and stress than languages with uniform criteria, 26 vs. 16. The bulk of the cases of weight uniformity (13 of 16) are languages in which the criterion for both phenomena is CVV(C) and CVC heavy.[92] If one examines weight for minimal word requirements independently of stress, this is not a particularly surprising result given the fact that approximately 80% of languages with monosyllabic minimal word criteria observe this weight distinction (see Chapter Five). For this reason, it is also not surprising that the majority of the cases of weight conflict (21 of 26) arise when the minimal word requirement observes the CVV(C), CVC heavy criterion and stress respects a different weight distinction. The large number of mismatches in weight between stress and minimal word requirement is striking, however, from the point of view of theories that assume a close association between minimal word requirements and weight-sensitive stress (e.g. McCarthy and Prince 1986, 1995a, Hayes 1995).

Because there is a relatively large number of languages with both weight-sensitive stress and a minimal word requirement, we are also in a position to measure statistically, using a χ^2 test, the degree of weight uniformity between these two processes in individual languages (see table 2.11).

The χ^2 analysis indicates, in fact, that there is no significant interaction between weight criteria for one stress and weight criteria for minimal word requirements, $\chi^2 = .569$, p=.4506. Thus, the statistical analysis corroborates the absence of a language dependent correlation between weight criteria for stress and minimal word requirements. This fits in with the general lack of a correlation between weight criteria for stress and other weight-sensitive phenomena examined (with the exception of metrics).

2.13.1.5. The Uniformity of Stress and Other Weight-Based Phenomena: A Summary

In summary, comparison of weight-sensitive stress systems with other weight-sensitive processes indicates that stress systems show virtually no consistent tendency to employ the same weight criteria as other weight-sensitive phenomena. Cases of weight mismatches between different processes in the same language are approximately equally as common as, and in some cases more common than, cases of weight uniformity. Thus, comparison of stress with other weight-sensitive processes argues against the standard view that weight is determined on a language specific basis. The one exception to the dominant trend against language internal homogeneity of weight criteria is provided by stress and metrics. These two phenomena tend, more often than not, to obey the same weight criterion within languages, suggesting that they operate along similar phonetic dimensions. This hypothesis is supported by phonetic measurements in Chapter Four.

2.13.2. Weight for Tone as Compared to Weight for Other Processes

We now consider the evidence for uniformity of weight criteria between tone and other phenomena. Table 2.12 depicts the number of languages displaying weight uniformity as compared to the number of languages in which weight conflicts occur. Weight criteria in individual languages appear in Table 2.13. Hearts in Table 2.13 indicate a converge in weight criteria and diamonds indicate a conflict in weight criteria. For processes marked by a diamond in Table 2.13, the weight criterion observed by the conflicting process appears after the diamond.

Once again, the number of weight conflicts and weight matches are, in general, fairly close with the exception of minimal word requirements which overwhelmingly tend to diverge from tone in their weight criteria. None of the other phenomena show a strong tendency to observe the same weight criterion as tone.

Although surprising from the point of view of theories in which weight is predicted to be uniform within languages, the tendency for weight criteria for tone to conflict more often than not with weight criteria for other phenomena is not surprising when one considers weight from a process specific point of view. In particular, the sheer frequency of tonal weight distinctions based on sonority combined with the extreme rarity of the CVV(C), CVR heavy criterion for other phenomena accounts for the large number of weight conflicts between tone and other phenomena.

We now consider the relationship between weight for tone and weight for phenomena other than stress in detail.

Table 2.12. Weight uniformity between contour tone restrictions and other phenomena

	Agree	Disagree
Stress	2	2
Compensatory Lengthening	1	3
Metrics	2	2
Syllable templates	**6**	**3**
Minimal Word	3	12

Table 2.13. Languages with weight restrictions for contour tones

Notes: Superscripted [a] indicates lack of codas. Superscripted [b] indicates lack of phonemic long vowels. Superscripted [d] indicates lack of obstruent codas. Superscripted [f] indicates syllabic nasals that bear tone. Superscripted [n] indicates that heavy syllables carry fuller range of tones than light syllables, though light syllables may carry certain phonetic contour tones. R = sonorant coda. Shaded languages do not contain coda consonants.

Language	Macro-Phylum	Tone	Stress	Metrics	Comp Length	Syll. Templ.	Minim. Word
Abau	Sepik-Ramu	CVV(C)					
Andoke	isolate	CVV(C)[93]					♥
Anufo[d f]	Niger-Congo	CVV(C)[94]					
Apache, Chiracahua[f]	Na Dene	CVV(C)					
Bete[a]	Niger-Congo	CVV(C)					
Bushong	Niger-Congo	CVV(C)					
Cherokee	Iroquoian	CVV(C)	♥				
Crow	Siouan	CVV(C)					♥ ??
Didinga	Nilo-Saharan	CVV(C)					
Duala[f]	Niger-Congo	CVV(C)					
Greek (Classical)	Indo-European	CVV(C)	♦ CVV(C), CVC	♦ CVV(C), CVC			♦ CVV(C), CVC
Ijo[a]	Niger-Congo	CVV(C)	♥				
Jukun[a f]	Niger-Congo	CVV(C)					

Krongo	Niger-Congo	CVV(C)	♥	◆ CVV(C), CVC			
Kru	Niger-Congo	CVV(C)[95]					
Kung (Zu|'Hõasi)[d f]	Khoisan	CVV(C)					
Mumuye[f]	Niger-Congo	CVV(C)					
Mura-Pirahã[a]	Mura	CVV(C)	♥				
Navajo[f]	Na Dene	CVV(C)					
Ocaina	Witotoan	CVV(C)[96]					
Sarsi	Na Dene	CVV(C)					
Shilluk	Nilo-Saharan	CVV(C)[97]					◆ CVV(C), CVC
Somali	Afro-Asiatic	CVV(C)					◆ CVV(C), CVC
Telefol	Trans New Guinea	CVV(C)					◆ CVV(C), CVC
Tubu	Nilo-Saharan	CVV(C)					

(continued)

Table 2.13. Languages with weight restrictions for contour tones *(continued)*

Language	Macro-Phylum	Tone	Stress	Metrics	Comp Length	Syll. Templ.	Minim. Word
Acoma[a]	Keres	CVV(C), CVR[98]					
Ai-Cham	Daic	CVV(C), CVR[n]					
Caddo	Caddoan	CVV(C), CVR					
Cantonese[b f]	Sino-Tibetan	CVV(C), CVR[99]					◆ CVV(C), CVC
Ching	Daic	CVV(C), CVR[n]					
Dzongkha	Sino-Tibetan	CVV(C), CVR			◆ CVV(C), CVC		
Gana-Khwe (‖ Ani)[d]	Khoisan	CVV(C), CVR					♥
Kabiye[d]	Niger-Congo	CVV(C), CVR				♥	
Khamti	Daic	CVV(C), CVR					◆ CVV(C), CVC

Kiowa	Kiowa-Tanoan	CVV(C), CVR				◆ CVV(C), CVC	◆ CVV(C), CVC
Kissi	Niger-Congo	CVV(C), CVR[100]					
Khmu	Austro-Asiatic	CVV(C), CVR[101]					
Kitsai	Caddoan	CVV(C), CVR					◆ ?:
Lao	Daic	CVV(C), CVR					◆ CVV(C), CVC
Lithuanian	Indo-European	CVV(C), CVR				◆ ♥	◆ CVV(C), CVC
Maru[b]	Sino-Tibetan	CVV(C), CVR				◆ CVV(C), CVC	◆ Full V
Mbai[d]	Nilo-Saharan	CVV(C), CVR					
Muong[b]	Austro-Asiatic	CVV(C), CVR[n]					

(continued)

Table 2.13. Languages with weight restrictions for contour tones (*continued*)

Language	Macro-Phylum	Tone	Stress	Metrics	Comp Length	Syll. Templ.	Minim. Word
Nama	Khoisan	CVV(C), CVR					❤
Naro[d]	Khoisan	CVV(C), CVR					◆
Nung	Sino-Tibetan	CVV(C), CVR^n					◆ CVV(C), CVC
Saek	Daic	CVV(C), CVR^n					
Shan	Daic	CVV(C), CVR^n					
Tai, Lung Ming	Daic	CVV(C), CVR^n					
Tewa	Kiowa-Tanoan	CVV(C), CVR					
Thai	Daic	CVV(C), CVR		◆ CVV(C), CVC	◆ CVV(C), CVC		◆ CVV(C), CVC

Language	Family		CVV(C)		CVV(C), CVC	
Tibetan (Lhasa)	Sino-Tibetan	CVV(C), CVR[102]	◆		◆	
Tura[d]	Niger-Congo	CVV(C), CVR				♥
Turkana	Nilo-Saharan	CVV(C), CVR[103]				
Vietnamese[b]	Austro-Asiatic	CVV(C), CVR[104]				
Hausa	Afro-Asiatic	CVV(C), CVC		♥		♥
Luganda	Niger-Congo	CVV(C), CVC		♥		♥
Musey	Afro-Asiatic	CVV(C), CVC			♥	♥

2.12.2.1. Tone vs. Compensatory Lengthening

Comparison of weight criteria for tone with weight criteria for compensatory lengthening is not particularly probative, since only four languages in the survey display both weight-sensitive tone and compensatory lengthening. Of the four languages, three (Thai, Dzongkha, and Lhasa Tibetan) disagree in their weight criteria and one agrees (Musey). The Lhasa Tibetan case was discussed above in section 2.5.1; the Dzongkha case is similar. The crucial data on Thai comes from northern Thai dialects which have lost coda /k/ historically and underwent compensatory lengthening of the preceding vowel, even though syllables closed by obstruents (including /k/) are treated as light by the tonal system. The one case of agreement in weight criteria between tone and compensatory lengthening comes from Musey which displays compensatory lengthening triggered by coda /r/ loss and treats closed syllables as heavy in its tonal system.

2.12.2.2. Tone vs. Metrics

The number of languages displaying both weight-sensitive tone and weight-sensitive poetic metrics is quite small, only four. Of these four languages, two (Hausa and Luganda) agree in their weight criteria for the two phenomena. In both Hausa and Luganda, CVV(C) and CVC are heavy for tone and for metrics. In the other two languages (Thai and Classical Greek) weight criteria for tone and metrics conflict. In Thai and Classical Greek, both CVV(C) and CVC are heavy in the metrical system, but the tonal system of Thai observes the CVV(C), CVR heavy criterion while the tonal system of Classical Greek exploits the CVV(C) heavy criterion.

2.12.2.3. Tone vs. Syllable Template Restrictions

We now turn to the relationship between weight criteria for tone and weight criteria for syllable template restrictions. There are six languages in which weight criteria for the two phenomena agree. In three languages (Hausa, Luganda, and Musey), CVV(C) and CVC are heavy both for tone and syllable templates. In one language (Lithuanian), CVV(C) and CVR are heavy for syllable templates and tone. There are 2 languages (Tura and Kabiye), in which both CVV(C) and CVR are heavy for syllable templates and tone, but which lack obstruent codas, and are therefore not able to diagnose weight distinctions based on coda sonority.

Weight criteria disagree between tone and syllable templates in three languages. In one language, Krongo, CVV(C) is heavy for tone, whereas CVV(C), CVC is heavy for syllable templates. In two languages (Kiowa and Maru), both CVV(C) and CVC count as heavy for syllable templates, but only CVV(C) and CVR are heavy for tone. The greater restrictedness of weight criteria for tone than for syllable templates is related to the fact that the CVV(C) and CVC weight criterion is so rare for tone (see section 2.3.2.1), unlike for syllable templates, for which it is so common.

Despite the overall lack of uniformity between tone and syllable template restrictions, it is worth noting that the few cases of uniformity are interesting in that they are unexpected given the overall distribution of weight criteria for the two processes. The only three languages in the survey that treat all codas as weighted for tone (Hausa, Luganda, and Musey) also have restrictions against long vowels in all closed syllables. Furthermore, observance of the CVV(C), CVR heavy criterion for tone in Lithuanian coincides with a restriction against long vowels in syllables closed by a sonorant, a restriction that is itself quite rare cross-linguistically. It is also worth noting that another language not included in the survey (or, more precisely, another historical stage of a language in the survey), Early Greek, observes the CVV(C), CVR heavy criterion for both tone and syllable template restrictions. Perhaps even more striking is the fact that the relaxation of the restriction against long vowels in sonorant closed syllables occurred during the development from Early to Classical Greek, a time frame in which CVR also shifted from heavy to light for tone. This case and other striking cases of uniformity of weight criteria between tone and other phenomena will be explored in Chapters Three and Five.

2.12.2.4. Tone vs. Minimal Word Requirements

The comparison of weight for tone and weight for minimal word requirements provides one of the more robust arguments against uniformity of weight criteria within languages. Of the 15 languages in the survey with both weight restrictions on tones and a minimal word requirement, only three (Andoke, Naro, and Gana-Khwe) observe the same weight criterion for these two phenomena: CVV(C) heavy.[105] Another 12 languages display different criteria for the two phenomena. Of these 12 cases of conflicting weight criteria, 7 use the CVV(C), CVC heavy criterion for their minimal word requirement but the CVV(C), CVR heavy criterion for tone. A further 4 exploit the CVV(C), CVC heavy criterion for the minimal word but treat CVV(C) as heavy for tone. One language (Maru) treats full vowels as heavy for the minimal word requirement, but CVV(C), CVR as heavy for tone. The large number of weight conflicts between tone and minimal word requirements is not surprising when one considers that only three languages treat both CVV(C) and CVC as heavy for tone, while approximately 80%

of languages (see Chapter Five) observe the CVV(C), CVC heavy weight criterion for minimal words.

2.12.2.5. The Uniformity of Tone and Other Weight-Based Phenomena: A Summary

In summary, comparison of weight criteria for tone with weight criteria for other phenomena demonstrates very little propensity for uniformity of weight criteria within individual languages. In fact, more often than not, weight criteria for tone disagree with weight criteria for other weight-sensitive phenomena, a finding which contradicts the hypothesis of uniformity of weight criteria. Amid the overwhelming lack of uniformity, however, there are a mere few scattered cases of convergence in weight criteria which appear not to be attributed to chance: the convergence between weight for tone and weight for syllable template restrictions in Hausa, Musey, Luganda, Lithuanian, and Early Greek. In Chapters Three and Five, the link between weight-sensitive tone and both weight-sensitive metrics and syllable template restrictions will be explored.

Chapter Three
Weight-Sensitive Tone

3.0. THE TYPOLOGY OF WEIGHT FOR TONE

In this chapter, we consider in more detail the motivation behind the cross-linguistic distribution of weight criteria for weight-sensitive tone. As a starting point in this endeavor, the standard formal account given for weight-sensitive tone restrictions is recapitulated here repeating the discussion in Chapter Two.

It is typically assumed that contour tones result from the combination of two level tones (e.g. Woo 1969, Hyman 1985, Duanmu 1994a,b). Thus, a rising tone results from the combination of a low tone followed by a high tone, while a falling tone is represented as a combination of a high tone followed by a low tone. Given the compositionality of contour tones, restrictions against contour tones are assumed to arise from a prohibition against associations between more than one tone and a single timing position (either skeletal slot or mora). Because a contour tone consists of two tones, it requires two timing positions on which to be realized, one for each element of the contour. For example, the restriction against contour tones on CVO and CV, which is common across languages, follows if we assume that tones may only be linked to sonorants.[1]

Although this analysis accounts for contour tone restrictions, it fails to capture certain distributional generalizations characteristic of weight-sensitive tone that were described in Chapter Two. Recall that languages with weight-sensitive tone or pitch accent follow an implicational hierarchy in terms of the ability of different syllable types to carry contour tones. This implicational hierarchy becomes clear if we consider the four basic patterns attested in languages that allow contour tones. In some languages (e.g. Somali), contour tones are limited to CVV(C). In other languages (e.g. Kiowa), contour tones are restricted to CVV(C) and CVR.[2] In other languages (e.g. Hausa), contour tones may occur on any syllable except CV, i.e. contour tones may occur on CVV(C), CVR, and CVO. The final type of language allows contour tones on all syllable types, even CV. Languages of this last type, which are relatively rare as discussed in Chapter Two, are less interesting for present purposes, since they lack weight-sensitive restrictions on contour tones. Recall from Chapter Two that, like other weight-sensitive processes, onsets are ignored for purposes of tonal weight.[3] The four types of languages and the syllables that tolerate contour tones in each are summarized in tabular form in Table 3.1. "Yes" indicates that the given syllable type may carry a contour in the given language type, "No" indicates that it may not.

Looking at Table 3.1, an implicational hierarchy is apparent, as pointed out in Chapter Two. If a language allows contour tones on CV, it also tolerates them on CVO, CVR, and CVV(C). If a language allows contours on CV and CVO, it also allows them on CVR and CVV(C). Finally, if a language tolerates contour tones on CV, CVO, and CVR, it also allows them on CVV. If we conflate these implicational statements, we are left with the hierarchy in Figure 3.1 in which tolerance of contours on a given syllable type implies tolerance of contours on syllable types to its left.

Figure 3.1. Hierarchy of weight for tone

There are two classes of exceptions to this hierarchy. First, certain languages, including Cantonese, which is discussed in section 3.2.2, allow contour tones on CV but not CVO. Cantonese also instantiates the second type of exception to the hierarchy: CVR but not CVVO can carry a contour tone.

As discussed in Chapter Two, if we look at languages that display at least one other weight-sensitive phenomenon in addition to weight-sensitive contour

Table 3.1. Patterns of contour tone restrictions

Syllable	Language			
	Type 1	Type 2	Type 3	Type 4
CVV(C)	**Yes**	**Yes**	**Yes**	**Yes**
CVR	No	**Yes**	**Yes**	**Yes**
CVO	No	No	**Yes**	**Yes**
CV	No	No	No	**Yes**

tone restrictions, we see that there is no tendency for different weight-sensitive phenomena to display the same weight criterion within the same language. Crucially, this is a rather unexpected finding if we assume, following standard theories, that weight is a function of languages, but it may find an explanation in a theory of weight in which process specificity plays an important role. In this chapter, we will explore the phonetic basis for weight-sensitive tone.

3.1. A PHONETIC BASIS FOR CONTOUR TONE RESTRICTIONS

Recall from Chapter Two, the striking difference in distribution of weight criteria for tone as compared to other weight-sensitive phenomena. In this section, we will see that these differences find an explanation in terms of the phonetic requirements of tone. Because these phonetic prerequisites are unique to tone among the weight-sensitive phenomena considered, the phonological asymmetry between weight for tone and weight for other processes turns out to be exactly what we would expect to find.

The physical correlate of tone is fundamental frequency, which is only present in voiced segments. In fact, the property that defines a voicing contrast is the fundamental frequency: voiceless segments lack a fundamental, voiced segments have one. Thus, the only type of segment on which tone may be *directly* realized is a voiced one.[4]

Crucially, the fundamental frequency profile of a segment or syllable (and hence its tonal profile) is cued not only by the fundamental frequency itself but also by other information. In particular, the presence of harmonics in the signal assists the recovery of the fundamental frequency. The reason for this is that harmonics occur at frequencies that are multiples of the fundamental frequency. Thus, a signal with a fundamental frequency of 200Hz will have harmonics at 400Hz, 600Hz, 800Hz, 1000Hz, and at 200Hz increments thereafter. The presence of harmonics greatly enhances the salience of the fundamental frequency, and can even allow for recovery of the tone when the fundamental itself has been extracted from the signal (see House 1990 and Moore 1995 for review of the relevant psychoacoustic literature).

While the relationship of harmonics to the fundamental in the frequency domain is the same for all segments (harmonics occur at multiples of the fundamental), voiced segments differ in terms of the intensity of their harmonics. Because vowels typically have the most energy at higher frequencies, their higher harmonics have greater intensity than those of consonants. Voiced sonorant consonants also possess a fairly energetic harmonic structure relative to voiced obstruents, but typically do not possess as intense harmonics as vowels. Nevertheless, the more crucial harmonics for the perception of the fundamental, the second through fourth (House 1990), are typically quite intense in sonorants.

In contrast to sonorants, obstruents provide either minimal or no cues to fundamental frequency. Voiceless consonants, including obstruents, do not have a fundamental or harmonics. In voiced obstruents, harmonics above the fundamental typically have very little energy; furthermore, the fundamental itself is typically substantially less intense than in sonorants. The absence of a salient harmonic structure in obstruents and the low intensity of the fundamental frequency are due to the narrow constrictions associated with obstruents. Thus, voiced obstruents are inherently impoverished relative to voiced sonorants in terms of their tonal salience. We would thus expect voiced obstruents to contribute extremely little to the ability of a syllable to carry a contour tone or not. This fact, taken together with the inability of voiceless obstruents to carry tone and the rarity of voiced coda obstruents relative to voiceless coda obstruents, means that the class of obstruents considered as a whole is quite poorly suited to supporting tonal information.

The relative ability of different segment types to carry tone can be made more vivid by considering a narrowband spectrogram of different types of voiced segments in Figure 3.2.

In Figure 3.2, we see that the vowel has the greatest number of visible harmonics (i.e. those with sufficient intensity to show up in the narrow band spectrogram) above the fundamental and also the most intense ones (as

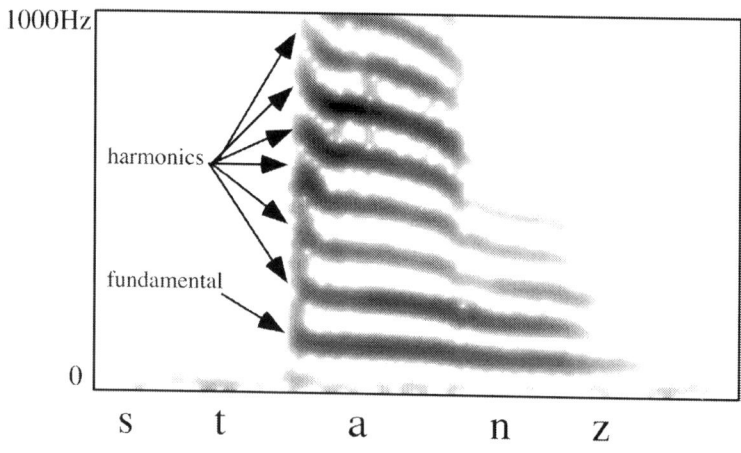

Figure 3.2. Narrowband spectrogram of voiced segments

reflected in the darkness of the harmonics). The sonorant consonant also has a relatively rich harmonic structure and relatively intense harmonics, though the sonorant consonant's harmonics are visibly fewer in number (again due to decreased intensity at higher frequencies) and less intense than the vowel's. The two voiceless consonants, a fricative and a stop, provide no fundamental frequency or harmonics.

The relative salience of tonal information realized on different segment types offers an explanation for the distribution of weight-sensitive contour tone restrictions discussed earlier. Recall the implicational hierarchy of syllable types that may bear contour tones: CVV is heaviest, followed by CVR, followed by CVO, followed by CV. This hierarchy mirrors the phonetic hierarchy of tonal salience in Figure 3.2 under the assumption that contour tones require a longer duration to be realized than level tones. It is thus crucial that not only the initial portion of the rime but also the *latter* portion of the rime possess properties that will allow for recovery of the tonal information. Thus, it is the second half of the long vowel in CVV and the coda consonant in CVR and CVO that serve to differentiate them from each other and from CV in terms of relative ability to carry a contour tone. The hierarchy of syllable types in Figure 3.1 thus reduces to a hierarchy characterizing the relative ability of different segment types to carry the latter portion of the contour: V > R > O > Zero, (where the difference between O (an obstruent) and zero is not particularly robust; see the discussion in section 3.1 above). This hierarchy corresponds to the phonetic hierarchy of segments in Figure 3.2 and also to the phonological hierarchy of syllable types in Figure 3.1. Languages with weight-sensitive restrictions on contour tones draw different "cut-off" points along this hierarchy, as in Figure 3.3.

Figure 3.3. Different cut-off points for weight-sensitive tone

In any given language, contour tones are permitted on syllable types to the left of the line, but not on syllable types to the right of the line, reflecting the fact that syllable types further left on the continuum are phonetically better suited to carry a contour tone. Thus, the licensing of contour tones on syllables that are less well suited to supporting a contour tone implies the licensing of contour tones on syllables that are phonetically better suited to supporting a contour.

Gordon (2001) quantifies the difference in harmonic structure between vowels, sonorant consonants, and voiced obstruents by summing the intensity (in decibeles) of the first five harmonics for the three classes of sounds. Results indicate that vowels have the greatest intensity over the first five harmonics, followed by sonorant consonants, and then voiced obstruents. Furthermore, the difference in intensity between sonorant consonants and voiced obstruents is far greater than the difference between vowels and sonorant consonants. This finding matches up well with the typological commonness of the CVV heavy and CVV, CVR heavy criteria relative to the CVV, CVC heavy criterion.

The close link between sonority and contour tone licensing also offers an account for the observation that contour tones in many languages are limited to the right edge of a word. Vowels in word-final position are typically (though not universally) longer than their word-medial counterparts due to final lengthening (Wightman et al. 1992). By virtue of its additional phonetic duration, a word-final vowel is thus better able to support a contour tone than a word-medial one. Similar duration-based asymmetries that impact tonal weight hold of stressed vs. unstressed syllables (see Zhang 2002 for discussion of final vs. non-final and stressed vs. unstressed tonal asymmetries).

3.2. APPARENT EXCEPTIONS TO THE TONAL WEIGHT HIERARCHY

3.2.1 Languages with a CVV(C), CVC Heavy Criterion for Tone

Positing a phonetic explanation for contour tone restrictions raises an interesting question about the three languages in the survey, Hausa, Musey, and Luganda, which draw their cut-off point in Figure 3.3 between CVO and CV. Assuming that obstruents are particularly ill-equipped to carry tonal information, there is then little reason to think that a CVO syllable would be much, if at all, better suited to carry a contour tone than CV. The Hausa, Musey, and Luganda pattern is especially surprising when one considers the fact that many of the coda obstruents in these languages are voiceless and thus cannot carry tone at all.

3.2.1.1. Phonetic Experiment: Hausa

In order to examine whether this a priori unexpected distribution of contour tones finds a phonetic explanation, a small experiment was conducted on Hausa. Hausa possesses the following syllable types: CV, CVC, and CVV

(Newman 1990, Wolff 1993, Russ Schuh p.c.). CVVC is not a permissible syllable type in Hausa. Contour tones, which can be falling tone but not rising, are limited to CVC and CVV syllables.

One speaker of Hausa was recorded (using an analog cassette recorder via a table top condenser microphone) repeating a list of words in isolation eight times in a sound proof booth. The list consisted of disyllabic words in which the rime of the first syllable was systematically varied such that various syllable types were represented in the list. The measured syllables contained the low vowel /a/ followed variously by the coda sonorant /n/ and the obstruent /s/. The list of words recorded appears in Appendix Three. Data were digitized at a 10kHz sampling rate using the Kay CSL speech analysis system. The duration of segments in the rime of the first syllable, the target syllable, was measured from a waveform in conjunction with a spectrogram and an energy display. The intensity of the first five harmonics was also calculated and multiplied by the duration of the targeted segments in order to directly assess tone bearing ability (see Gordon 2001 for results and expanded discussion of duration patterns). Differences in harmonic energy between different rime types were largely predictable from duration; for this reason, only duration results are presented below.

Average measurements (in milliseconds) appear in Table 3.2, which separates the four syllable types CV, CVO, CVR, and CVV, and the three tone types, high, low, and falling, found in Hausa. The crucial measurements for present purposes are those of CVO syllables (boxed off in the table).

Interestingly, the measurements in boldface, those for CVO, suggest that it is not the coda obstruent in CVO which makes CVO a better licenser of contours than CV, but rather it is the *vowel* in CVO which bears the burden of carrying the contour tone. The crucial evidence for this is that vowels carrying contour tones in CVO syllables are substantially longer than vowels carrying level tones in CVO syllables. The vowel carrying a falling tone in CVO averages 133 milliseconds as compared to 112 and 105 milliseconds for vowels

Table 3.2. Duration measurements for Hausa rimes

	Syllable Type										
	CV		CVO			CVR			CVV		
	H	L	H	L	HL	H	L	HL	H	L	HL
Vowel	103	98	112	105	133	115	132	126	272	262	263
Sonorant phase	103	98	112	105	133	271	279	238	272	262	263

carrying level high and level low tones, respectively. This difference between CVO carrying a contour tone and CVO carrying a level tone is responsible for the highly significant interaction between rime type (CVV, CVR, and CVO; i.e. those which carry contours) and tone type (contour vs. level) in an analysis of variance with vowel duration as the dependent variable and rime type and tone type as independent variables (F [2, 66]=7.317, p=.0013). The duration difference between vowels carrying a falling tone and vowels carrying both types of level tone in CVO is highly significant as indicated by a Fisher's PLSD posthoc test: p=.0008 for falling vs. high tone in CVO, p<.0001 for falling vs. low tone in CVO. The duration difference between the two level tones was statistically insignificant.[5] Furthermore, vowels carrying contour tones in CVR and CVV syllables were *not* longer when they carry contour tones. This indicates that it is only the vowel in CVO that is in need of phonetic lengthening to support a contour tone.

Nor is the total sonorous duration of the rime longer in CVR and CVV when they carry a contour tone as opposed to a level tone. An ANOVA examining the effect of rime type and tone type (contour vs. level) on the total sonorant duration of the rime indicated a non-significant effect of tone type on sonorant duration (F [1,66]=2.838, p=.0968). The substantial difference in sonorant duration between CVO carrying a level tone and CVO carrying a contour tone, however, contributed to a highly significant interaction between rime type and tone type (F [1,66]=28.746, p<.0001).

These data suggest that the vowel in CVO syllables carrying a contour tone is lengthening in order to aid in the realization of the contour, because the coda obstruent itself provides little assistance. Lengthening is not necessary in CVR and CVV, because the rime in these syllables consists entirely of sonorants, which, for reasons enumerated earlier, are well suited to supporting tonal information.

One might reasonably ask whether there are any independent factors unique to Hausa that contribute to or facilitate the substantial amount of subphonemic lengthening seen in CVO syllables carrying a contour tone. A related question concerns the asymmetrical ability of CVO but not CV to carry a contour tone in Hausa. One might ask why Hausa does not also allow contour tones on CV syllables and just lengthen the vowel in order to accommodate the contour tone.

There is a related fact about Hausa syllable structure that suggests an answer to this question. Hausa has a vowel length contrast in open but not closed syllables. It is conceivable that the subphonemic lengthening in CVO carrying a contour tone is allowed because there is no phonemic contrast in vowel length that could be jeopardized through subphonemic lengthening.

In open syllables, on the other hand, subphonemic lengthening could potentially jeopardize the salience of the phonemic length contrast. This account assumes that certain phonological conditions are a prerequisite for the Hausa weight distinction, but that the adoption of the phonological distinction is actually triggering the phonetic lengthening.

In summary, despite initial appearances to the contrary, Hausa actually provides further evidence that it is really the duration of the sonorant portion of the rime that serves as the basis for determining syllable weight for tone. Thus, the presence of an obstruent does not itself contribute to the ability of a syllable to carry a contour tone. It is only when the presence of the obstruent allows for lengthening of the preceding vowel as in Hausa that CVO is better able to support a contour tone than CV. The Hausa pattern also suggests that the ability of a syllable to carry a contour tone is really a property of the entire syllable and not merely a property of individual segments within the syllable summed together. It is the presence of the coda which licenses vowel lengthening in CVO syllables bearing a contour tone, but it is the vowel that actually carries the burden of realizing the tone.[6]

Let us now briefly consider the two other languages in the survey which superficially appear to allow contours on CVO but not on CV: Luganda and Musey. Luganda, as it turns out, also lacks CVVC syllables. Furthermore, in Luganda, CVO syllables with a phonological falling tone, the only type of contour in Luganda, are reported by Tucker, in his introduction to Snoxall's (1967) dictionary to carry only a "psychological low tone." Phonetically, only the high part of the contour is realized on the CVO syllable while the low tone is phonetically realized through its lowering effect on the tone of the following syllable. Snoxall's observations were confirmed through examination of tapes of Luganda in the UCLA Phonetics Laboratory (see Zhang 2002 for more discussion and phonetic data). Thus, Luganda is not an exceptional language that realizes the latter part of a contour tone on an obstruent coda itself.

Interestingly, like Hausa, Musey, the third language in the survey that appears to allow contour tones on CVO but not CV, also does not possess a vowel length contrast in closed syllables. Although I do not have phonetic data to bear on the issue, it is thus plausible that vowels carrying contour tones in Musey are phonetically lengthened in CVO syllables relative to vowels carrying level tones. Aaron Shryock's impressions of Musey data (p.c.) suggest that this is indeed the case.

3.2.2. Cantonese

Cantonese is one of the few languages in the survey that does not observe the implicational weight hierarchy in Figure 3.1. The Cantonese tone facts are as follows, following Kao (1971) and Bauer and Benedict (1997). Contour tones (which include a high rising, a low rising, and a falling tone) are permitted on phonemic short vowels in open syllables (CV) and on syllables closed by a sonorant, whether they contain a short vowel (CVR) or a long vowel (CVVR). Contour tones in morphologically simple forms do not occur on syllables closed by an obstruent, regardless of whether the vowel is short (CVO) or long (CVVO).[7] Syllables closed by an obstruent carry either level low, level mid, or level high tones. Crucially, Cantonese lacks a vowel length distinction in open syllables.

Given these facts, Cantonese appears to be an exception in more than one way to the implicational hierarchy in Figure 1. First, phonemic CV may bear a contour but CVO may not, a pattern that is the opposite of the Hausa type distribution. Second, both CV and CVR may bear a contour but CVVO may not, an apparent exception to the general pattern of CVV being heavier than both CV and CVR.

3.2.2.1. Cantonese: A Phonetic Experiment

In order to test whether the exceptional distribution of Cantonese tones finds a phonetic explanation, measurements of various Cantonese rimes were collected from a native speaker of Cantonese under conditions similar to those used to record Hausa. The subject read a list of words in isolation eight times. The data consisted of monosyllabic words in which the rime was systematically varied between /a/, /am/, /ap/, /aːm/, and /aːp/, which represent the principle prosodic shapes of rimes in Cantonese: V, VO, VR, VVO, VVR. All words were low-toned, since it was possible to find the closest minimal set of words for this tone. The Cantonese corpus appears in Appendix Three. Words were digitized and measured according to the same procedure described for Hausa above.

Although confining the data set to low toned syllables does not allow for examination of either the effect of tone type on duration or interactions between syllable type and tone, it does allow for controlled comparison of the durations of different syllable types. Any duration differences found in the low-toned rime types cannot be attributed to the presence of a contour tone.

In Table 3.3, we see mean duration values of the vowel and the entire sonorant phase of the rime (i.e. everything except the obstruent coda, if present), the relevant portion of the syllable for assessing the ability of a syllable to carry a contour tone or not. Syllables that can carry contour tones appear to the right of the boldface line; those to the left of the line cannot carry contours.

Table 3.3 Duration measurements (in milliseconds) for different rimes in Cantonese

	Syllable Type				
	CVO	**CVVO**	**CV**	**CVR**	**CVVR**
Vowel	77	150	283	99	208
Sonorous phase	77	150	283	275	301

Interestingly, the three syllable types that can carry contours in Cantonese (CV, CVR, CVVR) are those with the longest sonorant duration in the rime. The vowel in CV is quite long phonetically, much longer than V in either CVR or CVO, or for that matter, than the phonemic long vowels in CVVR and CVVO. Kao (1971) reports similar phonetic results in her study of Cantonese, which, unlike the present study, did not control for vowel quality or the type of coda consonant. The vowel in CV is also qualitatively quite similar to the long vowels in CVVR and CVVO, which are more peripheral than the short vowels in CVO and CVR. Thus, although there is no phonemic contrast in length in open syllables, the vowel in CV is more accurately treated as a long vowel than as a short vowel, both in terms of quality and in terms of quantity. The assignment of the vowel in CV to the long category is also corroborated by the judgment of my consultant and also those of other investigators (e.g. Kao 1971, also cf. Duanmu (1994b) on Mandarin). Presumably the length of the vowel in open syllables is a function of a minimal word requirement that words be minimally a certain duration (cf. Duanmu 1994a). Most words are monosyllabic in Cantonese. The long duration of the sonorant portion in CV relative to that in CVO and CVVO offers an explanation for why phonemic CV but neither CVO nor CVVO can carry a contour tone in Cantonese. Sonorant duration also accounts for the greater weight of CVR relative to CVVO in Cantonese.

Before concluding the discussion of Cantonese, it is worth noting that the tone restrictions in Cantonese cannot be attributed merely to moraic structure. CVVO must be at least bimoraic, since vowel length is contrastive in closed syllables. If one adopts the standard assumption that a mora may carry a maximum of one tone in languages with weight-sensitive tone restrictions, the vowel in CVVO would incorrectly be expected to be able to support a contour tone. The phonetic data in this section demonstrate that the relevant property for predicting weight for tone is the phonetic property of sonorant duration, not the moraic structure of the syllable.

3.3. THE ROLE OF PHONETICS IN LANGUAGE SPECIFICITY OF TONAL WEIGHT

Thus far, we have seen that weight-sensitive restrictions on contour tones have a phonetic basis in terms of the ability of different syllable types to support a contour tone. Syllables containing a long vowel are best suited to licensing a contour tone due to the rich and intense harmonic structure of vowels. Hence, it is correctly predicted that many languages only allow contour tones on syllables containing a long vowel. Syllables closed by a sonorant also provide a good platform for realizing contour tones (though not as good as a long vowel). The relatively large number of languages that allow contours on both CVV and CVR thus also follows from phonetic considerations. Finally, CVO and CV syllables are largely equivalent in terms of their phonetic ability to carry contour tones. It follows that CVO and CV are characteristically treated identically by phonologies when it comes to contour tone restrictions. Languages that appear to contradict the phonetic motivations for tone restrictions (e.g. CVO and CV behaving differently from one another in Hausa, and CVR and CV but not CVVO carrying contours in Cantonese) turn out, upon closer evaluation, to result from language specific phonetic patterns which themselves can be linked to other independent properties of the language. In Hausa, the absence of a vowel length contrast in closed syllables creates conditions that allow for the vowel in CVO to undergo substantial lengthening to support a contour tone. In Cantonese, a minimal word restriction against CV words ensures that vowels in open syllables are phonetically long and thus able to support a contour tone. Similarly, the relatively short phonetic duration of the sonorant portion of the rime in both CVO and CVVO in Cantonese makes them a poor docking site for contour tones.

A reasonable question to ask at this point is whether the language specific choice of weight distinctions, among those that fall within the universal set of phonetically permissible distinctions, is predictable on phonetic grounds. We have seen that phonetic factors constrain the set of possible weight distinctions for tone. Thus, languages do not allow contour tones on syllable types with relatively little overall sonority while simultaneously prohibiting contour tones on syllables with greater overall sonority. Such a hypothetical weight distinction would be at odds with the phonetic considerations underlying weight-sensitive tone.

What we have not established yet is whether language specific differences in weight criteria for tone are correlated with phonetic differences as well. For example, we might ask whether a language which makes a CVV(C), CVR heavy distinction for tone differs phonetically (in aspects relevant for tone) from one which treats only CVV(C) and not CVR as heavy. A reasonable place to look for such differences is in the duration domain. Thus, CVV(C) might be substantially longer than CVR in languages in which CVV(C) but not CVR is heavy, whereas CVV(C) and CVR might be roughly equivalent in duration in languages in which both syllable types are heavy. If this hypothesis were corroborated, we could presume that syllable weight for tone is purely a function of the duration of the sonorant portion of the rime and is not sensitive to differences in the relative sonority of sonorant segments. In other words, in languages in which CVV(C) is heavier than CVR, this weight distinction would not be attributed to the greater sonority of the second portion of the rime (V vs. R), but rather would be due to the greater total duration of the sonorant portion of the rime.

3.3.1. Navajo

As a test of the hypothesis that weight for tone is sensitive to the total sonorant duration of the rime, an experiment on Navajo, a language which treats only CVV as heavy for tone, was conducted. Both rising and falling contour tones occur on CVV syllables in Navajo but not on other syllable types (Sapir and Hoijer 1967). If CVV were longer than CVR in Navajo we would find support for the view that tonal weight is projected from sonorant duration.

A Navajo speaker was recorded reading a list of words in isolation eight times in a sound proof booth. The six words in the corpus each contained a different rime type in the target syllable: CV, CVR, CVO, CVV, CVVO and CVVR. The target syllable in each case carried a low tone and contained the vowel /a/. The corpus appears in Appendix Three. Data were digitized and analyzed using the same procedure as in the Hausa and Cantonese experiments discussed earlier.

Average duration measurements (in milliseconds) for Navajo appear in Table 3.4. Of particular relevance are measurements for the syllable types CVR and CVV, which are in boldface in Table 3.4.

Contra the hypothesis advanced above, CVV is not longer than CVR, even though it is heavier for tone. In fact, the total sonorant duration of

Table 3.4. Duration measurements (in milliseconds) for different rimes in Navajo

	Syllable Type					
	CV	CVO	**CVR**	**CVV**	CVVO	CVVR
Vowel	107	119	**153**	**173**	153	239
Sonorous phase	107	119	**208**	**173**	153	321

Table 3.5. Duration measurements (in milliseconds) for coda sonorants in Navajo, Cantonese, and Hausa

	Coda sonorant duration in different rime types		
	CVR	**CVVR**	**Ave.**
Navajo	55	81	**68**
Cantonese	176	93	**135**
Hausa	147	n.a.	**147**

CVR is substantially greater than that of CVV,[8] indicating that the weight for tone is not sensitive only to the total duration of the sonorant portion of the rime. Rather, these data appear to suggest that the weight of CVV relative to CVR is due at least partially to factors other than duration (see Zhang 2002).

There is, however, an interesting durational difference between, on the one hand, Navajo, which observes the CVV(C) heavy criterion, and, on the other hand, Cantonese and Hausa, which both allow CVR to carry contour tones. The coda sonorant in Cantonese and Hausa is much longer than the coda sonorant in Navajo, as shown in Table 3.5, which compares the duration of coda nasals in the three languages (/n/ in Hausa and Navajo and /m/ in Cantonese; syllables in all three languages carry level low tones and contain /a/). Note that coda sonorants do not follow long vowels.

Whereas the nasal coda averages only 68 milliseconds in Navajo, it averages 135 and 147 milliseconds, respectively, in Cantonese and Hausa. That these absolute differences in duration are attributed neither to differences in speaking rate between the speakers of the languages nor to differences in the number of syllables in the measured words (three in Navajo vs. two in Cantonese and Hausa) can be seen by comparing in Table 3.6 the duration ratio of the sonorant coda to the short vowels in the three languages. This was done for all three languages by dividing the duration of the sonorant coda by the duration of short vowels averaged over CV, CVO and CVR.

Table 3.6. Duration ratio of coda sonorant to preceding vowel in Navajo, Cantonese, and Hausa

Navajo	.54
Cantonese	1.78
Hausa	1.53

Based on these data, it is conceivable that sonorant codas only contribute to the ability of a syllable to carry a contour tone if they are sufficiently long. Under this account, sonorant codas in Navajo do not contribute to the weight of the syllable for tone, because they are not long enough. In Cantonese and Hausa, on the other hand, sonorant codas are long enough to add weight to the syllable. What we do not know on the basis of these data is the duration (either absolute or relative to the duration of some other element) which serves as the cut-off point for determining whether a language adopts the CVV(C) heavy or the CVV(C), CVR heavy criterion for tone. The data seen thus far are compatible with the relatively simple and least arbitrary hypothesis that a coda to vowel ratio of greater than one is sufficient to trigger adoption of the CVV(C), CVR heavy criterion in a language. Clearly, this value must be regarded merely as a working hypothesis subject to further investigation. What is crucial for the present argument is not the actual threshold value above which coda sonorants contribute weight, but the observation that coda sonorants must possess some, as yet undetermined, duration to count as weighted.

3.3.2. Phonetic Evidence for Coda Duration as a Predictor of Weight Criteria: The Case of Lithuanian

Phonetic data from Lithuanian, another language which observes the CVV(C), CVR heavy criterion for tone (Senn 1957–1966, Kenstowicz 1972, Halle and Vergnaud 1987, Zec 1988, Young 1991) supports the hypothesis that coda duration is a predictor of syllable weight for tone. In Lithuanian, CVV and CVR may either contain a rising accent (phonetically, a rising tone), a falling accent (phonetically, a falling tone), or no accent (phonetically, a low tone). CV and CVO syllables do not contrast rising and falling accents; syllables are either accented (i.e. high-toned) or unaccented (i.e. low-toned).

A native speaker of Lithuanian was recorded reading a list of disyllabic words in which the first syllable was systematically varied between CV, CVO and CVR. The tonal properties of the various syllable types were also varied. The corpus of words appears in Appendix Three. Six tokens of each word were read in isolation in a sound proof booth. Data were digitized and analyzed using the same procedure as in the Hausa, Cantonese, and Navajo experiments discussed earlier.

For purposes of the present discussion, the relevant measurement for comparison with Navajo, Cantonese, and Hausa is of the coda nasal (an /n/ in the present experiment) following /a/ in a low-toned (i.e. unaccented) syllable; the first syllable in bandá 'herd.' Averaged over six tokens, the /n/ was 159 milliseconds. If this figure is divided by the duration of short vowels averaged over

CV, CVO, and CVR in low-toned (i.e. unaccented) syllables, we get a coda sonorant to vowel ratio of 1.42, a figure which falls close to values reported for Cantonese and Hausa in Table 3.6 and which is much larger than Navajo, a language in which coda sonorants are not treated as heavy for tone.

In summary, the data from Cantonese, Hausa, Lithuanian, and Navajo offer support for the view that coda duration is a predictor of the language specific choice of weight criterion between CVV(C), CVR heavy and CVV(C) heavy. If sonorant codas are long enough in a given language, that language employs the CVV(C), CVR heavy criterion. If not, the language opts for the CVV(C) heavy criterion. This hypothesis awaits further corroboration (or disconfirmation) as data from other languages are examined. Assuming that the data here are mirrored by data from other languages, we have evidence that phonetic factors not only constrain the set of possible weight distinctions employed by tonal systems, but also predict the language-specific choice of weight criteria. The phonetic underpinnings of syllable weight will be further exemplified in the discussion of weight-sensitive stress.

The fact that the phonetic factors motivating tonal weight are sharply divergent from those driving other weight-sensitive phenomena, a point which will become clearer in the discussion of stress in Chapter Four, explains the observation made in Chapter Two and again earlier in this chapter that phonological weight for tone displays a much different distribution than weight for other processes. In contrast, the distribution of tonal weight is not accounted for by current theories of weight that assume language internal uniformity of weight to be the normal scenario.

3.4. THE DIRECTIONALITY OF THE PHONETICS/ PHONOLOGY RELATIONSHIP FOR TONE

This chapter has thus far demonstrated a close link between phonological weight criteria for tone and the sonorant energy of syllables. The close correspondence between the phonology of weight and the phonetic dimension of sonorant energy is apparent on two levels. First, the hierarchy of weight for tone corresponds to a universal phonetic hierarchy of sonority. CVV(C) is heaviest by virtue of its long sonorant phase and its rich harmonic structure, both of which are important in the phonetic realization of tone. CVR is intermediate in weight, as it has a longer sonorant phase than either CV or CVO, but is not as rich as CVV(C) in terms of its harmonic structure. Finally, CV and CVO are roughly equivalent in weight since they differ very little in their phonetic ability to support contour tones. Cases of languages in which an obstruent coda appears to carry tone itself were demonstrated to be only apparent exceptions, at least phonetically on the surface. In one set of such cases, including Hausa and probably Musey, a vowel carrying a contour tone in CVO is phonetically lengthened to support the contour tone. In another language, Luganda, the second half of the contour tone is not actually realized on CVO but is phonetically realized through its effect on the tone of the following vowel.

The second level on which the link between phonetics and the phonology of weight-sensitive tone manifests itself involves the language specific choice of weight criteria from the set of criteria that are phonetically sensible for tone. We have seen that the rarely attested CVV(C), CVC heavy weight criterion is associated with increased phonetic length of the vowel in CVO syllables. Evidence has also suggested that the difference between the CVV(C) heavy and the CVV(C), CVR heavy criteria is reflected in phonetic differences: coda sonorants are longer in languages in which CVR counts as heavy than in languages in which only CVV(C) is heavy.

In summary, there is ample evidence for a close correspondence between the phonetics and phonology of weight. What we have not yet investigated as thoroughly is the directionality of the relationship between phonetic and phonological aspects of weight. It must still be determined whether the phonology of weight is projected from phonetic considerations, or alternatively, whether the phonetic patterns observed are the result of tailoring the phonetic system to maximize the salience of existing phonological properties. Under the first scenario, phonetics can, roughly speaking, be construed as driving the phonology, whereas, under the second scenario, the roles are reversed and phonology is driving the phonetics. Yet another possibility is that the phonetics/phonology relationship is bi-directional, whereby certain aspects of the phonology help to create certain phonetic conditions, which in turn are responsible for other phonological properties. Although teasing apart the various possibilities is rather difficult, data suggests that the third possibility is most accurate and that the phonetic and phonological subsystems are interleaved. Let us now consider the evidence bearing on this position.

The strongest piece of evidence for the phonetics-drives-phonology position comes from the process specificity of weight. In particular, the fact that the sharp divergence in the cross-linguistic distribution of weight criteria between tone and stress corresponds to a difference in phonetic dimensions along which the two phenomena operate provides solid evidence that phonetic considerations drive the phonology of weight. If the relationship were reversed and phonology drove the phonetics, we would have no explanation for why the weight criteria observed by tonal systems are so closely related to a measure of sonorant energy whereas those observed by stress systems are closely linked to a measure of total energy, as we will see in Chapter Four. If phonology were basic and phonetics were secondary, we could just as easily expect the distribution of weight criteria for tone and stress to be reversed and to find numerous tone systems which make a weight distinction between CVO and CV and numerous stress systems which distinguish between CVR and CVO. That this is not the actual situation in languages of the world is accounted for if we assume that the choice of weight criteria for a given phenomenon is constrained by the phonetic dimensions along which that phenomenon operates.

There are also phonetic properties relevant for shaping the phonology of weight, which appear to be linked to other aspects of the phonology. Some of the relevant data demonstrating this comes from Hausa in which one weight-sensitive phenomenon, the restriction against phonemic long vowels in closed syllables, helps to create the phonetic conditions allowing for the adoption of the CVV(C), CVC heavy criterion for tone. Recall from section 3.2.1.1 that the vowel in a CVO syllable carrying a contour tone is phonetically lengthened relative to vowels carrying level tones in CVO. The fact that lengthening is limited to syllables carrying a contour tone indicates that it is the presence of the contour tone that is responsible for the lengthening effect. The choice of the CVV(C), CVC heavy criterion in Hausa was argued to be linked to the language specific restriction in Hausa against phonemic long vowels in closed syllables. This gap in the phonological inventory of syllable types creates an environment that is conducive to substantial subphonemic vowel lengthening in closed syllables containing a contour tone. Thus, one aspect of the phonological system, the inventory of syllables, creates the phonetic conditions that favor a particular choice of phonological weight criterion. We may further speculate that the restriction against long vowels in closed syllables in Hausa has a phonetic basis in terms of syllable isochrony; this argument will be developed in Chapter Five.

Although the existence of languages like Kiowa which lack phonemic long vowels in closed syllables but observe the CVV(C), CVR heavy criterion for tone demonstrates that a restriction against phonemic long vowels in closed syllables does not guarantee adoption of the CVV(C), CVC heavy criterion for tone, we can at least speculate that the absence of phonemic CVVC is a precondition for observing the CVV(C), CVC heavy criterion. This condition sharply limits the pool of languages that are eligible for employing the CVV(C), CVC heavy criterion for tone, and thereby goes a long way toward explaining the extreme rarity of the CVV(C), CVC heavy in tonal systems.

Cantonese provides another example of one aspect of the phonological system triggering a phonetic response, which in turn impacts the choice of weight criterion for tone. Recall from section 3.2.2 that vowels in open syllables, which a purely phonemic analysis would describe as short, can carry contour tones even though neither CVO nor CVVO tolerate contours. The tolerance of contour tones on what, at first glance, appears to be CV but on neither CVO nor CVVO contradicts the universal hierarchy of weight for tone. It turned out, however, that vowels in open syllables are phonetically long in Cantonese, i.e. they are actually CVV; this additional length was argued to be responsible for the ability of vowels in open syllables to support contour tones. It was also suggested that a minimal word requirement was responsible for the lengthening of vowels in open syllables in Cantonese. Thus, one aspect of the phonological system (in fact a property of the weight system), the minimal word requirement, triggers a phonetic response, vowel lengthening in open syllables, which in turn impacts another aspect of the phonological system, weight requirements for tone.

In summary, we have seen evidence that the phonology of tonal weight is to a large extent driven by phonetic considerations, which often can ultimately be attributed to another aspect of the phonological system. This is not to say that all phonetic properties relevant for tonal weight are predictable from other phonological phenomena. For example, phonetic differences in the duration of coda consonants, such as those found between Navajo, on the one hand, and Hausa, Cantonese, and Lithuanian, on the other hand, do not appear to be attributed in any obvious way to other independent phonological properties. It is possible that this variation is arbitrary and exists alongside phonologically predictable phonetic variation. Alternatively, the interlanguage variation in coda duration could be attributed to phonetic enhancement of phonological weight contrasts. The data considered here do not allow us to tease apart these two possibilities. What is clear, however, is that the phonetic facts and the phonological weight criteria align with each other.

3.5. AN OPTIMALITY-THEORETIC ANALYSIS OF CONTOUR TONE RESTRICTIONS

Thus far, we have seen that both the range of variation in weight-sensitive contour tone restrictions as well as the language specific choice of weight criteria for tone are grounded in phonetic considerations. In this section, I develop a formal analysis of these restrictions within an Optimality-Theoretic (OT) framework (Prince and Smolensky 2004). The basic approach adopted here is similar to one adopted in much work within OT: that the ranking of constraints is governed to a large extent by phonetic scales (e.g. Prince and Smolensky 2004, Kenstowicz 1997, Jun 1995, 1996, Hayes 1999, Steriade 1999, Kirchner 1998, Boersma 1998, etc.). The idea is that certain constraint rankings are universally impermissible, since they would contradict these phonetic scales. For example, consonants are never selected as syllable peaks preferentially over vowels, because consonants are less sonorous than vowels (Prince and Smolensky 2004), where sonority is ultimately a function of phonetic properties. This is also reflected in the constraint rankings: a constraint against vocalic nuclei is never ranked above a constraint against consonantal nuclei. Similarly, high vowels are never heavier than low vowels in stress systems, because high vowels are less sonorous than low vowels (Kenstowicz 1997).[9] This is reflected in constraint rankings: the constraint prohibiting stress on low vowels is in no language ranked above the constraint against stress on high vowels. By appealing to phonetic scales, the range of cross-linguistic variation in constraint ranking, and hence the range of grammars attested cross-linguistically, is greatly constrained.

Now let us turn to the matter of formalizing restrictions against contour tones. There are three types of weight-sensitive tonal systems as discussed earlier. Some languages, e.g. Navajo, only allow contour tones on long vowels. Other languages, e.g. Kiowa, allow contour tones on both long vowels and syllables closed by a sonorant consonant. Finally, a few languages, e.g. Hausa, allow contour tones on long vowels and on all closed syllables. Although we have seen evidence that, in languages belonging to this last type, it is a neighboring vowel that actually assumes the burden of bearing the tonal information, I will nevertheless assume that the relevant constraints in the formal system are expressed in terms of phonemic contrasts and not phonetic duration. In other words, I assume that the structural description of the Hausa type contour tone restriction refers to closed syllables and not directly to the phonetic duration of the vowel preceding the coda consonant.

The approach I assume here follows recent work in Optimality Theory, which assumes constraints that differ in their scope. For example, in her account of default-to-opposite stress systems, Zoll (1997) assumes a series of broad constraints requiring that stress be aligned with a certain edge of a word, either the right or left edge, in addition to narrower constraints requiring specifically that light syllables be aligned with a certain edge of the word. By ranking the narrow constraint referring to light syllables above the broad constraint referring to all syllable types, we get the default-to-opposite stress systems attested in languages like Kwakw'ala and Classical Arabic. By ranking the broad constraint above the narrower constraint, on the other hand, the result is stress at the same edge regardless of the weight of syllables in the word.

Following this general approach, we may assume that constraints on weight-sensitive tone are sensitive to two factors: the complexity of the tone associated with the syllable and the type of syllable on which that tone may be realized (cf. Zhang 2002 for a similar approach). Constraints prohibit tonal complexity of a certain degree except on syllables of sufficient weight. Each constraint specifies a tonal target and a minimal syllable weight that may license that target. Constraints thus take the form *Target tone type *x* unless licensed by syllable type *y*. For example, one set of constraints, the most crucial one for our purposes, specifies a simple contour tone consisting of two tonal units as its target. Members of this constraint set include the following. One constraint bans contour tones unless licensed by a rime containing two sonorant timing positions. This constraint is formulated in (5).

(5) $\overset{*T\,T}{\underset{R}{V}}$ unless $\overset{[XX]}{V}{}_R$ [+sonorant]: A contour tone is licensed by a rime with two sonorant timing slots.

Any rime carrying a contour tone which contains at least two sonorant timing positions honors (5). Thus, a rime of the form VVO or VRO carrying a contour tone does not violate (5). A VO or V rime carrying a contour tone, however, would incur a violation of (5), since it contains only one sonorant timing position.

Another constraint prohibits contour tones except if licensed by a rime containing two syllabic timing positions. This constraint appears in (6).

(6) $\overset{*T\,T}{\underset{R}{V}}$ unless $\overset{[XX]}{V}{}_R$ [+syllabic]: A contour tone is licensed by a rime with two syllabic timing slots.

Only contour toned rimes containing a long vowel (or diphthong) honor (6). Thus, VV and VVC carrying a contour tone do not incur any violations of (6). V, VO, and VR carrying contour tones, however, all violate (6).

Yet another constraint bans contour tones unless the licenser rime contains two timing positions (7).

(7) $\overset{*T\,T}{\underset{R}{V}}$ unless $[XX]{}_R$: A contour tone is licensed by a rime with two timing slots.

Only V with a contour tone violates (7). Any branching rime successfully passes inspection by (7).

The violations of (5), (6), and (7) incurred by different rime types are summarized in tableau (8).

(8)

	$\overset{*T\,T}{\underset{R}{\vee}}$ unless $[XX]_R$	$\overset{*T\,T}{\underset{R}{\vee}}$ unless $\overset{[XX]}{\underset{[+sonorant]}{\vee}}{}^R$	$\overset{*T\,T}{\underset{R}{\vee}}$ unless $\overset{[XX]}{\underset{[+syllabic]}{\vee}}{}^R$
V̂	*	*	*
V̂O		*	*
V̂R			*
V̂V			
V̂RO			*
V̂VO			
V̂VR			

In addition, we may also assume a broad constraint banning contour tones on all rimes (9).

(9) $\overset{*T\,T}{\underset{R}{\vee}}$: A contour tone is not licensed by any rime.

This constraint is highly ranked in languages that categorically prohibit contour tones on all syllables; it will play a minimal role in the discussion of weight-sensitive tone in this chapter.

In addition, we may tacitly assume another set of constraints which specifies rimes containing complex tones, i.e. three tonal units, as their target. Parallel to the set of constraints which take contour, i.e. bitonal, tones as their targets, one member of this constraint requires that complex tones be licensed by a rime containing two syllabic timing positions. Another constraint requires that complex tones be licensed by a rime containing two sonorant timing positions. A third constraint requires that complex tones take a rime containing two timing positions of any featural content as their licenser. Yet another broad constraint bans complex tones on all rime types. We may also assume, at least in principle, the existence of different constraint subfamilies taking rimes with greater than three tonal units as their targets, though they will not come into play in the discussion that follows.

We turn now to the three weight-sensitive constraints in (5), (6), and (7) which are most crucial for the data discussed here. Constraints (5), (6), and (7) refer to cut-off points in the hierarchy of weight which are observed in the tone data we have considered thus far. In languages like Navajo that employ the VV(C) heavy criterion, the constraint requiring that contour tones be licensed by rimes containing two syllabic timing positions (6) is higher ranked than the other two constraints formalized in (5) and (7). In languages like Kiowa that observe the VV(C), VR heavy criterion, the constraint requiring that contour tones be licensed by rimes with two sonorant timing positions ranks highest among the weight-sensitive tone constraints formalized thus far. Finally, in the few languages like Hausa which observe the VV(C), VC heavy criterion, the crucial highly ranked constraint is one that requires contour tones be associated with rimes containing two timing positions. The relevant highly ranked constraint governing the licensing of contour tones in a given language is ranked above any faithfulness constraints requiring that underlying tones surface. For example, the constraint requiring that contour tones be licensed by rimes containing two sonorant timing positions is ranked above faithfulness to underlying tone in a language like Kiowa that allows contour tones only on VV(C) and VR. The evidence for these rankings will become clearer in the formal analyses in section 3.6.

The relevant highly ranked constraint(s) on tonal associations in a given language is also ranked above constraints responsible for the construction of the lexicon, for example Flemming's (1995) Maximize Contrasts constraint, which requires that a language maximize the number of contrasts. Due to the complexity of the issue and its tangential relevance to the present discussion, I will not explore the role of constraints in lexicon construction.

The language specific ranking of constraints described in the preceding paragraph is largely projected from phonetic scales. A language determines its ranking of the constraints by examining the relevant phonetic properties driving tonal weight. Thus, for example, because its sonorant codas are relatively long, Lithuanian ranks the constraint requiring that contour tones be licensed by rimes containing two sonorant timing positions above other constraints governing the licensing of contour tones. Navajo, on the other hand, because its sonorant codas are short, ranks the constraint requiring that contour tones be licensed by rimes containing two syllabic timing positions above other constraints governing the licensing of contour tones. What has not yet been determined and must be left to future research is whether there are any phonetic dimensions which predict the adoption of the VV(C), VC heavy weight criterion, and thus the high ranking of the corresponding constraint, in a given language. It has only been suggested that the absence of a vowel length contrast in closed syllables is a prerequisite for high ranking of the constraint requiring that contour tones be licensed by rimes containing two timing positions. It remains to be seen whether it is possible to predict the actual choice of this weight criterion in languages that lack phonemic vowel length in closed syllables. On the basis of the evidence suggesting that the language-specific choice of criteria between VV(C), VR heavy is predictable on phonetic grounds, I will tentatively assume that the language specific employment of the VV(C), VC criterion also has a phonetic basis, though this basis remains to be determined.

3.6. ANALYSES OF WEIGHT-SENSITIVE TONE

3.6.1. Kiowa

Kiowa (Watkins 1984) is a Kiowa-Tanoan language in which contour tones are tolerated on syllables containing long vowels and on syllables closed by a sonorant coda (10a). Falling tones (the only type of contour tone found in Kiowa) are not permitted on CVO and CV syllables; in fact, an active process that shortens long vowels in closed syllables triggers the simplification of underlying contour tones in syllables that come to be closed by an obstruent (10b).

(10)   Kiowa contour tones (from Watkins 1984)
a. kʰînmɔ̀ 'cough' imperfective (from underlying kî:nmɔ̀), sô:gù 'sew' imperfective
b. kʰút 'pull off' perfective (from underlying kʰû:l-t)

Let us now consider the novel constraints that are relevant for the analysis of tonal weight in Kiowa. The first constraint that is necessary is a well-formedness constraint that accounts for the shortening of underlying long vowels in closed syllables. The shortening of long vowels in closed syllables is actually one manifestation of a broader constraint against overlong syllables, i.e. syllables containing three timing positions in the rime. The relevant constraint, which is highly ranked in a number of languages as will be shown in Chapter Five, is formulated in (11).

(11) $*[XXX]_R$: A rime may not contain three (or more) timing positions.

This constraint conflicts with two faithfulness constraints, the first of which requires that underlying long vowels surface as long. This constraint is formulated in maximally transparent fashion as a correspondence constraint (McCarthy and Prince 1995b) in (12).

(12) IDENT-IO [V-LENGTH]: Vowel length in the input must correspond to vowel length in the output.

The second constraint with which *[XXX]$_R$ conflicts is a faithfulness constraint requiring that underlying segments surface (13). This constraint can be formulated in feature geometric terms as a correspondence constraint of the MAX family (McCarthy and Prince 1995b) requiring that underlying root segments surface.

(13) MAX-IO: A segment in the input has a correspondent in the output.

We are now in a position to formulate the constraints referring to tone. The first constraint is a simple faithfulness constraint requiring that underlying tones surface in the output. This constraint is a member of the MAX family of constraints and is defined in (14).

(14) MAX-IO [TONE]: A tone of the input has a correspondent in the output.

Yet another constraint must determine which of the two tones forming a contour tone is eliminated when conditions trigger contour tone simplification. The relevant constraint may be formulated as a member of the ANCHOR family of constraints (McCarthy and Prince 1995), which, in the case of Kiowa, ensures that it is the leftmost of the underlying tones in a syllable that is preserved on the surface (15).

(15) LEFT-ANCHOR-IO [TONE]: A tone at the left edge of a syllable rime, R$_1$, in the input has a correspondent at the left edge of R$_1$ in the output.

We now turn to the rankings that generate the observed data. First, let us consider the simple case of an underlying contour tone on a long vowel that preserves its length on the surface. This form demonstrates that the broad constraint prohibiting contour tones on all rime types is ranked below faithfulness to underlying tone, MAX-IO [TONE].

(16) sô:gù	MAX-IO [TONE]	*T T $\lor$ R
☞ sô:gù		*
só:gù	*!	

Another relatively simple case involves underlying contour tones associated with a short voweled syllable closed by a sonorant. In this case, the contour tone surfaces, indicating that the constraint requiring that contour tones be licensed by rimes containing two syllabic timing positions is also ranked below MAX-IO [TONE].

(17)

kʰǐːnmɔ̀	MAX-IO [TONE]	*T T ∨ unless [XX] ∨ R R [+syllabic]
☞ kʰĩnmɔ̀		*
kʰĩnmɔ̀	*!	

Another constraint comes into play in the selection of the winner in (17). *[XXX]$_R$ outranks IDENT-IO [V-LENGTH] as indicated by the shortening of the underlying long vowel in the winning candidate (18).

(18)

kʰǐːnmɔ̀	*[XXX]$_R$	IDENT-IO [V-LENGTH]
☞ kʰĩnmɔ̀		*
kʰǐːnmɔ̀	*!	

*[XXX]$_R$ must also be ranked above the constraint requiring that contour tones be licensed by a rime containing two syllabic timing positions, as shown in (19).

(19)

kʰǐːnmɔ̀	*[XXX]$_R$	*T T ∨ unless [XX] ∨ R R [+syllabic]
☞ kʰĩnmɔ̀		*
kʰǐːnmɔ̀	*!	

MAX-IO is ranked above IDENT-IO [V-LENGTH] as indicated by the repair strategy adopted to truncate an overlong syllable. The underlying long vowel shortens while the coda consonant is preserved (20).

(20)

kʰǐːnmɔ̀	MAX-IO	IDENT-IO [V-LENGTH]
☞ kʰĩnmɔ̀		*
kʰǐːmɔ̀	*!	

We now turn to the interesting case of an underlying contour tone that must be simplified on the surface because it comes to stand in a syllable closed by an obstruent. Here we consider the form [kʰút] stemming from underlying /kʰûːl-t/ 'pull off-perfective.' The surface form differs from its corresponding underlying form in three respects: the vowel is short on the surface, the underlying /l/ is absent on the surface, and the contour tone on the first syllable has been simplified to a level tone. We will first account for the loss of the /l/ and the shortening of the underlying long vowel, two phenomena that both occur in response to the constraint against overlong rimes which outranks both MAX-IO and IDENT-IO [V-LENGTH] as shown in (21).

(21)

kʰûːl-t	*[XXX]ᵣ	MAX-IO	IDENT-IO [V-LENGTH]
☞ kʰút		*	*
kʰûlt	*!		*
kʰûːt	*!	*	

The shortening of the long vowel and the loss of the coda sonorant triggers simplification of the contour tone, since syllables closed by an obstruent cannot carry contour tones. This indicates that the constraint requiring that contour tones be licensed by rimes containing two sonorant timing positions is ranked above MAX-IO [TONE] (22).

(22)

kʰûːl-t	*T T / V unless [XX] / V ᵣ / R [+sonorant]	MAX-IO [TONE]
☞ kʰút		*
kʰût	*!	

Still left unanswered is the question of why the coda /l/ fails to surface while the coda /t/ is preserved. This is particularly mysterious when one considers that preservation of the /l/ rather than the /t/ would have the advantage of allowing for realization of the contour tone. The reason why /t/ rather than /l/ surfaces is, I conjecture, related to the fact that /t/ is the only overt realization of the perfective morpheme. A constraint requiring that underlying morphemes surface (cf. Lin 1993) is thus ranked highly in Kiowa. The relevant constraint can simply be stated as MAX-IO[MORPHEME] (23).

(23) MAX-IO[MORPHEME]: Every morpheme in the input has a correspondent in the output.

Max-IO[MORPHEME] is ranked above Max-IO [TONE], as tableau (24) demonstrates.

(24)

kʰûːl-t	MAX-IO [MORPHEME]	MAX-IO [TONE]
☞ kʰút		*
kʰûl	*!	

A final fact left to account for is the preservation of the high tone rather than the low tone component in cases of contour tone simplification. This result is achieved by ranking LEFT-ANCHOR-IO [TONE] over its counterpart RIGHT-ANCHOR-IO [TONE] (25).

(25)

kʰûːl-t	LEFT-ANCHOR-IO [TONE]	RIGHT-ANCHOR-IO [TONE]
☞ kʰút		*
kʰùt	*!	

3.6.2. *Krongo*

Krongo (Reh 1985) is a Niger-Congo language spoken in Sudan. Contour tones in Krongo (both falling and rising tones occur, although rising tones appear to be quite rare) are restricted to syllables containing long vowels (26a). Contour tones are not permitted on syllables containing short vowels, whether they are open or closed. This restriction manifests itself in the asymmetrical tonal spreading triggered by an optional process of vowel deletion applying to word-final vowels in words containing at least three syllables. The process of vowel deletion strands the tone originally associated with the deleted vowel and causes the immediately preceding syllable to become closed. If this syllable contains a long vowel, the stranded tone associates with it, as shown by the form in (26b); if not, the stranded tone is deleted (26c).

(26)   Krongo tone
       a. cǎːw 'go'
       b. àbâːn 'strike' (from underlying àbáːnà)
       c. ná.ŋgùrúʃ 'money'~ ná.ŋgùrúʃì, tùkúl 'side (of body)' ~ tùkúlì[10]

The Krongo data necessitates a new constraint: one that drives the optional process of final vowel deletion applying in words containing at least three syllables. I will simply state the relevant constraint as *FINAL VOWEL (27) (cf. Prince and Smolensky's 2004 FREE-V in their discussion of Lardil).

(27) *FINAL VOWEL: A word does not end in a vowel.

*FINAL VOWEL is freely ranked relative to the faithfulness constraint requiring that underlying segments surface, MAX. When *FINAL VOWEL is ranked above MAX, we get loss of the final vowel, as shown in (28).

(28)

àbá:nà	*FINAL VOWEL	MAX-IO
☞ àbâ:n		*
àbá:nà	*!	

If the opposite ranking obtains, the vowel is preserved (29).

(29)

àbá:nà	MAX	*FINAL VOWEL
☞ àbá:nà		*
àbâ:n	*!	

*FINAL VOWEL is ranked below a minimal word constraint requiring that words contain at least two syllables. This constraint is formulated in (30).

(30) $*[\sigma]_{PrWd}$: A word may not contain only a single syllable.

The ranking of *FINAL VOWEL below $*[\sigma]_{PrWd}$ is exemplified in (31) for the word /ʈá:rù/ 'sheets.'

(31)

ʈá:rù	$*[\sigma]_{PrWd}$	*FINAL VOWEL
☞ ʈá:rù		*
ʈâ:r	*!	

Interestingly, the disyllabic minimal word requirement is violated by numerous lexical items which are underlyingly monosyllabic, e.g. /ró/ 'breast,' /rú/ 'rope.' The presence of monosyllabic words on the surface indicates that $*[\sigma]_{PrWd}$ is ranked below a constraint prohibiting the insertion of material which is not present underlyingly. The relevant constraint is formulated in (32) as a DEP-IO constraint that requires that material in the output has a correspondent in the input (McCarthy and Prince 1995b). It will suffice for present purposes to state the DEP constraint with reference to timing positions.

(32) *DEP-IO [X]: A timing position in the output has a correspondent in the input.

The ranking of *DEP-IO [X] above [σ]$_{PrWd}$ is demonstrated in (33).

(33)

ró	*DEP-IO [X]	*[σ]$_{PrWd}$
☞ ró		*
róta	*!*	

We now return to the more interesting data for purposes of the discussion of tone: the fate of the stranded tone in case of vowel apocope. If, as we have seen, the syllable which becomes final due to vowel loss contains a long vowel, it accepts the stranded tone, indicating that the constraint banning contour tones on all rime types is ranked below MAX-IO [TONE], as shown in (34).

(34)

àbá:nà	MAX-IO [TONE]	*T T V R
☞ àbâ:n		*
àbá:n	*!	

If, however, the new final syllable contains a short vowel, the stranded tone fails to dock on it; this reveals that the constraint requiring that contour tones be licensed by a rime containing two syllabic timing positions is ranked above MAX-IO [TONE] (35).

(35)

tùkúlì	*T T unless [XX] V V R R [+syllabic]	MAX-IO [TONE]
☞ tùkúl		*
tùkûl	*!	

LEFT-ANCHOR-IO [TONE] ensures that another potential rival candidate in (35), tùkùl, does not surface. This candidate would violate LEFT-ANCHOR-IO [TONE], because the leftmost tone anchored to the penultimate rime in the input does not have a correspondent in the input (36).

(36)

tùkúlì	LEFT-ANCHOR-IO [TONE]
☞ tùkúl	
tùkùl	*!

3.6.3. Hausa

Hausa (Newman 1990, Wolff 1993, Russ Schuh p.c.) tolerates contour tones (only falling tones occur) on CVV and all CVC syllables, including those closed by an obstruent, as the examples in (37) show. Contour tones may either be underlying (37a), or may result from a suffix that leaves a tone on the preceding syllable (37b), or, in the case of some contours on CVC, may result from the shortening of long vowels in closed syllables (37c).

Hausa does not tolerate contour tones on CV syllables, as discussed in section 3.2.1.1. Although the restriction against contour tones on CV operates primarily as a lexical phenomenon, the addition of the verbal suffix -`wá: to verbs provides evidence that the constraint is also active in the grammar.[11] This suffix carries a low tone which attaches to the immediately preceding syllable, but only if this syllable is CVV or CVC (37b). If the immediately preceding syllable is CV, the floating tone is eliminated, since it has no place to dock (37d).

(37) Hausa tones
a. lâ:lá: 'indolence,' mântá: 'forget,' râs:á: 'branches'
b. ká:wô:wá: 'bringing' (from ká:wó: -`wá:), sájârwá: 'selling' (from sájár-`wá:)
c. mà:tât 'the wife' (Northwest dialects; standard Hausa má:târ) (from underlying mà:tá:-`t)
d. tà:rúwá: 'gathering (intr.)' (from underlying tà:rú-`wá:)

Let us first account for the presence of contour tones on heavy syllables. The fact that an underlying long vowel carrying a contour tone preserves its contour tone when shortened in closed syllables indicates that MAX-IO [TONE] is ranked above all the constraints on contour tones except the one requiring that contour tones be licensed by a syllable containing two rimal timing positions (38).

(38)

mà:tá:-`t	MAX-IO [TONE]	*T T $\underset{R}{V}$ unless $\underset{[+syllabic]}{[XX]}$ $\overset{}{V}$ R	*T T $\underset{R}{V}$ unless $\underset{[+sonorant]}{[XX]}$ $\overset{}{V}$ R	*T T $\underset{R}{V}$
☞ mà:tât		*	*	*
mà:tát	*!			

The constraint against overlong syllables is also ranked above the first two of these constraints on contour tones (39).

(39)

màːtáː˙t	*[XXX]ᵣ	*TT / V / R unless [XX]/V ᴿ [+syllabic]	*TT / V / R unless [XX]/V ᴿ [+sonorant]
☞ màːtât		*	*
màːtâːt	*!		

*[XXX]ᵣ is also ranked above Ident [V-length] (40).

(40)

màːtáː˙t	*[XXX]ᵣ	Ident [V-LENGTH]
☞ màːtât		*
màːtâːt	*!	

We now turn to the case of floating tones carried by suffixes. Although these floating tones can dock on heavy syllables thereby creating contour tones on underlying high-toned syllables, they fail to associate with CV syllables. This indicates that the constraint requiring that contour tones be licensed by syllables containing two rimal timing positions is ranked above Max-IO [tone], as shown in (41).

(41)

tàːrúˉwáː	*TT / V / R unless [XX]ᵣ	Max-IO [TONE]
☞ tàːrúwáː		*
tàːrûwáː	*!	

Note that we do not have a basis for ranking Max-IO [morpheme] relative to the constraint requiring that contour tones be licensed by syllables containing two rimal timing positions, since the loss of the floating low tone associated with the suffix does not constitute loss of the entire morpheme.

The fact that the vowel does not lengthen to accommodate the contour tone indicates that Ident [V-length] is ranked above Max-IO [tone] (42).

(42)

tàːrúˉwáː	Ident [V-LENGTH]	Max-IO [TONE]
☞ tàːrúwáː		*
tàːrûːwáː	*!	

Still left to determine is the constraint ranking that ensures that the underlying tone of the short vowel surfaces rather than the floating tone of the suffix. There are various constraints and rankings that could account for the output pattern. One possibility is a highly ranked IDENT-IO constraint requiring that associations between tones and syllables in the input have a correspondent in the output. Another possibility and one I will assume here is the ranking of LEFT-ANCHOR-IO [TONE] above a constraint requiring that underlying suffixal tones have a correspondent in the output, MAX-IO [TONE, SUFFIX]. LEFT-ANCHOR-IO [TONE] also rules out the third candidate in (43), in which the floating low tone carried by the suffix is docked on the final long vowel, since the leftmost tone on the final rime in the input does not fall at the left edge of the rime in the output.[12]

(43)	tàːrúˋwáː	LEFT-ANCHOR-IO [TONE]	MAX-IO [TONE, SUFFIX]
☞ tàːrúwáː			*
tàːrùwáː		*!	
tàːrùwǎ		*!	

3.6.4. Cantonese

We now turn to a language, Cantonese, in which a weight-sensitive restriction on contour tones holds of monomorphemic lexical items but is violated in case a tonal morpheme is added to a root. The basic Cantonese facts were discussed in section 3.2.2 and are summarized here again, summarizing the discussion in Kao (1971) and Bauer and Benedict (1997). Contour tones are permitted in roots consisting of an open syllable (CVV; see section 3.2.2.1), as well as roots that are closed by a sonorant consonant (CVR, CVVR). Contour tones do not occur on simple roots that are closed by an obstruent (CVO, CVVO).

What is interesting about Cantonese tonal weight is that the restriction against contour tones on CVO and CVVO is violated in many cases in forms containing the so-called *piːn-jam* or 'changed tones' which convey a change in the meaning of the root with which they are associated (Bauer and Benedict 1997). Bauer and Benedict (1997) contains a thorough discussion of the *piːn-jam*; I summarize here some of the more general points of their discussion. The *piːn-jam* are characteristic of colloquial Cantonese speech and can be classified according to their tonal configuration, which can be either high level, high rising, or mid-low falling. The *piːn-jam* convey a broad range of types of semantic information, including but not limited to derivation, aspectual information, diminutiveness, emphasis, and intensification. Although they have been lexicalized in some cases, they generally bear a close semantic relationship to the forms on which they are based.

For our purposes, the more crucial changed tones to consider are those involving contour tones (high rising and mid-low falling), since they create surface violations of the restriction against contour tone on CVO and CVVO. For example, the word /kʷʰaːk/ (25) 'circle, ring, loop' in which the first syllable contains a high rising changed tone is related to the base form /kʷʰaːk/ (33) with a mid level tone (Bauer and Benedict 1997:196) (tones indicated in parentheses where a higher number indicates a higher tone; contours consist of two different tones).

Interestingly, the *piːn-jam* differ in terms of their frequency of occurrence. The mid-low falling *piːn-jam* is rare according to Bauer and Benedict (1997) while the high level changed tone is more common, but nevertheless much less frequent than the high rising tone. What is most interesting is that the only frequently attested changed tone consisting of a contour, the high rising one, does not attach with equal frequency to all types of syllables. It does not occur with CVO or CVVO roots containing a high tone, and, furthermore, of the syllable types with which it does occur, it is rarest with CVO and CVVO containing tones other than high. Thus, the high rising changed tone is least likely to occur on precisely those roots (CVO and CVVO) that categorically reject contour tones in bare roots. Although the formal modeling of this gradient well-formedness would go beyond the scope of this work, it is nevertheless interesting to note how the direction of this gradience mirrors the categorical restriction against contour tones in bare CVO and CVVO roots. It is also interesting that Yu (2003) finds that CVVO syllables carrying a rising tone have phonetically longer vowels than their level toned counterparts. This phonetic lengthening effect is predicted given the phonetic requisites for tone.

For purposes of the present formal analysis, we will limit ourselves to the analysis of roots that contain a contour *piːn-jam*. As a first step, we must assume an additional constraint governing the license of contour tones. This constraint is needed to capture the fact that CVVO does not carry contour tones except in *piːn-jam* environments. Recall the implicational hierarchy between CVV and CVR: tolerance of contour tones on CVR implies tolerance of contours on CVV. Thus, all else being equal, were it not for the extremely short phonetic duration of the vowel in CVVO in Cantonese (see section 3.2.2.1), we would expect CVVO to be able to support a contour tone, since CVR can.

The relevant constraint needed to rule out contours on CVVO is one that requires that contour tones be licensed by a syllable containing a rime with only sonorant timing positions. This constraint is formulated in (44), where the presence of only the feature [+sonorant] in the rime refers to a rime which consists entirely of sonorants.

(44) $\overset{\displaystyle{}^{*}\text{T T}}{\underset{\displaystyle\text{R}}{V}}$ unless $[+\text{sonorant}]_{\text{R}}$: A contour tone is licensed by a rime with only sonorant timing slots.

This constraint requires that contour tones be licensed by a syllable consisting entirely of sonorants; any syllable carrying a contour tone and containing an obstruent (i.e. either CVO or CVVO) thus violates it.

Since Cantonese does not have any active phonological processes, as far as I know, which turn open syllables or syllables closed by a sonorant into obstruent-closed syllables, there is no evidence for ranking MAX [TONE] relative to the constraint requiring that contour tones be licensed by syllables containing only sonorants in the rime. We may assume, however, that the constraint requiring that contour tones occur in syllables containing only sonorants in the rime is ranked above any lexicon optimization constraints, such as Flemming's (1995) Maximize Contrasts constraint, which operate over the lexicon to maximize the number of phonologically distinctive lexical items.

We do have evidence, however, for the ranking of the constraint requiring that contour tones be licensed by rimes containing only sonorants below the constraint requiring that morphemes be realized, MAX-IO [MORPHEME]. This ranking is demonstrated in (45).

(45)

k^{wh}aːk + (25)	MAX-IO [MORPHEME]	$\overset{\displaystyle{}^{*}\text{T T}}{\underset{\displaystyle\text{R}}{V}}$ unless $[+\text{sonorant}]_{\text{R}}$
☞ k^{wh}aːk (25)		*
k^{wh}aːk (33)	*!	

The winning candidate is the one with the high rising changed tone, whereas the losing candidate is the one with a level tone. Cantonese thus demonstrates that phonological well-formedness constraints on tonal weight can be ranked below constraints requiring that morphology be overtly realized.

3.7. CONCLUSIONS

In this chapter, we have seen that weight-sensitive tone restrictions have a phonetic basis in terms of a syllable's overall sonorant energy. Syllables that have greater overall sonorant energy are better equipped to support contour tones than syllables with lesser sonorant energy. Because the phonetic requirements motivating weight-sensitive tone are different from those driving other weight-sensitive phenomena, it is predicted that the phonology of weight for contour tones will be different from the phonology of weight for other weight-based processes. This prediction is borne out by the typology of weight for tone, which displays far greater sensitive to sonority than other weight-sensitive phenomena. Languages that appear to contradict the phonetic basis for contour tone restrictions turn out, upon closer phonetic examination, to be only apparent exceptions that offer further support for the phonetically-driven nature of weight-sensitive tone and the process specificity of syllable weight. In the next chapter, we turn to another weight-sensitive phenomenon, weight-sensitive stress, which will be shown to be sensitive to quite different phonetic considerations from weight-sensitive tone.

Chapter Four
Weight-Sensitive Stress

4.0. INTRODUCTION

In this chapter, we turn to the analysis of weight-sensitive stress, a phenomenon that provides an instructive contrast to weight-sensitive tone, both in terms of its phonetic underpinnings and its phonological distribution. Weight-sensitive stress also provides crucial evidence for the notion that phonology is guided not only by phonetic considerations but also by principles of structural complexity.

4.1. A TYPOLOGY OF WEIGHT FOR STRESS

Recall from Chapter Two that, of the various weight-sensitive phenomena, weight-sensitive stress displays the greatest diversity of weight criteria cross-linguistically. Several types of weight distinctions not observed by other weight-sensitive processes are exploited by stress systems. Furthermore, several languages have stress systems that are sensitive to more than two levels of weight. In this section, we will amplify on the typology of weight for stress presented in Chapter Two, beginning with binary weight distinctions and then proceeding to more complex weight hierarchies. Note that several languages not included in the typology of stress in Chapter Two are included here in order to provide maximal coverage of the range of weight-sensitive stress systems found in the world.

4.1.1. A Typology of Binary Weight Distinctions for Stress

The two most common weight distinctions in stress systems cross-linguistically are CVV(C) heavy, found for example in Khalkha (Bosson 1964, Walker 1995, 1996), Malayalam (Mohanan 1986), and Menonimi (Bloomfield 1962), and CVV(C), CVC heavy, as found in languages like Latin

(Allen 1973) and Arabic (McCarthy 1979a,b). A variant of this latter distinction which also treats long vowels and closed syllables as heavy, draws a cut between heavy CVVC, CVCC and light CVV, CVC, CV. This distinction is found in Stoney Dakota in final syllables (Shaw 1985).

The third most common weight distinction for stress is the Full vowels heavy distinction, which is observed by languages like Javanese (Herrfurth 1964, Prentice 1990), Chuvash (Krueger 1961), Mari (Itkonen 1955).[1] A variant of the Full vowels heavy distinction treats only reduced vowels in open syllables as light, as in Malay (Winstedt 1927, Prentice 1990), Aljutor (Kodzasov and Muravyova 1978) and certain Mari dialects (Itkonen 1955; Kenstowicz 1997). Yet another type of weight system that is sensitive to the full vs. reduced vowel distinction treats all full voweled syllables as heavy but only reduced vowels followed by a coda sonorant as heavy, as for example in Lamang (Wolff 1983). The crucial difference between reduced and full vowels in languages in which they differ in weight lies in the relatively great durational differences between the two vowel types and not merely on qualitative differences. For example, in Chuvash, the reduced vowels are "fleetingly pronounced, and sometimes so reduced as to sound almost coalesced with the following consonant . . ." (Krueger 1961:71). Similarly, in Ossetic, the reduced vowels "tend more easily to reduction, contraction, and disappearance [than the full vowels]" (Abaev 1964:4). Similar duration differences between full and reduced vowels are found in the Javanese data examined later in section 4.7.2.6.

There are a few languages in which CVV and CVR, but not CVO, are heavy, e.g. Kwakw'ala (Boas 1947, Bach 1975, Wilson 1986), closely related Nuuchahnulth (Wilson 1986, Stonham 1990), and Inga Quechua (Levinsohn 1976). Interestingly, glottalized sonorants do not count as sonorants in languages with a weight distinction between CVR and CVO, e.g. Kwakw'ala, Nuuchahnulth. There are also a few languages, e.g. Kamchadal (Volodin 1976), Mundari (Sinha 1975), Mam (England 1983, 1986 in Maldonado Andres et al.), in which syllables containing a glottal stop (or in the case of Mundari, preglottalization) are heavier than syllables closed by other consonants. Although the heavy status of glottal stop may a priori seem somewhat curious, it is plausible that, in these languages, vowel plus glottal stop sequences in the rime are realized phonetically as a long vowel with glottalization on the latter half rather than as a short vowel plus complete glottal stop. This possibility finds support from casual observations I have made of a number of languages, as well Doherty's (1993) finding that what phonemic descriptions of Cayuga had described as a sequence of vowel plus coda glottal stop is phonetically a long vowel whose second half is glottalized. Phonetic descriptions of Cahuilla (Seiler 1965) suggest a similar realization. Glottal stop in Mam is also more a prosodic feature than a full glottal stop (England 1983).

I am aware of two languages, Maori (Bauer 1993) and Kara (De Lacy 1997), which treat phonemic long vowels as heavier than diphthongs. It is plausible that diphthongs are phonetically shorter than phonemic long vowels in languages in which they differ in weight. This hypothesis finds support from Maori, which contrasts short diphthongs which are lighter than long vowels and long diphthongs which are as heavy as long vowels: fa.**kai**.ri 'elevate' vs. ka:i.ŋ̂ga 'home' (examples from Bauer 1993). The Kara weight distinction between long vowels and diphthongs is also not so surprising when one considers that the only long vowel which occurs is long /aː/, the most sonorous of vowels; thus, any combination of different vowels is likely to be phonetically less weighty than long /aː/.

Another important class of weight divisions is based on vowel height. In languages that draw weight distinctions based on vowel height, it is the lower vowels that are universally heavier than the higher vowels. For example, at an earlier historical stage of the Jaz'va dialect of Komi (Lytkin 1961, Itkonen 1955), non-high vowels are heavy for stress, whereas high vowels are light. There are also certain languages that draw a distinction between low vowels and other vowels: e.g. Kara (De Lacy 1997), Gujarati (Cardona 1965), Yimas (Foley 1991) and Kobon (Davies 1980, Kenstowicz 1997).

There is a typologically interesting feature of languages that base their weight distinctions on vowel quality, including languages with weight distinctions between full and reduced vowels. Virtually all stress systems that I have located which are sensitive to vowel quality distinctions (including some not presented in the typology in Chapter Two) do not possess phonemic vowel length distinctions, as shown in Table 4.1. Of the 28 languages which make weight distinctions between vowels of different qualities, only three also have phonemic long vowels: Siraiki (Shackle 1976), Kara (De Lacy 1997) and Asheninca (Payne 1990). One of these three, Kara, has a single long vowel, /aː/. Interestingly, all three languages with phonemic long vowels and a weight distinction based on vowel quality also make other weight distinctions in addition to the distinction based on vowel quality. Thus, in these three languages, the distinction based on vowel quality implies the presence of another weight distinction. An explanation for the virtual confinement of weight distinctions based on vowel quality to languages without phonemic long vowels will be offered in section 4.9.1.

Table 4.1. Languages with weight distinctions based on vowel quality

Language	Genetic affiliation	Weight distinction(s)	Vowel length distinction	Source(s)
Aljutor	Chukcho-Kamchatkan	Red V in open σ light	No	Kodzasov and Muravyova (1978)
Asheninca	Arawakan	CVV > Ca(C), Ce(C), Co(C), CiC > Ci > Ci[2]	Yes	Payne (1981, 1990)
Au	Torricelli	Full V heavy	No[3]	Scorza (1985)
Chukchi	Chukcho-Kamchatkan	Low V, Mid V > HighV > Reduced V	No	Skorik (1961)
Chuvash	Altaic	Full V heavy	No	Krueger (1961)
Gujarati	Indo-European	LowV > RedVC > Non-loV > RedV in open σ	No	Cardona (1965)
Javanese	Austronesian	Full V heavy	No	Herrfurth (1964)
Kara	Austronesian	CVː > CaV, CaC > Ca > CV_iV_k, CVC > CNon-loV[4]	Yes	De Lacy (1997)
Karo Batak	Austronesian	Red V in open σ light	No	Woollams (1966)
Kobon	Trans New Guinea	Low V> MidV > High V > Red V	No	Davies (1980) in Kenstowicz (1997)
Komi	Uralic	Non-high V heavy	No	Itkonen (1955), Lytkin (1964)
Lamang	Afro-Asiatic	Full V, CVR heavy	No[5]	Wolff (1983)

(continued)

Table 4.1.—*(continued)*

Language	Genetic affiliation	Weight distinction(s)	Vowel length distinction	Source(s)
Lillooet	Salishan	Full V heavy	No	van Eijk (1997)
Lushootseed	Salishan	Full V heavy	No	Hess (1976, 1995)
Malay	Austronesian	Red V in open σ light	No	Prentice (1990)
Mari	Uralic	Full V heavy[6]	No	Gruzov (1960), Kenstowicz (1997)
Mayo	Sepik-Ramu	Low V heavy	No	Foreman and Marten (1973)
Mordvin	Uralic	Full V heavy	No	Kenstowicz (1997), Tsygankina (1980)
Moro	Niger-Congo	CVC > Full V > Red V	No	Black and Black (1971)
Nankina	Trans New Guinea	Full V heavy	No	Spaulding and Spaulding (1994)
Ngada	Austronesian	Full V heavy	No	Djawanai (1983)
Patep	Austronesian	Full V heavy	No	Adams and Lauck (1975)
Sarangani Manobo	Austronesian	Full V heavy	No	DuBois (1976)
Sentani	Trans New Guinea	CVC > Full V > Red V in open σ light	No	Cowan (1966), Elenbaas (1992, 1998)
Siraiki	Indo-European	CVV(C), CVC > Full V > RedV	Yes	Shackle (1976)

(continued)

Table 4.1. Languages with weight distinctions based on vowel quality *(continued)*

Language	Genetic affiliation	Weight distinction(s)	Vowel length distinction	Source(s)
Vach Ostyak	Uralic	Full V heavy	No	Gulya (1966)
Yil	Torricelli	Full V heavy	No	Martens and Tuominen (1977)
Yimas	Sepik-Ramu	Low V heavy	No	Foley (1991)

4.1.2. Ternary and Other Complex Distinctions

Up to now, discussion has been largely limited to simple weight distinctions involving a two-way split between heavy and light syllables. There are also languages that treat weight in a scalar fashion, drawing more than a binary distinction between heavy and light; some of these hierarchies appear in Table 4.1. We will now consider others.

One example of a fairly common three-way weight hierarchy is found in Klamath (Barker 1964), in which long vowels are at the top of the hierarchy, followed by closed syllables containing short vowels, followed at the bottom of the hierarchy by open syllables containing a short vowel: i.e. CVV > CVC > CV. Other languages displaying this type of three-way weight distinction include Kashmiri (Kenstowicz 1994b, Morén 2000), Chickasaw (Munro and Willmond 1994), and Yapese (Jensen 1977).

Another complex weight distinction is found in the Pulaar dialect of Fula (Niang 1995) and in Eipomek (Heeschen 1983) in which CVVC > CVV, CVC > CV. Kelkar (1968) describes a similar hierarchy for Hindi with the addition of CVCC (lacking in Fula and Eipomek) which is equivalent in weight to CVVC. The Hindi weight distinction, however, is the subject of controversy (see Ohala 1977).

There are other cases of complex weight hierarchies. For example, Asheninca (Payne 1990) is also sensitive to a complex weight distinction: CVV > Ca(C), Ce(C), Co(C), CiC > Ci > Cɨ. An interesting feature of this hierarchy is that a short /i/ in an open syllable is lighter than a closed syllable containing a short /i/. Asheninca is discussed further in section 4.4.1. Chukchi displays a three-way weight distinction that is sensitive only to vowel quality. In Chukchi (Skorik 1961; Kenstowicz 1997), the low vowel /a/ and the mid vowels /e, o/ are heaviest, followed by the high vowels /i, u/. At the bottom of the hierarchy is the reduced vowel, schwa. Kobon (Davies 1980, Kenstowicz 1997) draws a four-way distinction based entirely on vowel quality. The low vowel /a/ is heaviest, followed by the mid-vowels /e, o/, followed by the high vowels /i, u/ and finally by the central vowels /ɨ, ə/.[7] Other complex weight distinctions appear in Table 4.1 and are discussed in Chapter Two.

4.2. UNIVERSAL HIERARCHIES OF WEIGHT FOR STRESS

Parallel to weight-sensitive tone, weight-sensitive stress also observes implicational hierarchies of weight. One of these hierarchies is, in fact, identical to that observed by tonal systems. According to this hierarchy, CVV(C) is heaviest followed by CVR followed by CVO followed by CV, as shown in Figure 4.1. Note, though, that the distinction between CVO is CV is widely attested in stress systems, unlike in tonal systems (see Chapter Three).

Figure 4.1. First hierarchy of weight for stress

Along the hierarchy in Figure 4.1, a rime type may be equivalent in weight to a rime to its left but never heavier. Thus, VR is never heavier than VV(C), VO is never heavier than VR, and V is never heavier than VO. Most languages draw a cut-off point between one of the syllable types in Figure 4.1; syllables to the left of this cut-off point are heavy and syllables to the right are light. Thus, Khalkha draws its division between heavy and·light between VV and VR. Kwakw'ala makes its cut between VR and VO. Latin's demarcation point falls between VO and V. To the hierarchy in Figure 4.1, we might also add a pair of additional rimes. First, on the basis of data from Maori and Kara, we might include diphthongs just to the right of long vowels. Second, the existence of at least two languages in which CVVC is heavier than CVV, Eipomek (Heeschen 1983) and Pulaar Fula (Niang 1995) suggests that CVVC falls to the left of CVV. Finally, there is some evidence that the ranking of CVCC relative to CVV is language dependent. In virtually all languages, CVV is heavier than CVCC, but in the controversial variety of Hindi described by Kelkar, CVCC is heavier than CVV. Stoney Dakota (Shaw 1985) potentially provides stronger evidence for the language specific ranking of CVCC over CVC.

The second hierarchy of weight for stress involves vowel height and fullness. According to this hierarchy, low vowels are heaviest, followed by mid vowels, followed by high vowels, followed by reduced vowels, as shown in Figure 4.2.

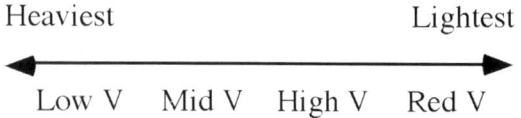

Figure 4.2. Second hierarchy of weight for stress

The three heaviest vowels in this hierarchy are distinguished by their height, while the lightest vowel is distinguished from the others by virtue of its being reduced. As pointed out above, reduced vowels are phonetically much shorter than full vowels in languages in which they differ in weight. In fact, the phonological hierarchy in Figure 4.2 may be essentially regarded as a hierarchy of duration, since lower vowels characteristically are longer than higher vowels (Lehiste 1970). These duration differences contingent on vowel height will be shown later in this chapter to contribute to differences in total energy between the vowels in the hierarchy.

4.3. WEIGHT AS A COMBINATION OF PHONETIC EFFECTIVENESS AND PHONOLOGICAL SIMPLICITY

The general hypothesis we explore in this chapter is that the phonology of weight is sensitive to two considerations: phonetic effectiveness and phonological simplicity. In Chapter Three, we saw evidence that the first of these ingredients, phonetic effectiveness, played a role in weight-sensitive tone. The basic argument was that languages choose weight distinctions for tone that are best suited to the phonetic demands imposed by tone. This sensitivity to phonetic conditioning factors accounts for both the range of variation in weight criteria employed by tone systems and (somewhat less clearly) the language specific choice of weight criteria for tone.

In this chapter, we will see further evidence for the role of phonetic effectiveness in syllable weight, this time in the context of weight-sensitive stress. Phonetic considerations will be shown to both constrain the range of cross-linguistic variation in weight criteria for stress and also the language specific parameterization of weight criteria.

Another ingredient that will be shown to be essential to the discussion of weight-sensitive stress is phonological simplicity, a notion that was introduced briefly in Chapter Two. The basic idea to be developed in this chapter is that languages treat natural and symmetrical classes of sounds uniformly with respect to weight. For example, as we have seen, many languages treat long vowels as uniformly heavy for purposes of stress or tone.

Other languages (more commonly for stress than tone) treat syllables with branching rimes, i.e. CVV(C) and CVC, as heavy. Still other languages treat syllables with two sonorant timing positions in the rime as heavy. What we typically do not find are languages that make weight distinctions that are simultaneously sensitive to vowel height and length, e.g. languages in which long, non-high vowels are heavy, or that are sensitive to both vowel height and sonority, e.g. languages in which syllables containing a low vowel plus a sonorant are heavy. There thus seems to be some pressure on weight systems to manipulate relatively simple classes of syllables that refer to a minimal set of phonological dimensions. Limiting the set of weight distinctions to simple ones has the obvious advantage of constraining the set of possible weight distinctions which a language learner must entertain when constructing or analyzing a weight system.

The notions of "simple classes" and "minimal set of phonological dimensions" will be made explicit in the discussion of weight-sensitive stress in this chapter, as will the definition of phonetic effectiveness in the context of weight-sensitive stress. The overall picture that will emerge from the discussion of stress in this chapter is that the phonology of weight is the result of a compromise between choosing weight distinctions that are ideal phonetically, but that are also structurally simple in terms of the phonological predicates that they manipulate. Although the evidence for this combination of phonetic effectiveness and phonological simplicity presented in this chapter is gleaned from stress systems, both ingredients are assumed to be relevant for other weight-sensitive phenomena, such as tone. In fact, the discussion of tone in Chapter Three demonstrated the important role of phonetic effectiveness in tonal systems. The fact that tone systems employ weight distinctions that are analogous in their simplicity to those used by stress systems suggests that phonological simplicity is relevant for tone as well as stress. Phonetic evidence for the role of simplicity in tonal systems is presented in Chapter Five.

In the next section, the notion of phonological simplicity is explored in detail. In section 4.5, we shift attention from phonological simplicity to the definition of phonetic effectiveness for weight-sensitive stress.

4.4. THE ROLE OF STRUCTURAL COMPLEXITY IN SYLLABLE WEIGHT

As a starting point in the investigation of complexity, let us consider some phonological predicates that define heavy and light syllables. The overall goal of this endeavor is to provide representations that offer a means of characterizing weight distinctions. Clearly, two crucial elements that must be encoded in these representations are a formalism for capturing phonological duration and a set of features describing the acoustic and/or articulatory properties of segments. In Chapter Two, a means for representing phonological duration, namely the timing slot, was adopted. Recall from the discussion in Chapter Two that phonologically short segments are assumed to project one timing position, while phonemically long segments project two timing positions. The one exception to the generalization that all segments project at least one timing position is provided by segments that are phonetically too short to receive a timing position, e.g. reduced vowels. Implicit in this system of timing slot assignment is the view that segments must be of a certain minimal duration to carry a timing slot.[8]

We now turn to the phonological features used to differentiate segments. Note that the phonological features discussed in this section are not intended to be an exhaustive set of features employed by phonological systems. Rather, they are the ones that are relevant for syllable weight. The non-place features include [syllabic], [sonorant], and the laryngeal feature [constricted glottis]. We may assume conventional definitions of these features with the exception of [syllabic]. As pointed out in Chapter Two, a segment is [+syllabic] by virtue of having acoustic properties that make it the most prominent segment of the syllable, not by virtue of merely being in a position that is defined as the syllable nucleus. For the present discussion, the primary function of the [syllabic] feature is to distinguish between syllables containing long vowels and those containing short vowels. The feature [syllabic] could thus, for practical purposes, be substituted by a feature that differentiates between vocalic and non-vocalic segments. I will (somewhat tentatively) assume the feature [syllabic], however, given that [+syllabic] nasals but not [-syllabic] nasals can carry tonal contrasts in certain languages (see Chapter Two).

The feature [sonorant] is relevant for defining the CVV(C), CVR heavy distinction, which is found in a few languages, including Kwakw'ala, Nuuchahnulth, and Inga Quechua. Interestingly, two of these languages, Nuuchahnulth and Kwakw'ala, contrast modal voiced and glottalized sonorants, the latter of which are treated as light for stress. We thus need a way to differentiate modal voiced and glottalized sonorants. One possibility is to adopt a slight amendment to the standard definition of [sonorant]. We might adopt Stevens and Keyser's (1989) acoustic-based definition of [sonorant] with one additional condition. Stevens and Keyser state that [+sonorant] segments are "characterized by continuity of the spectrum amplitude at low frequencies in the region of the first and second harmonics—a continuity of amplitude that extends into an adjacent vowel" (p. 87). If it were stipulated that the energy in the first harmonic must be periodic for a segment to be considered a sonorant, we would have a way to differentiate between modal voiced and glottalized sonorants. This assumption captures the uniformity of weight between CVV and CVR to the exclusion of CV plus glottalized sonorant in languages like Kwakw'ala. Another possibility, and one which will be tentatively adopted here, would be to employ the feature [constricted glottis] which is independently needed to account for the heavy status of glottal stop (perhaps phonetically realized as glottalization on an adjacent vowel) in languages like Kamchadal (Volodin 1976), Mundari (Sinha 1975), and Mam (England 1983). Since Mam possesses phonemic long vowels that are also heavy, a single representation encompassing both long vowels and syllables containing a glottal stop is needed. Pursuing the suggestion that phonemic glottal stop is phonetically realized as a long vowel whose latter portion is glottalized in languages in which it is heavy (see section 4.1.1), I will assume that syllables containing a "glottal stop" contain two [+syllabic] timing positions in languages in which glottal stops are heavy.

Weight-sensitive stress necessitates the introduction of certain place features. First, features are needed to differentiate vowels of different heights. Vowel height can be defined as follows, adopting traditional assumptions. High vowels are [+high], whereas low vowels are [+low]. Mid vowels are [-high] and [-low].

One final phonological predicate is necessary to capture the Maori weight hierarchy: CV: > CV_iV_k > CV. If we assume as suggested in section 4.1.1, that the diphthongs which count as lighter than long vowels are phonetically shorter than long vowels, we can assume that they are two segments linked to one timing slot, in which case long vowels and short diphthongs are differentiated by number of timing positions in the rime. Short diphthongs would then be differentiated from short monophthongs in terms of number of root nodes: monophthongs have one and diphthongs have two, one for each of the vowel qualities that comprise the diphthong.

Let us consider in Figure 4.3 representations characterizing the set of heavy syllables for the weight distinctions discussed in the typology in Chapter Two and above in section 4.1.

The representations in Figure 4.3 define the set of heavy syllables in a language and serve to differentiate them from the light syllables in that language. For example, according to the CVV(C) heavy criterion, all syllables containing two syllabic timing positions in the rime are heavy. Rimes which satisfy this structural description are all those which minimally contain two syllabic timing positions, e.g. all CVV syllables whether they contain long

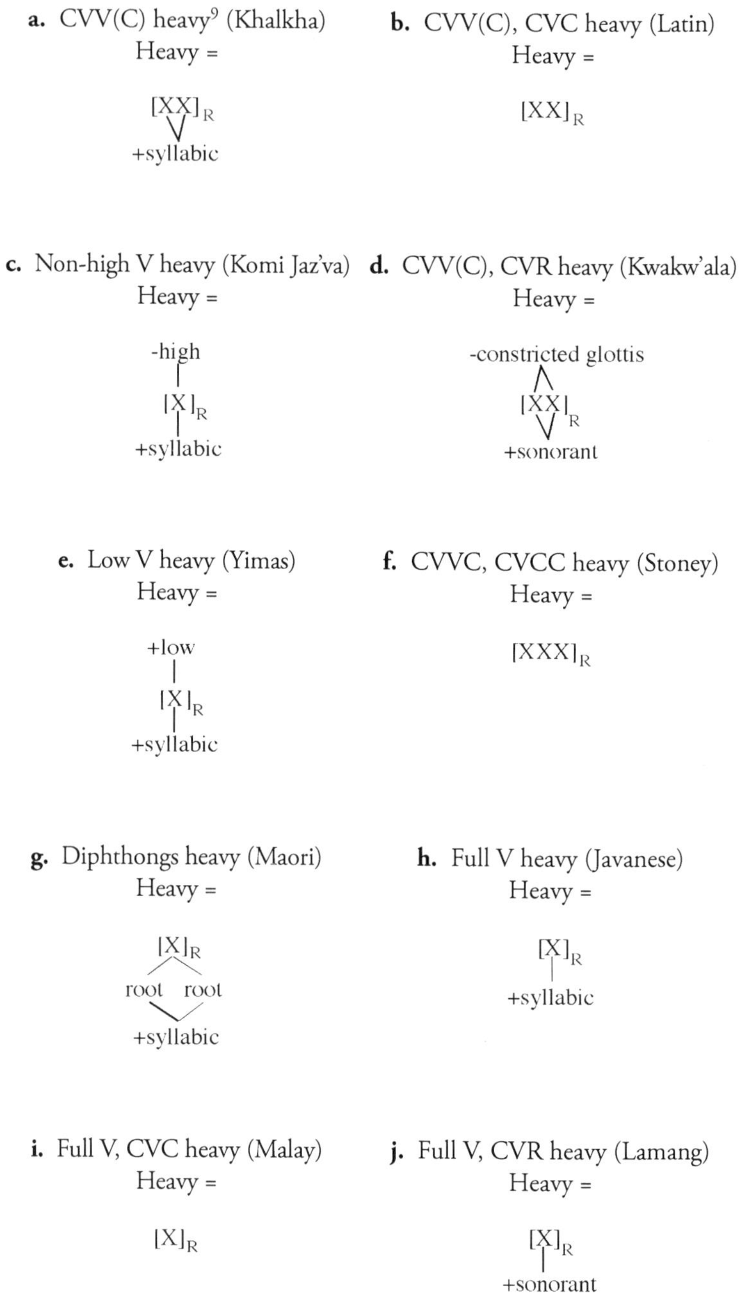

a. CVV(C) heavy[9] (Khalkha)
Heavy =

$$[\underset{\vee}{XX}]_R$$
+syllabic

b. CVV(C), CVC heavy (Latin)
Heavy =

$$[XX]_R$$

c. Non-high V heavy (Komi Jaz'va)
Heavy =

-high
|
$$[\overset{|}{X}]_R$$
|
+syllabic

d. CVV(C), CVR heavy (Kwakw'ala)
Heavy =

-constricted glottis
$$[\underset{\vee}{\overset{\wedge}{XX}}]_R$$
+sonorant

e. Low V heavy (Yimas)
Heavy =

+low
|
$$[\overset{|}{X}]_R$$
|
+syllabic

f. CVVC, CVCC heavy (Stoney)
Heavy =

$$[XXX]_R$$

g. Diphthongs heavy (Maori)
Heavy =

$$[\overset{|}{X}]_R$$
root   root
+syllabic

h. Full V heavy (Javanese)
Heavy =

$$[\overset{|}{X}]_R$$
|
+syllabic

i. Full V, CVC heavy (Malay)
Heavy =

$$[X]_R$$

j. Full V, CVR heavy (Lamang)
Heavy =

$$[\overset{|}{X}]_R$$
|
+sonorant

Figure 4.3. Simple and attested weight distinctions

vowels or diphthongs, as well as CVVC(C) syllables with one or more coda consonants. Similar, the CVV, CVC heavy criterion treats as heavy all syllables containing two timing positions in the rime. Thus, any CVC syllable or any syllable containing a long vowel or diphthong, whether open or closed, is considered heavy. Note that, for the Low Vowels heavy distinction, the [+syllabic] feature is only necessary in languages with [+low] consonants, which are relatively uncommon.

Most of the other representations in 4.3 are straightforward with the possible exception of those in (h), (i) and (j). Recall from Chapter Two the assumption that reduced vowels lack a timing position of their own. Under this assumption, the Full Vowels heavy distinction (h) treats syllables containing a syllabic timing position as heavy. The Full V, CVR heavy distinction (j) considers heavy any syllables containing at least one sonorant timing position, whether a syllabic one or a non-syllabic one. The Full V, CVC heavy distinction (i) considers syllables containing at least one timing position as heavy.

Weight systems that are sensitive to more than a binary distinction are composed of a combination of two or more simple weight distinctions. For example, the Chickasaw hierarchy, in which CVV > CVC > CV, is composed of two weight distinctions: a distinction of the Khalkha type (CVV(C) heavy) and a distinction of the Latin type (CVV(C), CVC heavy). Combining these two distinctions produces the three-way hierarchy CVV > CVC > CV.

In evaluating the phonological complexity of weight distinctions it is useful to consider the type of phonological predicates, or dimensions, needed to bifurcate the set of rimes into heavy and light groups according to various weight distinctions. To do this, we may adopt a division of predicates into two dimensions, a place dimension, which includes place features such as [high], [low], and [back], as well as [labial], [dorsal], [coronal], and a non-place dimension, which includes any phonological predicates not specifying place of articulation. These include timing positions, root nodes, and manner and laryngeal features such as [syllabic], [sonorant], [voice], [nasal], [continuant], [constricted glottis], etc.

In order to provide a working definition of complexity it is useful to recast the representations of weight in Figure 4.3. in terms of associations between features and individual timing positions, and, in the case of diphthongs, between features and individual root nodes.

Table 4.2 classifies the weight distinctions in Figure 4.3 according to the featural specifications of each timing position and the number of predicates (timing positions, root nodes, and features) referred to by each distinction. Thus, for example, the CVV(C) heavy distinction specifies that syllables containing two rimal timing positions, each of which is linked to the feature [+syllabic], are heavy. This distinction thus refers to four predicates in total: two timing positions and two [+syllabic] features. The CVV(C), CVC heavy distinction refers to two timing positions and thus two predicates in total. The predicates referred to by other distinctions appear in Table 4.2.

Using Table 4.2 as a guide, we may hypothesize on the upper limit of complexity tolerated by weight distinctions. Most weight distinctions involve reference to non-place predicates. The two that refer to both place and non-place predicates only refer to a single place feature. Given the set of distinctions in Table 4.2, I will offer the following measure of complexity as a working hypothesis. A weight distinction is too complex if it refers to more than one place feature. That all distinctions in Table 4.2 are simple can be easily verified by checking the number of place features referenced by each distinction. Most distinctions in Table 4.2 satisfy the complexity requirement because they only refer to non-place elements, i.e. skeletal slots, root nodes, and non-place features. The two weight distinctions in Table 4.2 that involve the place dimension only refer to a single place predicate; they thus fall within the complexity threshold.

We may also assume that weight distinctions that require disjoint representations of the heavy syllables are trivially complex, even if they only refer to a single dimension. Thus, for example, a weight distinction which treats long vowels and syllables closed by a lateral as heavy is complex, since there is no single representation of the syllable which encompasses both long vowels and syllables closed by lateral. The reason for this is that long vowels contain no [+lateral] timing positions; there is thus no way for the second timing position in the rime to be both simultaneously [+lateral] and [+syllabic]. The definition of complexity is formalized in (46).

(46) Definition of complexity
     A weight distinction is complex iff:
         It refers to more than one place predicate.
                          OR
         It makes reference to disjoint representations of the syllable.

At this point, one might ask why place is the dimension that is relevant for assessing complexity. I conjecture that the reason why place features are penalized more than other types of features stems from considerations

Table 4.2. Weight distinctions and their phonological dimensions			
	Predicates	Dimension	
		Non-place	Place
CVV(C) heavy	$[\overset{\mid}{X}]_R$ $[\overset{\mid}{X}]_R$ +syllabic +syllabic	4	0
CVV(C), CVC heavy	$[X]_R$ $[X]_R$	2	0
CVV(C), CVR heavy	-const.gl. -const.gl. $[\overset{\mid}{X}]_R$ $[\overset{\mid}{X}]_R$ +sonorant +sonorant	6	0
CVVC, CVCC heavy	$[X]_R$ $[X]_R$ $[X]_R$	3	0
Non-high V heavy	-high $[\overset{\mid}{X}]_R$ +syllabic	2	1
Low V heavy	+low $[\overset{\mid}{X}]_R$ +syllabic	2	1
Full V heavy	$[X]_R$ +syllabic	2	0
$CV_iV_k(C)$ heavy	$[X]_R$ $[X]_R$ root root +syllabic +syllabic	6	0
Full V, CVC heavy	$[X]_R$	1	0
Full V, CVR heavy	$[X]_R$ +sonorant	2	0

related to the size of the hypothesis space being tested by learners of a weight system. Place features are distinctive for all segments in a syllable rime, including both vowels and consonants. Non-place features, on the other hand, are characteristically redundant for at least the vowel in a syllable. With rare exceptions, manner and voicing features are non-contrastive and thus redundant for vowels. Thus, the set of possible contrasts in place of articulation for the entire rime is larger than the set of possible contrasts in manner or voicing. For this reason, it is plausible that the discrimination against place features by the complexity metric merely reflects an attempt to reduce the hypothesis space of the learner.

In summary, we may hypothesize that languages do not exploit weight distinctions that exceed an upper limit of phonological complexity. A weight distinction is complex if it either requires reference to a disjoint set of syllable types or if it is sensitive to more than one place predicate.

This discussion is not to say that no language ever employs a complex weight distinction. There is for example a complex distinction in Munster Irish, which treats long vowels and /ax/ as heavier than other syllables (Ó Siadhail 1989). Such cases of complexity "creeping" into the phonology of weight appear to be exceedingly rare, however. We will thus adopt the condition of complexity proposed in this section as a working hypothesis that is compatible with virtually all of the observed data. Investigation of how Munster Irish developed its highly unusual and complex weight criterion in the face of the pressure for structural simplicity must be left to future research.

4.4.1. An Apparent Complex Weight Distinction: The Case of Asheninca

Before concluding the discussion of complexity, there is one weight distinction that superficially resembles one of the simple weight distinctions in Figure 4.3 and Table 4.2, but that is predicted to be complex by the complexity metric developed thus far. Asheninca treats the high vowel /i/ (the only high vowel in the language) in an open syllable as lighter than other syllable types, including closed syllables containing /i/. As discussed in section 4.1, /i/ in an open syllable is in fact merely one level of weight along a complex weight hierarchy operative in Asheninca: CVV > Ca(C), Ce(C), Co(C), CiC > Ci > Cɨ. The vowel in the weakest syllable in the hierarchy, Cɨ, is the phonetic realization of /i/ in syllables beginning with a strident coronal onset, /ʃ/ (underlying /s/ palatalized before /i/), and /t͡s/. Cɨ has a straightforward representation like that of other reduced vowels that lack their own timing position. Likewise, the weight distinctions between CVV and other syllables and between the non-high vowels /a, e, o/ and other syllables is compatible with representations in Figure 4.3. What is problematic under the definition of complexity adopted here is the distinction between CiC and Ci. CiC must somehow be grouped together with all syllables containing a non-high vowel, whether open or closed, to the exclusion of Ci.

Though superficially problematic, the Asheninca facts are effectively analyzed if one adopts the assumption advanced here that segments must exceed a minimum duration threshold to receive a timing position. Recall that this requirement is compatible with observations about the extremely short phonetic duration of reduced vowels in languages in which they count as light for stress. There is ample evidence that /i/ is phonetically very short in open syllables in Asheninca and therefore plausibly does not carry its own timing position. Let us consider this evidence now.

Facts about the qualitative realization of /i/ in different environments and the relationship between speech rate and its ability to attract stress suggest a continuum of phonetic duration for /i/. First, /i/ in an open syllable is centralized after coronal stridents; the centralization of /i/ in this environment is compatible with the assumption that it is shorter in duration and that this durational reduction prevents the tongue from reaching the peripheral high front target required for the canonical realization as [i]. The result is a hypoarticulated /i/ which is phonetically realized as a central vowel. In fact, this central vowel is phonetically so short that it is completely overlapped by the laryngeal opening gesture of a following voiceless consonant; the result is acoustic deletion of the vowel, e.g. ʃiʦa → ʃɨʦá 'intestinal worm' (Payne 1990:190). /i/ is not subject to centralization in closed syllables, even when following a coronal strident, suggesting that, unlike /i/ in open syllables, it is long enough for the tongue to reach a more forward articulation.[10] A process of stress deletion applying at fast speech rates and affecting secondary stressed /i/ in Ci adjacent to a heavier syllable (stressed or unstressed) also suggests a phonetic continuum of duration along which /i/ in an open syllable ranks lowly (Payne 1990:201). Stress deletion does not target any syllables that are heavier than Ci suggesting that /i/ is substantially shorter than other vowels.

Given these facts, we can plausibly assume that the vowel in Asheninca Ci has the durational properties of a reduced vowel in a language that treats reduced vowels as light for stress. It is thus reasonable to assume that /i/ in Ci lacks its own timing position. The weight distinction between heavier Ca(C), Ce(C), Co(C), CiN and lighter Ci can thus be assumed to be represented as in (i) in Figure 4.3, Heavy= $[X]_R$, where all heavy syllables have at least one timing position in the rime.

The distinction between light Ci and extra-light Cɨ following a coronal strident onset then becomes a matter of assigning representations that distinguish between high front and high central vowels. Since the representation of distinctions of this type is an unresolved issue in phonological theory (see Clements 1991 for a proposal to represent such distinctions), a precise representation of the distinction between Ci and Cɨ must await further research. Whatever the ultimate representation of this distinction turns out to be, however, it will presumably involve place features (as Clements proposes).

4.4.2. Other Phonologically Simple Weight Distinctions

The set of attested weight distinctions in Figure 4.3 does not exhaust the logically possible set of weight distinctions that would be considered simple by the complexity metric introduced above. There are, in fact, other weight distinctions that qualify as simple according to the complexity metric postulated here. Let us consider some of them in Figure 4.4. Note that +S = a continuant consonant, +G = a voiced consonant.

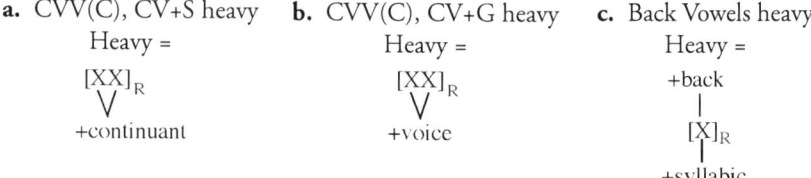

Figure 4.4. Other structurally simple weight distinctions

The first of these distinctions treats long vowels and syllables closed by a continuant as heavy. This distinction is equivalent in complexity to the CVV(C), CVR heavy distinction. The second distinction in Figure 4.4 treats long vowels and syllables closed by a voiced consonant as heavy. Yet another simple distinction, the one in (c), groups together back vowels to the exclusion of non-back vowels, i.e. /ɑ, u/ heavy, or /a, i/ heavy depending on whether the low vowel is back or not. This distinction is identical to the distinction between high and non-high vowels, except for the replacement of the height feature with a backness feature.

All of these distinctions are simple according to the definition adopted above. As shown in Table 4.3, none of them require disjoint representations of the syllable and none of them make references to more than one place predicate.

4.4.3. Structurally Complex Weight Distinctions

Thus far we have only considered structurally simple weight distinctions. We now consider some complex weight distinctions in Figure 4.5. The distinction in (a) is the representation of a weight distinction between long low vowels and all other rimes, in a language lacking [+low] consonants. (Note that a language with [+low] consonants would also require a [+syllabic] feature linked to the two rimal timing positions.) Conversely, a language whose only long vowels were low (e.g. Kara) would not require the [+low] feature and could instead be expressed using the feature [+syllabic], which would make it a simple distinction.

Table 4.3. Other Simple distinctions and their phonological dimensions			Disjoint	Dimension	
	Predicates			Non-place	Place
CVV(C), CV+S heavy	$[X]_R$ +continuant	$[X]_R$ +continuant	No	4	0
CVV(C), CV+G heavy	$[X]_R$ +voice	$[X]_R$ +voice	No	4	0
Back Vowels heavy	+back $[X]_R$ +syllabic		No	2	1

The distinction in (b) is the representation of a weight division according to which long vowels and diphthongs and rimes containing a non-high vowel followed by a nasal coda are heavy, while (c) is the representation of the distinction according to which long vowels and diphthongs and syllables containing a non-high vowel and a sonorant coda are heavy. The distinction in (d) represents a system in which long vowels and syllables containing a non-high vowel followed by a bilabial coda are heavy. The distinction in (e) treats long vowels and syllables closed by a nasal as heavy. These weight distinctions are unattested in languages of the world to the best of my knowledge.

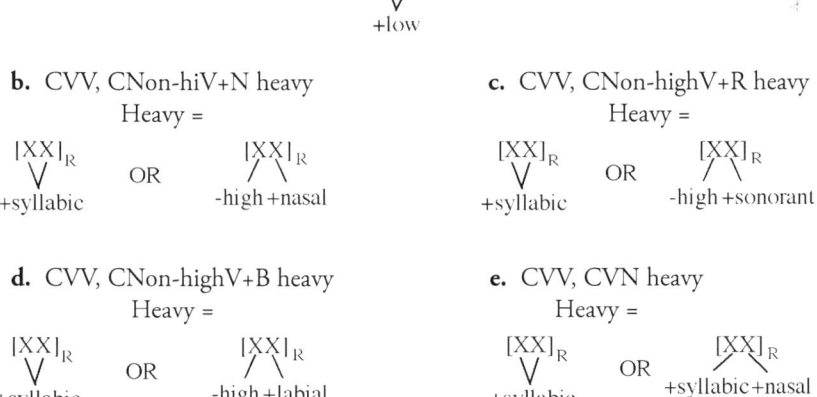

Figure 4.5. Structurally complex and unattested weight distinction

Table 4.4. Complex weight distinctions and their phonological dimensions

	Predicates	Disjoint	Dimension	
			Non-place	Place
Long low V heavy	$[X]_R$ $[X]_R$ $\mid$ $\mid$ +low +low	No	2	2
CVV, CNon-hiV+N heavy	$[X]_R$ $[X]_R$ $[X]_R$ $[X]_R$ $\mid$ $\mid$ $\mid$ $\mid$ +syllabic +syllabic -high +nasal	Yes	7	1
CVV, CNon-hiV+R heavy	$[X]_R$ $[X]_R$ $[X]_R$ $[X]_R$ $\mid$ $\mid$ $\mid$ $\mid$ +syllabic +syllabic -high +sonorant	Yes	7	1
CVV, CNon-hiV+B heavy	$[X]_R$ $[X]_R$ $[X]_R$ $[X]_R$ $\mid$ $\mid$ $\mid$ $\mid$ +syllabic +syllabic -high +labial	Yes	6	2
CVV, CVN heavy	$[X]_R$ $[X]_R$ $[X]_R$ $[X]_R$ $\mid$ $\mid$ $\mid$ $\mid$ +syllabic +syllabic +syllabic +nasal	Yes	8	0

Table 4.4 classifies the weight distinctions in Figure 4.5 according to their associations (if any) between features and timing predicates, such as skeletal slots and root nodes. Table 4.4 also summarizes the number of place and non-place predicates invoked by each weight distinction.

All of these weight distinction are relatively complex in comparison to both the attested weight distinctions in Figure 4.3, as well as the simple but unattested weight distinctions in Figure 4.4. In Figure 4.5, the distinction between long low vowels and other syllables (a) is sensitive to two place predicates, since the [+low] feature is linked to two timing positions. The distinctions in (b-e) are also complex but for a different reason; each of them makes reference to disjoint representations of the syllable, one representation for long vowels and another representation for other heavy syllable types: in (b) a non-high vowel followed by a nasal, in (c), a non-high vowel followed by a sonorant, in (d), a non-high vowel and a bilabial, and, in (e), a syllable closed by a nasal.

Because the weight distinctions in Figure 4.5 are phonologically complex, they are not expected to be exploited by the phonology, even if they are phonetically superior to other structurally simpler weight distinctions. We will see in section 4.7 that the notion of phonological complexity is important in ruling out weight distinctions which are phonetically more effective than weight distinctions actually observed by phonological systems. In fact, the distinctions in Figure 4.5 will be shown in this chapter and Chapter Five to be phonetically more effective than actual phonological distinctions: for (a), see the discussion of Chickasaw (section 4.7.2.1) and Telugu (section

4.7.2.5); for (b), see section 4.7.2.1 on Chickasaw and section 4.7.2.3 on Khalkha; for (c), see section 4.7.2.1 on Chickasaw; for (d) see section 4.7.2.3 on Khalkha; for (e), see section 5.5 on Lithuanian.

4.5. PHONETIC EFFECTIVENESS

4.5.1. The Phonetic Correlates of Weight-Sensitive Stress

In this section, we turn to the second ingredient in syllable weight: phonetic effectiveness. We have already seen in Chapter Three the relevance of phonetic effectiveness for syllable weight in the context of weight-sensitive tone. Recall from Chapter Three that phonetic effectiveness for tone is evaluated along the dimension of the sonorant energy of the rime. Syllables that have greater sonorous energy are heavier than those with less sonorous energy. On a language specific basis, we also saw evidence that the duration of coda sonorants may be relevant for determining the relative effectiveness of the CVV(C) heavy criterion as compared to the CVV(C), CVR heavy criterion. The CVV(C), CVR heavy criterion appeared to be phonetically more effective in languages with relatively long sonorant codas, whereas the CVV(C) heavy criterion was phonetically superior in languages with short sonorant codas.

In the case of stress, the phonetic correlates of weight are less obvious a priori. Two plausible conditioning properties, however, are total energy and duration of the syllable rime. Duration and energy appear to be plausible correlates of weight for stress for two reasons. First, duration and energy are closely linked to the realization of stress in many languages. It is a well-known observation that both energy (and its perceptual correlate loudness) and duration are common phonetic correlates of stress. In many languages, stressed syllables are either longer or louder than unstressed syllables or are *both* longer *and* louder than unstressed syllables. The correlation between stress and increased duration and/or loudness has been experimentally shown for many languages, including English (Fry 1955, 1958, Beckman 1986), French (Rigault 1962), Russian (Bondarko et al. 1973), Polish (Jassem and Steffen-Batóg 1968), Mari (Baitschura 1976), Indonesian (Adisasmito-Smith and Cohn 1996), Tagalog (Gonzalez 1970), Dutch (Sluijter and van Heuven 1996), etc. and impressionistically noted for many other languages. It would thus not be surprising that languages might use these same phonetic properties not only to signal stress, but also perhaps to determine the position of stress in a word.[11] A measure of total energy rather than another measure of energy such as average energy is most relevant for testing the link between energy and weight-sensitive stress, as psychoacoustic experiments suggest that the ear integrates energy and time up to durations under which most syllable durations fall (see Moore 1995 for a review of the relevant literature). Total energy may be visually represented as the area under the curve in Figure 4.6, where the curve represents a continuous intensity display over a syllable rime.

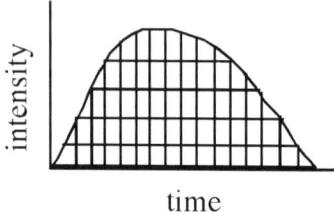

Figure 4.6. Measurement of total energy

Interestingly, work by Broselow et al. (1997) has suggested that one of the properties examined in this chapter, duration, is closely correlated with phonological weight distinctions. In their study of four languages with different weight systems (Malayalam, Hindi and two dialects of Arabic), they found duration differences corresponding to the different phonological weight criteria of these languages. Their work is reviewed in the context of the present results in section 4.8. We now turn to the phonetic data examined in this chapter.

4.5.2. Phonetic Effectiveness and Weight-Sensitive Stress

For purposes of weight, phonetic effectiveness may be defined as the degree to which a particular weight division separates syllables into two maximally distinct groups. In other words, the most optimal division of syllables creates a distribution with two peaks and no overlap between the two groups. Since this ideal division is seldom found in the real world, we may for practical purposes define the optimal weight distinction as the one which separates syllables into two groups with the least overlap between the two groups and the greatest separation of average values for the groups. In contrast, the least optimal division is the one with the most overlap and smallest difference in average values between the two groups.

The difference between an effective and an ineffective weight distinction can be illustrated by means of two histograms from Khalkha shown in Figures 4.7 and 4.8. The x-axis in both figures represents arbitrary units used for measuring energy, while the y-axis is the number of tokens of each syllable falling within the energy values along the y-axis. The peak of each curve represents the average for a given group. In Figure 4.7, the CVV vs. CVC,

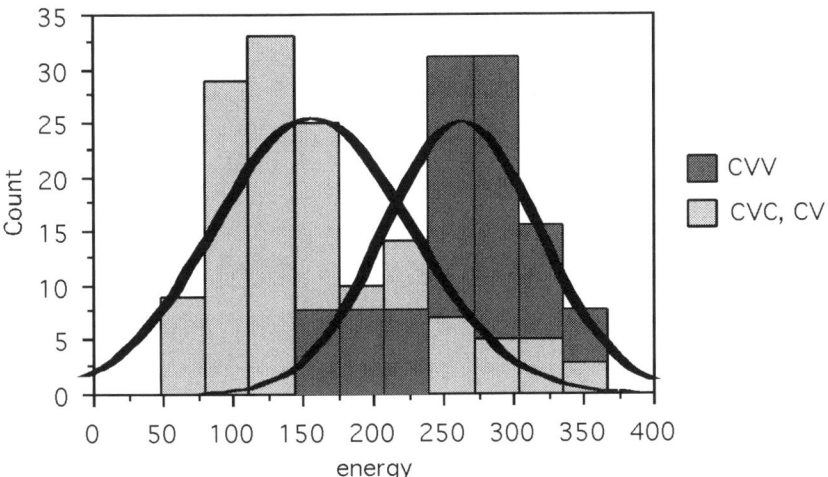

Figure 4.7. Effective distinction (Khalkha energy: CVV > CVC, CV)

CV distinction is shown. This distinction is quite effective as indicated by the relatively small amount of overlap between the two groups of syllables and the large difference between average values for the two groups. In Figure 4.8, on the other hand, an ineffective weight distinction is shown, one based on vowel height. Notice the almost complete overlap between rimes containing a high vowel and rimes containing a low vowel.

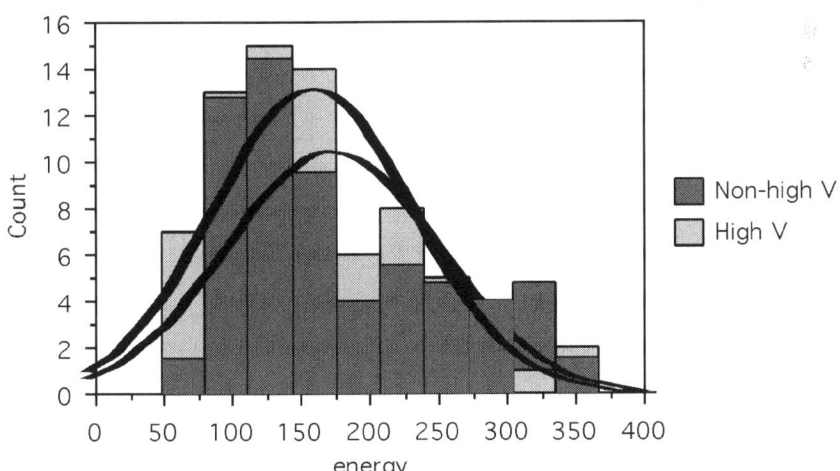

Figure 4.8. Ineffective distinction (Khalkha energy: Non-high V > High V)

The motivation for this metric of phonetic effectiveness is perceptual in nature. It is claimed that languages prefer weight distinctions based on the largest phonetic differences, since distinctions based on larger phonetic differences are easier to perceive and also to learn than distinctions based on smaller differences. Phonetic and perceptual distinctness (or conversely, lack of distinctness) have been shown to play an important role in phonology in such diverse areas as the construction of segment inventories that maximize the phonetic space (cf. Liljencrants and Lindblom 1972, Lindblom 1986), neutralization processes eliminating phonetic contrasts that are difficult to implement in a perceptually salient manner (Flemming 1995, Steriade 1999), and phonological processes that preserve or create maximally distinct segments or combinations of segments (Flemming 1995).

4.6. METHODOLOGY OF THE PRESENT STUDY

4.6.1. *Languages*

To examine the phonetic basis for weight in relation to stress, six languages displaying various weight distinctions were investigated. These weight distinctions are primarily observed by stress systems, although weight distinctions used by metrical systems were examined for two languages in the study. Data from metrical systems were included, since stress and metrics appear to be closely linked, as demonstrated in Chapter Two.

Two languages with a binary distinction of the CVV(C), CVC heavy type, Finnish and Japanese, were included in the study. One language employing the CVV(C) heavy criterion, Khalkha, was examined. Two languages with a ternary distinction CVV(C) > CVC > CV, Chickasaw and Telugu, were investigated. One language, Javanese, makes a weight distinction between full and reduced vowels for stress.

Finally, four languages with weight-insensitive prominence systems were included in the study: Bole, Farsi, Russian, and French. Languages without weight-sensitive stress serve as experimental controls, in the sense that, if they display similar phonetic patterns to those found in weight-sensitive languages, we avoid a potential circular relationship between phonetics and syllable weight whereby phonetic patterns could be argued to be purely the result of phonological criteria. See section 4.9 and Chapter Three for discussion of the direction of the relationship between phonetics and phonology. The ten languages in the current study are listed in Table 4.5 with the relevant distinctions employed by each language, along with sources for the phonological data. Evidence for the weight hierarchies in

Table 4.5. Ten language study of vowel and consonant duration and energy

	Weight distinction	**Source(s)**
Finnish	CVV, CVC > CV	Kiparsky (1968), Sadeniemi (1949), Hanson and Kiparsky (1996)
Japanese	CVV, CVC > CV	Vance (1987)
Khalkha	CVV > CVC, CV	Bosson (1964), Walker (1995, 1996)
Telugu	CVV > CVC > CV	Brown (1981), Petrunicheva (1960), Krishnamurti and Gwynn (1985), Sitapati (1936)
Chickasaw	CVV > CVC > CV	Munro and Willmond (1994), Munro (1996b), Gordon (1999)
Javanese	Full V > Reduced V	Herrfurth (1964), Horne (1974), Ras (1982)
Russian	weight-insensitive stress	Comrie (1990)
Farsi	weight-insensitive stress	Windfuhr (1990)
French	weight-insensitive stress	Delattre (1966)
Bole	no stress; tonal	Lukas (1969)

each of the examined languages is considered in more detail in the sections detailing the results for individual languages.

4.6.2. Measure of Energy

A corpus of two syllable words of the form (C)V(ː)C.CV(C) was constructed for each language, varying the rime of the first syllable, the target syllable, (except in Javanese—see below) and keeping the vowel in the other syllable constant.[12] Within each language, the first syllable had the same stress level for all words in the corpus, as did the second syllable. The first syllable was stressed for all tokens in all languages except for Farsi, Chickasaw, French. In these three languages, stress fell on the second syllable of words in the corpus. Also, the Javanese reduced vowel in an open syllable had to be measured in the first syllable due to a restriction against absolute word-final reduced vowels in the native vocabulary. By keeping stress uniform for all target syllables, a difference in stress level between different syllable types is eliminated as a potential confounding factor. Due to the lack of a consensus regarding syllable affiliations, only open syllables were examined in Russian. The rimes appearing in the first syllable were varied according to the vowel quality and length (if long vowels occurred in the language) of the syllable nucleus. Three vowel qualities were examined: /i, u/ and a low vowel, either /a/ or /ɑ/. In

Javanese, the reduced (i.e. central) vowel was also examined. Rimes containing /i/ were not measured in Khalkha due to confounds created by the vowel harmony system. Rimes containing /u/ were not measured for Chickasaw due to the absence of this vowel in the inventory. In order to create a more manageable data set for measurement, diphthongs and mid vowels were not examined in any of the languages; thus, the phonetic basis for weight distinctions between long vowels and diphthongs and between mid vowels and other vowel qualities was not examined experimentally. Short vowels were examined in both open syllables and syllables closed by various coda consonants; for example, by different sonorant codas and coda obstruents (if tolerated by the language). Geminates were not measured, as they cannot be acoustically segmented into coda and onset phases. The set of coda consonants and vowels examined for each language is listed in Table 4.6. The complete corpus recorded for each language appears in Appendix Four.

Six to eight tokens of each word were recorded from one speaker in each language. Data were recorded in a soundproof booth onto an analog cassette via a table top condenser microphone. Words were read in random order and appeared in a carrier phrase that is listed for each language in Appendix Four. Data were digitized at 16kHz using Kay Computerized Speech Lab. Two measurements were made for each rime: duration and total perceptual energy (the integration of energy over time in the perceptual domain). Duration was measured for each segment in the rime using a waveform in conjunction with a spectrogram and an energy display. Discontinuities in one or

Table 4.6. Vowels and codas measured for ten languages

Language	Vowels and codas examined
Telugu	a, i, u, aː, iː, uː, m, l, r, s, k, g
Chickasaw	a, i, aː, iː, m, n, l, ʃ, ɬ, b, k
Khalkha	ɑ, u, ɑː, uː, m, n, l, r, s, ʃ, x, k, g
Finnish	ɑ, i, u, ɑː, iː, uː, m, l, r, s, t
Javanese	a, i, u, ə, r, n, s, t
French	a, i, u, l, ʁ[13], s
Farsi	ạ, i, u, m, n, l, r, f, s, z, ʃ, ʒ, x, k, g
Russian	a, i, u (only open syllables)
Japanese	a, i, u̥, aː, iː, u̥ː, m, n
Bole	a, i, u, aː, iː, uː, m, n, l, r

more of these displays were used for segmentation purposes. For vowels, the onset of the second formant was treated as the beginning point and the offset of the second formant was treated as the end.

The procedure for measuring total perceptual energy was as follows. First, in order to control for token to token variation in speaking level, average amplitude (RMS) in decibels for each target vowel and the following coda consonant (if any) was calculated relative to a reference vowel in the other syllable which, as mentioned earlier, was kept constant. Second, the average amplitude of each segment in the target rime was converted to a value representing perceived loudness relative to the reference vowel in the second syllable. Perceived loudness was computed from a graph in Warren (1970: 1399) based on experiments designed to measure relative perceived loudness of tones. While Warren's results are based on a different type of stimulus than real speech, they serve as a reasonable and also tractable estimate of the relationship between acoustic energy and perceived loudness. Third, the relative loudness value for each segment was multiplied by the duration of the segment to yield a total energy value for the segment. Finally, if the rime contained a coda, total energy values for the vowel nucleus and the coda were added together yielding a total energy value for the rime. An example of the method of calculating total energy is provided here. Let us take the first syllable of the word /**pan**ta/. Let us suppose that the /**a**/ of the first syllable is 80 milliseconds and the /**n**/ is 60 milliseconds. First, the average energy of /a̱/ is subtracted from the average energy of /**a**/ and the average energy of /**n**/. Let us suppose the average energy of /**a**/ is 6dB greater than the average energy of /a̱/, and the average energy of /**n**/ is 3dB greater than the average energy of /a̱/. 6dB corresponds to a twofold increase in perceived loudness, while 3dB corresponds to a 1.55 increase in perceived loudness. The duration of /**a**/ (80 milliseconds) in /**pan**ta/ is thus multiplied by 2, and the duration of /**n**/ (60 milliseconds) in /**pan**ta̱/ is multiplied by 1.55 yielding total energy values for /**a**/ and /**n**/ of 160 and 93 (in arbitrary units), respectively. Finally, the products of these operations are summed together providing a total energy value for the rime as a whole, 253.

Results of the energy and duration phases of the measurements will be presented in section 4.7 and 4.8, respectively. In the next section, we turn to the role of phonetic effectiveness and phonological simplicity in weight-sensitive stress systems.

4.6.3. Phonetic Evaluation of Potential Weight Criteria

We are now in a position to consider the actual phonetic data collected for the ten languages examined in this paper. Along the two phonetic parameters of duration and total energy, the set of syllables measured in a given language were bisected a number of different ways, with each bisection representing a different weight distinction, just as syllables containing long vowels were grouped together to the exclusion of syllables containing short vowels in Figure 4.7 and high vowels were grouped together to the exclusion of non-high vowels in Figure 4.8. In determining the phonetic effectiveness of different weight distinctions, the goal was to test all reasonable distinctions against the phonetic data. This resulted in testing a total of 55 weight distinctions, though not all weight distinctions were tested in every language due to gaps in the inventory of syllable types in certain languages. Thus, for example, the division between full and reduced vowels could only be tested in Javanese, since the other examined languages do not make a distinction between full and reduced vowels. Furthermore, in some cases, two different distinctions provide the same division of the data. Thus, for example, distinctions based on the voicing of the coda and those based on the sonorancy of the coda divide the data in the same way for Finnish, as the only sonorants in Finnish are voiced and the only obstruents in Finnish are voiceless.

A large number of plausible weight distinctions were tested against the data in the ten languages. We now examine the method for creating the set of candidate weight distinctions to be tested. The tested weight distinctions were based on several featural parameters. The relevant features were place features ([high] in the case of vowels, and [coronal] [dorsal] and [labial] for consonants) and manner features ([voice], [sonorant] and [continuant]). Vowels were considered as one dimension, and consonants another. For each of the features pertaining to consonants, consonants were divided into two groups, those that lack the feature and those that have the feature. The same was done for the vowels using the vocalic feature [high]. Consonants and vowels were combined in all possible ways. The corpus did not include mid vowels; thus, there was no basis for distinguishing between [high] and [low] for vowels.

To take an example, assume that the relevant consonant feature is [sonorant]. For convenience, let us represent [+sonorant] consonants as +R and [-sonorant] consonants as -R. Assuming that both sonorant and non-sonorant codas appear following both [+high] and [-high] vowels, there are thus four logical combinations of vowels and consonants (where /i/ stands for high vowels, and /a/ for non-high vowels): a+R, a-R, i+R, i-R. If we align the consonants and vowels on different axes we get Figure 4.9.

i-R   i+R

a-R   a+R

Figure 4.9. Matrix of vowel height and coda sonority

If we put short vowels in open syllables on the left side of this matrix and long vowels on the right side, we get a continuum ranging from phonologically heavy to light on both axes, as in Figure 4.10.

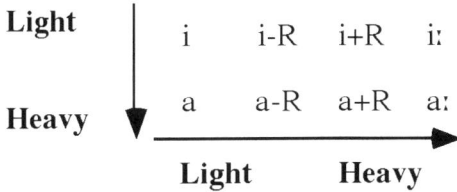

Figure 4.10. Matrix of syllable weight

Along the x-axis, rimes to the right are heavier, and along the y-axis, rimes at the bottom are heavier. This matrix can be bisected in many different ways that would be likely to split the data into two phonetically distinct groups. We now consider in Figure 4.11 eight distinctions that would appear to be reasonably plausible.

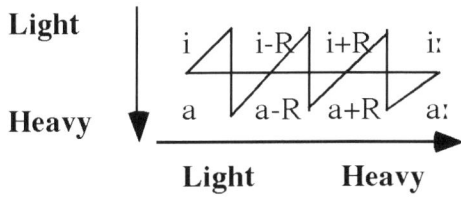

Figure 4.11. Weight divisions tested in study

There are three vertical divisions. According to one vertical division, indicated by the rightmost vertical line, long vowels are separated from all other rimes. This is the distinction shown in Figure 4.7 for Khalkha. The center vertical line represents the weight distinction according to which long vowels and syllables closed by a sonorant coda are separated from short vowels in open syllables and syllables closed by an obstruent. Recall that this weight distinction is exploited in Kwakw'ala. Yet another division, marked by the leftmost vertical line, groups together all closed syllables and syllables containing a long vowel to the exclusion of short vowels in open syllables. This distinction is found in languages like Latin. Finally, the horizontal division separates high and non-high vowels, the distinction employed by Komi.

We now proceed to some more complex divisions of the matrix, which are represented with diagonal lines; most of these distinctions are either unattested or vanishingly rare, but are plausible from a phonetic standpoint given standard assumptions about sonority. One distinction separates long /aː/, the most sonorous long vowel, from all other rimes. Another distinction groups together long vowels and syllables containing a low vowel followed by a sonorant coda, the most sonorous rimes. Yet another division groups together long vowels, syllables closed by a sonorant, and syllables containing /a/ followed by a non-sonorant coda. Finally, it is possible to divide the matrix such that all syllables are grouped together to the exclusion of /i/ in an open syllable. This final distinction is attested in Asheninca.

Note that it would be possible to test other weight distinctions represented with diagonal lines on a negative slope. However, these would not be phonetically "sensible" weight distinctions.

The same procedure of splitting the matrix in various ways was done using the laryngeal feature [voice], the manner features [nasal] and [continuant], and the place features capturing the difference between labials, coronals, and velars: [labial], [coronal], and [dorsal], respectively. Even though languages do not appear to be sensitive to these features in determining weight distinctions, they are a priori plausible weight distinctions, particularly those involving the manner features [voice] and [continuant], which play a role in sonority hierarchies. The relevant matrices involving these features appear in Figure 4.12. Note the following abbreviations: +G represents a voiced consonant, -G a voiceless consonant, +S a continuant, -S a non-continuant, +N a nasal, -N a non-nasal, +B a labial, -B a non-labial, +T a coronal, -T a non-coronal, +K a velar and -K a non-velar.

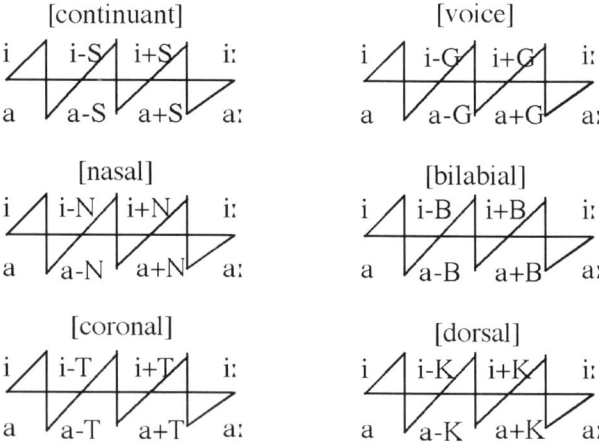

Figure 4.12. Weight distinctions divided according to vowel height and coda type

Because it is unclear for certain of the consonant classes, which are "heavier," both possibilities were considered by switching the order of the two. For the sake of symmetry, this was done for all consonant features, including [sonorant] as in Figure 4.13.

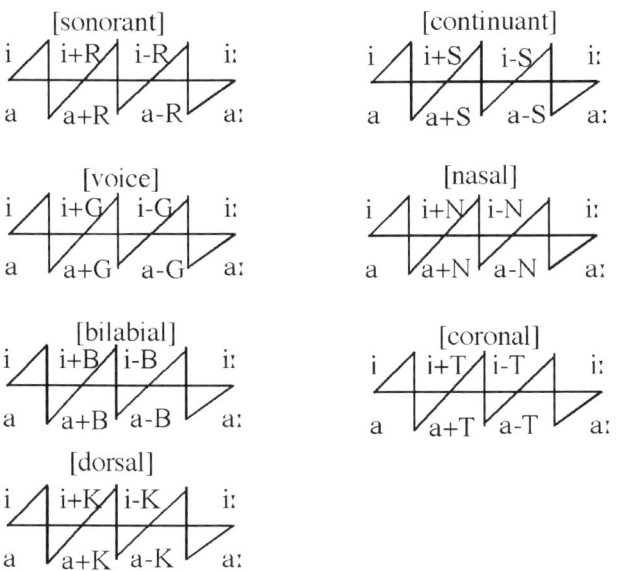

Figure 4.13. Further weight distinctions examined in the study

Finally, coda consonants of different types can be collapsed yielding the matrix in Figure 4.14, where C refers to any type of coda consonant.

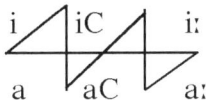

Figure 4.14. Weight distinctions based on presence/absence of coda consonant

Note that many of the divisions tested are duplicated in more than one matrix; for example, the distinction between low and high vowels appears as a horizontal line in every matrix.

In addition to the distinctions considered in the matrices in Figures 4.12–4.14, a few other distinctions were tested. The distinction between CVVC (superheavy) and other syllables was tested for Chickasaw, and the full vs. reduced vowel distinction was examined for Javanese. Additionally, the Malay type distinction according to which only open syllables containing reduced vowels are light was examined in Javanese. Finally, distinctions between long /aː, iː/ and other rimes, and between long /aː, uː/ and other rimes were examined in languages with phonemic long vowels. All told 55 possible weight distinctions were tested, though the total for any one language did not reach 55 due to gaps in the inventory of coda consonants in certain languages as noted above.

4.6.4. A Quantitative Metric of Phonetic Effectiveness

For the parameters of duration and total energy, distinctions were compared in a three step process. First, a one factor analysis of variance was performed treating rime type (e.g. /an/, /am/, /is/, /uk/, etc.) as the independent variable and duration and energy as the dependent variables. The purpose of this initial analysis was merely to determine whether syllable type had an effect on duration and energy values.

The second step was to compare the mean values for heavy and light syllables for each weight distinction. Weight distinctions for which the means for heavy and light syllables were most divergent were deemed to be the most effective weight distinctions. As an example of this criterion for establishing phonetic effectiveness, let us compare, using hypothetical energy values, the distinction between non-high and high vowels with the distinction between long vowels and other rimes. Suppose that both of these distinctions divide the set of syllables into two groups that are statistically different from each other. Suppose further that high vowels average 85 units of energy and non-high vowels 110 units. The difference between the heavier group, i.e. the non-high vowels, and the lighter group, the high vowels, is thus 25 units. Now assume that long vowels average 140 units of energy and the combination of all other rimes average 120 units. This difference of 20 units of energy is smaller than the difference between high and non-high vowels (25 units). Thus, the high vs. non-high vowel weight distinction is a better discriminator along this dimension because it has the greater separation between mean values. Because they are not dependent on number of tokens, differences in means were used to determine the relative effectiveness among the weight distinctions. The metric of phonetic effectiveness adopted as a differentiator of weight criteria is formalized in (47).

(47) Definition of phonetic effectiveness
      A weight distinction x is more effective than a weight distinction y, if the difference between the mean energy of heavy syllables and the mean energy of light syllables for distinction x is greater than the difference between

the mean energy of heavy syllables and the mean energy of light syllables for distinction *y*.

The final step involved in examining the phonetic effectiveness of different weight distinctions was to perform a discriminant analysis for each distinction to determine how well each one sorted syllables into heavy and light groups. Each weight distinction was treated as a categorical variable with two values, one for light syllables and another for heavy syllables. Significance levels and Wilkes' lambda values for each weight distinction were examined to determine how reliable various weight distinctions were in differentiating heavy and light syllables. Wilkes' lambda serves as a way of comparing the amount of variance in the data attributed to differences within groups to the amount of variance attributed to differences between groups. Wilkes' lambda thus serves as a way as assessing the reliability of a result. The lower the Wilkes' lambda value, the greater the amount of variance is attributed to differences between the heavy and light syllables and the less the variance is attributed to differences among members of the heavy group or the light group. Because the Wilkes' lambda values are affected by factors such as sample size which are not claimed to be relevant to the hypothesis examined here, they were not used as the definitive criterion for ranking weight distinctions in order of phonetic effectiveness; rather, as pointed out above, mean values were used to rank the relative phonetic effectiveness of distinctions.

4.7. RESULTS: TOTAL ENERGY

We turn now to the results of the phonetic study of energy. Several major results emerged from this study. First, the phonological weight hierarchies for stress presented earlier in Figures 4.1 and 4.2 corresponded to phonetic hierarchies along the energy dimension. Second, a measure of total energy corresponded remarkably well to a variety of weight distinctions in several languages; the phonological weight distinctions adopted by languages were those that were the phonetically most effective distinctions. At the same time, however, phonetic data demonstrates that a notion of phonological simplicity plays an important role in excluding certain phonetically optimal weight distinctions. Another result, which should be borne in mind when considering the energy results, is that duration did *not* offer an explanation for certain weight distinctions. Discussion of the duration results will be postponed until section 4.8 after the energy data are considered in detail.

4.7.1. The Correspondence Between Phonological Weight Hierarchies and a Measure of Phonetic Energy

Recall from section that a cross-linguistic survey of weight distinctions for stress indicated two core implicational hierarchies of phonological weight. The first of these hierarchies involves sensitivity to phonemic vowel length, number of segments in the rime and the sonority of coda consonants. It is repeated as Figure 4.15.

Figure 4.15. First hierarchy of weight for stress

The second of the weight hierarchies involves vowel height and vowel fullness and is repeated as Figure 4.16.

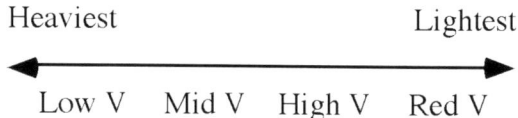

Figure 4.16. Second hierarchy of weight for stress

Within each of these hierarchies, a rime may be equivalent in weight but not heavier than a rime to its left. In phonological theory, the representations that capture these hierarchies are projected from phonemic contrasts in vowel length and segment count in conjunction with sonority scales. The last of these elements, sonority scales (Steriade 1982, Selkirk 1984, Clements 1990), plays an important role in deriving distinctions between VR and VO and between different vowel qualities.

The present study demonstrated that the weight hierarchies in Figures 4.15 and 4.16 correspond (with one exception to be discussed below) closely to phonetic hierarchies of total energy, according to which a rime may not have more energy than a rime to its left on along either of the hierarchies. Thus, for example, in none of the languages examined, does V have greater energy than VO. Nor do high vowels have greater energy than low vowels in the examined data.

The relevant data demonstrating the correlation between energy and the weight hierarchy in Figure 4.15 appears in Figure 4.17, which contains average

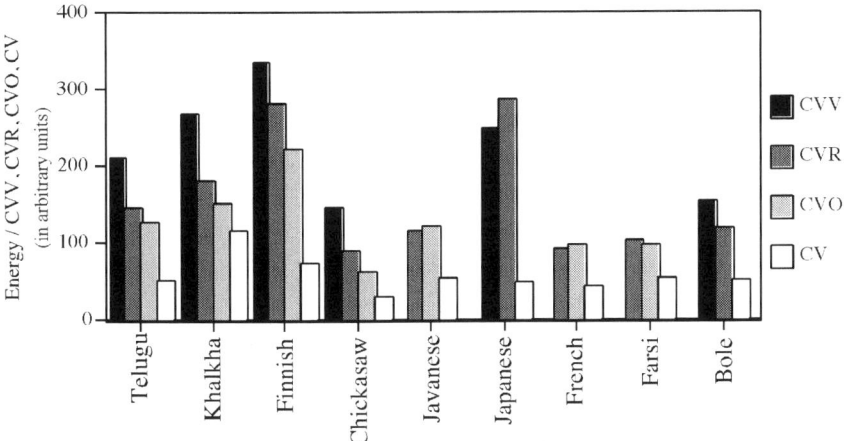

Figure 4.17. Average energy values for CVV, CVR, CVO, and CV in 9 languages

energy values for VV, VR, VO and V in the nine languages in the survey for which at least two of these rimes were examined (i.e. all except Russian). Energy values and statistical comparison according to unpaired t-tests appears in Table 4.7. Differences that are statistically insignificant (assuming significance at $p<.01$ level, due to the large number of comparisons) appear in shaded cells.

With one exception (Japanese, which is discussed below) all of the languages display the same overall pattern whereby rimes have at least as much energy as rimes to their left in the hierarchy in Figure 4.15.

It is also interesting to note that the energy difference between CVR and CVO is fairly small in most languages relative to the other differences. In only two languages (Finnish and Chickasaw) does the difference in energy between CVR and CVO reach significance at the $p<.01$ level. The overall weakness of the CVR and CVO distinction accords with the phonological observation of Chapter Two and section 4.1 of this chapter that languages which make a weight distinguish between CVR and CVO for stress and exceedingly rare.

Average energy data for low and high vowels, the two vowel qualities examined in the present study, appear in Figure 4.18 for ten languages. In the figure, the difference in means between the low and high vowels is represented. Results include both short and long vowels (if they occur in a given language). A line extending above zero on the y-axis indicates that low vowels have greater energy than high vowels (the more common situation); a line extending below zero indicates that low vowels have less energy than high vowels. Differences in average energy and statistical comparison according to

Table 4.7. Differences in energy between CVV, CVR, CVO, and CV in 9 language

	CVV-CVR	CVV-CVO	CVV-CV	CVR-CVO	CVR-CV	CVO-CV
Telugu	65.7, t=-4.668, p<.0001	85.2, t=6.612, p<.0001	159.4, t=10.350, p<.0001	19.5, t=2.198, p=.0303	93.7, t=7.997, p<.0001	74.2, t=7.694, p<.0001
Khalkha	85.9, t=-3.965, p=.0002	115.3, t=6.163, p<.0001	148.7, t-9.334, p<.0001	29.4, t=2.322, p=.0219	62.8, t=3.126, p=.0026	33.4, t=1.940, p=.0560
Finnish	53.3, t=4.219, p<.0001	112.4, t=9.953, p<.0001	262.1, t=22.510, p<.0001	59.1, t=6.150, p<.0001	208.8, t=17.133, p<.0001	149.7, t=14.226, p<.0001
Chickasaw	55.0, t=4.703, p<.0001	81.6, t=7.986, p<.0001	114.7, t=6.424, p<.0001	26.6, t=6.211, p<.0001	59.8, t=9.940, p<.0001	33.1, t=6.016, p<.0001
Javanese				3.6, t=.418, p=.6770	63.2, t=7.358, p<.0001	66.8, t=6.908, p<.0001
Japanese	-37.4, t=4.145, p<.0001		201.1, t=23.022, p<.0001	238.5, t=30.433, p<.0001		
French				-4.9, t=.370, p=.7124	36.4, t=2.377, p=.0218	41.3, t=3.434, p=.0010
Farsi				7.229, t=1.787, p=.0751	49.0, t=8.985, p<.0001	41.7, t=5.750, p<.0001
Bole	33.1, t=2.806, p<.0059		104.5, t=6.197, p<.0001	71.4, t=7.924, p<.0001		

unpaired t-tests follow in Table 4.8. Differences that are statistically insignificant (assuming significance at p<.01 level) appear in shaded cells.

We may also consider the energy difference between full and reduced vowels in Javanese, another distinction which is relevant for the hierarchy in Figure 4.16. The energy difference between full and reduced vowels in Javanese is 52.04, a highly significant difference according to an unpaired t-test: p<.0001, t=6.515. The fact that full vowels have greater energy than reduced vowels in Javanese accords with the observation that full vowels are at least as heavy as reduced vowels cross-linguistically.

Returning to the comparison of high and low vowels in Figure 4.18, energy values for low vowels are at least as great as energy values for high vowels, a fact that corresponds to the phonological observation that low

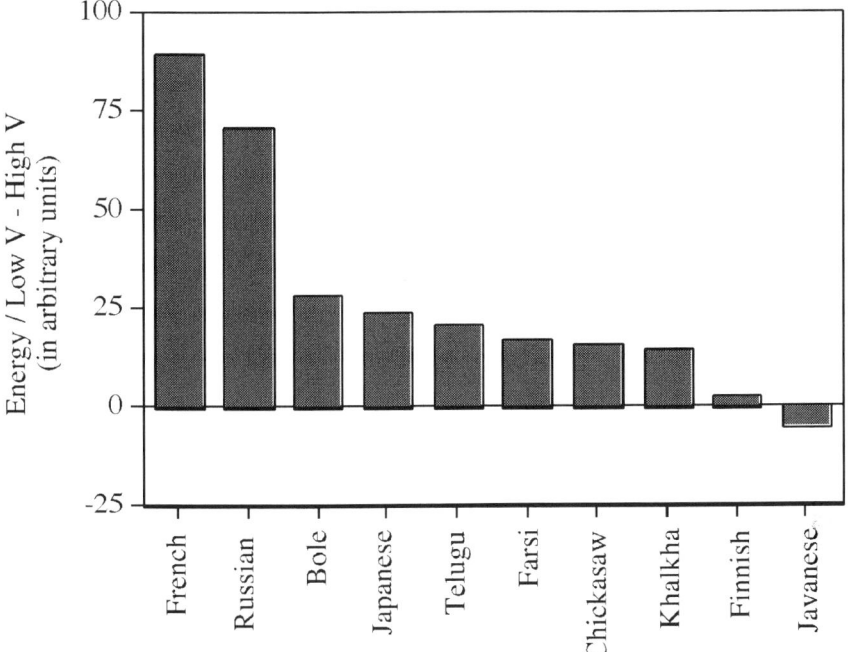

Figure 4.18. Average energy values for low and high vowels in 10 languages

vowels are at least as heavy as high vowels in weight systems. Note that the one exceptional language in this regard, Javanese, is only an apparent one, since the difference in energy between high and low vowels is statistically insignificant. The particularly large energy difference high and low vowels in French and Russian is also noteworthy; the magnitude of this difference is due in large part to the large durational differences between the two vowels, as will be shown in section 4.9.

Before concluding this section, we must return to the one exception (in Figure 4.17) to the otherwise quite consistent correlation between phonological weight hierarchies and phonetic energy. In Japanese, VR has greater energy than VV, an unexpected result given that VR appears to never be heavier than VV phonologically. Assuming the Japanese phonetic data is not unique among the world's languages, one might expect to find languages in which VR is heavier than VV phonologically.

Despite initial appearances, however, there are two factors that conspire to account for the absence of languages in which VR is heavier than VV. As argued in section 4.5, in order for a weight distinction to be

Table 4.8. Differences in energy between low and high vowels in 10 languages

	Low V- High V		Low V- High V
French	89.5, t=12.914, p<.0001	Farsi	16.9, t=4.360, p<.0001
Russian	70.6, t=.4622, p=.0003	Chickasaw	15.5, t=2.124, p=.0351
Bole	27.9, t=2.744, p=.0069	Khalkha	14.1, t=1.169, p=.2441
Japanese	23.8, t=1.059, p=.2924	Finnish	2.8, t=.184, p=.8541
Telugu	20.4, t=1.852, p=.0662	Javanese	-5.2, t=.563, p=.5747

exploited phonologically, it must be the phonetically most effective of the phonologically simple weight distinctions. It is thus not enough for a rime to have slightly more energy than another rime; rather, this difference in energy must be large enough relative to other differences to be exploited by the phonology. Even though VR has slightly more energy than VV in Japanese, this difference is far smaller, as Figure 4.17 shows, than the difference between VR and V. Thus, VR and VV are likely to be treated uniformly with respect to weight and together differentiated from V, as in fact the phonology of Japanese does.

As a follow-up question, one might ask whether one might in fact encounter a more extreme version of Japanese in which VR has substantially greater energy than VV, in which case VR might be expected to be treated as heavier than VV. While in principle such languages might be found, their existence seems rather unlikely when one considers the primary source of the energy discrepancy between VV and VR in Japanese. Figure 4.19 shows duration values for the vowel in CV, CVR, and CVV in Japanese.

As Figure 4.19 shows, the vowel in CVR is much longer than in CV; in fact, it is closer in length to the long vowel in CVV than the vowel in CV.[14] All else being equal, a vowel of greater duration will also have greater total energy; the occurrence of longer vowels in closed syllables thus makes less puzzling the result that CVR has slightly greater energy than CVV in the Japanese data. The question then becomes, whether one could reasonably expect to find a language in which the vowel in CVR would be so lengthened that the difference in energy between CVR and CVV would be exploited as a phonological weight distinction. There are reasons to doubt that this situation would arise. Although the lengthening of vowels before voiced consonants is relatively common cross-linguistically (Lehiste 1970), the extent of the lengthening effect is characteristically much smaller than that seen in the Japanese data. In order for VR to be treated as heavier than VV, the lengthening effect would likely need to be even larger than that found in Japanese. It seems rather unlikely that such a language would be found. It is thus not surprising that there do not appear to be languages that preferentially stress CVR over CVV. As an aside, one might conjecture that the lengthening effect is rather large in Japanese, because vowel length is only marginally contrastive in closed syllables (Vance 1987). Thus, in closed syllables, vowels that are phonetically prone to lengthening may comfortably lengthen without jeopardizing the perception of a phonemic length contrast.

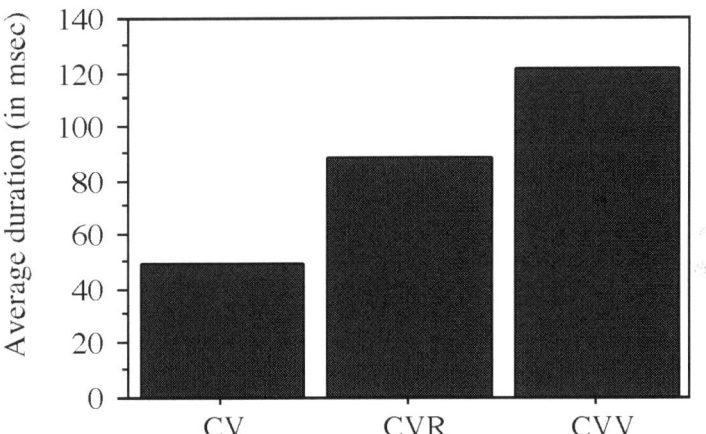

Figure 4.19. Average vowel duration in three rime types in Japanese

In summary, a measure of total energy is a good predictor of phonological weight hierarchies. The results presented here thus demonstrate that the phonetic property of total energy predicts, to a large extent, the range of variation displayed by weight-sensitive stress systems. In particular, it explains why certain syllable types are not treated as heavier than others cross-linguistically. The only case in which we would have the potential for a reversal in the hierarchies of weight in Figures 4.15 and 4.16 would occur in a language with exceptional phonetic properties, for example, in a language in which high vowels had greater energy than low vowels, or in a language like the hypothetical variant of Japanese with even greater phonetic vowel lengthening before sonorants than in real Japanese.

4.7.2. The Correlation Between Energy and Language-Specific Weight Distinctions

In this section, we examine the extent to which a measure of energy predicts the language specific choice of weight distinctions among those that fall within the range of phonetically plausible distinctions. We will examine the relative effectiveness of different weight distinctions, both structurally simple and structurally complex, along the energy dimension in a variety of languages. In sections 4.7.2.1–4.7.2.6, we consider weight-sensitive languages, in which the link between phonological syllable weight, phonetic energy, and phonological simplicity can be most clearly explored. In section 4.7.2.7–4.7.2.10, we turn to weight-insensitive languages, which allow for observation of the intrinsic energy properties of different syllable types unconfounded by the presence of phonological weight distinctions.

4.7.2.1. Chickasaw: CVV(C) > CVC > CV

We begin the discussion with Chickasaw, a language which makes a ternary weight distinction in which long vowels are heaviest, followed by closed syllables containing a short vowel, followed by open syllables containing a short vowel. This weight hierarchy is evident both in phrase-medial words and, even more clearly, in phrase-final words, which will be the focus of discussion here (see Munro 1996 for general discussion of Chickasaw stress and Gordon 1999 for discussion of word-level versus phrase-level prominence).

At the phrase level, primary stress, which is phonetically realized as the nuclear pitch accent, draws the same tripartite distinction: CVV(C) > CVC > CV. This distinction only emerges in questions; in statements, the nuclear pitch accent characteristically falls on the final syllable (see Gordon 1999 for discussion). In questions, the pitch accent falls on the final syllable if it contains a long vowel, where long vowels include phonemic long vowels, nasalized vowels, and, in non-final syllables, rhythmically lengthened vowels arising through lengthening of the second vowel (if non-final) in a sequence of two CV syllables (Munro 1996, 2005, Munro and Ulrich 1984, Munro and Willmond 1994) (48a). Otherwise it falls on a penult that is either closed or contains a long vowel (48b). If these conditions are not met, the nuclear pitch accent falls on the antepenult (48c). Note that rhythmic lengthening ensures that the nuclear pitch accent always falls on either a CVV or a CVC syllable in words of at least three syllables. The nuclear pitch accent is indicated by an acute accent and falls on the same syllable that receives primary stress.

(48) Nuclear pitch accent placement in Chickasaw

a. (katahtãː) tʃihaːʃá: 'Who are you angry at?,' (kataːt) malːitóːk '(Who) jumped (distant past)?'

b. malíːtam 'Did he run?,' (nantaːt) hatáːt͡ʃim 'What turned color (ripen)?' (kataːt) atóbːim 'Who paid for it?,' (kataːt) malíːli 'Who's running?,' (nantaːt) istóktʃank 'What's a watermelon?,' (katiːjakta) akánka? 'Where's the chicken?

c. málːitam 'Did he jump?,' (nantaːt) abóːkoʃi? 'What's a river?'

Because it possesses more than a binary weight distinction, Chickasaw provides a relatively tough testing ground for establishing a correlation between phonetics and syllable weight. As a first step, an analysis of variance was conducting to determine whether rime type had a significant effect on energy values. This ANOVA indicated a highly significant effect of rime type on energy values: $F (21,153) = 15.215$, p<.0001.

In Table 4.9, the relative effectiveness of different weight distinctions in Chickasaw is compared. Distinctions are ordered from top to bottom with the phonetically more effective distinctions (according to differences in mean energy values between heavy and light syllables as described in section 4.6.4) on top. Simple distinctions are indicated by a heart and complex distinctions by a diamond. Mean values are normalized as a ratio relative to the top ranked distinction, which is assigned an arbitrary value of 100. For example, a weight distinction with a value of 50 has a 50% smaller difference in energy between heavy and light syllables than the top ranked distinction. Table 4.9 also includes (in shaded cells) Wilkes' lambda values and significance levels according to the discriminant analyses.

Note that all of the ties in Table 4.9 between two weight distinctions are the result of two weight divisions completely overlapping. For example, the first two distinctions, the distinction between long low vowels and other rimes (i.e. /aː/ heavy) and the distinction between long back and long low vowels and other rimes (i.e. /aː/ and /uː/ heavy), are equivalent for the data set examined, since Chickasaw does not have a long /uː/. Equivalent weight distinctions of this sort are followed by the same set of statistical values. The bold-faced distinctions are the ones actually employed by the language being examined, in this case, Chickasaw. Due to space constraints, only the complex distinctions that are superior to at least one of the actual phonological distinctions are listed in Table 4.9, and in subsequent tables for other languages. All of the simple distinctions after the phonological ones are listed in order of relative phonetic effectiveness according to mean values. The interested reader is referred to Appendix Five for the complete list of all weight distinctions, both simple and complex, and their relative rankings in terms of effectiveness in the energy domain. Note the following abbreviations in Table 4.9 and subsequent tables: +G represents a voiced consonant, -G a voiceless consonant, +S a continuant, -S a non-continuant, +N a nasal, -N a non-nasal, +B a labial, -B a non-labial, +T a coronal, -T a non-coronal, +K a velar and -K a non-velar.

Strikingly, the two phonetically most effective weight distinctions among the simple distinctions are precisely the ones exploited by the phonology of Chickasaw. The optimal simple distinction is the one referring to the heaviest member of the weight hierarchy, CVV(C), while the second best simple distinction refers to the two heaviest syllable types in Chickasaw (CVV(C), CVC). The three-way phonological hierarchy thus results from the combination of the two phonetically best simple weight distinctions. The Chickasaw data thus provides strong evidence for a correlation between syllable weight and phonetics. The Chickasaw data also provides corroboration

Table 4.9. The most effective weight distinctions in Chickasaw			
DISTINCTION	DIFF	W-λ	P-VAL.
♦ /aː/ heavy ♦ /aː,uː/ heavy	100	.657425	.0000
♥ VV(C) heavy ♦ /aː,iː/ heavy	80.6	.603375	.0000
♦ VV, a+R heavy	73.3	.581391	.0000
♦ VV, a+N heavy	72.5	.612845	.0000
♦ V, hiV+K light	71.6	.796293	.0000
♥ VV(C), VC heavy	71.5	.862489	.0000
♥ VVC, (VCC) heavy	67.8	.799441	.0000
♥ VV, V+R heavy	64.8	.661233	.0000
♥ VV, V+G heavy	56.3	.760122	.0000
♥ VV, V+S heavy	55.9	.747150	.0000
♥ VV, V-N	31.7	.934154	.0006
♥ +low V heavy	17.7	.974586	.0351

for the important role of phonological simplicity in syllable weight. Six of the top eight weight distinctions are ruled out only by virtue of their complexity. If phonological complexity did not play a role in the phonology of weight, we would incorrectly expect the phonology to observe the Caː heavy criterion (among many other complex ones) before observing the CVV(C), CVC heavy criterion.

4.7.2.2. Japanese: CVV(C), CVC heavy

Japanese treats closed syllables and syllables containing a long vowel as heavy in both its system of recited poetry and in songs (Vance 1987). In (49a) and (49b), a haiku by Bashoo Matsuo and a verse from a poem by Bonchoo Nozawa, respectively (from Vance 1987:64; transcription altered to fit IPA), demonstrate the metrical equivalence of CVV and CVC as distinct from CV. The first line and third line in each sample contains a total of five moras, while the second line contains seven moras (using 'moras' in the traditional sense in which it is used by Japanese linguists), where CVV and CVC are bimoraic and CV is monomoraic.

(49) Japanese weight-sensitive metrics
a. ɹa$^\mu$n$^\mu$ no$^\mu$ ka$^\mu$ ja$^\mu$ 'The fragrant orchid
t͡ʃoː$^{\mu\mu}$no$^\mu$ t͡su$^\mu$ba$^\mu$sa$^\mu$ ni$^\mu$ Into a butterfly's wings
ta$^\mu$ki$^\mu$mo$^\mu$no$^\mu$ su$^\mu$ It breathes the incense.'
b. go$^\mu$ɹo$^\mu$p$^\mu$po$^\mu$N$^\mu$ 'Five or six pieces
na$^\mu$ma$^\mu$ki$^\mu$ t͡su$^\mu$ke$^\mu$ta$^\mu$ɹu$^\mu$ Of freshly cut timber
mi$^\mu$zu$^\mu$ta$^\mu$ma$^\mu$ɹi$^\mu$ Over a muddy pool.'

In (49a), the long vowel in the word /t͡ʃoː/ contributes two moras, as does the syllable closed by a nasal in the word /ɹan/. In (49b), the syllable closed by the first half of a geminate in the word /goɹoppoN/ is bimoraic, as is the syllable closed by a nasal in the same word.

An analysis of variance conducted on the Japanese data demonstrated a highly significant effect of syllable type on energy: $F_{(11, 82)} = 100.596$, $p < .0001$. Table 4.10 lists the most effective weight distinctions in Japanese following the protocol explained above in the discussion of Chickasaw.

The most effective weight distinction (CVV, CVC heavy) is also the one exploited by the phonology in Japanese. Thus, Japanese provides evidence for a correlation between the phonology of syllable weight and a phonetic measure of total energy. Note that other weight distinctions are equally as effective as the phonological distinction; however, they all involve the same division of rimes, since the only codas measured in Japanese were sonorants.

Table 4.10. The most effective weight distinctions in Japanese			
DISTINCTION	DIFF	W-λ	P-VAL.
♥ **VV(C), VC heavy**			
♥ VV(C),V+R heavy			
♥ VV(C),V+G heavy			
♥ VV(C),V+N heavy			
♦ V, hiV-N light			
♦ V, hiV+S light	100	.435783	.0000
♦ V, hiV-R light			
♦ V, hiV-G light			
♦ V, hiV+K light			
♦ VV,V-K heavy			
♦ VV, V-S heavy			
♥ VV(C) heavy			
♥ VV(C), V+S heavy			
♥ VV(C), V-N heavy	17.5	.982682	.1767
♦ VV(C), V-G heavy			
♦ VV(C), V-R heavy			
♥ +low V heavy	11.3	.991636	.3488
♥ -back V heavy	5.6	.997915	.6405

Thus, Japanese is a less rigorous test of the correlation between energy and phonological weight, since many weight criteria are conflated.

4.7.2.3. Khalkha: CVV(C) Heavy

Like Japanese, Khalkha Mongolian observes a simple binary weight distinction. However, the Khalkha stress system treats CVV(C), but not CVC, as heavy (Bosson 1964, Walker 1995, 1996). In Khalkha, primary stress falls on the rightmost non-final long vowel or diphthong (50a). If the only long vowel in a word occurs in the final syllable, it is stressed (50b). In words lacking long vowels and diphthongs, primary stress falls on the initial syllable (50c). (Examples in (50) are from Walker 1995, 1996 minus secondary stresses.)

(50) Khalkha Mongolian stress
     a. 'aːruːl 'dry cheese curds,' 'uitgartae 'sad,' doloːdugaːr 'seventh,' xøndiːˈryːlen 'to separate (modal),' ulaːnˈbaːtaraːs 'Ulaanbaatar (ablative),' baeˈguːlagdax 'to be organized'
     b. daˈlae 'sea,' gaˈluː 'goose'
     c. 'axa 'brother,' 'unʃisan 'having read'

Table 4.11. The most effective weight distinctions in Khalkha			
DISTINCTION	DIFF	W-λ	P-VAL.
♦ VV, a+N heavy	100	.634865	.0000
♦ VV, a+B heavy	99.1	.707726	.0000
♥ **VV(C) heavy**	**89.7**	**.832069**	**.0000**
♥ VV(C), VC heavy	48.1	.948532	.0047
♥ VV(C), V+R heavy	43.9	.878960	.0000
♥ VV(C), V+G heavy	38.8	.905707	.0001
♥ VV(C), V+S heavy	13.9	.988034	.1769
♥ VV(C), V-N heavy	13.5	.990921	.2398
♥ +low V heavy	11.9	.991083	.2441
♦ VV(C), V-R heavy	2.9	.999471	.7770

An analysis of variance indicated a highly significant effect of syllable type on energy: $F_{(21, 132)} = 5.857$, $p<.0001$. Individual distinctions are compared in Table 4.11.

Table 4.11 shows that the phonological weight distinction between CVV(C) and other rimes is the phonetically most effective distinction among the structurally simple weight distinctions. There are only two distinctions which are superior phonetically to the actual phonological distinction: CVV, a+N heavy and CVV, a+B heavy; however, both of these distinctions are structurally complex. Thus, Khalkha provides evidence both for the correlation between syllable weight and total energy, and also the importance of phonological simplicity in the determination of syllable weight.

4.7.2.4. Finnish: CVV(C), CVC Heavy

The Finnish stress system treats both CVV(C) and CVC as heavy (Sadeniemi 1949) for purposes of determining the location of secondary stress. Primary stress in Finnish falls on the first syllable of the word. Under most circumstances, secondary stress falls on odd-numbered syllables after the first syllable (51a), though the final syllable of a word is typically unstressed. However, in words of at least five syllables, secondary stress skips over a light third syllable and instead falls on a heavy fourth syllable, where heavy is equivalent to CVC or CVV(C) (51b).

(51) Finnish stress
   a. 'opetˌtajana 'teacher (essive sg.),' 'kuvasˌtuvat 'they are reflected,' 'læhteˌmæisillæ 'to be about to depart (3sg.),' 'ikæˌvæna 'tedious (essive sg.)'

b. 'luonnolli͵sestæ 'natural (elat. sg.),' 'la:jene͵vaksi 'expanding (transl. sg.),' 'læhettæ͵kæ:mme 'let us send'

In addition to its stress system, Finnish employs a weight-sensitive tradition of poetic metrics that treats CVV(C) and CVC equivalently for purposes of metrical scansion (Kiparsky 1968, Hanson and Kiparsky 1996).[15] An analysis of variance found a highly significant effect of syllable type on energy values: F $(21,149)$ = 34.300, p<.0001. Table 4.12 lists the relative phonetic effectiveness of different weight distinctions in Finnish.

As Table 4.12 shows, the link between phonetics and phonology is quite strong, as in other languages: the phonological weight distinction is also the most effective distinction phonetically. It is ranked ahead of all other weight distinctions, both simple and complex.

4.7.2.5. Telugu: CVV > CVC > CV

Like Chickasaw, Telugu, with its three-way weight hierarchy, CVV(C) > CVC > CV, provides a good testing ground for examining the correlation between total energy and syllable weight. The Telugu weight hierarchy is evident if one collapses the weight system for stress with that employed for poetic metrics. The stress system treats CVV(C) as heavier than both CVC and CV (Petrunicheva 1960, Brown 1981). Stress falls on the first syllable in words containing only CVC and CV syllables (52a).[16] In words containing long vowels, stress falls on the rightmost long vowel (52b).

Table 4.12. The most effective weight distinctions in Finnish			
DISTINCTION	DIFF	W-λ	P-VAL.
♥ **VV(C), VC heavy**			
♦ V, hiV+K light	100	.431361	.0000
♦ V, V+K light			
♦ VV,V-K heavy			
♦ hiV in open σ light	99.5	.603583	.0000
♥ VV(C),V+R heavy	62.6	.554805	.0000
♥ VV(C),V+G heavy			
♥ VV(C), V+S heavy	57.2	.628306	.0000
♥ VV(C) heavy	53.8	.835684	.0000
♥ VV(C), V-N heavy	52.8	.735541	.0000
♥ -back V heavy	12.0	.985190	.1161
♥ +low V heavy	1.1	.999879	.8872

(52) Telugu stress
  a. 'padi 'ten,' 'telugu 'Telugu,' 'ʃatakam 'collection of 100 poems'
  b. kuːdaː 'also,' gur'raːlu 'horse' genitive

Telugu has a system of quantitative poetic metrics that treats CVV(C) and CVC uniformly as heavy syllables (Sitapati 1936, Brown 1981). The combination of the CVV(C) heavy distinction for stress and the CVV(C), CVC heavy distinction for metrics thus yields the three-way weight hierarchy CVV(C) > CVC > CV.

An analysis of variance indicates a highly significant effect of rime type on energy values: F (23, 111) = 25.207, $p<.0001$. The phonetically most effective weight distinctions are listed in Table 4.13.

The two phonetically most effective of the simple weight distinctions are also the two phonological distinctions as predicted. Table 4.13 provides further confirmation of the important role of phonological complexity in syllable weight: there are three complex weight distinctions that are phonetically superior to the actual phonological weight distinctions in Telugu. These are prohibited from playing a role in the phonology only by virtue of their exceeding the upper threshold of phonological complexity.

4.7.2.6. Javanese: Full Vowels Heavy

We now examine the relative effectiveness of different weight distinctions in Javanese, a language that makes a weight distinction between full and reduced vowels. The stress facts that demonstrate this distinction are as follows. Stress

Table 4.13. The most effective weight distinctions in Telugu

DISTINCTION	DIFF	W-λ	P-VAL.
♦ /aː,iː/ heavy	100	.677287	.0000
♦ /aː/ heavy	89.0	.866058	.0000
♦ hiV in open σ light	85.4	.764897	.0000
♥ VV(C), VC heavy	79.5	.709650	.0000
♥ VV(C) heavy	72.3	.760039	.0000
♥ VV(C), V+G heavy	66.1	.613276	.0000
♥ VV(C), V-N heavy	47.7	.823348	.0000
♥ VV(C), V+R heavy	47.1	.780127	.0000
♥ VV(C), V+S heavy	36.7	.866472	.0000
♥ -back V heavy	30.5	.916773	.0007
♥ +low V heavy	1.1	.999879	.8872

in Javanese (Herrfurth 1964, Horne 1974, Ras 1982[17]) falls on the penult if it contains a full vowel (53a), otherwise on the final syllable if the penult contains a reduced vowel (53b). Stress does not fall farther to the left than the penult, even if both the penult and the final syllable contain a reduced vowel and an earlier syllable contains a full vowel.

(53) Javanese stress
    a. 'badan 'body,' 'balur 'type of fish,' 'marmər 'marble,' 'padət 'compact'
    b. kəm'pal 'gather,' tə'ka 'come,' bə'nər 'correct,' gatə'lən 'itch'

    Beside the fact that it possesses a different weight distinction from the other languages examined experimentally in this paper, Javanese is also different in another respect: it lacks both phonemic long vowels and diphthongs.[18] There is thus no potential for making a weight distinction in Javanese between CVV(C) and CVC. The absence of long vowels and diphthongs also means that certain distinctions that were unlikely to surface in languages with long vowels or diphthongs have a better chance of surfacing in Javanese. The reason for this is that certain distinctions that are complex in other languages are simple in Javanese. For example, the V+N heavy distinction is simple in languages lacking long vowels and diphthongs, because it does not require disjoint representations for long vowels and syllables closed by a nasal.

    An analysis of variance demonstrated a highly significant effect of rime type on energy values: $F_{(19, 92)} = 15.080$, $p<.0001$. The most effective weight distinctions in Javanese appear in Table 4.14. Because none of the complex weight distinctions are superior to the phonological weight distinction, only the simple distinctions appear in Table 4.14.

    Javanese presents the first conflict between phonetics and syllable weight. The actual phonological distinction active for Javanese stress assignment is not the phonetically most optimal of the simple weight distinctions. Rather the Malay type distinction according to which only open syllables containing a reduced vowel are light is phonetically better than the actual Javanese distinction that treats *all* syllables containing a reduced vowel as light.

    Interestingly, there is an asymmetry in Javanese between the distribution of reduced vowels in closed syllables and reduced vowels in open syllables that arguably falls under the rubric of weight, though it does not, strictly speaking, involve stress. Reduced vowels do not appear in open word-final syllables in the native vocabulary, presumably in order to avoid lengthening reduced vowels in final position, a common position for vowel lengthening (Wightman et al. 1992). A similar avoidance of lengthened

Table 4.14. The most effective weight distinctions in Javanese			
DISTINCTION	DIFF	W-λ	P-VAL.
♥ RedV in open σ light	100	.828389	.0000
♥ **Red V light**	65.5	.721594	.0000
♥ V+S heavy	55.9	.740907	.0000
♥ VC heavy			
♥ V-K heavy	53.3	.864457	.0001
♥ V-B heavy			
♥ V+T heavy			
♥ Hi V in open σ light	46.7	.950932	..0189
♥ V-N heavy	44.8	.839328	.0000
♥ -back V heavy	42.7	.884289	.0002
♥ +low V	36.1	.890146	.0004
♥ V-S heavy	20.3	.978710	.1248
♥ V-G heavy	19.0	.970622	.0708
♥ V-R heavy			
♥ V+N heavy	18.3	.980861	.1458
♥ CaC heavy	17.2	.983084	.1717
♥ V+R heavy	12.0	.988028	.2508
♥ V+G heavy			

reduced vowels is found in Yupik in which underlying reduced vowels in word-final position become the low vowel /a/ which is more amenable to lengthening (Reed et al. 1977). Word-internally, reduced vowels in stressed open syllables also do not lengthen in Yupik, unlike full vowels in the same environment. Assuming that the restriction against reduced vowels in final open syllables in Javanese and Yupik is due to a difference in weight between open syllables containing a reduced vowel and closed syllables containing a reduced vowel, this distinction is compatible with the energy data for Javanese in Table 4.14.

As a final note, we may also note that the actual phonological criterion in Javanese has a lower Wilkes' lamda value, indicating that, from a purely statistical point view, it is in some sense superior to the distinction that is better from the point of view of separation of means. It is thus conceivable that a more sophisticated method of evaluating phonetic effectiveness that factored in the relative balance in the number of heavy and light syllable types according to a given distinction could provide an even closer fit to the data.

4.7.2.7. French

French is a weight-insensitive stress language in which stress falls on the final syllable of the phrase (Delattre 1966). French, like other weight-insensitive languages, provides a valuable testing ground for examining the phonetic effectiveness of different weight distinctions without interference from phonological weight distinctions. In particular, we can examine whether certain weight distinctions are inherently more effective from a phonetic standpoint. Weight-insensitive languages thus act as experimental controls, in the sense that, if a weight distinction is phonetically effective in a weight-insensitive language, it cannot be the case that the effectiveness of that distinction is due to phonological weight patterns.

As in the weight-sensitive languages, rime type had a highly significant effect on energy values in French: F (11,83) = 30.067, p<.0001. The most effective weight distinctions in French appear in Table 4.15. Only simple distinctions are considered, since weight-insensitive stress systems are not relevant for testing the hypothesis that phonological complexity plays a role in syllable weight.

Interestingly, the most effective of the simple distinctions, is the Non-high vowels heavy distinction. This fact suggests that the Non-high vowels heavy distinction is inherently an effective distinction. The fact that this distinction is in fact found in other languages offers support for the view that the phonology of weight is sensitive to phonetic considerations.

4.7.2.8. Bole

Like French, Bole is a weight-insensitive language; however, unlike French, it is a tonal language and has a phonemic contrast in vowel length, though

Table 4.15. The most effective weight distinctions in French

DISTINCTION	DIFF	W-λ	P-VAL.
♥ -high V heavy	88.7	.357994	.0000
♥ -back V heavy	49.9	.800531	.0000
♥ VC heavy			
♥ V+S heavy	39.3	.896293	.0015
♥ V-S heavy			
♥ V-N heavy			
♥ V-G heavy	9.2	.994205	.4634
♥ V+R heavy	8.4	.995096	.5001
♥ V+G heavy			

DISTINCTION	DIFF	W-λ	P-VAL.
♥ VV, VC heavy			
♥ VV, V+R heavy	65.8	.728823	.0000
♥ VV, V+G heavy			
♥ VV(C) heavy	40.2	.898783	.0002
♦ VV, V-R heavy			
♥ VV, V+S heavy	27.8	.914060	.0006
♥ VV, V-N heavy			
♥ -high V heavy	23.5	.946411	.0069
♥ -back V heavy	21.1	.954628	.0131

Table 4.16. The most effective weight distinctions in Bole

only in open syllables (Lukas 1969). An analysis of variance found a highly significant effect of rime type on energy in Bole: $F(17,117) = 21.641$, $p<.0001$. The phonetically most effective weight distinctions in Bole appear in Table 4.16.

Although a number of the weight criteria are conflated in Bole, it is interesting to note that two of the conflated criteria which are most effective in Bole, CVV(C), CVC heavy and CVV(C), CVR heavy, are attested in other languages. This suggests that these criteria are inherently more effective than certain other simple weight criteria. Under the view that the phonology of weight is largely phonetically driven, it is thus not surprising that a language might exploit these distinctions.

4.7.2.9. Farsi

Farsi is a weight-insensitive language with stress on the final syllable of words (Windfuhr 1990). Unlike the other languages examined in this paper, the synchronic status of the Farsi vowel system is unclear. Historically, Farsi displayed a phonemic vowel length contrast, which is still preserved in some dialects (Windfuhr 1990) and in the archaic poetic traditions of the standard language (Elwell-Sutton 1976, Hayes 1979). However, modern standard Farsi does not contrast vowels only on the basis of length; rather vowels contrast on the basis of quality, though subphonemic phonetic differences in length are typically assumed to be present synchronically (Windfuhr 1990).

An analysis of variance found a highly significant effect of rime type on energy in Farsi: $F(38,242) = 10.996$, $p<.0001$. The phonetically most effective weight distinctions in Farsi appear in Table 4.17.

Table 4.17. The most effective weight distinctions in Farsi

DISTINCTION	DIFF	W-λ	P-VAL.
♥ VC heavy	100	.863679	.0000
♥ V-K heavy	84.8	.709590	.0000
♥ V+T heavy	81.9	.685262	.0000
♥ V+S heavy	81.5	.705819	.0000
♥ V+K heavy	61.5	.873516	.0000
♥ V-S heavy	57.0	.872014	.0000
♥ V-T heavy	55.6	.862002	.0000
♥ V-B heavy	53.5	.904505	.0000
♥ aC heavy	50.1	.894606	.0000
♥ V-N heavy	47.5	.925919	.0000
♥ -high V heavy	38.4	.936202	.0000
♥ V+G heavy	28.4	.962062	.0010
♥ V+R heavy	27.0	.971198	.0043
♥ V+B heavy	17.5	.992722	.1538
♥ -back V heavy	13.1	.993218	.1686
♥ V+N heavy	8.4	.998352	.4979
♥ V-R heavy	6.6	.998034	.4591
♥ V-G heavy	.07	.999981	.9419

As in the other weight-insensitive languages examined, the top ranked of the simple weight distinctions in Farsi, CVV(C), CVC heavy, is instantiated in other languages.

4.7.2.10. Russian

The final weight-insensitive language examined was Russian, in which stress is morphologically and lexically contrastive (Comrie 1990). Because of the uncertainty of syllable boundaries in Russian, only three types of syllables were measured: open syllables containing /a, i, u/. Russian does not have phonemic long vowels.

An analysis of variance found a highly significant effect of rime type on energy in Russian: $F(2,15) = 21.639$, $p<.0001$. Table 4.18 lists the simple weight distinctions (only two in the Russian data) and their relative effectiveness.

As in the other languages with weight-insensitive stress, the most effective weight distinction of the ones tested in Russian is one employed in other

Table 4.18. The most effective weight distinctions in Russian			
DISTINCTION	DIFF	W-λ	P-VAL.
♥ -high V heavy	100	.428184	.0003
♥ -back V heavy	2.7	.999592	.9366

languages, the distinction between high and non-high vowels. The simple but unattested distinction between back and non-back vowels is highly ineffective: it does not even divide syllables into two groups that are significantly distinct from each other.

4.7.3. The Phonetics of Syllable Weight: A Summary

The experimental data in the preceding sections indicate a number of important facts. First, in all of the languages with weight-sensitive stress and/or metrical traditions, with the possible exception of Javanese, the phonological weight distinction(s) are also the phonetically most sensible of the simple distinctions. This is true not only of languages with binary weight distinctions like Japanese, Finnish, and Khalkha, but also those with three-way weight hierarchies like Chickasaw and Telugu. These data suggest a strong general correlation between the phonology of weight-sensitive stress/metrics and a measure of total energy.

An equally important fact emerging from the data is that syllable weight is not projected only from phonetics. Rather, phonological simplicity plays an important role in Chickasaw, Khalkha, and Telugu in filtering out weight distinctions that may be phonetically quite effective but nevertheless are too complex. Thus, the overall picture that emerges is that the phonology of syllable weight is the result of compromise between achieving the, often conflicting, goals of constructing a phonetically sensible grammar that also manipulates a relatively simple set of phonological predicates.

4.8. DURATION AS A POTENTIAL CORRELATE OF SYLLABLE WEIGHT

The previous sections demonstrated that a measure of integrated energy was correlated quite closely with phonological weight in a number of languages with different weight distinctions. Duration was also examined in all ten languages, but unlike energy, failed to display a correlation with phonological weight in many languages.

In Tables 4.19 (weight-sensitive languages) and 4.20 (weight-insensitive languages), duration is considered as a correlate of syllable weight, comparing all of the structurally simple distinctions. Complex weight distinctions are not considered in Table 4.19 and 4.20, as they are eliminated from consideration independently of phonetic effectiveness. The difference (in milliseconds) between the means for heavy and light rimes according to each distinction appears along with a ranking indicating the effectiveness of a given weight distinction relative to others. Thus, the first ranked weight distinction is the most effective one, followed by the second ranked one, etc. Negative values in a given language indicate that the syllables marked as heavy in the leftmost column are shorter than the light syllables in that language. The weight distinction(s) actually employed by the phonology of a given language is indicated by boldface. Simple weight distinctions that do not surface in the phonology appear in lightly shaded cells. If a weight distinction is complex in a given language, the corresponding cell is shaded darkly. A boldface line separates distinctions that are attested cross-linguistically from those that are not. Blank cells indicate weight distinctions that were not tested in a given language. Ties in ranking are indicated by a lower-case "t" in the rank column. The reader is referred to Appendix Six for duration measurements of all the simple weight distinctions. Note the following abbreviations: +G represents a voiced consonant, -G a voiceless consonant, +S a continuant, -S a non-continuant, +N a nasal, -N a non-nasal, +B a labial, -B a non-labial, +T a coronal, -T a non-coronal, +K a velar and -K a non-velar.

The CVV(C), CVC heavy distinction is among the two most effective distinctions in all languages examined. This includes languages in which this distinction is actually employed (Japanese, Telugu, Finnish, Chickasaw), languages that employ weight distinctions other than the Latin one (Khalkha, Javanese), languages that are synchronically weight-insensitive for stress or metrics (Farsi, French), as well as non-stress languages (Bole). The CVV(C), CVC heavy is thus a good distinction from a durational standpoint.

However, other phonological weight distinctions do not provide as good a phonetic fit in terms of duration. For example, the distinction by which CVV(C) but not CVC is heavy is ranked far behind the CVV(C), CVC heavy distinction in all languages, including one which exploits the CVV(C) distinction but not the CVV(C), CVC heavy distinction: Khalkha. In Khalkha, the CVV(C) vs. CVC, CV distinction does not even divide syllables into two groups that are significantly different from one another. Furthermore, in two other languages which exploit both the CVV(C) heavy

Table 4.19. Effectiveness of simple weight distinctions in terms of duration in six weight-sensitive languages												
Weight distinction Heavy	Chickasaw		Telugu		Khalkha		Finnish		Japanese		Javanese	
	Diff.	Rank	Diff.	Rank	Diff.	Rank	Diff.	Rank	Diff.	Rank	Diff.	Rank
CVV(C) heavy	14.4	7	13.1	6	2.3	6	22.3	6	9.1	5t		
CVV(C), CVC heavy	101.2	1	66.5	1	76.3	1	95.5	1	81.5	1t	68.1	2
CVV(C), V+R heavy	23.5	6	14.5	4	-6.1	5	39.7	4t	81.5	1t	5.4	11t
+low V heavy	8.6	8	7.9	8	-1.3	7	10.0	7	12.1	4	-16.7	7
-back V heavy			11.3	7			1.3	8	5.4	8	-8.5	10
Red V light											29.4	4
Red V in open • light											109.8	1
CVVC, CVCC heavy	30.3	4										
CVV(C), V+G heavy	28.8	5	30.3	3	-9.2	4	39.7	4t	81.5	1t	5.4	11t
CVV(C), V+S heavy	32.6	3	13.4	5	26.3	3	44.9	3	9.1	5t	29.3	5
CVV(C), V-N heavy	35.6	2	34.4	2	33.4	2	46.1	2	9.1	5t	37.4	3
CVV(C), V-T heavy												
CVV(C), V-S heavy											11.1	8t
CVV(C), V-R heavy												
CVV(C), V-K heavy												
CVV(C), V-B heavy												
CVV(C), V-G heavy											11.1	8t
CVV(C), V+T heavy												
CVV(C), V+N heavy											4.3	13
CVV(C), V+K heavy												
CVV(C), V+B heavy												
CVV(C), CaC heavy											17.0	6

and the CVV(C), CVC heavy distinctions (Chickasaw and Telugu), the CVV(C) heavy distinction is surpassed by several other simple weight distinctions which do not emerge in the phonology. The failure of duration to account for the observed weight facts is also apparent in Javanese, in which the full vs. reduced vowel distinction only provides the fourth best fit in duration even though it is the distinction actually exploited. In summary, the duration data correlate well with the Latin type distinction according to which CVV and CVC are heavy, but do not provide a good fit to other weight distinctions such as the Khalkha one (CVV(C) heavy) and the Javanese one (Full vowels heavy).

Nor does another duration measure encompassing only coda consonants correlate with language specific differences in weight criteria. Average duration values for coda consonants in three languages appear in Table 4.21. In two of these languages, Japanese and Finnish, coda consonants contribute weight to the syllable, whereas, in one of these languages, Khalkha, coda consonants do not add to the weight of the syllable. Parallel to the data on weight-sensitive tone in Chapter Three, one might expect coda consonants to be longer in languages in which they carry weight.

Table 4.20. Effectiveness of simple weight distinctions in terms of duration in four weight-insensitive languages

Heavy	Bole Diff.	Rank	Farsi Diff.	Rank	French Diff.	Rank	Russian Diff.	Rank
CVV(C) heavy	2.8	7						
CVV(C), CVC heavy	79.6	1t	83.8	1	69.8	1t		
CVV(C), V+R heavy	79.6	1t	1.1	18	-14.5	6		
Non-high V heavy	20.0	4	21.4	11	25.3	4	39.9	1
Non-back V heavy	1.8	8	10.2	14	11.8	7	16.3	2
Full V heavy								
Red V in open σ light								
CVVC, CVCC heavy								
CVV, V+G heavy	79.6	1t	5.7	16	16.0	5		
CVV(C), V+S heavy	5.4	5t	47.3	2	69.8	1t		
CVV(C), V-N heavy	5.4	5t	37.0	4	69.8	1t		
CVV(C), V-T heavy			-11.9	13				
CVV(C), V-S heavy			-24.1	9				
CVV(C), V-R heavy			24.8	8				
CVV(C), V-K heavy			46.3	3				
CVV(C), V-B heavy			28.5	7				
CVV(C), V-G heavy			19.6	12				
CVV(C), V+T heavy			35.7	5				
CVV(C), V+N heavy			-3.1	17				
CVV(C), V+K heavy			-21.7	10				
CVV(C), V+B heavy			8.2	15				
CVV(C), CaC heavy			30.9	6				

In fact, the language in which codas are weightless for stress, Khalkha, has a longer average coda duration value than the two languages in which codas carry weight.

Table 4.21. Average duration (in milliseconds) of coda consonants in 3 languages

Language	Weight distinction	coda (duration)
Khalkha	CVV(C) > CVC, CV	79.8
Japanese	CVV(C), CVC > CV	54.5
Finnish	CVV(C), CVC > CV	73.8

Table 4.22. Average duration (in milliseconds) of coda /m/ in 3 languages

Language	Weight distinction	coda (duration)
Khalkha	CVV(C) > CVC, CV	71.9
Japanese	CVV(C), CVC > CV	57.8
Finnish	CVV(C), CVC > CV	80.7

Table 4.22 presents average duration values from a controlled comparison of coda /m/, the coda for which data from all three languages is available.

Although coda /m/ in one of the languages with weighted codas, Finnish, is slightly longer than the comparable coda in Khalkha, this difference is statistically insignificant as revealed by an unpaired t-test conducted over syllables containing /u/ or /a/ as their nucleus (the two nuclei examined in all three languages): p=.0798, t=1.816. More importantly, the other language with weighted codas, Japanese, has a shorter coda /m/ than both Finnish and Khalkha: Japanese vs. Finnish, p<.0001, t=6.634; Japanese vs. Khalkha, p=.0114, t=2.702. The controlled comparison thus does not provide evidence for a link between coda duration and choice of weight criteria.

Let us now consider, following work by Broselow et al. (1997), another way in which duration values could be argued to be correlated with differences in weight criteria. In their study of Malayalam, Hindi and various dialects of Arabic, Broselow et al. (1997) argue that differences in phonological weight distinctions between these languages/dialects are reflected in durational differences as well. To take a striking example of the match between phonological structure and phonetic duration evident in Broselow et al.'s data, consider the difference between Malayalam and Hindi. Malayalam employs the Khalkha type weight distinction according to which long vowels but not closed syllables containing short vowels are heavy. Hindi, on the other hand, is like Latin: both long vowels and closed syllables are heavy. Broselow et al. make the interesting discovery that vowels are substantially shorter in closed than in open syllables in Malayalam but not Hindi. They suggest that this is a result of the different moraic structures in the two languages. The vowel and a coda consonant share a mora in Malayalam but not in Hindi. The sharing of the mora in Malayalam is reflected phonetically in the shortening of vowels in closed syllables (see Figure 4.20).

In the present experiment, there is no evidence for mora sharing in Khalkha, a language with the same weight distinction as Malayalam. Compare in Table 4.23 the duration of vowels in open and closed syllables in Khalkha versus vowels in the same environments in two languages (Japanese and Finnish) with a Hindi like weight distinction of the form CVV, CVC heavy.

Table 4.23. Duration (in milliseconds) of short vowels in open and closed syllables in 3 languages

Language	Weight distinction	open syll.	std.dev.	closed syll.	std.dev.
Khalkha	CVV(C) > CVC, CV	**70.3**	8.7	**67.5**	14.0
Japanese	CVV(C), CVC > CV	**49.9**	7.2	**88.2**	10.7
Finnish	CVV(C), CVC > CV	**75.8**	13.2	**95.9**	11.7

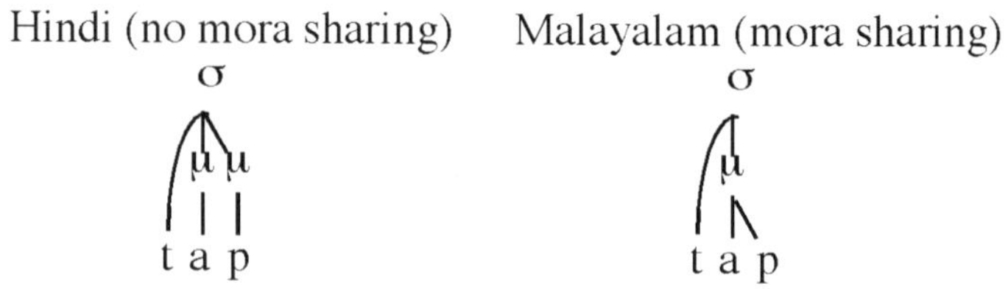

Hindi (no mora sharing)   Malayalam (mora sharing)

Figure 4.20. Moraic representations for CVC in two languages (After Broselow et al. 1997)

Although there are clearly differences in vowel duration between Khalkha, on the one hand, and Finnish[19] and Japanese, on the other hand, they do not tie into moraic structure in any obvious way. Vowels are only marginally longer in open than in closed syllables in Khalkha contra what one would expect if vowels and coda consonants shared a mora. This difference between open and closed syllables does not reach statistical significance for Khalkha according to an unpaired t-test: $p = .4411$, $t = .773$.

A controlled comparison was made for only syllables containing a low vowel or /u/ followed by the coda consonant /m/ (the nuclei and coda which are common to the data set for all three languages). Measurements of vowel duration appear in Table 4.24.

As in the data in Table 4.23, vowels are not substantially longer in open than closed syllables in Khalkha. In fact, vowels are slightly longer in closed syllables in the data in Table 4.24, an unexpected phonetic result if the vowel and coda consonant were sharing a mora in Khalkha.

Table 4.24. Duration (in milliseconds) of short /a/ɑ/ and u/ in open syllables and syllables closed by /m/ in 3 languages

Language	Weight distinction	open syll.	std.dev.	closed syll.	std.dev.
Khalkha	CVV(C) > CVC, CV	**70.3**	8.9	**78.4**	13.7
Japanese	CVV(C), CVC > CV	**49.3**	7.4	**87.3**	11.2
Finnish	CVV(C), CVC > CV	**73.0**	15.2	**95.7**	10.6

Table 4.25. Duration (in milliseconds) of short /ɑ/ and u/ in open syllables and syllables closed by /m, r, l, s/ in 2 languages

Language	Weight distinction	open syll.	std.dev.	closed syll.	std.dev.
Khalkha	CVV(C) > CVC, CV	**70.3**	8.9	**70.2**	12.6
Finnish	CVV(C), CVC > CV	**73.0**	15.2	**99.3**	10.5

Finally, the duration of vowels in open and closed syllables was compared for Khalkha and Finnish, languages for which a larger set of coda consonants were examined than for Japanese. The duration of /ɑ/ and /u/ (vowels measured for both languages) were measured in the environment before /m, r, l, s/ (coda consonants examined in both languages) in Finnish and Khalkha. Results appear in Table 4.25.

Parallel to results in Tables 4.23 and 4.24, there is no duration difference between vowels in open and vowels in closed syllables in Khalkha. The difference of .1 milliseconds is insignificant according to an unpaired t-test: t =.026, p=.9790.

In summary, seen from a variety of angles, duration does not appear to fit as closely with phonological syllable weight as a measure of total energy.

4.9. THE DIRECTIONALITY OF THE PHONETICS/ PHONOLOGY RELATIONSHIP FOR STRESS

Thus far, this chapter has demonstrated a close match between phonological weight for stress and a phonetic measure of energy. The relationship manifests itself both in the range of cross-linguistic variation in weight criteria as well as in the language specific choice of weight criterion. What we have not yet explored in the context of weight-sensitive stress is the directionality of the relationship between phonetics and phonology. Thus, parallel to the question raised in the discussion of weight-sensitive tone in Chapter Three, we may ask whether languages tailor their stress systems to fit their phonetic characteristics or whether languages adapt their phonetic patterns to maximize the salience of their stress systems. A third and intermediate possibility is that the relationship between phonetics and phonology is bi-directional in that both systems mutually influence each other.

This issue was explored in the context of weight-sensitive tone in Chapter Three, where it was argued that phonetics plays a large role in shaping the phonology of weight, but that certain phonetic patterns may themselves be attributed to other aspects of the phonological system. Arguments that phonetics drives phonology came from a few sources. First, the sharp divergence in the cross-linguistic distribution of weight criteria between stress and tone systems has been shown to result from differences in the phonetic factors underlying each phenomenon. Tone is sensitive to the sonorant portion of the rime, whereas stress distinctions are sensitive to the total energy of the rime. Additional arguments that phonetics influences phonology came from data on Cantonese tone restrictions. In Cantonese, evidence suggested that the weight-criterion observed by the given phenomena arose in response to language specific durational properties. These language specific durational features could be linked to another aspect of the phonological system, the minimal word requirement. The Cantonese facts thus suggest a fairly complex relationship between phonetics and phonology, whereby one aspect of the phonological system is responsible for certain phonetic patterns which in turn influence another aspect of the phonology. A similar relationship between phonetics and phonology was argued in Chapter Three to be relevant for the distribution of contour tones in Hausa.

Weight-sensitive stress provides additional arguments for an integrated model of the phonology/phonetics relationship whereby one aspect of the phonology influences phonetic properties, which in turn influence another phonological phenomenon. The first argument for this model comes from examination of the relationship between vowel duration and weight distinctions based on vowel quality. The second piece of evidence is gleaned from comparison of language-specific aspects of syllable structure with language-specific choices in weight criteria.

4.9.1. The Influence of Structure on Phonetics: Vowel Quality vs. Quantity

Recall from section 4.1 that virtually all languages that make weight distinctions based on vowel quality do not possess phonemic long vowels. Those that have phonemic long vowels and make a weight distinction based on vowel quality exploit another weight distinction in addition to the one based on vowel quality. Assuming that weight-sensitive stress is phonetically driven, this observation would strongly suggest that energy differences between vowels of different qualities tend to be larger in languages without phonemic vowel length than in languages with phonemic vowel length.

This prediction is borne out for the most part in the data presented earlier in Figure 4.18, with the exception of Farsi, whose vowel system is in a state of transition from being based on quantity to being based on quality (Windfuhr 1990). Javanese also appears at first glance to be exceptional in lacking phonemic long vowels and having small energy differences between high and non-high vowels. It should be borne in mind, however, as pointed out in section 4.7.1, that Javanese does display a vowel quality based energy difference of considerably greater magnitude, the difference between full and reduced vowels.

The different duration patterns characteristic of languages with and without phonemic vowel length can be seen in the plot of duration differences between high and non-high vowels in Figure 4.21. Statistical comparison of the vowels appears in Table 4.26. Cells containing differences which are not statistically significant (according to t-tests) at the p<.01 level are shaded. Data from one male Italian speaker (8 tokens of each word, first syllable targeted in disyllabic words, words with /a, i, u/ in open syllables and syllables closed by /m, n, r, l, s/; corpus in Appendix Four) are also included in Figure 4.21. and Table 4.26. Both phonemic short vowels and phonemic long vowels (in languages in which they occur) were measured. For Javanese, both the difference between full and reduced vowels and the difference between high and non-high vowels are shown.

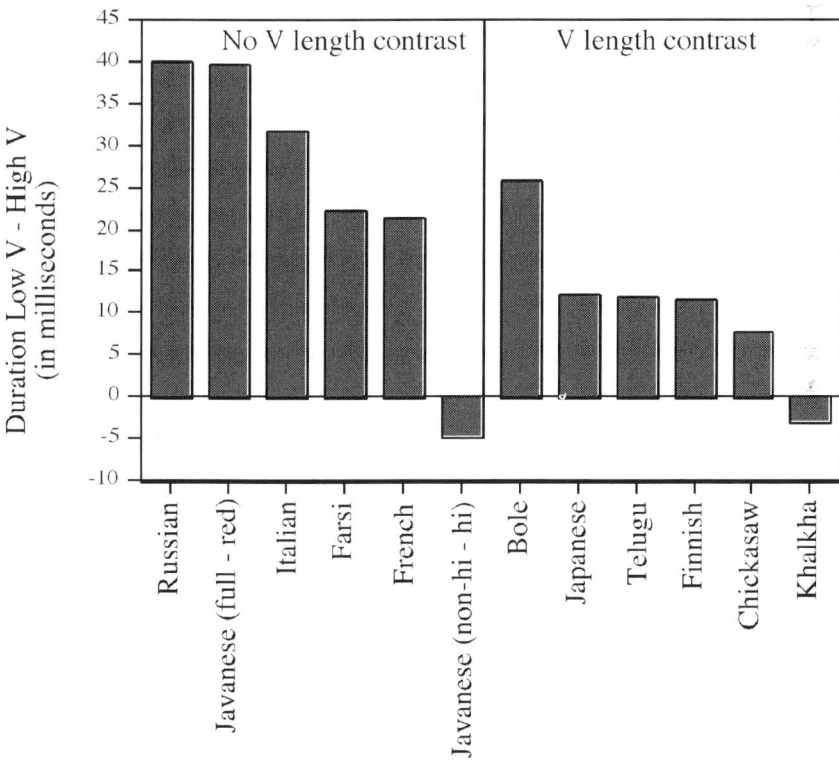

Figure 4.21. Duration difference between vowels of different qualities (low V- high V, except where noted)

Table 4.26. Duration differences between vowels of different qualities in 11 languages

Language	Low V- High V	t-value	Significance Level
Russian	39.9	7.536	p<.0001
Javanese (full V - red V)	39.6	12.395	p<.0001
Italian	31.6	9.805	p<.0001
Farsi	22.1	11.810	p<.0001
French	21.1	11.447	p<.0001
Javanese (Non-hi V - hi V)	-4.8	1.126	p=.2635
Bole	25.9	5.900	p<.0001
Japanese	12.4	2.087	p=.0397
Telugu	11.8	2.417	p=.0170
Finnish	11.7	2.238	p=.0265
Chickasaw	7.6	1.747	p=.0824
Khalkha	-3.0	.733	p-.4644

In virtually all cases, languages without phonemic vowel length display greater durational differences between vowels of different qualities. The exceptional languages in this regard are Bole, in which vowel length is phonemic only in open syllables, and Javanese, which makes a large duration difference between full and reduced vowels but not between high and non-high vowels. The different duration patterns found in languages with and without phonemic vowel length contrasts impact total energy measurements, since the measurement of total energy factors in duration. Thus, the longer the vowel, the more energy it will have, all else being equal.

These data offer an explanation for the fact that virtually all languages with weight distinctions based on vowel quality do not possess phonemic contrasts in vowel length. Because the energy differences between low and high vowels are greater in languages without phonemic long vowels than in languages with phonemic long vowels, languages without phonemic long vowels are more likely to make a phonological weight distinction based on vowel height. Those languages with phonemic vowel length and a weight distinction based on vowel quality draw an additional weight distinction (e.g. CVV(C) heavy in Asheninca) that we may presume is phonetically superior to the distinction based on vowel quality. Assuming this to be true, the general hypothesis advanced here that phonetically superior weight distinctions are adopted before distinctions that are phonetically less favorable is further supported.

The tendency for energy differences between vowels of different qualities to be more pronounced in languages without phonemic vowel length has a functional basis. There is a well-documented tendency for low vowels to be cross-linguistically longer than high vowels (Lehiste 1970), a fact which is typically attributed to the additional time needed for the jaw lowering needed to produce a low vowel (Westbury and Keating 1980). In languages with phonemic length contrasts there is less room for the intrinsically longer low vowels to enhance their inherent length by undergoing additional lengthening, because additional subphonemic lengthening would potentially jeopardize phonemic length distinctions. In contrast, in languages without phonemic vowel length contrasts, the low vowels can safely lengthen without endangering any phonemic length contrasts.

In summary, comparison of duration and energy measurement in languages with phonemic vowel length contrasts and languages without phonemic vowel length demonstrates one way in which phonological patterns of syllable weight are grounded in phonetic patterns which themselves are attributed to another aspect of the phonology.

4.9.2. The Function of Syllable Structure in Language Specificity of Weight Criteria

Data discussed in this section suggest another way in which cross-linguistic variation in a basic phonological property of a language, its syllable structure, triggers phonetic differences between languages, which in turn lead to variation in weight criteria for stress.

The relevant data comes from comparison of languages observing the CVV(C) heavy criterion for stress and those displaying the CVV(C), CVC heavy criterion for stress. The exemplar language discussed in this chapter which instantiates the CVV(C) heavy criterion is Khalkha, while Japanese and Finnish both employ the CVV(C), CVC heavy distinction. As we have seen, for all three languages, the phonological weight criterion is also the phonetically most effective of the simple weight distinctions. Khalkha thus differs substantially from both Japanese and Finnish in terms of the phonetic measure of energy.

Interestingly, Khalkha also differs from Finnish and Japanese in terms of its inventory of coda consonants. Let us consider this difference along two dimensions: the number of permissible voiced codas relative to the number of permissible voiceless codas, and the number of sonorant codas relative to the number of obstruents codas. The reasons for examining voicing and sonorancy will become apparent shortly.

Both the voiceless to voiced ratio and the obstruent to sonorant ratio is larger in Khalkha than in either Finnish or Japanese. This structural difference can be seen just by comparing the set of attested codas in the three languages, without weighing their relative lexical frequencies; for example, if we assume that all codas (excluding recent loans) are weighted equivalently whether they occur in 10 words or 100 words. Thus, what is argued to be relevant here is the type frequency, and not necessarily the token frequency (but see discussion later). Furthermore, I will tentatively assume here that not only codas that are contrastive but also major allophones of coda phonemes contribute to the type frequency.

According to Poppe (1951), Khalkha has the following inventory of coda consonants, including codas that are clearly phonemic and those that are allophonic: [p, t, ts, tʃ, kʲ, k, s, ʃ, x, m, n, ŋ, l, r, b, g]. If we split this inventory along the voicing dimension, we get slightly more voiceless codas than voiced codas: nine voiceless codas, [p, t, ts, tʃ, kʲ, k, s, ʃ, x] as compared to seven voiced codas, [m, n, ŋ, l, r, b, g]. Divided along the sonorancy dimension, we get eleven obstruent codas, [p, t, ts, tʃ, kʲ, k, s, ʃ, x, b, g] and five sonorant codas, [m, n, ŋ, l, r].

Japanese (Vance 1987), on the other hand, has five voiced codas (including codas which are clearly phonemic and those which are allophonic), [m, ɲ, n, ŋ, ɴ] and five voiceless codas, [p, t, ts, tʃ, k]. Because all of the voiced codas are sonorants and all of the voiceless ones are obstruents, the division is the same along the sonorancy dimension. Finnish has five sonorant codas, all of them voiced [m, n, ŋ, r, l], and four obstruent codas, all of them voiceless [s, p, t, k].[20]

The reason sonorancy and voicing are relevant to the present discussion is that differences between segments along these dimensions are reliably associated with differences in energy. Sonorants characteristically have greater energy than obstruents and voiced sounds typically have greater energy than voiceless sounds, all else being equal. Although these generalizations are not without exception, sonorancy and voicing are two of the best, if not the best, features for predicting energy values.

If we consider the energy of CVC syllables as a whole, CVC will, all else being equal, have greater energy if a larger proportion of the coda consonants are voiced rather than voiceless. Similarly, CVC will have greater energy if a larger subset of the coda consonants are sonorants rather than obstruents. This argument of course adopts the assumption made above that all coda consonants are weighted equally in the calculation of energy for CVC as a whole.

Following this line of reasoning, CVC in Khalkha would thus be expected to have less energy than in either Japanese or Finnish, since Khalkha has both a greater obstruent-to-sonorant ratio and a greater voiceless-to-voiced ratio of coda consonants than both Japanese and Finnish. This hypothesis can, in fact, be tested by examining the energy of CVC relative to both CV and CVV in Khalkha and Finnish. Japanese is not a fair test case, since no obstruent codas were included in the corpus (see Table 4.6). The Khalkha data includes three sonorant codas (m, r, l) and five obstruent codas (s, ʃ, x, k, g). Considered along the voicing dimension, four voiced consonants (m, r, l, g) and four voiceless consonants (s, ʃ, x, k) were included. The Finnish data includes three sonorant codas, all of them voiced, (m, r, l) and two obstruent codas, both of them voiceless (s, t). The corpora for the two languages thus roughly reflect differences between the two languages in the type frequency of voiced relative to voiceless codas and in the type frequency of sonorant codas relative to obstruent codas.

Given the differences in the set of codas examined for Finnish and Khalkha, we would expect differences in the energy of CVC relative to CVV and CV. In particular, CVC should be closer in energy to CVV in Finnish than in Khalkha. Conversely, CVC should be closer in energy to CV in Khalkha than in Finnish. This hypothesis is tested in Figure 4.22, which contains energy values for CVV, CVC, and CV in Khalkha and Finnish.

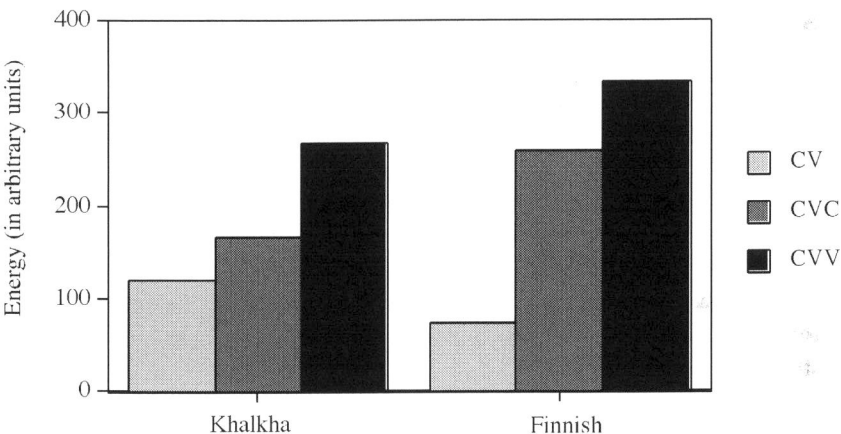

Figure 4.22. Energy values for CV, CVC, and CVC in Khalkha and Finnish

As predicted, CVC is closer to CV than CVV in Khalkha, whereas CVC is closer to CVV than to CV in Finnish. This results corresponds to the difference in the weight of CVC in the two languages. In Khalkha, CVC is light, whereas, in Finnish, CVC is heavy. The overall picture that thus emerges is that one language-specific aspect of the phonological system, syllable structure, leads to phonetic differences between languages, which in turn are responsible for differences in weight criteria. Positing this link between structural properties and syllable weight via the intermediary of phonetics makes the quite interesting prediction borne out by

Khalkha, Japanese, and Finnish, that weight distinctions are at least partially predictable if one considers the syllable structure of a language. This prediction can be tested by examining the inventory of coda consonants in other languages employing either the CVV(C) heavy or the CVV(C), CVC heavy distinctions for stress and/or metrics. The account given here would predict that languages with the CVV(C) heavy criterion should have a greater obstruent-to-sonorant coda ratio and/or a greater voiceless-to-voiced coda ratio than languages employing the CVV(C), CVC heavy criterion.

This prediction was tested in Gordon (2002) by examining the set of coda consonants in 62 languages which observe either the CVV(C) heavy or the CVV(C), CVC heavy criteria for stress and/or poetic metrics and possess closed syllables and either long vowels or diphthongs. I summarize the methodology and results of Gordon (2002) here; the reader is referred to the original work for further discussion and data. Languages in which both criteria are observed for either stress or poetic metrics or a combination of both were not included, since they are not probative in testing the hypothesis. Data were collected for all languages for which the set of codas could reliably be determined from available sources. All segments analyzed by the author(s) as coda segments were counted, excluding /h/ and glottal stop, since their phonetic realization, which is relevant for assessing their energy profile, usually could not be inferred from published descriptions. For languages in which it was difficult to determine which codas are limited to recent loans, all codas were included.

Because the hypothesis is that both the sonorancy and voicing of codas are predictors of the weight of CVC, the most probative languages fall into two classes: those that have neither more sonorant than obstruent codas nor more voiced than voiceless codas and those that have both as many or more sonorant than obstruent codas and as many or more voiced than voiceless codas. Languages falling into the former group would be expected to observe the CVV(C) heavy criterion and languages falling into the latter group would be expected to observe the CVV(C), CVC heavy criterion.

In general, languages employing the CVV(C) heavy criterion and those employing the CVV(C), CVC heavy criterion turned out to be well differentiated on the basis of their voiced to voiceless coda ratio. Languages with the CVV(C) heavy criterion, for the most part, had a smaller voiced to voiceless ratio than those with the CVV(C), CVC heavy criterion, as predicted by the hypothesis that syllable structure is a predictor of weight criteria. All else being equal, a greater proportion of voiced codas would be expected to boost the energy of CVC as a whole relative to languages with a smaller proportion of voiced codas. If a ratio of one is treated as a demarcation point separating languages with a CVV(C) heavy criterion from languages with a CVV(C), CVC heavy criterion, voicing correctly predicts weight criteria for 55 of 62 (88.7%) languages. Coda voicing acts as a particularly good predictor of the CVV(C), CVC heavy criterion; 32 of the 33 languages (all except Yana) with this criterion have at least as many voiced codas as voiceless codas. The success rate for the CVV(C) heavy criterion is somewhat lower but nevertheless fairly high: 23 of 29 with the CVV(C) heavy criterion have more voiceless codas than voiced codas. This leaves 6 exceptional languages with at least as many voiced as voiceless codas.

Turning to sonority, the ratio of sonorant to obstruent codas also is a fairly reliable predictor of weight criteria as predicted. Of the 29 languages with the CVV(C) heavy criterion, 27 have fewer sonorant than obstruent codas. Of the 33 languages with the CVV(C), CVC heavy criterion, 23 have at least as many sonorant as obstruent codas.

Now let us consider the languages that are most probative in testing the hypothesis that coda inventories are a predictor of weight criteria. There are 24 languages in which both the sonorant-to-obstruent ratio and the voiced-to-voiceless ratio are less than one, while there are 25 languages in which both the sonorant-to-obstruent ratio and the voiced-to-voiceless ratio are at least one. As it turns out, virtually all languages (23 of 24) in which both the sonorant-to-obstruent ratio and the voiced-to-voiceless ratio are less than one, employ the CVV(C) heavy criterion, just as predicted by the hypothesis that weight is ultimately determined by coda inventory. The only exceptional language is Yana, which has the CVV(C), CVC heavy criterion yet has sonorant-to-obstruent and voiced-to-voiceless ratios of less than one. Of the 25 languages in which both the sonorant-to-obstruent ratio and the voiced-to-voiceless ratio are at least one, almost all (23 of 25) have the CVV(C), CVC heavy criterion, again as predicted. The four exceptional languages which have both at least as many voiced as voiceless codas and at least as many sonorant as obstruent codas are Nyawaygi and Tidore.

A chi-squared test in which languages were coded categorically as either containing sonorant-to-obstruent and voiced-to-voiceless ratios of less than one or containing sonorant-to-obstruent and voiced-to-voiceless ratios of at least one confirmed that the close link between coda inventory and weight is not due to mere chance: $\chi^2=37.802$, $p<.0001$.

It is clear that factoring in both sonority and voicing as predictors of weight criteria expands the predictive power of the hypothesis that syllable structure is ultimately responsible for language-specific choice of weight criteria. However, based on the data analyzed in this book, languages vary in terms of whether weight distinctions sensitive to coda voicing or coda sonority are phonetically more effective. In Chickasaw and Khalkha, the CVV(C), CVR heavy criterion is phonetically more effective than the CVV(C), CV+G heavy criterion. In Telugu, Farsi, and French, on the other hand, the CVV(C), CV+G heavy criterion is phonetically superior to the CVV(C), CVR heavy criterion. This variation suggests that languages differ in terms of whether sonority or voicing is a better predictor of weight criteria. Future research should investigate the extent to which the phonological weight criteria are the phonetically most effective criteria in languages that are exceptional in either their voiced-to-voiceless coda ratio or their sonorant-to-obstruent coda ratio, or, even more importantly, languages that are exceptional along both dimensions (see Gordon 2002 for discussion). As far as the present research is concerned, though, it is striking that both sonority and voicing independently act as very good predictors of both the CVV(C) and the CVV(C), CVC criteria cross-linguistically. When both features are considered, coda inventories serve as an excellent predictor of weight criteria, as predicted by the proposed account in which syllable weight is ultimately dependent on syllable structure. As a final note, it is conceivable that a more sophisticated weighting of codas factoring in lexical frequency could provide an even better fit to the data. Thus, for example, it is possible that, in CVV(C), CVC heavy languages with fewer obstruent than sonorant codas (e.g. Turkish), sonorant codas occur with greater frequency in the lexicon than obstruents. Unfortunately given the difficulty involved in such a study, investigation of lexical frequency as a factor in choice of weight criteria must await further research.

4.9.3. The Phonetics-Phonology Relationship: A Summary

In summary, data presented in this section suggest that syllable structure plays an important role in establishing phonetic patterns, which in turn are responsible for language-specific choices in weight criteria for stress. We have seen evidence for this relationship both in the examination of vowel inventories and coda inventories. As a final note, languages with weight-insensitive stress systems provide one piece of additional evidence that phonetic considerations drive the phonology of weight-sensitive stress. Recall from sections 4.7.2.7–4.7.2.10 that the phonetically most effective weight distinctions in the weight-insensitive stress systems examined here were attested in languages with weight-sensitive stress systems. If the phonology of weight were not projected from phonetic factors, this fact would be an accident. We might just as well expect an unattested weight distinction to be the most effective weight distinction in weight-insensitive stress systems.

4.10. RARER CONDITIONING FACTORS IN WEIGHT: ONSETS AND TONE

In this section, we briefly explore possible phonetic motivations for two factors that occasionally, though rarely, play a role in syllable weight: syllable onsets and tone.

4.10.1. Syllable Onsets in Stress Systems

Recall that virtually all languages ignore syllable onsets in the calculation of weight for stress. There are, however, some exceptional cases of onset sensitivity in languages of the world. The most famous case is probably that of Mura-Pirahã (Everett and Everett 1984, Everett 1988), which observes a five way weight distinction primarily differentiated on the basis of the presence and type of onset: KVV > GVV > VV > KV > GV, where K stands for a voiceless consonant and G for a voiced consonant. Other cases of onset sensitivity in the survey (see Gordon 2005 for a more exhaustive survey of onset-sensitive stress) include Banawá (Ladefoged et al. 1997) and Júma (Abrahamson and Abrahamson 1984), in which syllables with onsets are heavier than those without onsets, and Nankina (Spaulding and Spaulding 1994), in which syllables with complex onsets are heavier than those with simple onsets. Bislama (Camden 1977) also treats syllables with complex onsets as heavier than those with simple onsets. Davis (1988) discusses additional cases of onset sensitivity in Arrernte and in Italian.[21] In Manam, onsetless syllables tend to resist stressing in penultimate position (Lichtenberk 1983). Sensitivity to onsets in a limited morphological context is also observed in English. Nanni (1977) shows that the first syllable in the English suffix -ative tends to destress immediately following either a vowel or a sonorant onset consonant (e.g. palli[ə]tive, cumul[ə]ative) but not following an obstruent onset or a cluster consisting of at least one obstruent (e.g. legisl[èɪ]tive, qualit[èɪ]tive).

There are at least two possible places to search for the basis of onset sensitivity in stress systems. The most obvious possibility is that the onset itself contributes to the weight of the syllable just as the presence of a coda consonant makes syllables heavy in many languages with purely rime-sensitive stress. Under this view, we would probably assume that the presence of an onset consonant contributes to the total energy and hence the weight of a syllable in some languages. While this approach would certainly be compatible with the position advanced in this chapter that energy is the primary correlate of weight for stress, there are certain aspects of onset sensitivity that make this hypothesis appear less tenable. Pirahã and English treat syllables with voiceless onsets as heavier than syllables with voiced onsets. A priori this is somewhat surprising given that voiced consonants characteristically have greater energy than voiceless ones. If onset sensitivity were simply the result of summing together the energy of the rime and the energy of the onset, we could not easily account for the fact that voiceless onsets are heavier than voiced onsets in languages like Mura-Pirahã. Furthermore, the destressing of the -ative suffix in English following a sonorant onset but not following an onset containing at least one obstruent would also be curious, since sonorants have greater energy than obstruents.

There is an answer to this conundrum in terms of auditory considerations (see Gordon 2005 for further discussion). The auditory system's response to a stimulus, as reflected in nerve firing rates, is strongest at the onset of the stimulus following a period of silence or a stimulus of lesser intensity and gradually displays a decline in response over time, a phenomenon termed auditory adaptation (see Delgutte 1982, as well as Bladon 1986 and Silverman 1995, 1997 for its influence on phonological patterns). A period of relatively less intensity thus allows the auditory system an opportunity to recover from the previous stimulus. It is thus plausible that a rime receives a boost in perceptual loudness when it follows an onset consonant. In contrast, a rime without an onset does not receive this perceptual boost.

Because a complex onset offers a longer recovery period than a simple onset, one might predict that a language might treat syllables with complex onsets as heavier than syllables with simple onsets. This prediction is in fact corroborated by the existence of languages like Nankina and Bislama that treat syllables with complex onsets as heavier than syllables with simple onsets.

This account also offers an explanation for the heavier status of syllables with voiceless onsets than syllables with voiced onsets in Pirahã and, in a more limited way, in English. Because voiceless consonants characteristically are less intense than voiced ones, a rime following a voiceless onset sounds louder, all else being equal, than a rime following a voiced onset.

Gordon (2005) quantitatively models the perceptual boost provided by onsets, especially low energy onsets, showing that onset-sensitive weight systems from three languages (Pirahã, Banawá, and Arrernte) match up well with a measure of perceptual energy factoring in recovery. He also compares the recovery-based account of onset sensitivity to the phonetically-grounded approach to onset-sensitive stress proposed by Goedemans (1998).[22]

4.10.1.1. Onset Sensitivity and Phonological Complexity

The presence of onset sensitivity in certain languages provides a testing ground for the metric of phonological simplicity developed in section 4.4. Recall that weight distinctions were argued to be too complex if they either referred to disjoint representations of the syllable rime possible or if they referred to more than one place predicate. Let us now consider how onset sensitive stress fits in with the metric of complexity proposed here. To see this, let us consider the case of Pirahã which observes the weight hierarchy KVV > GVV > VV > KV > GV, where K stands for a voiceless consonant and G for a voiced consonant. Two distinctions in this hierarchy are distinguished by the voice feature of the onset: KVV > GVV and KV > GV. Let us consider in Figure 4.23 the representation of the first of these two distinctions, the more complex one. If the first distinction is treated as simple, the second one will thus be simple too. Note that the subscripted $_O$ in Figure 4.23 indicates the onset.

$$[X]_O \; [XX]_R$$
$$+\text{voice} \; +\text{syllabic}$$

Figure 4.23. The representation of onset-sensitive stress

The dimensions to which this distinction refers appear in Table 4.26.

Because the distinction in Figure 4.23 does not refer to disjoint representations of the syllable and because it refers to only non-place predicates, it is simple and does not constitute an exception to the complexity metric proposed earlier (see Gordon 2005 for a constraint-based approach to onset-sensitive stress that employs the representations in Figure 4.23).

4.10.2. Tone As a Factor in Syllable Weight

We saw in Chapter Two that several languages of the world preferentially stress syllables that carry high tones over syllables carrying mid or low tones (see DeLacy 2002 for similar typological conclusions). We do not find, to

Table 4.26. Onset sensitive weight in Pirahã					
		Predicates		Disjoint	Dimension	
					Non-place	Place
KVV > GVV	$[X]_O$ -voice	$[X]_R$ +syllabic	$[X]_R$ +syllabic	No	6	0

the best of my knowledge, stress systems that treat syllables with mid or low tones as heavier than syllables with high tones. A reasonable question to ask is why several languages, e.g. Crow (Kaschube 1967) and Iraqw (Mous 1993) (see Chapter Two for other examples) either treat simple high-toned syllables or syllables containing a high tone, i.e. syllables with tonal contours, as heavier than low or mid tones. One plausible answer to this question is that syllables carrying a high tone simply have greater acoustic intensity than syllables with mid or low tones. A small experiment using a subset of the Hausa data examined in the discussion of tone in Chapter Three was performed to test the hypothesis that higher tone is associated with greater intensity. The average amplitude (RMS) of the low-toned vowel in the first syllable of the word ràndá: 'large water pot' was compared to that of the high-toned vowel in the first syllable of the word mándá: 'dark Bornu medicinal salt.' The comparison was made by calculating the RMS of each target vowel and subtracting it from the RMS for the vowel in the second syllable, which served as a control against token-to-token fluctuations in amplitude and distance from the microphone.

Results indicated that the high-toned vowel had greater average amplitude than the low-tone vowel by a difference of 3.14 decibels. This difference was found to be statistically highly significant by an unpaired t-test: $t=6.562$, $p<.0001$. The difference is particularly large when considered in the perceptual domain. Recall that a difference of only approximately 6dB in intensity corresponds to roughly a twofold difference in loudness. This result supports the view that weight-sensitive stress is energy-driven.

4.11. A CONSTRAINT SET FOR WEIGHT-SENSITIVE STRESS SYSTEMS

Thus far, we have seen that the phonological weight distinctions in languages are those that are phonetically most effective but are also structurally simple in terms of the phonological dimensions to which they are sensitive. Discussion of the formal representation of weight-based stress has been kept to a minimum thus far, used only in the discussion of structural complexity in sections 4.4 and 4.10.1.1. In this section, I explore the way in which phonetic conditioning factors can be incorporated into a formal theory of weight. The discussion here will basically follow that adopted in the discussion of weight-sensitive tone in Chapter Three. Before proceeding in this endeavor, a caveat is necessary. The present proposal is not intended to be a comprehensive metrical theory, which although an integral part of a complete account of syllable weight, goes well beyond the scope of this chapter.

The model which I briefly sketch here as a formalism of syllable weight is couched within an Optimality-theoretic framework (Prince and Smolensky 2004) and follows work by Prince and Smolensky (2004), Kenstowicz (1997) and others in which much of the burden of phonology is shifted from representations to constraints. In their accounts of weight-sensitive stress, Prince and Smolensky (2004) and Kenstowicz (1997) posit constraints referring to different syllable types involved in a hierarchy of prominence. These constraints capture what Prince and Smolensky (2004:38) term "prominential enhancement that calls directly on contrasts in the intrinsic prominence of syllables."

Prince and Smolensky posit a series of Peak-Prominence constraints referring to syllable types of differing degrees of prominence. Similarly, Kenstowicz (1997) posits constraints of the form *P/x, where x is a member of a set of different vowel types participating in weight distinctions based on vowel quality: *P/a, *P/e,o, *P/i,u, etc. These constraints each require that stress not occur on the vowel mentioned in the constraint. Thus, *P/a requires that /a/ not be stressed.

In the present account, I assume that structurally simple weight distinctions are reflected in constraints referring to weight-sensitive stress. We may also speculate that constraints referring to complex weight distinctions also exist in the grammar but are destined to be mired at the bottom of the constraint hierarchy, precisely because they are complex and thus are unlikely to be entertained by the language learner evaluating simple criteria before complex one. Under this view, the learner first tests simple weight criteria against the phonetic map and only proceeds to more complex criteria after the simple ones have proven themselves to be phonetically ill suited to the language. Thus, what is innate is not the set of constraints but the learning algorithm that tests simple weight distinctions before complex ones.[23]

Most of the relevant constraints discussed here refer to stress. We have already seen in Chapter Three that similar constraints account for the facts of weight-sensitive tone and pitch accent. All of the representations in section 4.4 which refer to heavy syllables appear as positively stated constraints requiring that the given syllable be stressed. For example, the CVV heavy distinction is reflected in the constraint in (54).

(54) STRESS $[X_{[+syll]}X_{[+syll]}]_R$: A CVV syllable is stressed.

One violation of the constraint is incurred for each instance of an unstressed syllable containing a long vowel.

Similarly, the CVV, CV+R heavy distinction is reflected in the constraint in (55):

(55) STRESS $[X_{[+son,-cgl]}X_{[+son,-cgl]}]_R$: CVV and CVR syllables are stressed.

The structurally simple constraints are ranked on a language specific basis on the basis of how well different weight distinctions fit the phonetic map. More effective weight distinctions in a given language are ranked ahead of less effective distinctions in the family of weight-sensitive constraints. For example, if the CVV heavy distinction is the optimal phonetic distinction in a language, that language will rank STRESS $[X_{[+syll]}X_{[+syll]}]_R$ above all the other stress constraints. Similarly, if the Non-high V heavy distinction provides the best fit to the phonetic map, the constraint STRESS $[X_{[+syll,-hi]}]_R$ will be ranked higher than stress constraints referring to other weight distinctions. Under this view, the default ranking of constraints in a given language is determined on the basis of phonetic effectiveness. There is limited opportunity for purely inductive learning of the rankings, as, for example, in a hypothetical language in which the observed weight criterion is not the phonetically most effective one.

We have seen in the case of Telugu, that it is possible for a weight distinction employed by a metrical system to be phonetically superior to one operative in a stress system. For example, CVV is heavier than CVC for stress in Telugu, but both CVV and CVC are heavier than CV for metrics. The most effective weight distinction phonetically in Telugu is CVV, CVC heavy, i.e. the distinction used for metrics. Thus, although the ranking of constraints referring to stress is not completely predictable on the basis of phonetic effectiveness, the optimal phonetic effectiveness of the CVV, CVC heavy distinction is reflected in constraint rankings operative in the metrical system of Telugu. Thus, the Telugu data is compatible with the view that the ranking of constraints referring to metrics may be projected from the same phonetic dimension as the ranking operative for stress.

Javanese is a possible exception to the general rule that rankings of constraints are projected from phonetics. The phonetically most optimal weight distinction in Javanese, the one between reduced vowels *in open syllables* and other syllables, is ranked ahead of the distinction between full and reduced vowels. One might have expected the distinction between full and reduced vowels to be phonetically more effective in Javanese given its status as a phonological weight distinction.

The constraints on stress are interleaved with other constraints; for example, constraints against more than one stress per word, constraints requiring stress in a word, constraints against stress clashes, etc.

In complex weight hierarchies like those found in Telugu, Chickasaw or Finnish, more than one constraint is ranked highly enough in the grammar to impact the language.

For example, both STRESS $[X_{[+syll]}X_{[+syll]}]_R$ and STRESS $[XX]_R$ are highly ranked in Chickasaw.

In the next section, a sample typology illustrating the interaction between the STRESS constraints and other constraints is presented.

4.12. A FACTORIAL TYPOLOGY OF STRESS SYSTEMS

We evaluate here the types of stress systems generated by interleaving various metrical constraints with the STRESS constraints referring to the three most common types of weight distinctions: the Khalkha type distinction treating long vowels as heavy, the Javanese type distinction according to which full vowels are heavy, and the Latin type distinction in which both long vowels and closed syllables are stress attracting.

The five constraints relevant for the mini-typology are given in (56).

(56) • ALIGN (ớ, L, PRWD): Stress must fall on the first syllable of the prosodic word; one violation incurred for every syllable separating stress from left edge of word (violations cumulative for each stress). (McCarthy and Prince 1993)

• ONE STRESS: A word has one and only one stress. (cf. Culminativity in Prince 1983).

• STRESS $[XX]_R$: CVV, CVC syllables are stressed

• STRESS $[X_{[+syll]}X_{[+syll]}]_R$: CVV syllables are stressed.

• STRESS $[X_{[+syll]}]_R$: Non-central (i.e. full) vowels are stressed.

In order to constrain the typology, I will assume that ONE STRESS is undominated.

First, let us consider the system generated by ranking STRESS $[X_{[+syll]}X_{[+syll]}]_R$ below ONE STRESS but above ALIGN (ớ, L, PRWD), which in turn is higher ranked than the other two STRESS constraints considered here. This set of rankings yields a language that stresses the leftmost CVV syllable, otherwise the initial syllable, a system found in Murik (Abbott 1985). Schematic forms illustrating the attraction of stress by the leftmost heavy syllable are shown in (57). In case of a word with all light syllables, ALIGN (ớ, L, PRWD) ensures that the stress falls on the initial syllable.

(57)

Input tətatapta:	ONE STRESS	STRESS [X̯X̯]$_R$ +syllabic	ALIGN (ϭ, L, PRWD)	*STRESS [XX]$_R$	STRESS [X]$_R$ +syllabic
☞ tətatap'ta:			***	*	**
'tətatapta:		*!		**	***
tə'tatapta:		*!	*	**	**
təta'tapta:		*!	**	*	**
'tətatap'ta:	*!		***	*	**

If the ranking in (57) remains unchanged except that STRESS [XX]$_R$ is promoted above the other weight-sensitive stress constraints, a system with stress on the first CVV or CVC syllable, otherwise the initial syllable, is generated. This pattern corresponds to the stress system of Yana (Sapir and Swadesh 1960) and is depicted in (58).

(58)

Input tətatapta:	ONE STRESS	*STRESS [XX]$_R$	ALIGN (ϭ, L, PRWD)	STRESS [X̯X̯]$_R$ +syllabic	STRESS [X]$_R$ +syllabic
tətatap'ta:		*	***!		**
'tətatapta:		**!		*	***
tə'tatapta:		**!	*	*	**
☞ təta'tapta:		*	**	*	**
'tətatap'ta:	*!	*	***		**

If the highest ranked constraint is the constraint requiring that stress fall on full vowels, a system is generated that stresses the leftmost full vowel otherwise the initial syllable. This system corresponds to that found in Au (Scorza 1985). It is illustrated in (59).

(59)

Input tətatapta:	ONE STRESS	STRESS [X]$_R$ +syllabic	ALIGN (ϭ, L, PRWD)	STRESS [X̯X̯]$_R$ +syllabic	*STRESS [XX]$_R$
tətatap'ta:		**	**!*		*
'tətatapta:		***!		*	**
☞ tə'tatapta:		**	*	*	**
təta'tapta:		**	**!	*	*
'tətatap'ta:	*!	**	***		*

The final possibility obtains if ALIGN (ϭ, L, PRWD) is ranked above all the constraints requiring that heavy syllables be stressed. This is shown in (60) and corresponds to a language, such as Chitimacha (Swadesh 1946), that stresses the leftmost syllable regardless of the weight of syllables after the first one.

(60)

Input tətatapta:	ONE STRESS	ALIGN (σ, L, PrWd)	STRESS [X̌X]$_R$ +syllabic	STRESS [X]$_R$ +syllabic	STRESS [XX]$_R$
tətatap'ta:		*!**		**	*
☞ 'tətatapta:			*	***	**
tə'tatapta:		*!	*	**	**
təta'tapta:		*!*	*	**	*
'tətatap'ta:	*!	***		**	*

4.13. SUMMARY

In this chapter, we have seen that phonological weight distinctions for stress and poetic metrical systems closely match up with the phonetic property of total energy. Languages choose weight distinctions that divide syllables into two groups of maximally differentiated syllables along the phonetic/perceptual parameter of total energy. Total energy, in turn, appears to be largely predictable on the basis of certain structural properties of languages, such as the structure of the vowel and coda inventory.

However, languages are not blindly faithful to phonetic properties when evaluating weight distinctions. Languages eschew weight distinctions that are structurally too complex, even if they provide an optimal fit to the phonetic map. Syllable weight for stress thus represents a compromise between phonetic effectiveness and structural symmetry, parallel to the situation for weight-sensitive tone presented in Chapter Three.

We also examined further the issue of the directionality of the phonetics/phonology relationship. Evidence was presented for a model of this relationship in which universal phonetic properties constrain the range of weight-sensitive stress systems attested cross-linguistically, while language specific phonetic properties guide languages in their choice of particular weight criteria. These language specific phonetic features were shown to be largely conditioned by differences in other aspects of the phonological system, including syllable structure and vowel inventories. The result is a fairly complex relationship between phonetic and phonological systems, whereby different subcomponents of each system are interleaved and mutually dependent.

Chapter Five
Other Weight-Sensitive Phenomena

5.0. INTRODUCTION

In this chapter we pick up the discussion of weight criteria for four weight-based phenomena other than stress and tone: metrics, compensatory lengthening, syllable template restrictions, and minimal word requirements. The distribution of weight criteria for each of these phenomena will be discussed and compared to each other, following the structure of the comparison in Chapter Two of stress and tone with each other and with the other four weight-based phenomenon. In addition, some (rather tentative) speculations on the motivations behind these phenomena will be offered. Finally, we explore the basis for one of the more intriguing cases of weight uniformity discussed in the literature: the convergence of weight criteria for tone and syllable template restrictions in Lithuanian and Greek.

5.1. COMPENSATORY LENGTHENING

There were 29 languages with compensatory lengthening triggered by coda loss among the languages surveyed. In 10 of these languages, more than one segment triggered compensatory lengthening. Of the 29 languages with compensatory lengthening, in 14 it was a historical process, at least for certain segments. There are 17 languages in which there are synchronic compensatory lengthening alternations, though the productivity of the alternations is not clear in certain cases. The consonant type that most frequently triggered compensatory lengthening were rhotics (9 languages), followed by nasals (7 languages) stops (6 languages), /h/ (5 languages), and /l/ (4 languages).

Looking at these figures, we see a general tendency for sonorants to more readily trigger compensatory lengthening than obstruents, an observation made by DeChene and Anderson (1979), Rialland (1993), and Kavitskaya (2002).[1]

This skewing is stronger if we include among the sonorants non-strident voiced fricatives, such as those made in the velar and uvular regions, which are often approximant-like. Note, however, as pointed in Chapter Two, that we cannot conclude from this survey that the loss of obstruents more rarely results in compensatory lengthening than the loss of sonorants, since the survey did not catalog the consonants that were lost but did *not* trigger compensatory lengthening. Thus, the fact that sonorants appear superficially to trigger compensatory lengthening more often than obstruents could, in principle, turn out to be the result of a tendency for sonorants to delete more readily than obstruents. In order to draw more definitive conclusions about the type of segments that trigger compensatory lengthening, one would need to know which segments were lost but failed to trigger compensatory lengthening. The survey presented here is not designed to examine this question, though it is interesting to note that there are documented languages in which sonorant loss but not obstruent loss triggers compensatory lengthening, e.g. Classical Greek (Ingria 1980), Kasem (Rialland 1993). Data such as these suggest that the compensatory lengthening asymmetry between sonorants and obstruents observed here might be a robust phenomenon.

There is another limitation of any survey of compensatory lengthening. Even if coda loss does not trigger compensatory lengthening in a given language, we cannot conclude that consonants are weightless in that language. The reason for this is that an absence of compensatory lengthening could be due to independent factors such as an avoidance of long vowels, either due to a prohibition against long vowels in the language or a desire to preserve the underlying duration of short vowels. Thus, unlike for processes like stress, tone, metrics and minimal word requirements, there is no positive evidence for a weight distinction between consonants and vowels in compensatory lengthening. A similar impasse emerges if one considers the evidence provided by compensatory lengthening for differentiating the weight of CVC and CVCC syllables. In certain languages, e.g. Cretan Greek (Ingria 1980) and Komi Izhma (Harms 1968, Hayes 1989), compensatory lengthening applies in syllables closed by a single consonant but not in syllables closed by two consonants. The asymmetry in such cases could be due to an independent syllable template restriction against long vowels in closed syllables.[2]

If, however, a language has compensatory lengthening due to coda loss but one or more other weight-sensitive processes such as stress, tone bearing units, metrics or minimal word requirements, indicate that codas consonants are weightless, we can infer a weight mismatch. Thus, for example, stress in Huallaga Quechua ignores coda consonants; thus, the weight uniformity as a function of language hypothesis would (incorrectly) expect the loss of a coda consonant *not* to trigger compensatory lengthening in Huallaga Quechua.

Cases of compensatory lengthening found in the survey are listed in Table 5.1. Table 5.1 also compares weight criteria used for compensatory lengthening with weight criteria employed by other weight-sensitive processes.

The number of matches and mismatches (hearts and diamonds in parentheses not included) are presented in tabular form in Table 5.2. Cases where the number of weight matches exceeds the number of weight mismatches appear in bold.

As Table 5.2 shows, compensatory lengthening is in complete (or near complete) agreement with three processes (metrics, syllable templates, and minimal word requirements). For two other processes (stress and tone), there is a greater degree of conflict, as discussed in Chapter Two.

On the basis of the robust correlation between weight criteria for compensatory lengthening and weight criteria for the three other processes: metrics, syllable templates, and minimal words), we might conclude that we have evidence for the hypothesis that weight is a property of languages and not of processes. However, a closer look at the nature of the processes providing the strongest corroboration of weight uniformity as a function of language suggests that the evidence is not as strong as it seems.

The processes that provide the strongest evidence for weight uniformity as a function of language (metrics, syllable templates and minimal word requirements) are inherently biased toward agreements in weight criteria with compensatory lengthening. We consider these processes in turn.

First, we turn to the uniformity of weight criteria between compensatory lengthening and syllable template restrictions. Like compensatory lengthening, syllable templates do not allow for comparison of the weight of vowels and consonants, since an absence of a constraint against long vowels in closed syllables does *not* demonstrate that codas are weightless. Codas may bear weight, but faithfulness to underlying vowel length (either synchronically or diachronically) may have priority over an avoidance of long vowels in closed syllables. Thus, just as lack of compensatory lengthening does not prove that codas are weightless, the absence of a restriction against long vowels in closed syllables also does not prove that codas are weightless. Thus, the deck is inherently stacked in favor of matches between compensatory lengthening and syllable templates. The nature of these two processes (at least as considered in this book) allows no opportunity for a conflict of weight criteria.

Second, we turn to weight uniformity between compensatory lengthening and metrics. As discussed in Chapter Two and further in section 5.2, all languages in the survey with weight-sensitive metrics employ the same weight

Table 5.1. Languages with compensatory lengthening triggered by loss of coda consonant(s).

Notes: A superscripted ᵃ indicates that the language does not have codas. A super-scripted ᵇ indicates an absence of phonemic long vowels. A superscripted ᵇ indicates an absence of long vowels and diphthongs. A superscripted ᶜ indicates an historical compensatory lengthening process involving the loss of *segments preceding the* ᶜ.

Language	Phylum	Comp Length	Stress	Metrics	Syll. Templ.	Tone	Minim. Word
Belizean Creole	Creole	r					♥
Chitimacha	Gulf	hᶜ					♥
Diegueño	Hokan	ʔ					
Dzongkha	Sio–Tibetan	l, r, ŋ, t, k, s ᶜ					♥
English	Indo-European	rᶜ (dialect)	♥	♥			
Gurage	Afro-Asiatic	r, l, pharyng.ᶜ					♥
Hindi	Indo-European	C (thru degem.)	(♥)	♥	(♥)		♥
Irish (Munster)	Indo-European	g, n ᶜ		♥			
Kabardian	North Caucasian	h					
Kalispel	Salishan	rʷ ᶜ					
Lamangᵇ ³	Afro-Asiatic	ŋ					
Latin	Indo-European	s	♥				♥
Lillooet	Salish	u̜, ʕ, ʕʷ	♦ Full V				
Marubo	Panoan	n					♦ CVV
Musey	Afro-Asiatic	r			♥	♥	

Language	Family	Segment					
Nyawaygi	Australian	r[c]	♦ CVV(C)				♥
Oneida	Iroquoian	h			♥		
Pomo, Eastern	Hokan	n[c]					
Pomo, Kashaya	Hokan	l, n[c]	(♥)[4]				
Quechua, Huallaga	Quechan	q	♦ CVV(C)		♥		
Telugu	Dravidian	m	♦ CVV(C)	♥			♥
Thai	Daic	k[c] [5]		♥		♦ CVV(C), CVR	♥
Tibetan (Lhasa)	Sino-Tibetan	s[c], r, p, k	♦ CVV(C)			♦ CVV(C), CVR	
Turkish	Altaic	v [6]	♥				♥
Uzbek	Altaic	r[c], ʔ					♥
Veps[b][7]	Uralic	l[c] (South Veps)	♥				
Wichita	Caddoan	k[c], h					
Yapese	Austronesian	j, w	(♥, ♦)				
Yurok	Algic	h[8]					♥

Table 5.2. Weight uniformity between compensatory lengthening and other phenomena

	Agree	Disagree
Metrics	**5**	**0**
Stress	4	5
Syllable Templates	**3**	**0**
Tone	1	2
Minimal Word	**11**	1

distinction: both CVV(C) and CVC are heavy. If we consider the internal consistency of weight criteria used by metrical systems and the inherent inability of compensatory lengthening to shed light on the relative weight of obstruents, sonorants, and vowels, one would not expect weight conflicts between compensatory lengthening and metrics. 100% of languages in the survey with weight-sensitive metrics treat coda consonants as weighted, and 100% of languages in the survey with compensatory lengthening treat codas as weighted. Thus, the uniformity of weight criteria for compensatory lengthening and metrics is an artifact of the rigid consistency of weight criteria for both of these phenomena, and does not provide any support for the hypothesis that weight is a function of language.

The correlation between compensatory lengthening and minimal word requirements is also most likely attributed to the process internal consistency of weight criteria for minimal word requirements. Approximately 80% of languages with monosyllabic minimal word requirements have CVC as their minimal word (see section 5.3). Thus, there is inherently a strong bias against weight mismatches between minimal word requirements and compensatory lengthening; this fact diminishes the significance of the consistency in weight criteria between the two phenomena. Though the number of languages in the survey displaying both of these phenomena is too small to demonstrate statistically that the strong correlation between weight criteria for minimal words and compensatory lengthening is an artifact of the internal consistency of weight criteria for each of these phenomena, this hypothesis can be evaluated with some simple arithmetic. Given that there is an approximately 80% chance that any individual language will treat codas as weighted for minimal word requirements and that 100% of the languages in the survey treat codas as weighted for compensatory lengthening, we would expect just on the basis of the process internal weight criteria for these phenomena, that 80% of languages with both of the processes would agree in their weight criteria.

Given this strong bias in favor of uniformity of criteria between compensatory lengthening and minimal word requirements, we do not find support for the weight uniformity hypothesis.

In summary, what at first glance looked like robust evidence supporting the hypothesis that weight is a function of language, upon closer inspection was reduced to other independent properties: an inherent deficiency in the set of possible weight criteria exploited by compensatory lengthening and syllable template restrictions combined with the internal consistency of weight criteria for metrics and minimal word requirements.

5.1.2. The Basis for Compensatory Lengthening

Compensatory lengthening has the effect of preserving the duration of the rime in the face of the deletion of the coda consonant. The coda consonant deletes and the preceding vowel lengthens to take up the duration originally occupied by the consonant.

Moraic and skeletal slot theories treat compensatory lengthening as a weight-preserving phenomenon that preserves the prosodic structure of the original string. Although moraic models capture the fundamental nature of compensatory lengthening, they encounter problems in defining exactly what aspects of the prosodic structure are being maintained. The existence of many languages in which compensatory lengthened is triggered by the loss of coda consonants which are otherwise weightless for other phenomena (see section 2.3.1) demonstrates that compensatory lengthening cannot simply be viewed as preservation of the same prosodic "weight" relevant for other phenomena. Rather, weight as it pertains to compensatory lengthening must be explicitly defined along some particular prosodic dimension, just like weight for other phenomena.

The most obvious candidate is duration, since compensatory lengthening of a vowel has the effect of approximating the underlying or original duration of the rime, since VV and VC tend to be roughly equivalent in duration cross-linguistically (see, for example, measurements in Chapter Four). If we follow skeletal slot models of the syllable in assuming that each segment is linked to a timing position and long segments are linked to two timing positions, then we can formalize the duration preserving nature of compensatory lengthening. Compensatory lengthening ensures that underlying timing positions surface. Formally, compensatory lengthening can be captured in a constraint-based paradigm like Optimality Theory using a relatively small set of constraints. First, one may assume a highly ranked member of the MAX family of constraints (McCarthy and Prince 1995) requiring that rimal timing positions in the input have a correspondent in the output, i.e. MAX-IO $[X]_R$. By ranking this constraint above a constraint requiring that underlying vowel length surface unaltered, compensatory lengthening is accounted for. For concreteness sake, I formulate this latter constraint as a member of the IDENT-IO family of constraints (McCarthy and Prince 1995) requiring that vowel length in the input be preserved in the output (see Chapter Three for this constraint in tone systems). The final constraint is highly ranked (above the IDENT-IO constraint) and drives the deletion of the coda. It is stated here simply as *CODA (Prince and Smolensky 2004). The analysis of a schematic case of compensatory lengthening is given in (64).

(64)

Input: VC]σ	*CODA	MAX-IO [X]$_R$	IDENT-IO [V-LENGTH]
☞ a) V:]σ			*
b) VC]σ	*!		
c) V]σ		*!	

Recall that there appears to be some tendency for compensatory lengthening to be triggered most commonly by the loss of a coda sonorant. Unfortunately, because the data sample does not include languages in which codas are lost but compensatory lengthening does not occur, we do not know how robust this asymmetry is. We do know, however, that there are at least some languages (e.g. Classical Greek and Kasem; see discussion above) in which compensatory lengthening is asymmetrically triggered by loss of a sonorant but not by loss of an obstruent. In these languages, the weight criterion for compensatory lengthening is thus CVV(C), CVR heavy. For such cases, we must assume a more specific MAX-IO constraint referring not to all rimal timing positions but only ones associated with the feature [sonorant]. The IDENT-IO constraint is ranked below this constraint but above the generic MAX-IO constraint referring to all rimal timing positions. In (64) we see tableaux for two syllables, the first of which is closed by a sonorant, the second of which is closed by an obstruent.

(65)

Input: VR]σ	*CODA	MAX-IO [X]$_R$ | [sonorant]	IDENT-IO [V-length]	MAX-IO [X]$_R$
☞ a) V:]σ			*	
b) VR]σ	*!			
c) V]σ		*!		*
Input: VO]σ	*CODA	MAX-IO [X]$_R$ | [sonorant]	IDENT-IO [V-length]	MAX-IO [X]$_R$
☞ a) V]σ				*
b) V:]σ			*!	
c) VO]σ	*!			

5.2. METRICS

We now turn to the results of the typology of metrics. There were 17 languages with weight-sensitive metrics in the survey; these languages appear in Table 5.3 along with hearts and diamonds indicating weight convergences and weight inconsistencies, respectively.

All of the languages found make the same weight distinction: both CVC and CVV(C) are heavy. In one of them, Fijian, CVC does not occur; there is thus no basis for establishing the relative weight of CVV(C) and CVC. Berber has a slight variation on this pattern: only syllables either closed by an entire geminate (e.g. CVC:) or by a coda consonant which is not the first half of a geminate (e.g. $CVC_1.C_2V$) are heavy; Berber lacks phonemic long vowels. Two languages in the survey (Hindi and Persian) are sensitive to a third level of weight for metrics, thus yielding the hierarchy CVVC, CVCC > CVV, CVC > CV.

In considering the significance of these results, it is important to bear in mind that not only is the number of languages displaying quantity-sensitive metrics relatively small, but that many of these systems have a common source. Thus, six of the seventeen languages are Indo-European; a further three languages in the survey borrowed their weight-sensitive metrical systems from an Indo-European language. Thai, Malayalam, and Telugu borrowed the Indo-Aryan type system, which is still preserved in certain Indo-Aryan languages like Hindi and Sindhi. Hungarian also modeled its weight-sensitive metrical systems after the Latin and Classical Greek models. It is also possible that the source for the Finnish quantitative metrical system is ultimately Indo-European. In North Africa, the Arabic metrical system potentially served as the model for the Hausa weight-sensitive system. Furthermore, Berber is in close contact with Arabic. This leaves us with only a few weight-sensitive metrical systems that clearly appear to have independent origins: Japanese, Fijian, and Luganda. Furthermore, as pointed in section 2.12.1, there appears to be at least one language not in the survey, Kayardild (Evans 1995), which observes the CVV(C) heavy criterion in its meter. The basis picture that thus emerges is that, although the predominance of the CVV(C), CVC heavy criterion for metrics is certainly intriguing, one should probably regard this result with some caution. Table 5.4 shows the number of languages in which weight criteria between metrics and other phenomena match or mismatch.

As examination of Table 5.4 indicates, weight criteria for metrics show a strong tendency to agree with other weight-sensitive phenomena with the exception of tone. The convergence in weight criteria between stress and

Table 5.3. Languages with weight-sensitive metrics

Notes: A superscripted ᵃ indicates that the language does not have codas. A superscripted ᵇ indicates an absence of phonemic long vowels. A superscripted ᵈ indicates an absence of non-sonorant codas. A superscripted ᶜ indicates an absence of phonemic long vowels and diphthongs. VV stands for long vowels and diphthongs, unless otherwise noted. R stands for a sonorant coda. Shaded languages do not contain coda consonants and are not diagnostic for weight.

Language	Phylum	Metrics	Stress	Comp Length	Syll. Templ.	Tone	Minim. Word
Arabic	Afro-Asiatic	CVV(C), CVC	♥				♥
English	Indo-European	CVV(C), CVC		♥			♥
Estonian	Uralic	CVV(C), CVC	♥				
Fijianᵃ	Austronesian	CVV(C), CVC	♥				♥
Finnish	Uralic	CVV(C), CVC	♥		♥		◆ CVV(C)
Greek (Classical)	Indo-European	CVV(C), CVC	♥		♥	◆ CVV(C)	♥
Hausa	Afro-Asiatic	CVV(C), CVC			♥	♥	
Hindi	Indo-European	CVCC, CVVC> CVV, CVC >CV	♥⁹	(♥)	(♥)		♥

Hungarian	Uralic	CVV(C), CVC	♥				
Old Icelandic	Indo-European	CVV(C), CVC					♥
Japanese	Japanese	CVV(C), CVC			♥		
Latin	Indo-European	CVV(C), CVC	♥	♥	♥		♥
Luganda	Niger-Congo	CVV(C), CVC			♥		
Malayalam	Dravidian	CVV(C), CVC	♦ CVV(C)				
Persian	Indo-European	CVV(C), CVC		♥			
Tamazight Berber[c]	Afro-Asiatic	CVC[10]					
Telugu	Dravidian	CVV(C), CVC	♦ CVV(C)				♥
Thai	Daic	CVV(C), CVC				♦ CVV(C), CVR	

Table 5.4. Weight uniformity between metrics and other phenomena

	Agree	Disagree
Compensatory lengthening	4	0
Stress	7	2
Syllable Templates	4	0
Tone	2	2
Minimal Word	8	1

metrics was argued in Chapter Two to be non-accidental. In Chapter Four, it was claimed that weight criteria for both stress and metrics are linked to a measure of auditory energy.

The convergence of weight criteria for metrics with weight criteria observed by compensatory lengthening, syllable templates and minimal word requirements is, on the other hand, unlikely to offer any support for weight uniformity. Rather, these cases of weight agreement are artifacts of the inability of compensatory lengthening and syllable templates to demonstrate that codas are weightless, in conjunction with the internal consistency of weight criteria for the minimal word requirement.

Before concluding the discussion of metrics, it is interesting to note that virtually all languages with weight-sensitive metrical systems in the survey possess phonemic vowel length. The exception to this generalization is Berber. Assuming that this generalization holds up as our database expands, it would appear that a sufficiently robust quantitative system is a prerequisite for the development of a weight-sensitive metrical system. In support of this view, it is interesting to note that the Persian system of quantitative metrics has been largely abandoned, as the original vowel system based on quantity contrasts has been supplanted by one based on quality contrasts in modern Farsi (Bruce Hayes p.c.). Similarly, certain Russian poets tried unsuccessfully in the 17th century to adopt a system of quantitative verse; their lack of success may be attributed in large part to the lack of phonemic vowel length in Russian (Silbajoris 1968).

5.3. MINIMAL WORD REQUIREMENTS

144 languages in the survey possess a minimal word requirement; they are listed in Table 5.5.

Of the 144 languages, 22 have a disyllabic minimal word requirement.[28] Languages of this sort do not shed any light on the question of

Table 5.5. Languages with minimal word requirements

Notes: A superscripted a indicates that the language does not have codas. A superscripted b indicates an absence of phonemic long vowels. A superscripted d indicates that the language does not have obstruent codas. A superscripted c indicates an absence of long vowels and diphthongs. VV stands for both long vowels, if found in a language, and diphthongs unless otherwise noted. Shaded languages either do not contain coda consonants or have disyllabic minimal word requirements.

Language	Macro-Phylum	Minim. Word	Stress	Metrics	Comp Length	Syll. Templ.	Tone
Kashuyana [c]	Carib	CCV, CVCV					
Czech	Indo-European	CCV, CVC					
Tsou [a11]	Austronesian	CCV, CVV					
Au	Torricelli	CFull V	♥				
Maru [b]	Sino-Tibetan	CFull V				♦ CVV(C)	♦ CVV(C), CVR
Kwak'ala	Wakashan	CLowV	♦ CVV(C), CVR				
!Xoo [d]	Khoisan	CVC				♥	
Aguacatec	Mayan	CVC	♦ CVV(C)				
Alamblak [c]	Sepik-Ramu	CVC					
Alawa [c]	Australian	CVC					

(continued)

Table 5.5. Languages with minimal word requirements (*continued*)

Language	Macro-Phylum	Minim. Word	Stress	Metrics	Comp Length	Syll. Templ.	Tone
Aleut	Eskimo-Aleut	CVC	◆ CVV(C)				
Arabic[12]	Afro-Asiatic	CVC	❥	❥			
Bashkir[b]	Altaic	CVC					
Basque[b]	isolate	CVC					
Buriat	Altaic	CVC	◆ CVV(C)				
Cakchiquel[e]	Mayan	CVC					
Capanahua	Panoan	CVC					
Chitimacha	Gulf	CVC			❥		
Chontal[e]	Mayan	CVC					
Diegueño	Hokan	CVC			❥		
Diola	Niger-Congo	CVC					
English	Indo-European	CVC	❥	❥	❥		
Even (=Lamut)	Altaic	CVC					
Evenki	Altaic	CVC	❥				
Fula (Pulaar)	Niger-Congo	CVC	❥				
Gana-Khwe (‖ Ani)[d]	Khoisan	CVC					❥

Language	Family						
Halang	Austro-Asiatic	CVC					
Hindi	Indo-European	CVC	♥	♥	(♥)	(♥)	
Hixkaryana	Carib	CVC[13]	♥	♥		♥	
Huasteco	Mayan	CVC	♥ CVV(C)				
Huave (de San Mateo del Mar)	Huavean	CVC	♥				
Hupa	Na Dene	CVC	♥ CVV(C)				
Inuktitut, North Alaskan	Eskimo-Aleut	CVC					
Iraqw	Afro-Asiatic	CVC	♥ CVV(C)				
Irish (Munster)	Indo-European	CVC	♥ [14] CVV > Cax > CV		♥		
Javanese[e]	Austronesian	CVC	♥ Full V				
Karok	Hokan	CVC	♥ CVV(C)				
Khalkha	Altaic	CVC	♥ CVV(C)				

(continued)

Table 5.5. Languages with minimal word requirements *(continued)*

Language	Macro-Phylum	Minim. Word	Stress	Metrics	Comp Length	Syll. Templ.	Tone
Khamti	Daic	CVC					◆ CVV(C), CVR
Khmer	Austro-Asiatic	CVC	♥				
Khmu	Austro-Asiatic	CVC					
Kiliwa	Hokan	CVC					◆ CVV(C)
Kiowa	Kiowa-Tanoan	CVC				♥	◆ CVV(C), CVR
Koasati	Muskogean	CVC	◆ CVV(C)			♥	
Kolami	Dravidian	CVC					
Koya	Dravidian	CVC	♥			(♥)	
Kung (Zu|ʼHõasĩ)[d]	Khoisan	CVC				♥	
Lao	Daic	CVC					◆ CVV(C), CVR

						CVV(C), CVR	CVV(C), CVR
Lithuanian	Indo-European	CVC				◆	◆
Luiseño	Uto-Aztecan	CVC	◆ CVV(C)			♥	
Malayalam	Dravidian	CVC	◆ CVV(C)	♥			
Malay[c]	Austronesian	CVC	◆ Full V, CVC				
Mam	Mayan	CVC	♥, ◆				
Mangbetu	Nilo-Saharan	CVC					
Miwok, Sierra	Penutian	CVC	♥			♥	
Mixe, Totontepec	Mixe-Zoque	CVC					
Moghol	Altaic	CVC					
Murik	Trans New Guinea	CVC	◆ CVV(C)				
Nahuatl	Uto-Aztecan	CVC					
Naro[d]	Khoisan	CVC					♥

(continued)

Table 5.5. Languages with minimal word requirements (*continued*)

Language	Macro-Phylum	Minim. Word	Stress	Metrics	Comp Length	Syll. Templ.	Tone
Nung	Sino-Tibetan	CVC				◆ CVV(C), CVR^n	
Old Icelandic	Indo-European	CVC		❤			
Oromo	Afro-Asiatic	CVC					
Paiwanᶜ	Austronesian	CVC					
Sapuan	Austro-Asiatic	CVC					
Sarangani Manoboᶜ	Austronesian	CVC	◆ Full V, CVC				
Shilluk	Nilo-Saharan	CVC					◆ [15] CVV(C)
Sierra Popoluca	Mixe-Zoque	CVC				◆ CVV?	
Somali	Afro-Asiatic	CVC					◆ CVV(C)
Tamil	Dravidian	CVC (CVCV)[16]	❤,◆	❤			
Telefol	Trans New Guinea	CVC					◆ CVV(C)

Language	Family						
Telugu	Dravidian	CVC	♦ CVV(C)	♥	♥		
Tepehuan	Uto-Aztecan	CVC	♥				
Ternate[e]	West Papuan	CVC					
Thai	Daic	CVC[17]		♥	♥[18]		♦ CVV(C), CVR
Tolojolabal[e]	Mayan	CVC	♦ CVV(C)				
Tonkawa	Coahuiltecan	CVC					
Totonac (Misantla)	Totonacan	CVC	♥				
Tubatulabal	Uto-Aztecan	CVC	♦ CVV(C)				
Turkish	Altaic	CVC[19]	♥		♥		
Tzutujil	Penutian	CVC					
Uzbek	Altaic	CVC			♥		
Wintu	Penutian	CVC	♦ CVV(C)				
Wolof	Niger-Congo	CVC	♦ CVV(C)				
Yucatecto	Mayan	CVC					
Yukaghir	Yukaghir	CVC					

(continued)

Table 5.5. Languages with minimal word requirements (*continued*)

Language	Macro-Phylum	Minim. Word	Stress	Metrics	Comp Length	Syll. Templ.	Tone
Yupik, Central	Eskimo-Aleut	CVC	(♥)			♥	
Yupik, Pacific Gulf	Eskimo-Aleut	CVC	(♥)			♥	
Yupik, Sirenik^e	Eskimo-Aleut	CVC					
Yurok	Algic	CVC			♥		
Estonian	Uralic	CVCCC, CVVV	♥				
Greek (Classical)	Indo-European	CVVC, CVCC	♥	♥			♦ CVV(C)
Menomini	Algic	CVVC	♦ CVV(C)				
Arabela	Zaparoan	CVCV					
Arawak^e	Arawakan	CVCV					
Aymara	Aymara	CVCV					
Cashinahua	Panoan	CVCV					
Cayuga	Iroquoian	CVCV					
Chamorro	Austronesian	CVCV					
Coreguaje^a,e	Tucanoan	CVCV					
Djingili	Australian	CVCV					

Language	Family										
Inuktitut, Greenlandic	Eskimo-Aleut	CVCV									
Jaqaru	Aymara	CVCV									
Karao[e]	Austronesian	CVCV									
Nyawaygi	Australian	CVCV									
Ocaina[20]	Witotoan	CVCV									
Onondaga	Iroquoian	CVCV									
Quechua, Huallaga	Quechan	CVCV									
Quechua, Inga[e]	Quechan	CVCV									
Quechua, Junin–Huanca	Quechan	CVCV									
Quicha	Quechan	CVCV									
Seneca	Iroquoian	CVCV									
Sumbanese[a]	Austronesian	CVCV									
Warembori	isolate	CVCV									
Yawelmani	Penutian	CVCV									
Andoke[21]	isolate	CVV									♥
Banawá[a]	Arawakan	CVV									
Barasano[a,b]	Tucanoan	CVV									

(continued)

Table 5.5. Languages with minimal word requirements (*continued*)

Language	Macro-Phylum	Minim. Word	Stress	Metrics	Comp Length	Syll. Templ.	Tone
Cebuano	Austronesian	CVV	◆ CVV(C), CVC				
Chacobo	Panoan	CVV					
Chickasaw	Muskogean	CVV	♥, ◆			◆ CVV(C), CVC	
Comanche	Uto-Aztecan	CVV	♥				
Fijian[a]	Austronesian	CVV	♥				
Finnish	Uralic	CVV	◆ CVV(C), CVC	◆ CVV(C), CVC		◆ CVV(C), CVC	
Guahibo[a]	Arawakan	CVV					
Guarani[a]	Tupi	CVV					
Kavalan	Austronesian	CVV[22]					
Kawaiisu[a][23]	Uto-Aztecan	CVV	♥				
Ket	Yenisei Ostyak	CVV					
Larike	Austronesian	CVV					
Maithili[a][24]	Indo-European	CVV	♥, ◆				

Language	Family					
Malagasy[a]	Austronesian	CVV	♦			
Marubu	Panoan	CVV			♦ n	
Mocha	Afro-Asiatic	CVV				
Mura-Pirahã[a]	Mura	CVV	♦			
Murut	Austronesian	CVV				
Sámi, Eastern	Uralic	CVV				♦ CVV(C), CVC
Sámi, Northern	Uralic	CVV				♦ CVV(C), CVC
Siona[a]	Tucanoan	CVV				
Tiriyo[b]	Carib	CVV				
Tiwi[a] 25	Australian	CVV				
Urim[b] 26	Torricelli	CVV[27]	♦ Full V			
Votic	Uralic	CVV	♦ CVV(C), CVC			
Warao[a][b]	isolate	CVV				
Winnebago	Siouan	CVV	♦			

weight uniformity, since the disyllabic minimal word requirement operates on the level of the syllable rather than the segmental level. They are thus not considered in the discussion that follows.

In three languages (Czech, Tsou and Kashuyana), the minimal word is either CCV or CVC. In all three languages, the CCV words result from loss of the first vowel, either synchronically or diachronically, in an originally disyllabic word.

Of the 119 remaining languages with minimal word requirements greater than CV but less than disyllables and which are not sensitive to the onset, 13 lack both long vowels and diphthongs. Of the remaining 106 languages, 83 have a CVC minimal word requirement, and 18 have a CVV minimal word requirement (excluding languages without coda consonants). One language (Menomini) has a CVVC minimal word requirement and, in one language (Classical Greek), the minimal word is either CVVC or CVCC. In one language (Estonian), the minimal word is either an overlong vowel (CVVV) or a syllable closed by an overlong consonant (CVCCC). In two languages (Au and Maru), the minimal word must contain a full vowel. In one language (Kwakw'ala), the minimal word contains a low vowel. If we collapse all languages that have minimal word requirements that treat codas as weighted (CVC; CVC or CCV; CVVV or CVCCC; CVVC or CVCC; CVVC) and also possess codas and either long vowels or diphthongs, there are a total of 86 languages in which codas contribute toward the calculation of the minimal word. Thus, there is a heavy skewing in favor of languages in which codas contribute toward satisfying the minimal word requirement.

The uniformity of weight criteria for minimal word requirements and weight criteria for other processes has already been considered either in Chapter Two (stress and tone) or earlier in this chapter (compensatory lengthening, metrics, syllable template restrictions). The comparison of weight criteria for these processes with weight observed by minimal word requirements is summarized in Table 5.6.

Table 5.6. Weight uniformity between minimal word requirements and other phenomena

	Agree	Disagree
Compensatory lengthening	**9**	**1**
Stress	18	26
Metrics	**9**	**1**
Syllable templates	**9**	**8**
Tone	3	11

The number of weight matches and mismatches between minimal word requirements and syllable templates is nearly identical.[29] The number of mismatches far exceeds the number of matches in the case of tone bearing units; this result is not surprising given the predominance of the CVC minimal word requirement and the virtual absence of languages that draw a weight distinction between open and closed syllables for tone. The number of mismatches also is much greater than the number of matches in the case of stress.[30] The number of weight matches between minimal word requirements and both metrics and compensatory lengthening is quite high relative to the number of mismatches. However, this is more a result of the process internal distribution of weight for these phenomena rather than an indication of language internal weight uniformity. Recall that all metrical systems in the survey treat both CVV(C) and CVC as heavy. Thus, given the predominance of the CVC minimal word requirement, the large number of matches between metrics and compensatory lengthening is expected. The uniformity between compensatory lengthening and minimal word requirements is due to the fact that compensatory lengthening cannot diagnose the weight of CVV(C) syllables relative to CVC syllables.

In summary, comparison of weight criteria for minimal word requirements with weight criteria for other phenomena argues against the hypothesis that weight is a property of languages. Rather the overwhelming tendency toward language internal consistency of weight criteria for minimal word requirements across languages argues for the process specific basis of weight.

5.3.1. The Basis for Minimal Word Requirements

The minimal word requirement is perhaps the most difficult weight-sensitive phenomenon to explain, even though it is so pervasive cross-linguistically. The most common minimal word requirement is CVC, although the CVV and the disyllabic minimal word requirement are attested in a significant minority of languages. I will speculate here on some possible motivations for minimal word requirements.

It is possible that the minimal word requirement is motivated by a requirement that content words must possess sufficient amounts of some phonetic property, perhaps energy, to increase their perceptual salience. We might suppose that the CVC minimal word requirement is found in languages that set a relatively low limit on minimal energy in a word, whereas the CVV minimal word requirement is found in languages with a higher minimal threshold. Note, however, that this account does not explain in any obvious way the preference for a minimal word of CVCV over CVV found in many languages, assuming that the domain of energy calculation is the syllable rime and long vowels are approximately twice as long as short vowels.

An alternative, which perhaps seems more plausible, is that the CVC minimal word requirement is rooted in duration, while the CVV and the CVCV minimal word are grounded in intonational considerations. Thus, languages that tolerate both CVC and CVV words but not CV words require that words be a minimal duration. Languages which allow CVV but not CVC or CV words require that words support a minimal intonation contour, which, following the argument behind weight-sensitive tone and pitch accent in Chapter Three, must be realized on the most sonorant segments, vowels. This account, like the energy-based one proposed in the previous paragraph, does not provide an obvious account of the choice of a CVCV minimal word over a CVV one in many languages. Perhaps closer examination of these languages on a case-by-case basis would provide some insight into this issue. Furthermore, it would predict that many languages would observe a CVR minimal word requirement.

Another possibility, which *a priori* seems untenable in its strongest form is that minimal word requirements reflect an attempt to maximize the amount of total material in a morpheme (irrespective of whether the material occurs in the onset or rime), in order to increase the chances of its being recovered in a string of speech. Following this reason, a CVC word is better than a CV one, since there is more material in a CVC word to allow for easier lexical access. However, if this were the primary motivating force behind minimal word requirements, we might expect onsets to play a greater role in minimal word requirements. In other words, one might expect it to be less necessary for a word to have an onset consonant, the longer the word. One might thus expect there to be languages which do not tolerate VC words but which allow CVC and VCV words. However, onsets typically do not figure in the calculation of minimal word requirements, contra this prediction.

Another hypothesis suggested here might link minimal word requirements to a desire to avoid neutralization of phonemic contrasts in conjunction with some combination of stress, final lengthening and the tendency for segment duration to be inversely correlated with number of syllables. These latter three factors have been shown to be operative in many languages of the world. Stress syllables are longer than unstressed syllables in many languages, perhaps the result of hyperarticulation of stressed targets (De Jong 1995) or an attempt to enhance the perceptual prominence of stressed syllables, or some combination of both of these factors. Typically, segments, particularly vowels, are lengthened cross-linguistically at the right edge of prosodic domains (Wightman et al. 1992), reflecting the tendency for gestures in final position to be slowed down (Beckman et al. 1992). Finally, the length of segments is typically inversely correlated with the number of syllables in a word, i.e. the shorter the word, the longer individual segments are. This phenomenon may be viewed as a type of word isochrony, or an attempt to produce words of approximately equivalent durations, perhaps for rhythmic purposes (Lindblom and Rapp 1973).

Together, final lengthening, stress, and the short duration of monosyllabic words would conspire to have a dramatic lengthening effect on monosyllabic content words, most notably the vowels. For this reason, maintaining a contrast between phonemic short and phonemic long vowels could conceivably be difficult in monosyllabic words, particularly those not ending in a consonant, an environment likely to experience the greatest amount of final vowel lengthening. That a vowel length contrast in final position is difficult to maintain is demonstrated by the existence of a number of languages in which vowel length is not contrastive in word-final position, e.g. Kiowa, Wintu, Khmer, Halang, Lao, Thai. If, however, minimal word requirements were attributed solely to word-final vowel lengthening, then one would not expect minimal word requirements in languages without vowel length contrasts, where there is no threat of loss of contrast. In fact, a great many languages without vowel length contrasts have CVC minimal word requirements.

In summary, although many of the hypotheses about the motivation behind minimal word requirements seem promising in certain respects, there are pieces of data that are not readily accounted for. The basis for minimal word requirements clearly needs further investigation, including meticulous evaluation of criteria for establishing minimal word requirements and systematic searches of lexicons and dictionaries to determine statistical patterns. It is hoped that the discussion in this section may provide some useful ways of thinking about minimal word requirements. For further discussion of minimal word requirements and their possible motivations, the interested reader is referred to Garrett (1999).

5.4. SYLLABLE TEMPLATES

There were 58 languages with prohibitions against long vowels in either all closed syllables, syllables closed by two consonants, or syllables closed by a certain type of consonant, either a geminate or a sonorant. These languages are shown in Table 5.7.

Of the 58 languages, all but three are sensitive neither to the quality of the vowel nor to the sonority of the coda consonant nor to whether the

Table 5.7. Languages with restrictions on long vowels in closed syllables

Notes: A superscripted [a] indicates that the language does not have codas. A superscripted [b] indicates an absence of phonemic long vowels. A superscripted [c] indicates an absence of non-sonorant codas. A superscripted [d] indicates an absence of phonemic long vowels and diphthongs. R stands for a sonorant coda. OSVL stands for stressed vowel lengthening that is confined to open syllables.

Language	Macro-Phylum	Syll. Templ.	Stress	Metrics	Comp Length	Tone	Minim. Word
!Xoo[d]	Khoisan	*CVVC				♥	♥
Ainu [31]	isolate	OSVL	♥[32]				
Atayal	Austronesian	*CVVC					
Aymara	Aymara	*CVVC	♦ CVV(C)				
Berbice[b]	Creole	*CVVC					
Carib	Carib	*CVVC	♥				
Cayuga	Iroquoian	OSVL	♦ CVV(C)				
Chickasaw	Muskogean	OSVL	♥, ♦				♦ CVV(C)
Cora	Uto-Aztecan	*CVVC					
Cuna	Chibchan	*CVVC	♥				
Gana-Khwe (‖ Ani)[d]	Khoisan	*CVVC				♥	♥
Hausa	Afro-Asiatic	*CVVC		♥		♥	

Language							
Hindi	Indo-European	*CVVC[33]	(♥)[34]	(♥)	♥		(♥)
Hikkaryana[c]	Carib	OSVL	♥				♥[35]
Hmong, Green[b]	Miao-Yao	*CVVC					
Hualapai	Hokan	OSVL					
Japanese	Japanese	*CVVC		♥			
Kabiye[d]	Niger-Congo	*CVVC				♥	
Kiowa	Kiowa-Tanoan	*CVVC				♦ CVV(C), CVR	♥
Koasati	Muskogean	*CVVC	♦ CVV(C)				♥
Koya	Dravidian	*CVVC (gemin.)	(♥)				(♥)
Krongo	Niger-Congo	*CVVC	♦ CVV(C)			♦ CVV(C)	
Kunama	Nilo-Saharan	*CVVC	♦ CVV(C)				
Kung (Zu|'Hõasi)[d]	Khoisan	*CVVC				♦ CVV(C)	
Luganda	Niger-Congo	*CVVC				♥	

(continued)

Table 5.7. Languages with restrictions on long vowels in closed syllables *(continued)*

Language	Macro-Phylum	Syll. Templ.	Stress	Metrics	Comp Length	Tone	Minim. Word
Luiseño	Uto-Aztecan	*CVVC	● CVV(C)				●
Macushi	Carib	OSVL	●				
Maidu (Northeast)	Penutian	OSVL	●				
Maru[b]	Sino-Tibetan	*CVVC				● CVV(C), CVR	● Full V
Miwok, Sierra	Penutian	*CVVC	●				●
Mohawk	Iroquoian	OSVL					
Mulwi	Afro-Asiatic	*CVVC					
Mundari[b]	Austro-Asiatic	*CVVC	● VʔC)				
Musey	Afro-Asiatic	*CVVC			●	●	
Nambiquara, S.	Nambiquaran	*CVVC					
Nambiquara, N.	Nambiquaran	OSVL	●				

Oneida	Iroquoian	OSVL[36]	♥							
Onondaga	Iroquoian	OSVL[37]								
Patep	Austronesian	OSVL	◆ Full V		♥					
Quechua, Huallaga	Quechan	*CVVC	◆ CVV(C)							
Quechua, Junin-Huanca	Quechan	*CVVC	◆ CVV(C)							
Quileute	Chimakuan	OSVL								
Runga	Nilo-Saharan	*CVVC								
Selkup	Uralic	OSVL	◆ CVV(C)							
Tolowa	Na Dene	*CVVC								
Tura[d]	Niger-Congo	*CVVC								
Yana	Hokan	*CVVC	♥							
Yawelmani	Penutian	*CVVC								

(continued)

Table 5.7. Languages with restrictions on long vowels in closed syllables (*continued*)

Language	Macro-Phylum	Syll. Templ.	Stress	Metrics	Comp Length	Tone	Minim. Word
Yupik, Central	Eskimo-Aleut	OSVL³	(♥)				(♥)
Yupik, Pacific Gulf	Eskimo-Aleut	OSVL	(♥)				(♥)
Pacoh[b]	Austro-Asiatic	*CFullVC *CVVC[38]					
Lithuanian	Indo-European	*CVVR	.			♥	◆ CVV(C), CVC
Nootka	Wakashan	*CVVR	♥				
Finnish	Uralic	*CVVCC	♥	♥			◆ CVV(C)
Sámi, Eastern	Uralic	*CVVCC					◆ CVV(C)
Sámi, Northern	Uralic	*CVVCC					◆ CVV(C)
Zuni	isolate	*CVVCC					

coda is the first half of a geminate or not. In most languages, this prohibition holds both lexically and on the surface. In other languages (16 in the survey), however, the constraint does not operate on underlying forms or on forms created through morphological concatenation. Rather, in these languages, coda consonants block lengthening of vowels which would otherwise be expected to lengthen due to stress. If we combine languages that observe an absolute restriction against long vowels in closed syllables with languages that block vowel lengthening in all closed syllables but allow underlying CVVC to surface, most languages with weight-related restrictions on syllable templates treat all coda consonants uniformly, i.e. observe the CVV(C), CVC heavy criterion. (Long vowels are trivially heavy by virtue of the fact that they count toward the upper weight limit per syllable.)

Only two languages ban long vowels in syllables closed by a sonorant (Lithuanian, Nuuchahnulth), but allow long vowels in syllables closed by an obstruent. Thus, vanishingly few languages observe the CVV(C) and CVR heavy criterion for syllable templates. These cases will be discussed below in section 5.4.2. In Hindi and Koya, there is a restriction against long vowels in syllables closed by the first half of a geminate. One language (Pacoh) disallows closed syllables containing a full vowel or a diphthong.

An important fact when comparing weight criteria for syllable template restrictions with weight criteria for other phenomena is that syllable template restrictions inherently treat consonants as heavy, since it is the combination of a long vowel (or full vowel in the case of Pacoh) plus a coda consonant that violates the maximal template. Thus, unlike for processes such as stress, metrics, minimal words, and tone, there is no possibility of a language observing the CVV(C) heavy criterion.

In Table 5.8, we see that once again, there is no reliable tendency for weight as diagnosed by syllable templates to agree with weight as diagnosed by other processes. Note that, as before, hearts and diamonds in parentheses are not included in Table 5.8.

Table 5.8. Weight uniformity between syllable template restrictions and other phenomena

	Agree	Disagree
Compensatory lengthening	3	0
Stress	11	11
Metrics	3	0
Tone	7	4
Minimal Word	7	6

The number of matches and mismatches in weight criteria for syllable templates and weight criteria for stress and minimal word requirements is approximately equal or equal. The greatest uniformity is between syllable templates and metrics, tone, and compensatory lengthening. In the case of metrics and compensatory lengthening, once again the convergence is an artifact of the process specificity of weight for the phenomena being examined. Recall from earlier discussion that virtually all languages treat both long vowels and all coda consonants as heavy for syllable templates. If this fact is combined with the observation that all weight-sensitive survey metrical systems treat both CVV(C) and CVC as heavy (see section 5.2), there are virtually guaranteed to be no weight mismatches between syllable templates and metrics. Furthermore, compensatory lengthening can only diagnose the CVV(C), CVC heavy criterion; we would thus not expect there to be many, if any at all, disagreements between syllable templates and compensatory lengthening. There is also a tendency for weight for syllable templates to agree with weight for tone. This convergence in criteria is somewhat misleading, however, since three of the mismatches occur in languages lacking obstruent codas. Nevertheless, there are some striking cases of agreement between the two phenomena. Hausa, Luganda, and Musey have obstruent codas and treat all codas as weighted for both tone and syllable template restrictions. This convergence was addressed in Chapter Three, where it was suggested that the syllable template restriction facilitated the adoption of the CVV(C), CVC heavy criterion for tone. The employment of the CVV(C), CVR heavy criterion for tone and syllable templates in Lithuanian is also plausibly linked to the greater length of vowels in heavy syllables (see section 5.4.3 for phonetic data).

Let us now look more closely at weight criteria for syllable template restrictions as compared to weight criteria for minimal word requirements. There are 7 languages in which the weight criterion for syllable templates and the minimal word requirement match. There are 6 in which criteria for the two phenomena do not match. In four languages, both CVV(C) and CVC are heavy for syllable templates, whereas only CVV(C) is heavy for minimal words. In one language (Lithuanian), all coda consonants are heavy for minimal words, but only sonorants are heavy for syllable template restrictions. In another language (Maru), both CVV(C) and CVC are heavy for the syllable templates, but the minimal word treats full vowels as heavy. These results argue against consistency of weight criteria within individual languages. Furthermore, there is no consistent tendency for weight criteria to be any more or less restrictive for one phenomenon relative to the other.

In summary, the most robust observation that emerges from comparison of weight criteria for syllable templates with weight criteria for other processes is the overwhelming tendency for syllable templates to observe the same weight criterion (CVV(C) and CVC heavy) in all languages independent of weight criteria for other processes within those languages. Comparison of syllable templates and other weight-sensitive phenomena also argues against the hypothesis that weight is a function of languages.

5.4.1. The Basis for Syllable Template Restrictions

In considering possible explanations for syllable template restrictions, it is worthwhile to first explore the basis for the most common type of syllable template restriction, the one against long vowels in closed syllables. The avoidance of CVVC syllables plausibly follows from general principles of syllable isochrony that guide speech at some level. This principle of isochrony mandates that syllable durations fall within some prescribed language-specific range. The nearly universal phenomenon of closed syllable phonetic vowel shortening (Maddieson 1985) may be viewed as one manifestation of syllable isochrony; by shortening a vowel in a closed syllable, or, viewed the other way, lengthening a vowel in an open syllable, the duration difference between closed and open syllables is reduced. The tendency for the length of individual segments to be inversely correlated with the overall duration of a word (Lindblom and Rapp 1973) is another manifestation of isochrony applying at the level of a word. Prohibitions against long vowels in closed syllables plausibly reflect one manifestation of syllable isochrony, in this case by eliminating syllable types at the upper end of the duration hierarchy. Opposing the movement toward isochronous syllable durations are phenomena such as stressed syllable lengthening, vowel reduction, and final lengthening. Clearly the competition between these factors and the push for isochrony is sensitive to duration, as demonstrated by the asymmetrical lengthening of stressed vowels in open but not closed syllables in many languages. In such languages, it is desirable to lengthen stressed vowels in order to enhance their prominence, even though this potentially reduces isochrony. However, isochrony takes precedence when the lengthening of vowels would disrupt timing patterns substantially by creating a superheavy syllable containing both a coda consonant and a long vowel.

It can be seen from languages which restrict CVVC syllables but which treat codas as weightless for other weight-sensitive phenomena that syllable template restrictions are not sensitive to the "weight" of the syllable as traditionally conceived. Rather it is the phonological duration of the syllable, i.e. the length and number of segments, which is relevant for such restrictions. As a final note, there are some languages, e.g. Finnish, which set a higher upper limit of duration tolerated in a syllable. These languages allow CVVC and CVCC syllables but prohibit long vowels in doubly closed syllables, i.e. they do not allow CVVCC.

5.4.2. Prohibitions Against CVVR Syllables

There is one type of syllable template restriction that does not find an obvious explanation in terms of syllable isochrony: the restriction against long vowels in syllables closed by a sonorant. Though this restriction is quite rare compared to the restriction against CVVC syllables, where the sonority of the coda is irrelevant, it is nevertheless attested in two languages in the survey, Lithuanian and Nuuchahnulth. Early Greek is yet another language not included in the survey that prohibited long vowels in syllables closed by a sonorant (Allen 1973, Steriade 1991).

Strikingly, in all three of these languages, not only do sonorant coda consonants contribute weight for purposes of syllable template restrictions, they also contribute weight for either tone (Lithuanian, Early Greek) or stress (Nuuchahnulth). While the mere convergence of weight criteria between two phenomena in a pair of languages may perhaps itself not be any more than accidental, there are two pieces of data that suggests that the convergences under consideration here are due not just to chance. First, the restriction against CVVR syllables (Osthoff's Law) in Early Greek was lifted at the same time (or approximately the same time) as CVR syllables became no longer able to carry contour tones. The (virtually) simultaneous switching of weight criteria for the two phenomena in Greek seems unlikely to be mere coincidence. Furthermore, the Nuuchahnulth stress system treats both CVV(C) and CVR as heavy to the exclusion of CVO. This uniformity of weight criteria between syllable templates and stress in Nuuchahnulth is striking, since the CVV(C), CVR heavy weight criterion is cross-linguistically so rare for both phenomena.

In this section, we will explore not only the motivation behind the language specific observance of the CVV(C), CVR heavy criterion for syllable template restrictions, but also the convergence of this weight criterion with the weight criterion for tone in Lithuanian and Early Greek and for stress in Nuuchahnulth. The approach adopted here to account for the convergence of weight criteria between syllable template restrictions and other phenomena will be to focus in some depth on the syllable template restriction against CVVR and then, using the results from this study, conjecture on the relationship between syllable template restrictions and phenomena like tone and stress. To do this, we will consider data from Lithuanian, a language that both has a restriction against CVVR syllables and treats syllables containing sonorant codas as heavy for tone.

5.4.3. The Durational Basis of Syllable Template Restrictions: The Case of Lithuanian

The particularly challenging aspect of the Lithuanian weight system to account for is not the observance of the CVV(C), CVR heavy criterion for tone, since it was demonstrated in Chapter Three that not only is this criterion common for tone, but that a measure of coda duration predicts it to be the criterion employed by Lithuanian. Rather, the superficially problematic aspect of Lithuanian weight that must be accounted for is the restriction against long vowels in syllables closed by a sonorant,[39] since syllable template restrictions typically appear to be driven by considerations of syllable isochrony. In order for durational isochrony to account for the restriction against CVVR in languages like Lithuanian, Nuuchahnulth, and Early Greek, we would want evidence that CVVR, if it were to surface, would be much longer than CVVO. One way to garner such evidence is to compare the duration of short-voweled syllables closed by a sonorant (CVR) with the duration of short-voweled syllables closed by a obstruent (CVO). If CVR were substantially longer than CVO, one can assume, all else being equal, that CVVR, if tolerated, would be much longer than CVVO. Thus, the constraint against CVVR could be explained in terms of an upper limit on duration tolerated per syllable rime; CVVR is discriminated against, because it would be too long.

In order to test the hypothesis that the constraint against CVVR is durationally driven, several words containing CVR or CVO were read by a native Lithuanian during the same session in which words for the experiment described in Chapter Three were elicited. Six tokens of each word were read in isolation in a sound booth and then digitized and analyzed using Kay CSL. Words contained two syllables, the first of which was low-toned (i.e. unaccented) and served as the target syllable. The vowel was /a/ and the coda consonants were systematically varied between /n/, /l/, /r/ (sonorants) and /g/, /p/ (obstruents). The elicited words appear in Appendix Three. Average durations for the various rime types appear in Table 5.9, in which the total rime duration is in boldface.

Table 5.9. Duration of unaccented rimes (in milliseconds) in Lithuanian

	Sonorant codas			Obstruent codas	
	an	**al**	**ar**	**ag**	**ap**
Vowel	127	121	131	104	70
Coda	159	121	80	76	100
Total	**286**	**242**	**211**	**180**	**170**

Results indicate that the rime in CVR is in fact much longer than the rime in CVO, as predicted by the hypothesis that the restriction against CVVR is durationally driven. The difference between CVR and CVO was found to be statistically significant by an analysis of variance in which syllable type served as the independent variable: F [1, 27] = 34.039, p<.0001. The duration difference between CVR and CVO is most reliably attributed to differences in the duration of the vowel: the vowel is much longer before a tautosyllabic sonorant than before a tautosyllabic obstruent, a difference which was found to be statistically significant: F [1, 27] = 31.301, p<.0001. Coda duration is also significantly longer in CVR than in CVO: F [1, 27] = 7.659, p=.0101, though this effect is smaller than the one attributed to the vowel. Furthermore, across consonants, coda length is not as reliable as vowel length in separating CVR from CVO, since the coda sonorant /r/ is actually shorter than the coda obstruent /p/.

All else being equal and assuming, in particular, a fixed duration ratio between long and short vowels, the durational difference between CVVO and CVVR would be predicted to be even greater than that between CVO and CVR, due to the inherent vowel length difference between presonorant and preobstruent vowels. To verify the hypothesis that the restriction against CVVR is duration-based, one would want to examine a broader set of syllable types, including those closed by other nasals and stops and by fricatives. The results presented here, though, offer support for the view that the restriction against CVVR syllables is attributed to an upper threshold of duration tolerated in a single syllable.

Before concluding this section, let us consider some additional evidence suggesting that syllable isochrony plays a role in Lithuanian prosody. Lithuanian displays a process of vowel lengthening which affects non-final /a/ and /ɛ/ (there is no /ɔ/ in the native vocabulary) carrying a high tone (i.e. accented) subject to certain morphophonological restrictions, e.g. láːnda 'hole' (< lánda) (Kenstowicz 1972). These lengthened vowels are, in fact, marked as long in the Lithuanian orthography, suggesting that the lengthening effect is quite substantial. If the restriction against long vowels in syllables closed by a sonorant is due to an upper limit of duration allowed per syllable, one might expect accented vowel lengthening to be subject to some compression effect, whereby the phonetically longer vowels (i.e. those before sonorants) are limited in the degree of lengthening which they may undergo. Phonetically shorter vowels (i.e. those before obstruents), on the other hand, could lengthen to a greater degree without exceeding the duration threshold tolerated in a single rime.

In order to investigate this hypothesis, duration data for lengthened /a/ were collected from a series of disyllabic words in which the coda of the first syllable (the target syllable) was varied between /n/, /l/, /r/, /p/. The duration of the vowel and the total rime for the high-toned vowels appear in Table 5.10, along with the duration ratio of accented vowels to their unaccented counterparts. The words elicited appear in Appendix Three.

Interestingly, the unlengthened vowel which was shortest, the one before /p/, is the one which undergoes the greatest amount of accentual lengthening. Conversely, the unlengthened vowel which was longest, the one before /r/, undergoes the smallest amount of accentual lengthening. Although there is not a perfect inverse correlation between the duration of unlengthened vowels and the duration of lengthened vowels (unlengthened /a/ before /n/ is longer than unlengthened /a/ before /l/, but nevertheless undergoes slightly more lengthening), as a whole, vowels before sonorants undergo much less lengthening than vowels before obstruents. The gap between the longest and shortest lengthened vowel is only 23 milliseconds as compared to the gap of 61 milliseconds between the longest and shortest unlengthened vowel, suggesting that a compression effect is at work. If there were no compression effect and the degree of lengthening were the same across vowels we would have expected the gap to grow under accented conditions, contra the actual results. The compression of the lengthened vowels has the effect of reducing differences in the overall duration of rimes. Whereas the duration difference between the longest and shortest unaccented rime is 116 milliseconds, the comparable difference under accented conditions is only 70 milliseconds.

In summary, comparison of lengthened and unlengthened vowel duration suggests that Lithuanian syllable duration is constrained by an upper limit of duration allowed in a single syllable. In Lithuanian, the phonological cut-off corresponding to this phonetic threshold falls between CVVR and CVVO; CVVO is permitted whereas CVVR is not. The imposition of this

Table 5.10. Duration of accented rimes (in milliseconds) in Lithuanian

	Sonorant codas		Obstruent coda	
	aːn	aːl	aːr	aːp
Vowel	186	173	178	163
Rime	331	263	261	264
Ratio of accented to unaccented vowel	1.46	1.43	1.36	2.33

upper threshold may be viewed as one manifestation of a syllable isochrony effect that constrains the overall durational variation between syllables.

5.4.4. Convergence of Weight Criteria Between Tone and Syllable Template Restrictions: The Case of Lithuanian

We are now in a position to investigate the convergence in weight criteria between syllable templates and tone in Lithuanian and Early Greek and between syllable templates and stress in Nuuchahnulth. Having examined phonetic data on weight-based tone and syllable template restrictions, we are in a better position to account for the convergence in weight criteria in Lithuanian and Early Greek than the convergence in Nuuchahnulth.

Based on the data we have seen, it would appear that phonetic duration is ultimately responsible for the observance of the CVV(C), CVR heavy criterion by both tone and syllable template restrictions. Both phenomena are sensitive to the duration of the coda sonorant. We saw in Chapter Three that coda duration is a good predictor of whether a language will adopt the CVV(C) heavy or the CVV(C), CVR heavy criterion for tone. If coda sonorants are relatively long in a given language, then that language adopts the CVV(C), CVR heavy criterion. All else being equal, greater duration of the coda sonorant will also contribute to increased length in syllables closed by a sonorant, making them more prone to exceed the upper duration limit tolerated in a single syllable. Thus, greater duration in sonorant codas increases the likelihood of a language observing the CVV(C), CVR heavy criterion for both tone and syllable template restrictions. We might thus speculate that a single phonetic event, namely the shortening of coda sonorants, was responsible for the shift in Greek from the CVV(C), CVR heavy criterion to the CVV(C) heavy criterion for tone and the simultaneous lifting of the restriction against CVVR syllables.

The convergence of weight criteria between stress and syllable template restrictions in Nuuchahnulth is also plausibly linked to the duration of coda sonorants in the following way. Following the discussion of syllable template restrictions, one would predict that syllables closed by a sonorant are much longer than syllables closed by an obstruent in Nuuchahnulth. Assuming this to be true, the difference in total energy, which was argued in Chapter Four to be the phonetic correlate of weight-sensitive stress, between syllables closed by a sonorant and syllables closed by an obstruent would be much greater, all else being equal, than in languages in which CVR and CVO do not differ as much in length. CVR would thus be more likely to be treated as heavy in a language in which it has substantially greater energy than CVO.

5.5. THE ROLE OF STRUCTURAL COMPLEXITY IN WEIGHT-SENSITIVE TONE

The Lithuanian phonetic data in section 5.4.3 also provide evidence for the importance of structural complexity for phenomena other than stress. The evidence to be discussed here comes from weight-sensitive tone. Recall from Chapter Three that the language specific choice of weight criteria in Lithuanian between CVV(C) heavy and CVV(C), CVR heavy is plausibly linked to the long duration of coda sonorants relative to the preceding vowel. It was suggested that Lithuanian chooses the CVV(C), CVR heavy criterion over the CVV(C) criterion, because sonorant codas are relatively long in Lithuanian compared to languages like Navajo, which choose the CVV(C) heavy criterion. The relevant phonetic support for this hypothesis was drawn from comparison of coda /n/ in languages like Navajo with languages like Lithuanian.

Assuming that the duration values for /n/ presented in Chapter Three are comparable to those for other sonorant codas in Lithuanian, the uniform behavior of sonorant codas as a class finds phonetic support. If, however, certain sonorant codas were much shorter than others, the uniform behavior of sonorants finds less phonetic justification. Instead we might expect an asymmetrical weight distinction whereby longer sonorant codas are heavier than shorter ones.

In fact, phonetic data on two other sonorant codas in Lithuanian, /l/ and /r/, was presented in the course of the discussion of syllable template restrictions in section 5.4.3 of this chapter. Table 5.11 repeats from Table 5.9 the durations of coda /n/, /l/ and /r/ in low-toned (i.e. unaccented) syllables both in absolute values and relative to short vowels (averaged over CV, CVO, and CVR in low-toned syllables) in Lithuanian.

Looking at these figures, in particular the relative duration of the sonorant, the largest gap in duration falls between /al/ and /ar/. Coda /l/

Table 5.11. Duration of different sonorant codas in Lithuanian

	Rime type		
	an	**al**	**ar**
Absolute duration of R (in milliseconds)	159	121	80
Relative to V	1.42	1.08	.71
Relative to V (averaged over sonorants)	**.95**		

and /n/ are both at least as long as the preceding vowel, whereas /r/ is much shorter than the preceding vowel. In fact, the duration of /r/ is shorter than that of Navajo coda /n/ (84 milliseconds) which is weightless for stress; the duration ratio of /r/ to the preceding vowel is also not much greater in Lithuanian than the duration ratio of /n/ (the sonorant coda measured in Navajo) to the preceding vowel in Navajo, .71 vs. .61. While it is possible that this small difference between languages could account for the fact that sonorant codas are weightless in Navajo but coda /r/ contributes weight in Lithuanian, it seems more plausible that a purely phonetically-driven grammar would draw its cut-off point between heavy and light somewhere else and treat syllables closed by /r/ as light for tone in Lithuanian.

A more plausible explanation for the uniform weight of /r/, /l/ and /n/ in Lithuanian is that the three are treated identically because they all belong to the class of sonorants. Under this account, which appeals to the notion of phonological simplicity following the discussion in Chapter Four, the duration of all members of the class of coda sonorants are factored in to calculate a measure of average duration encompassing all sonorant codas. Phonetically more effective alternatives to the actual Lithuanian weight distinction would be considered complex by the definition of complexity developed in Chapter Four and would thus be rejected. A hypothetical distinction which treats long vowels and syllables closed by a nasal as heavy would be too complex, since it requires disjoint representations for the heavy syllables, one for the long vowels and another for the syllables closed by a nasal (see section 4.4.3). Similarly, the hypothetical distinction that treats long vowels and syllables closed by a lateral would also be complex, since it too necessitates disjoint representations for the class of heavy syllables.

5.6. SUMMARY OF THE RESULTS OF THE WEIGHT TYPOLOGY

Analysis of syllable weight for phenomena other than stress and tone has produced several results, which corroborate those presented in the discussion of tone and stress in Chapter Two. Most crucially, syllable weight has been further shown in this chapter not to be a property of languages, contra the predictions made by most current theories of weight. This conclusion was reached by showing that, within languages displaying more than one weight-sensitive phenomenon, there is very little tendency for different phenomena within the same language to display the same weight criterion independent of the processes being considered. Most cases of language internal uniformity were attributed to the process specificity of weight for certain processes. The isolated cases of language internal uniformity of weight criteria that are non-accidental, e.g. stress and metrics (Chapter Four), syllable templates and tone in Lithuanian and Early Greek (section 5.4.4), syllable templates and stress in Nuuchahnulth (section 5.4.4) were argued to result from convergences in the phonetic factors conditioning the two phenomena. Furthermore, we have seen additional evidence in this chapter for the role of structural simplicity in establishing weight criteria.

Chapter Six
Conclusions

6.1. SUMMARY OF THE PRINCIPAL FINDINGS

This work has argued for a process specific account of syllable weight grounded in a combination of phonetic factors and considerations of phonological simplicity. The analysis of weight proposed here is based on a synthesis of typological, phonological, and phonetic work.

As a starting point in the investigation of syllable weight, a survey of several weight-sensitive phenomena in a set of roughly 400 genetically and areally diverse languages was conducted, results of which were discussed in Chapters Two and Five. The purpose of this survey was to investigate on a broad scale the standard hypothesis that syllable weight is a property of languages that behaves uniformly for different phenomena within the same language. Results of the survey disconfirmed this hypothesis of language-internal weight uniformity. With few exceptions, there was no tendency toward uniformity of weight criteria within languages. In fact, for many pairs of phenomena, the number of mismatches in weight criteria exceeded the number of cases of weight uniformity.

Rather than displaying uniformity within languages, weight was shown to have different distributions for different processes. The cases of language internal weight mismatches resulting from the process-driven nature of weight suggest the need for amendments to representations of the syllable designed to encode weight, such as moraic theories. Perhaps even more importantly, the results of the survey cast doubt on the fruitfulness of viewing syllable weight as a property of languages as opposed to processes.

Chapters Three and Four develop an alternative conception of syllable weight grounded in phonetic considerations. Focusing on weight-sensitive tone and stress, these chapters show that different phenomena may be sensitive to different phonetic requirements. The fact that the processes differ in their phonetic prerequisites leads to divergences in phonological weight criteria for different phenomena. The portion of the rime characterized by sonorant energy is the relevant domain for determining weight for tone, whereas weight-sensitive stress is sensitive to the energy profile of the entire rime.

On the level of specific languages, phonetic considerations were also shown to account for cross-linguistic variation in weight criteria for a single process. The language specific choice in weight criteria for a given phenomenon is linked to language specific phonetic differences. Many, but not all, of these language specific phonetic differences can in turn be attributed to differences between languages in other aspects of the phonological system. The model that thus emerges is one in which phonetics and phonology are interleaved. Certain language specific aspects of the phonology, such as segment inventories and syllable structure, along with other phonetic properties which cannot reliably be attributed to syllable structure or phoneme inventories, shape the phonetic map against which the phonetic goodness of potential phonological weight criteria is evaluated. For example, the inventory of coda consonants and the nature of the vowel inventory were shown to influence the energy profile of syllables, which in turn impacts the choice of weight criteria for stress.

The selection of weight criteria is not completely driven by considerations of phonetic goodness, however. Rather, the set of weight criteria being evaluated is constrained by a notion of phonological simplicity, which either filters out completely more complex weight criteria, or at the very least, acts as a guide in establishing the order in which weight criteria are tested against the phonetic data. This reliance on a combination of phonetic effectiveness and phonological simplicity results in adoption of weight criteria that are simultaneously both phonetically and phonologically sensible.

6.2. DIRECTIONS FOR FUTURE RESEARCH

Although the present work attempts to offer a fairly explicit and comprehensive account of syllable weight, it also raises a number of issues that have been left unresolved. Some of the more obvious questions for future research include the following.

While the present work has discussed weight-sensitive stress and tone in some depth, it has left other weight-sensitive phenomena open to further investigation. In particular, results of cross-linguistic surveys of four other weight-sensitive phenomena besides stress and tone were presented, but were not analyzed as thoroughly as stress and tone. For example, minimal word requirements were shown to be predominantly CVC, but reasons for the predominance of this criterion were only explored in cursory fashion. Likewise, the motivation behind other weight-sensitive phenomena is worthy of more in-depth explication than that offered here.

Furthermore, in the domain of weight-sensitive stress, we have left to future research the more complete integration of the stress constraints into a formal theory of metrical structure which is standardly assumed to consist of other elements, such as constraints against stress lapses and stress clashes, and constraints governing the construction of metrical feet. Clearly, this is a large task, but one which is nevertheless essential.

Another issue raised in the chapter dealing with weight-sensitive stress concerns the relevance of type frequency vs. token frequency in the phonetic evaluation of different syllable types. A simple measure of type frequency which weighs syllables equally whether they occur in ten words or a thousand words was shown in Chapter Four to be a good predictor of whether a language adopts the CVV(C) heavy or the CVV(C), CVC heavy criterion for stress. However, the possibility was also raised that a measure of token frequency could provide an even closer fit to the choice of phonological weight criteria, perhaps eliminating the languages which appear to behave exceptionally and/or perhaps creating an even better separation of languages according to their sonorant-to-obstruent and voiced-to-voiceless coda ratios.

Another interesting area for further research concerns the evaluation of phonetic effectiveness of different weight criteria on a language-specific basis. We saw that a measure of phonetic effectiveness computed by comparing mean values for different weight criteria provided an excellent fit to phonological weight for a wide variety of weight criteria. However, the mismatch between phonetic effectiveness and phonological weight in Javanese raised the question of whether languages might also be sensitive to the relative robustness of weight criteria in terms of the balance between numbers of heavy syllables and numbers of light syllables for a given distinction. It could be the case that weight distinctions are discriminated against if they have too few syllable types belonging to either the light or heavy camp. For example, in Javanese, it could be the case that the "Full V, CVC heavy" distinction is disfavored, because there are so few light syllables according to this distinction.

Another learnability issue of a different sort is raised by the Munster Irish weight distinction (Chapter Four), which was shown to exceed the complexity threshold honored by other languages. The Munster Irish data raise questions about the size and scope of the hypothesis space in the acquisition process. Assuming that the notion of complexity is relevant in the grammar and assuming that the Munster Irish weight distinction is complex relative to other distinctions, then it is unclear how the Munster Irish stress system came into existence and why it continues to be perpetuated rather than simplified. Clearly, inductive learning is crucial in the perpetuation of the stress pattern, but the precise relationship between evaluation of complexity and raw induction of phonological weight remains to be determined. A related issue concerns the relationship between induction and phonetic evaluation in the acquisition process.

Although these issues (among many others) must be left for future research, it is hoped that the present work provides a springboard for further investigation of syllable weight and, more generally, the role of notions such as phonetic effectiveness and phonological simplicity in phonological theory.

Appendix One

LANGUAGES, GENETIC AFFILIATIONS, REFERENCES

Language	Macro-Phylum	Reference(s)
!Xoo	Khoisan	Traill (1985), Miller-Ockhuizen (1998)
Abau	Sepik-Ramu	Bailey (1975)
Abelam	Trans New Guinea	Laycock (1965)
Abkhaz	North Caucasian	Hewitt (1989)
Achagua	Arawakan	Wilson (1992)
Acoma (Western Keres)	Keres	Miller (1965)
Aguacatec	Mayan	McArthur and McArthur (1956)
Ai-Cham	Daic	Lin and Jianxin (1988)
Ainu	isolate	Batchelor (1938), Refsing (1986), Majewicz and Majewicz (1986), Shibatani (1990)
Alamblak	Sepik-Ramu	Bruce (1984)
Alawa	Australian	Sharpe (1972)
Albanian	Indo-European	Hetzer (1978)
Aleut	Eskimo-Aleut	Bergsland (1994), Rozelle (1997)
Aljutor	Chukotko-Kamchatkan	Kodzasov and Muravyova (1978)
Amahuaca	Panaoan	Osborn (1948)
Amami (Shodon)	Japanese	Martin (1970)
Amele	Trans New Guinea	Roberts (1987)
Amharic	Afro-Asiatic	Hartmann (1980)

(continued)

(continued)

Language	Macro-Phylum	Reference(s)
Andamanese	Andamanese	Manoharan (1989)
Andoke	isolate	Landaburu (1979)
Anem	East Papuan	Thurston (1982)
Anufo	Niger-Congo	Stanford and Stanford (1970)
Apache, Chiracahua	Na Dene	Hoijer (1946a)
Apalaí	Carib	Koehn and Koehn (1986)
Apinaye	Macro-Ge	Burgess and Ham (1968)
Arabela	Zaparoan	Rich (1963)
Arabic	Afro-Asiatic	Harrell (1957, 1960), Mitchell (1960), Wright (1971), McCarthy (1979a,b), Owens (1984), Angoujard (1990), Schuh (1996)
Aramaic	Afro-Asiatic	Segert (1983)
Arapesh	Torricelli	Conrad (1991)
Araucanian	Araucanian	Echeverría and Contreras (1965)
Arawak	Arawakan	de Goeje (1928)
Asheninca Campa	Arawakan	Payne (1981), Payne et al. (1982), Payne (1990)
Assiniboine	Siouan	Levin (1964)
Atakapa	Gulf	Swanton (1929)
Atayal	Austronesian	Egerod (1966, 1980)
Au	Torricelli	Scorza (1985)
Aymara	Aymara	Briggs (1976)
Bagirmi	Nilo-Saharan	Stevenson (1969)
Banawá	Arawakan	Ladefoged et al. (1997)
Barasano	Tucanoan	Smith and Smith (1971), Stolte and Stolte (1971)
Bashkir	Altaic	Poppe (1964)
Basque	isolate	Saltarelli (1988), Hualde (1991), Elordieta (1997)
Belizean Creole	Creole	Greene (1999)
Berbice	Creole	Kouwenberg (1994)

(continued)

(continued)

Language	Macro-Phylum	Reference(s)
Bete	Niger-Congo	Werle (1976)
Biangai	Trans New Guinea	Dubert and Dubert (1973)
Blackfoot	Algic	Frantz (1991)
Bobo	Niger-Congo	Le Bris (1981)
Boiken	Sepik-Ramu	Freudenberg and Freudenberg (1974)
Brahui	Dravidian	Bray (1934)
Brao	Austro-Asiatic	Keller (1976)
Buriat	Altaic	Poppe (1960), Walker (1995, 1996)
Burmese	Sino-Tibetan	Okell (1969), Wheatley (1990)
Burushaski	isolate	Tiffou (1982)
Bushong	Niger-Congo	Vansina (1959)
Caddo	Caddoan	Chafe (1976)
Cakchiquel	Mayan	Grimes (1972)
Canela-Krahô	Macro-Ge	Popjes and Popjes (1986)
Cantonese	Sino-Tibetan	Kao (1971), Bauer and Benedict (1997)
Capanahua	Panoan	Loos (1969)
Carib	Carib	Hoff (1968)
Cashinahua	Panoan	Kensinger (1963)
Cavinena	Tacanan	Key (1968)
Cayapa	Paezan	Lindskoog and Brend (1962)
Cayubaba	isolate	Key (1961, 1967)
Cayuga	Iroquoian	Chafe (1977), Doherty (1993), Foster (1982), Michelson (1988)
Cebuano	Austronesian	Bunye and Yap (1971), Shryock (1993)
Chacobo	Panoan	Prost (1960)
Chamorro	Austronesian	Topping (1973), Chung (1983)
Cherokee	Iroquoian	Feeling (1975), Pulte and Feeling (1975), Cook (1979), Foley (1980), Munro (1996a), Scancarelli (1987), Wright (1996)

(continued)

(continued)

Language	Macro-Phylum	Reference(s)
Chickasaw	Muskogean	Munro and Willmond (1994), Munro (1996b, 2005), Gordon et al. (1997), Gordon (1999)
Chinantec, Comaltepec	Oto-Manguean	Anderson (1989), Anderson et al. (1990)
Ching	Daic	Dabai (1988)
Chitimacha	Gulf	Swadesh (1946)
Chontal	Mayan	González (1985)
Chukchi	Chukotko-Kamchatkan	Skorik (1961)
Chumash, Barbareño	Hokan	Beeler (1976)
Chuvash	Altaic	Krueger (1961)
Cofán	Chibchan	Borman (1962)
Comanche	Uto-Aztecan	Robinson (1990), Charney (1993)
Comox	Salish	Hagege (1981)
Cora	Uto-Aztecan	Casad (1984), McMahon (1967)
Coreguaje	Tucanoan	Gralow (1985)
Crow	Siouan	Kaschube (1967)
Cuna	Chibchan	Holmer (1947)
Czech	Indo-European	Kucera (1961), Sroufkova et al. (1987)
Dani	Trans New Guinea	Bromley (1981)
Didinga	Nilo-Saharan	Rosato (1980), Odden (1983)
Diegueño	Hokan	Langdon (1970, 1977), Couro and Hutcheson (1973)
Diola	Niger-Congo	Sapir (1965)
Dizi	Afro-Asiatic	Breeze (1988)
Djingili	Australian	Chadwick (1975)
Duala	Niger-Congo	Ittmann (1978)
Dumi	Sino-Tibetan	Driem (1993)
Dzongkha	Sino-Tibetan	Mazaudon and Michailovsky (1988)

(continued)

(continued)		
Language	**Macro-Phylum**	**Reference(s)**
Eipomek	Trans New Guinea	Heeschen (1983)
Émérillon	Tupi	Rose (2002)
English	Indo-European	Kiparsky (1989), Finegan (1990)
Estonian	Uralic	Hint (1973), Lehiste (1978), Saagpakk (1982)
Even (Lamut)	Altaic	Benzing (1955), Doerfer (1980)
Evenki	Altaic	Konstantinova (1964)
Fijian	Austronesian	Schütz (1985)
Finnish	Uralic	Sadeniemi (1949), Wuolle (1962), Kiparsky (1968), Hanson and Kiparsky (1996), Anttila (1997), Sulkala and Karjalainen (1992)
Fong	Niger-Congo	Guédou (1985)
French	Indo-European	Harris (1990)
Fula (Pulaar)	Niger-Congo	Prunet and Tellier (1984), Niang (1995)
Fur	Nilo-Saharan	Beaton (1968)
Gana-Khwe (‖ Ani)	Khoisan	Vossen (1986)
Georgian	South Caucasian	Zhgenti (1964), Aronson (1991)
Gilyak	isolate	Panfilov (1962)
Gondi	Dravidian	Steever (1998)
Greek (classical)	Indo-European	Joseph (1990), Steriade (1991)
Guahibo	Arawakan	Queixalós (1985)
Guarani	Tupi	Ayala (1996)
Gujarati	Indo-European	Cardona (1965)
Gurage	Afro-Asiatic	Polotsky (1951), Leslau (1992)
Gurung	Sino-Tibetan	Glover (1969)
Haida	NaDene	Lawrence (1977), Enrico (1991)
Haitian Creole	Creole	d'Ans (1968)
Halang	Austro-Asiatic	Cooper and Cooper (1966)
Halkomelem	Salishan	Galloway (1993)

(continued)

(continued)

Language	Macro-Phylum	Reference(s)
Hatsa	Khoisan	Dempwolff (1916–7)
Hausa	Afro-Asiatic	Newman (1990), Schuh (1996)
Hewa	Sepik-Ramu	Vollrath (1985)
Hindi	Indo-European	Kelkar (1968), Ohala (1977, 1983), McGregor (1993)
Hixkaryana	Carib	Derbyshire (1985)
Hmong, Green	Miao-Yao	Lyman (1979)
Hopi	Uto-Aztecan	Whorf (1946), Jeanne (1982), Seaman (1985)
Hualapai	Hokan	Redden (1966)
Huasteco	Mayan	Larsen and Pike (1949), Beller and Beller (1979)
Huave	Huavean	Ruiz de Bravo Ahuja (1983)
Huitoto	Witotoan	Minor and Minor (1976), Burtch (1983)
Hungarian	Uralic	Szinnyei (1912), Hall (1938), Sovijärvi (1956), Kerek (1971)
Hupa	Na Dene	Golla (1970, 1996), author's fieldnotes
Icelandic (Old)	Indo-European	Gordon (1927), Árnason (1980), Robinson (1992)
Ijo	Niger-Congo	Williamson (1965)
Inuktitut, Greenlandic	Eskimo-Aleut	Kleinschmidt (1968), Rischel (1974), Thalbitzer (1976), Fortescue (1984)
Inuktitut, North Alaskan	Eskimo-Aleut	Kaplan (1981)
Iraqw	Afro-Asiatic	Mous (1993)
Irish	Indo-European	Lewis and Pedersen (1937), Ó Siadhail (1989), Doherty (1991)
Japanese	Japanese	Shibatani (1990), Vance (1987)
Jaqaru	Aymara	Hardman-de-Bautista (1966)
Javanese	Austronesian	Herrfurth (1964), Horne (1974), Ras (1982)

(continued)

(continued)

Language	Macro-Phylum	Reference(s)
Jemez	Kiowa-Tanoan	Bell (1993)
Jivaro	Jivaroan	Beasley and Pike (1957)
Jukun	Niger-Congo	Shimizu (1980)
Júma	Tupi	Abrahamson and Abrahamson (1984)
Kabardian	North Caucasian	Abitov et al. (1957)
Kabiye	Niger-Congo	Delord (1976)
Kaingang	Macro-Ge	Wiesemann (1972)
Kalispel	Salishan	Vogt (1940)
Kamayurá	Tupi	Saelzer (1976)
Kamchadal	Chukotko-Kamchatkan	Worth (1969), Volodin (1976)
Kara	Austronesian	DeLacy (1997)
Karao	Austronesian	Brainard (1994)
Karen	Sino-Tibetan	Jones (1961)
Karok	Hokan	Bright (1957)
Kashuyana	Carib	Paula (1980)
Kavalan	Austronesian	Li (1982)
Kawaiisu	Uto-Aztecan	Zigmond et al. (1991)
Kayabí	Tupi	Dobson (1988)
Kayapó	Macro-Ge	Stout and Thomson (1974)
Kedang	Austronesian	Samely (1991)
Ket	Yenisei Ostyak	Vall and Kanakin (1990)
Khalkha	Altaic	Poppe (1951), Bosson (1964),. Hangin (1986), Walker (1995, 1996)
Khamti	Daic	Weidert (1977)
Khasi	Austro-Asiatic	Singh (1983), Nagaraja (1985)
Khmer	Austro-Asiatic	Gorgoniyev (1966)
Khmu	Austro-Asiatic	Svantesson (1983)
Kiliwa	Hokan	Mixco (2000)
Kiowa	Kiowa-Tanoan	Watkins (1984)
Kiriwina	Austronesian	Senft (1986)

(continued)

(continued)

Language	Macro-Phylum	Reference(s)
Kisar	Austronesian	Christensen (1992)
Kisi	Niger-Congo	Childs (1995)
Kitsai	Caddoan	Bucca and Lesser (1969)
Klamath	Penutian	Barker (1963, 1964)
Koasati	Muskogean	Kimball (1991, 1994)
Kobon	Trans New Guinea	Davies (1980)
Kolami	Dravidian	Emeneau (1955)
Komi	Uralic	Itkonen (1955), Lytkin (1961), Wiedemann (1964)
Korean	isolate	Martin (1992)
Korlai	Creole	Clements (1996)
Koryak	Chukotko-Kamchatkan	Zhukova (1967, 1972)
Koya	Dravidian	Tyler (1969)
Kpelle	Niger-Congo	Westermann (1930), Welmers (1962), Leidenfrost (1973)
Krio	Creole	D'iachkov (1981)
Krongo	Niger-Congo	Reh (1985)
Kru	Niger-Congo	Rickard (1970), Thalmann (1980)
Kui	Dravidian	Winfield (1928)
Kunama	Nilo-Saharan	Thompson (1983), Böhm (1984)
Kung (Zu|'Hóaนี)	Khoisan	Snyman (1975)
Kwakw'ala	Wakashan	Boas (1947), Bach (1975), Wilson (1986), Stonham (1990)
Lahu	Sino-Tibetan	Matisoff (1973, 1988)
Lak	North Caucasian	Zhirkov (1955)
Lakota	Siouan	Boas and Deloria (1933, 1941)
Lamang	Afro-Asiatic	Wolff (1983)
Lango	Nilo-Saharan	Noonan (1992)
Lao	Daic	Morev et al. (1979)

(continued)

(continued)

Language	Macro-Phylum	Reference(s)
Larike	Austronesian	Laidig (1992)
Latin	Indo-European	Allen (1973, 1975), Mester (1994)
Laz	South Caucasian	Marr (1910)
Lillooet	Salish	van Eijk (1997)
Lithuanian	Indo-European	Senn (1957–1966), Kenstowicz (1972), Young (1991)
Loniu	Austronesian	Hamel (1994)
Luganda	Niger-Congo	Tucker (1962)
Luiseño	Uto-Aztecan	Kroeber and Grace (1960), Bright (1968), Munro and Benson (1973)
Lushootseed	Salishan	Hess (1976, 1995)
Macushi	Carib	Hawkins (1950), Abbott (1991)
Mai Brat	West Papuan	Brown (1991)
Maidu	Penutian	Shipley (1963, 1964), Robbins (1991)
Maithili	Indo-European	Jha (1940–4, 1958), Yadav (1984)
Malagasy	Austronesian	Dez (1980), Erwin (1996)
Malay	Austronesian	Winstedt (1927), Prentice (1990)
Malayalam	Dravidian	Prabodhachandran Nayar (1973), Mohanan (1986), Asher and Kumari (1997)
Malecite Passamaquoddy	Algic	Teeter (1971), Teeter and LeSourd (1983), LeSourd (1984, 1993)
Malto	Dravidian	Das (1973)
Mam	Mayan	England (1983, 1986 in Maldonado Andrés et al)
Mandan	Siouan	Kennard (1936)
Mandarin	Sino-Tibetan	Chao (1968)
Mangbetu	Nilo-Saharan	Larochette (1958)
Mari	Uralic	Serebrennikov (1956), Gruzov (1960), Sebeok and Ingemann (1961), Ivanov and Tuzharov (1970)
Maricopa	Hokan	Gordon (1982)

(continued)

(continued)

Language	Macro-Phylum	Reference(s)
Maru	Sino-Tibetan	Burling (1967)
Marubo	Panoan	Costa (2000)
Maung	Australian	Capell (1970)
Mayo	Sepik-Ramu	Foreman and Marten (1973), Foreman (1974)
Mazatec	Oto-Manguean	Pike and Pike (1947), Jamieson (1977a, b)
Mbai	Nilo-Saharan	Fortier (1971)
Mende	Niger-Congo	Crosby (1944), Innes (1962, 1969)
Menomini	Algic	Bloomfield (1962, 1975)
Miwok, Sierra	Penutian	Freeland (1951), Broadbent (1964), Callaghan (1987)
Mixe, Coatlán	Mixe-Zoque	Hoogshagen (1984)
Mixe, Totontepec	Mixe-Zoque	Crawford (1963)
Mixtec	Oto-Manguean	Bradley (1970)
Mocha	Afro-Asiatic	Leslau (1959)
Moghol	Altaic	Weiers (1972)
Mohawk	Iroquoian	Michelson (1973), Chafe (1977), Michelson (1988)
Mojave	Hokan	Munro (1976), Langdon (1977), Munro et al. (1992)
Mordvin	Uralic	Paasonen (1990–6), Tsygankina (1980)
Moro	Niger-Congo	Black and Black (1971)
Movima	unclassified	Judy (1962)
Mulwi	Afro-Asiatic	Tourneux (1978)
Mumuye	Niger-Congo	Shimizu (1983)
Mundari	Austro-Asiatic	Sinha (1975)
Munsee	Algic	Goddard (1979, 1982)
Muong	Austro-Asiatic	Solntsev et al. (1987)
Mura-Pirahã	Mura	Everett and Everett (1984), Everett (1986, 1988)

(continued)

(continued)

Language	Macro-Phylum	Reference(s)
Murik	Trans New Guinea	Abbott (1985)
Murut	Austronesian	Prentice (1971)
Musey	Afro-Asiatic	Shryock (1995)
Naga	Creole	Sreedhar (1985), Boruah (1993)
Nahuatl	Uto-Aztecan	Brockway (1979), Sischo (1979), Tuggy (1979), Wolgemuth (1981)
Nama	Khoisan	Hagman (1977)
Nambiquara, S.	Nambiquaran	Price (1976)
Nambiquara, N.	Nambiquaran	Eberhard (1995)
Nandi	Nilo-Saharan	Creider and Creider (1989)
Nankina	Trans New Guinea	Spaulding and Spaulding (1994)
Naro	Khoisan	Vossen (1997)
Navajo	Na Dene	Sapir and Hoijer (1967), Young and Morgan (1992)
Ndumbea	Austronesian	Rivierre (1973), Paita and Shintani (1983)
Ndyuka	Creole	Huttar and Huttar (1994)
Nenets	Uralic	Décsy (1966), Popova (1978)
Nez Perce	Penutian	Aoki (1970, 1994), Crook (1999)
Nganasan	Uralic	Tereshchenko (1979)
Nocte	Sino-Tibetan	Das Gupta (1971)
Nuuchahnulth	Wakashan	Sapir and Swadesh (1939), Wilson (1986), Stonham (1990)
Nubi	Creole	Heine (1983)
Nung	Sino-Tibetan	Saul (1980)
Nyawaygi	Australian	Dixon (1983)
Ocaina	Witotoan	Agnew and Pike (1957)
Ojibwa	Algic	Bloomfield (1956), Kaye (1973), Piggott (1980), Piggott and Grafstein (1983)
Oneida	Iroquoian	Chafe (1977), Michelson (1988)
Onge	Andamanese	Dasgupta (1982)

(continued)

(continued)

Language	Macro-Phylum	Reference(s)
Onondaga	Iroquoian	Chafe (1970, 1977), Michelson (1988)
Orokolo	Trans New Guinea	Brown (1986)
Oromo	Afro-Asiatic	Ali (1990)
Orya	Trans New Guinea	Field (1991)
Ostyak (Vach)	Uralic	Gulya (1966), Schiefer (1975)
Otomi	Oto-Manguean	Manuel (1955)
Pacoh	Austro-Asiatic	Watson (1966)
Paez	Paezan	Slocum (1985)
Pagu	West Papuan	Wimbish (1992)
Paipai	Hokan	Joel (1966), Langdon (1977)
Paiwan	Austronesian	Ferrell (1982)
Paraujano	Arawakan	Patte (1989)
Patep	Austronesian	Adams and Lauck (1975)
Pawnee	Caddoan	Parks (1976)
Pemon	Carib	Armellada (1943)
Persian (Farsi)	Indo-European	Elwell-Sutton (1976, 1983), Hayes (1979), Windfuhr (1990)
Pomo, Eastern	Hokan	McLendon (1975)
Pomo, Kashaya	Hokan	Oswalt (1961, 1988), Buckley (1994)
Quechua, Huallaga	Quechan	Weber (1989)
Quechua, Inga	Quechan	Levinsohn (1976)
Quechua, Junin-Huanca	Quechan	Cerrón-Palomino (1976)
Quicha	Quechan	Orr (1962), Grimes (1972)
Quileute	Chimakuan	Powell and Woodruff (1976)
Runga	Nilo-Saharan	Nougayrol (1990)
Russian	Indo-European	Wheeler (1984)
Saek	Daic	Morev (1988)
Sahu	West Papuan	Severn (1995)
Sámi, Eastern	Uralic	Äimä (1914), Itkonen (1986)

(continued)

Language	Macro-Phylum	Reference(s)
Sámi, Northern	Uralic	Nielsen (1926, 1932)
Sango	Creole	Samarin (1967)
Santali	Austro-Asiatic	Chakrabarti (1994)
Sanuma	Yanomam	Borgman (1989)
Sapuan	Austro-Asiatic	Jacq and Sidwell (1999)
Sarangani Manobo	Austronesian	DuBois (1976), Meiklejohn and Meiklejohn (1958)
Sarsi	Na Dene	Cook (1984)
Sawai	Austronesian	Whisler (1992)
Selknam	Chon	Najlis (1973)
Selkup	Uralic	Szabó (1967), Erdélyi (1970), Halle and Clements (1983)
Seneca	Iroquoian	Chafe (1977, 1996, 1998), Michelson (1988)
Senoufo	Niger-Congo	Chéron (1925), Mills (1984)
Sentani	Trans New Guinea	Cowan (1966), Elenbaas (1992, 1998)
Shan	Daic	Morev (1983), Young (1985)
Shilluk	Nilo-Saharan	Heasty (1974), Gilley (1992)
Sierra Popoluca	Mixe-Zoque	Foster (1948)
Siona	Tucanoan	Wheeler and Wheeler (1962)
Siriano	Tucanoan	Priest (1968), Schermair (1949)
Siwa	Afro-Asiatic	Walker (1921)
Slavey	Na Dene	Rice (1989)
Somali	Afro-Asiatic	Berchem (1993), Qani (1993), Saeed (1993)
Songai	Nilo-Saharan	Prost (1956)
Sre	Austro-Asiatic	Manley (1972)
Stieng	Austro-Asiatic	Miller (1976)
Stoney Dakota	Siouan	Shaw (1980, 1985)
Sumbanese	Austronesian	Klamer (1994)
Tacana	Tacanan	Key (1968)

(continued)

(continued)

Language	Macro-Phylum	Reference(s)
Tai, Lung Ming	Daic	Gedney (1991)
Tamazight Berber	Afro-Asiatic	Abdel-Massih (1971), Dell (1997)
Tamil	Dravidian	Andronov (1989), Christdas (1996)
Tangkhul	Sino-Tibetan	Arokainathan (1980, 1987)
Tangsa	Sino-Tibetan	Das Gupta (1980)
Taos (N.Tiwa)	Kiowa-Tanoan	Trager G. (1946), Trager F. (1971)
Tatar	Altaic	Poppe (1963)
Tauya	Trans New Guinea	MacDonald (1990)
Tehit	West Papuan	Flassy and Stokhof (1979)
Telefol	Trans New Guinea	Healey A. (1964), Healey P. (1977)
Telugu	Dravidian	Sitapati (1936), Petrunicheva (1960), Brown (1981), Krishnamurti and Gwynn (1985), Gwynn (1991)
Tepehuan	Uto-Aztecan	Willett (1991)
Ternate	West Papuan	Watuseke (1991)
Tetun	Austronesian	Morris (1984)
Tewa	Kiowa-Tanoan	Harrington (1910), Speirs (1966)
Thai	Daic	Noss (1964), Hudak (1990a,b)
Tibetan (Lhasa/ Refugee)	Sino-Tibetan	Odden (1979), Dawson (1980), Meredith (1990)
Tidore	West Papuan	Pikkert and Pikkert (1995)
Tigre	Afro-Asiatic	Raz (1983)
Tiriyo	Carib	Migliazza (1965)
Tiwi	Australian	Osborne (1974)
Tlingit	Na Dene	Boas (1917), Naish and Story (1963), Story and Naish (1973)
Toda	Dravidian	Sakthivel (1976), Emeneau (1984)
Tol (Jicaque) [e]	isolate	Holt (1999)
Tolojolabal	Mayan	Furbee-Losee (1976)
Tolowa	Na Dene	Bright (1964)
Tonkawa	Coahuiltecan	Hoijer (1946, 1949)

(continued)

(continued)

Language	Macro-Phylum	Reference(s)
Torres Strait	Creole	Shnukal (1988)
Totonac (Misantla)	Totonacan	MacKay (1999)
Trique	Oto-Manguean	Hollenbach (1977)
Tsimshian	Penutian	Dunn (1978, 1979)
Tsotsil	Mayan	Weathers (1947)
Tsou	Austronesian	Tung (1964), Wright and Ladefoged (1997)
Tübatulabal	Uto-Aztecan	Voegelin (1935), Crowhurst (1991)
Tubu	Nilo-Saharan	Lukas (1953)
Tunen	Niger-Congo	Dugast (1967, 1971)
Tunica	Gulf	Swanton (1921), Haas (1946)
Tura	Niger-Congo	Bearth (1971)
Turkana	Nilo-Saharan	Dimmendaal (1983)
Turkish	Altaic	Kaisse (1985, 1986), Barker (1989), Kornfilt (1990), Inkelas and Orgun (1995)
Tzutujil	Penutian	Dayley (1985)
Ubyx	North Caucasian	Dumézil (1959)
Urim	Torricelli	Luoma (1985)
Usan	Trans New Guinea	Reesink (1987)
Uzbek	Altaic	Poppe (1962)
Vai	Niger-Congo	Welmers (1976)
Veps	Uralic	Zaitseva (1972, 1981)
Vietnamese	Austro-Asiatic	Nguyen (1969), Van-Chinh (1970), Nguyen (1990)
Votic	Uralic	Ariste (1968), Posti (1980), Viitso (1997)
Waiwai	Carib	Hawkins (1952)
Wappo	Yuki	Radin (1929)
Warao	isolate	Osborn (1966)
Wardaman	Australian	Merlan (1994)
Warembori	unclassified	Donohue (1999)

(continued)

(*continued*)

Language	Macro-Phylum	Reference(s)
Wari'	Chapacura-Wanham	MacEachern et al. (1997)
West Tarangan	Austronesian	Nivens (1992)
Wichita	Caddoan	Rood (1976)
Winnebago	Siouan	Susman (1943), Lipkind (1945), Miner (1979, 1989), Hale and White Eagle (1980), Hale (1985), Morrison (1994)
Wintu	Penutian	Pitkin (1984, 1985)
Wolof	Niger-Congo	Suvageot (1965), Ka (1987), Gamble (1990), Munro and Gaye (1991)
Xavánte	Macro-Ge	McLeod and Mitchell (1977)
Yagua	Peba-Yaguan	Payne and Payne (1990)
Yana	Hokan	Sapir and Swadesh (1960)
Yapese	Austronesian	Jensen (1977)
Yawelmani	Penutian	Newman (1944), Archangeli (1984)
Yele	East Papuan	Henderson (1995)
Yil	Torricelli	Martens and Tuominen (1977)
Yimas	Sepik-Ramu	Foley (1991)
Yonaguni	Japanese	Hirayama and Nakamoto (1964)
Yucatecto	Mayan	Straight (1976)
Yuchi	isolate	Crawford (1973), Ballard (1975)
Yukaghir	Yukaghir	Kreinovich (1982)
Yulu	Nilo-Saharan	Santandrea (1970), Boyeldieu (1987)
Yupik, Central	Eskimo-Aleut	Reed et al. (1977), Woodbury (1981, 1985, 1987, 1989), Krauss (1985b), Jacobson (1984, 1985), Miyaoka (1985, 1996), Leer (1985b,c)
Yupik, Pacific Gulf	Eskimo-Aleut	Leer (1985a,b,c)
Yupik, Sirenik	Eskimo-Aleut	Krauss (1985a), Menovshchikov (1962, 1975)
Yurok	Algic	Robins (1958)
Zapotec, Mitla	Oto-Manguean	Briggs (1961)
Zoque	Mixe-Zoque	Wonderly (1951), Knudson (1975)
Zuni	isolate	Newman (1958, 1965)

Appendix Two

LANGUAGES APPEARING IN THE WEIGHT TYPOLOGY AND THEIR RELEVANT WEIGHT SENSITIVE PROCESSES IN TABULAR FORM

Notes: A superscripted ^{a} indicates that the language does not have codas. Except where noted in a footnote, these languages observe an outright ban on codas in any position. A superscripted ^{b} indicates an absence of phonemic long vowels. A superscripted ^{c} indicates an historical compensatory lengthening process involving the loss of segments *preceding* the ^{c}. A superscripted ^{d} indicates an absence of obstruent codas. A superscripted ^{e} indicates an absence of long vowels and diphthongs. A superscripted ^{f} in the tone column indicates the presence of syllabic nasals. A superscripted ^{g} indicates that long vowels and diphthongs do not occur in final syllables. q.i. indicates quantity insensitive stress; the location of stress in languages with quantity insensitive stress pertains to the main stress. A superscripted ^{h} indicates a quantity insensitive binary stress pattern, i.e. stress on every other syllable preceding/following the main stress. A superscripted ^{k} indicates a quantity insensitive ternary stress pattern, i.e. stress on every third syllable preceding/following the main stress. A superscripted ^{m} indicates an absence of contour tones. A superscripted ^{n} indicates that heavy syllables carry a fuller range of tones than light syllables, though light syllables may carry certain phonetic contour tones. VV stands for both long vowels and diphthongs unless otherwise noted (by subscripts). Onset consonants are irrelevant for the processes examined unless noted. R stands for a sonorant, O for an obstruent, K for a voiceless consonant, and G for a voiced consonant. OSVL stands for lengthening of vowels in certain open syllables, in most cases due to stress or rhythmic constraints, either synchronically or diachronically. "n.a." stands for not applicable; this designation is used in cases where the data examined did not contain information on the given process; it does not necessarily mean that the language lacks the relevant phenomenon. In the case of tone, "none" means that there are no weight-sensitive restrictions on which tones or pitch accents may occur on different syllable types. For syllable template phenomena, "none" indicates that long vowels, if there are any, may occur in both open and closed syllables. Question marks indicate uncertainty about weight distinction(s).

Language	Macro-Phylum	Stress (heavy)	Metrics	Comp Length	Syll. Templ.	Tone	Minim. Word
!Xoo[d]	Khoisan	n.a.	n.a.	n.a.	*CVVC	none	CVR
Abau	Sepik-Ramu	n.a.	n.a.	n.a.	none	CVV(C)	none
Abelam[b]	Trans New Guinea	CaV > CøV > Cij, Cuw > CV	n.a.	n.a.	none	n.a.	none
Abkhaz[1]	North Caucasian	q.i. (phonemic)	n.a.	n.a.	none	n.a.	none??
Achagua	Arawakan	q.i. (phonemic)	n.a.	n.a.	none	n.a.	CVV ??
Acoma (Western Keres)	Keres		n.a.	n.a.	none	CVV(C), CVR[2]	none
Aguacatec	Mayan	CVV(C)	n.a.	n.a.	none	n.a.	CVC
Ai-Cham	Daic	n.a.	n.a.	n.a.	none	CVV(C), CVR[n]	none
Ainu[3]	isolate	CVV(C), CVC[4]	n.a.	n.a.	OSVL	n.a.	none
Alamblak[e]	Sepik-Ramu	???	n.a.	n.a.	none	n.a.	CVC
Alawa[e]	Australian	q.i.. (penult)	n.a.	n.a.	none	n.a.	CVC
Albanian[5]	Indo-European	q.i.. (penult)	n.a.	n.a.	none	n.a.	none
Aleut	Eskimo-Aleut	CVV(C)	n.a.	n.a.	none	n.a.	CVC
Aljutor[e]	Chukotko-Kamchatkan	Red V in open syll light	n.a.	n.a.	n.a.	n.a.	none

Language	Family						
Amahuaca	Panoan	q.i. (phonemic)	n.a.	n.a.	none	n.a.	CVV[6]??
Amami (Shodon)	Japanese	CVV(C), CVC[7] (pitch accent)	n.a.	n.a.	none	n.a.	none
Amele[8]	Trans New Guinea	CVV(C), CVC	n.a.	n.a.	none	n.a.	none
Amharic[e]	Afro-Asiatic	n.a.	n.a.	n.a.	none	n.a.	none
Andamanese	Andamanese	q.i. (penult)	n.a.	n.a.	none	n.a.	none
Andoke[9]	isolate	n.a.	n.a.	n.a.	none	CVV(C)	CVV
Anem[e]	East Papuan	q.i. (penult)	n.a.	n.a.	none	n.a.	none
Anufo[d f]	Niger-Congo	n.a.	n.a.	n.a.	none	CVV(C)[10]	none
Apache, Chiracahua[f]	Na Dene	n.a.	n.a.	n.a.	none	CVV(C)	none
Apalaí	Carib	CVV(C), CVC[11]	n.a.	n.a.	none	n.a.	none
Apinaye	Macro-Ge	q.i. (final of root)	n.a.	n.a.	none	n.a.	none
Arabela	Zaparoan	q.i. (initial)	n.a.	n.a.	none??	n.a.	CVCV
Arabic	Afro-Asiatic	CVV(C), CVC[12]	CVV(C), CVC	n.a.	none[13]	n.a.	CVC
Aramaic	Afro-Asiatic	q.i. (final)	n.a.	n.a.	none	n.a.	CVC ??

(continued)

(*continued*)

Language	Macro-Phylum	Stress (heavy)	Metrics	Comp Length	Syll. Templ.	Tone	Minim. Word
Arapesh[b]	Torricelli	q.i. (penult)	n.a.	n.a.	none	n.a.	??
Araucanian[c]	Araucanian	q.i. (peninitial)[h]	n.a.	n.a.	none	n.a.	none
Arawak[a]	Arawakan	q.i.[14] (initial)	n.a.		none	n.a.	CVCV
Asheninca Campa	Arawakan	CVV > Ca(C), Ce(C), Co(C), CiC > Ci.[16]		n.a.	none	n.a.	none
Assiniboine[e]	Siouan	q.i. (peninitial)	n.a.	n.a.	none	n.a.	none
Atakapa	Gulf	???	n.a.	n.a.	none	n.a.	CVC??
Atayal	Austronesian	q.i. (final)	n.a.	n.a.	*CVVC	n.a.	none
Au	Torricelli	Full V	n.a.	n.a.	none	n.a.	CVfull
Aymara	Aymara	CVV(C)	n.a.	n.a.	*CVVC	n.a.	CVCV
Bagirmi	Nilo-Saharan	n.a.	n.a.	n.a.	none??	none??	none
Banawá[a]	Arawakan	onsets[17]	n.a.	n.a.	none	n.a.	CVV
Barasano[a b]	Tucanoan	H tone	n.a.	n.a.	none	none	CVV
Bashkir[b]	Altaic	q.i. (final)	n.a.	n.a.	none	n.a.	CVC
Basque[b]	isolate	q.i.[18]	n.a.	n.a.	none	n.a.	CVC
Belizean Creole	Creole	q.i. (penult)	n.a.	r	none	n.a.	none

		q.i.			*CVVC		
Berbice[b]	Creole	q.i. (penult)[b]	n.a.	n.a.	n.a.	n.a.	none
Bete[a]	Niger-Congo	n.a.	n.a.	n.a.	none	CVV(C)	none
Biangai	Trans New Guinea	q.i.	n.a.	n.a.	none	n.a.	CVCV??
Blackfoot	Algic	pitch accent	n.a.	n.a.	none	n.a.	CVC??
Bobo[a]	Niger-Congo	H tone > M tone > L tone	n.a.	n.a.	none	none	none
Boiken[b]	Sepik-Ramu	CVV(C), CVC[19]	n.a.	n.a.	none	n.a.	none
Brahui	Dravidian	CVV(C), CVC	n.a.	n.a.	none	n.a.	CVC??
Brao	Austro-Asiatic	q.i. (root)	n.a.	n.a.	none	n.a.	none[20]
Buriat	Altaic	CVV(C)	n.a.	n.a.	none	n.a.	CVC
Burmese[b][21]	Sino-Tibetan	n.a.	n.a.	n.a.	none	22	none
Burushaski	isolate	q.i. (phonemic)	n.a.	n.a.	none	n.a.	none
Bushong[b]	Niger-Congo	n.a.	n.a.	n.a.	none	CVV(C)	none
Caddo	Caddoan	n.a.	n.a.	n.a.	none	CVV(C), CVR	??
Cakchiquel[c]	Mayan	q.i. (final)	n.a.	n.a.	none	n.a.	CVC
Canela-Krahô	Macro-Ge	q.i (final)	n.a.	n.a.	none	n.a.	???

(continued)

(*continued*)

Language	Macro-Phylum	Stress (heavy)	Metrics	Comp Length	Syll. Templ.	Tone	Minim. Word
Cantonese[b f]	Sino-Tibetan	n.a.	n.a.	n.a.	none	CVV(C), CVR[23]	CVC[24]
Capanahua	Panoan	???	n.a.	n.a.	none	none[m]	CVC
Carib	Carib	CVV(C), CVC	n.a.	n.a.	*CVVC	n.a.	none
Cashinahua	Panoan	???	n.a.	n.a.	none	none[m]	CVCV
Cavinena[a e]	Tacanan	q.i. (penult)[h]	n.a.	n.a.	none	n.a.	none
Cayapa	Paezan	CVV(C), CVC except CVʔ	n.a.		none	n.a.	none
Cayubaba[a]	isolate	q.i. (antepenult)[k]	n.a.	n.a.	none	n.a.	none
Cayuga	Iroquoian	CVV(C)	n.a.	n.a.	OSVL[26]	n.a.	CVCV
Cebuano	Austronesian	CVV(C), CVC	n.a.	n.a.	none	n.a.	CVV
Chacobo	Panoan	n.a.	n.a.	n.a.	none	none[m]	CVV
Chamorro	Austronesian	q.i. (penult)	n.a.	n.a.	none	n.a.	CVCV
Cherokee	Iroquoian	CVV(C)	n.a.	n.a.	none	CVV(C)	CVCV??g??
Chickasaw	Muskogean	CVV(C) > CVC > CV	n.a.	n.a.	OSVL	n.a.	CVV

Chinantec, Comaltepec[27]	Oto-Manguean	n.a.	n.a.	n.a.	none	none	none
Ching	Daic	n.a.	n.a.	n.a.	none	CVV(C), CVR[n]	none
Chitimacha	Gulf	q.i. (initial)	n.a.	h[c]	none	n.a.	CVC
Chontal[e]	Mayan	q.i. (phonemic)	n.a.	n.a.	none	n.a.	CVC
Chukchi[e]	Chukotko-Kamchatkan	Low V, Mid V > HighV > Red V	n.a.	n.a.	none	n.a.	none
Chumash, Barbareño	Hokan	q.i. (penult)[28]	n.a.	n.a.	none	n.a.	??
Chuvash[e]	Altaic	Full V	n.a.	n.a.	none	n.a.	none
Cofán[b]	Chibchan	q.i. (penult)	n.a.	n.a.	none	n.a.	none
Comanche	Uto-Aztecan	CVV(C)	n.a.	n.a.	none	n.a.	CVV
Comox	Salishan	q.i. (initial)	n.a.	n.a.	none	n.a.	none
Cora	Uto-Aztecan	q.i. (antepenult)	n.a.	n.a.	*CVVC	none[m]	none
Coreguaje[a e]	Tucanoan	q.i. (initial of root)	n.a.	n.a.	none	none	CVCV
Crow	Siouan	H, HL tones	n.a.	n.a.	none	CVV(C)	CVV??
Cuna	Chibchan	CVV(C), CVC[29]	n.a.	n.a.	*CVVC	n.a.	none

(continued)

(*continued*)

Language	Macro-Phylum	Stress (heavy)	Metrics	Comp Length	Syll. Templ.	Tone	Minim. Word
Czech	Indo-European	q.i. (initial)	n.a.	n.a.	none	n.a.	CVC, CCV
Dani	Trans New Guinea	q.i. (final)	n.a.	n.a.	none	n.a.	none
Didinga	Nilo-Saharan	n.a.	n.a.	n.a.	none	CVV(C)	none
Dieguño	Hokan	q.i (root)	n.a.	?	none	n.a.	CVC
Diola	Niger-Congo	q.i. (initial)	n.a.	n.a.	none	n.a.	CVC
Dizi	Afro-Asiatic	q.i. (initial)	n.a.	n.a.	none	none[m]	none
Djingili	Australian	q.i. (penult)	n.a.	n.a.	none	n.a.	CVCV
Duala[f]	Niger-Congo	n.a.	n.a.	n.a.	none	CVV(C)	none
Dumi	Sino-Tibetan	q.i. (root-verbs, initial-nouns)	n.a.	n.a.	none	n.a.	none
Dzongkha	Sino-Tibetan	n.a.	n.a.	l, r, ŋ, t, k, s [c]	none	CVV(C), CVR	none
Eipomek[b]	Trans New Guinea	CVVC > CVV, CVC > CV	n.a.	n.a.	none	n.a.	none
Émérillon[b]	Tupi	q.i. (penult)	n.a.	n.a.	none	n.a.	none
English	Indo-European	CVV(C), CVC	CVV(C), CVC	, (dialectally)	none	n.a.	CVC

Estonian	Uralic	CVV(C), CVC[30]	CVV(C), CVC	n.a.	none	n.a.	CVCCC, CVV
Even (Lamut)	Altaic	q.i. (initial)	n.a.	n.a.	none	n.a.	CVC
Evenki	Altaic	CVV(C), CVC	n.a.	n.a.	none	n.a.	CVC
Fijian[a]	Austronesian	CVV(C)	CVV(C), CVC	n.a.	none	n.a.	CVV
Finnish	Uralic	CVV(C), CVC	CVV(C), CVC	n.a.	*CVVCC	n.a.	CVV
Fong[a f]	Niger-Congo	n.a.	n.a.	n.a.	none	none[31]	none
French[b]	Indo-European	q.i. (final-phrase)	n.a.	n.a.	none	n.a.	none
Fula	Niger-Congo	CVVC > CVV, CVC > CV	n.a.	n.a.	none	n.a.	CVC
Fur	Nilo-Saharan	n.a.	n.a.	n.a.	none	none	none
Gana-Khwe (≤ Ani)[d]	Khoisan	n.a.[32]	n.a.	n.a.	none	CVV(C), CVR	CVR
Georgian	South Caucasian	q.i. (initial)	n.a.	n.a.	none	n.a.	???
Gilyak[e]	isolate	q.i. (morph.)	n.a.	n.a.	none	n.a.	none
Gondi	Dravidian	q.i. (initial)	n.a.	n.a.	none	n.a.	CVC
Greek (classical)	Indo-European	CVV(C), CVC	CVV(C), CVC	n.a.	none	CVV(C)	CVCC, CVVC

(continued)

(continued)

Language	Macro-Phylum	Stress (heavy)	Metrics	Comp Length	Syll. Templ.	Tone	Minim. Word
Guahibo[a]	Arawakan	q.i. (phonemic)	n.a.	n.a.	none	n.a.	CVV
Guarani[a]	Tupi	q.i. (final)	n.a.	n.a.	none	n.a.	CVV
Gujarati	Indo-European	LowV >CəC > Non-loV >Cə	n.a.	n.a.	none	n.a.	none
Gurage	Afro-Asiatic	q.i. (final-verbs, penult-nouns)	n.a.	r, l, pharyngeals[c]	none	n.a.	none
Gurung	Sino-Tibetan	q.i. (initial); also pitch accent	n.a.	n.a.	none	n.a.	none
Haida	Na Dene	H tone[33]	n.a.	n.a.	none	n.a.	none
Haitian Creole[e]	Creole	q.i. (final)	n.a.	n.a.	none	n.a.	none
Halang	Austro-Asiatic	q.i. (root)	n.a.	n.a.	none	n.a.	CVC
Halkomelem	Salishan	q.i. (phonemic)[34]	n.a.	n.a.	none	n.a.	none
Hatsa[a b]	Khoisan	???	n.a.	n.a.	none	none???	none
Hausa	Afro-Asiatic	n.a.	CVV(C), CVC	n.a.	*CVVC	CVV(C), CVC	none
Hewa[b]	Sepik-Ramu	q.i. (initial)	n.a.	n.a.	none	n.a.	none

Language	Family						
Hindi	Indo-European	CVCC, CVVC > CVV, CVC > CV[35]	CVCC, CVVC > CVV, CVC > CV	C[36]	*CVVC[37]	n.a.	CVC
Hixkaryana[e]	Carib	CVC	n.a.	n.a.	OSSVL	n.a.	CVC[38]
Hmong, Green[b d]	Miao-Yao	n.a.	n.a.	n.a.	*CVVC	none	none
Hopi	Uto-Aztecan	CVV(C), CVC	n.a.	n.a.	none	n.a.	CVCVg[??]
Hualapai	Hokan	q.i. (initial)	n.a.	n.a.	OSVL	n.a.	none
Huasteco	Mayan	CVV(C)	n.a.	n.a.	none	n.a.	CVC
Huave (de San Mateo del Mar)	Huavean	CVV(C), CVC	n.a.	n.a.	none	none[m]	CVC
Huitoto[a]	Witotoan	q.i. (initial)	n.a.	n.a.	none	n.a.	none
Hungarian	Uralic	CVV(C), CVC[39]	CVV(C), CVC	n.a.	none	n.a.	none
Hupa	Na Dene	CVV(C)	n.a.	n.a.	none	n.a.	CVC
Old Icelandic	Indo-European	q.i. (initial)	CVV(C), CVC	n.a.	none	n.a.	CVC
Ijo[a]	Niger-Congo	H tone or contour heavy; also CVV(C)	n.a.	n.a.	none	CVV(C)	none

(continued)

(*continued*)

Language	Macro-Phylum	Stress (heavy)	Metrics	Comp Length	Syll. Templ.	Tone	Minim. Word
Inuktitut, Greenlandic	Eskimo-Aleut	q.i. (final)	n.a.	n.a.	none	n.a.	CVCV
Inuktitut, North Alaskan	Eskimo-Aleut	???	n.a.	n.a.	none	n.a.	CVC
Iraqw	Afro-Asiatic	CVV(C), H tone[40]	n.a.	n.a.	none	none[m]	CVC
Irish	Indo-European	CVV > Cax > CV	n.a.??	g, n[c]	none	n.a.	CVC
Japanese	Japanese	pitch accent	CVV(C), CVC	n.a.	*CVVC[41]	n.a.	none
Jaqaru	Aymara	q.i. (penult)	n.a.	n.a.	none	n.a.	CVCV[g]
Javanese[e]	Austronesian	Full V	n.a.	n.a.	none	n.a.	CVC
Jemez[42]	Kiowa-Tanoan	q.i. (initial)	n.a.	n.a.	none	none	none
Jivaro	Jivaroan	q.i. (phonemic)	n.a.	n.a.	none	n.a.	none
Jukun[a f]	Niger-Congo	n.a.	n.a.	n.a.	none	CVV(C)	none
Júma[e]	Tupi	onset[43]	n.a.	n.a.	none	n.a.	CVCV??
Kabardian[e]	North Caucasian	CVV(C), CVC	n.a.	h	none	n.a.	none
Kabiye[d f]	Niger-Congo	n.a.	n.a.	n.a.	*CVVC	CVV(C), CVR	none

Kaingang[c]	Macro-Ge	q.i. (phonemic)	n.a.	n.a.	none	n.a.	none
Kalispel	Salishan	q.i. (morph.)	n.a.	r^wc	none	n.a.	none
Kamayurá[b]	Tupi	q.i. (final)[h]	n.a.	n.a.	none	n.a.	CVC??
Kamchadal[c]	Chukotko-Kamchatkan	syllables containing ?	n.a.	n.a.	none	n.a.	none
Kara	Austronesian	CV: > CaV, CaC > Ca > $CV_i k$, CVC > CV[44]	n.a.	n.a.	none	n.a.	none
Karao[c]	Austronesian	q.i. (penult/final in free variation)	n.a.	n.a.	none	n.a.	CVCV
Karen[c] [45]	Sino-Tibetan	n.a.	n.a.	n.a.	none	none^m	none
Karok	Hokan	CVV(C)	n.a.	n.a.	none	n.a.	CVC
Kashuyana[c]	Carib	CVV(C), CVC	n.a.	n.a.	none	n.a.	CCV[46]
Kavalan[b]	Austronesian	q.i. (final)	n.a.	n.a.	none	n.a.	CVV[47]
Kawaiisu[a] [48]	Uto-Aztecan	CVV(C)	n.a.	n.a.	none	n.a.	CVV
Kayabí	Tupi	q.i. (final)	n.a.	n.a.	none	n.a.	???
Kayapó[c]	Macro-Ge	q.i. (final)	n.a.	n.a.	none	n.a.	none
Kedang[c]	Austronesian	??	n.a.	n.a.	none	n.a.	none

(continued)

(continued)

Language	Macro-Phylum	Stress (heavy)	Metrics	Comp Length	Syll. Templ.	Tone	Minim. Word
Ket	Yenisei Ostyak	??	n.a.	n.a.	none	n.a.	CVV
Khalkha	Altaic	CVV(C)	n.a.	n.a.	none	n.a.	CVC
Khamti[b]	Daic	n.a.	n.a.	n.a.	none	CVV(C), CVR	CVC
Khasi	Austro-Asiatic	???	n.a.		none	n.a.	none
Khmer	Austro-Asiatic	CVV(C), CVC	n.a.	n.a.	none	n.a.	CVC
Khmu	Austro-Asiatic	q.i. (root)	n.a.		none	CVV(C), CVR[m 49]	CVC
Kiliwa	Hokan	q.i. (penult)	n.a.	n.a.	none	CVV(C)	CVC?
Kiowa	Kiowa-Tanoan	n.a.	n.a.	n.a	*CVVC	CVV(C), CVR	CVC
Kiriwina[d]	Austronesian	CVV(C), CVC	n.a.	n.a.	none	n.a.	none
Kisar[e 50]	Austronesian	q.i. (penult of root)	n.a.	n.a.	none	n.a.	none
Kisi[51]	Niger-Congo	n.a.	n.a.	n.a.	none	CVV(C), CVR	none
Kitsai	Caddoan	??	n.a.	n.a.	none	CVV(C), CVR	CVVC, CVCC??

Klamath	Penutian	CVV(C) > CVC > CV	n.a.	n.a.	none	n.a.	none
Koasati	Muskogean	CVV(C)	n.a.	n.a.	*CVVC	n.a.	CVC
Kobon[a,b,52]	Trans New Guinea	Low V > MidV > High V > Reduced V	n.a.	n.a.	none	n.a.	none
Kolami	Dravidian	q.i. (initial)	n.a.	n.a.	none	n.a.	CVC
Komi (Jaz'va)[e]	Uralic	Non-high V	n.a.	n.a.	none	n.a.	none
Korean[e,53]	isolate	n.a.	n.a.	n.a.	none	n.a.	none
Korlai[b]	Creole	CVV(C), CVC	n.a.	n.a.	n.a.	n.a.	none
Koryak[e]	Chukotko-Kamchatkan	q.i. (peninitial)	n.a.	n.a.	none	n.a.	CVC??
Koya	Dravidian	CVV(C), CVC	n.a.	n.a.	*CVVC[54]	n.a.	CVC
Kpelle	Niger-Congo	H tone	n.a.	n.a.	none	none	none
Krio[b]	Creole	?:	n.a.	n.a.	none	n.a.	none
Krongo	Niger-Congo	H tone, CVV(C)[55]	n.a.	n.a.	*CVVC	CVV(C)	none
Kru[56]	Niger-Congo	n.a.	n.a.	n.a.	none	CVV(C)	none
Kui	Dravidian	q.i. (root)	n.a.	n.a.	none	n.a.	CVV??

(continued)

(*continued*)

Language	Macro-Phylum	Stress (heavy)	Metrics	Comp Length	Syll. Templ.	Tone	Minim. Word
Kunama	Nilo-Saharan	CVV(C)	n.a.	n.a.	*CVVC	none	none
Kung (Zu|'Hóasĩ)[d][f]	Khoisan	q.i. (initial of root)	n.a.	n.a.	*CVVC	CVV(C)	none
Kwakw'ala	Wakashan	CVV(C), CVR	n.a.	n.a.	none	n.a.	CLowV
Lahu[b][57]	Sino-Tibetan	n.a.	n.a.	n.a	none	none	none
Lak[e]	North Caucasian	q.i. (morph.)	n.a.	n.a.	none	n.a.	none
Lakota[e]	Siouan	q.i. (peninitial)	n.a.	n.a.	none	n.a.	none
Lamang[b][58]	Afro-Asiatic	Full V, CVR	n.a.	ŋ	none	none	none
Lango[b]	Nilo-Saharan	q.i. (final of root)	n.a.	n.a.	none	none[59]	none
Lao	Daic	n.a.	n.a.	n.a.	none	CVV(C), CVR	CVC
Larike	Austronesian	q.i. (penult of root)[h]	n.a.	n.a.	none	n.a.	CVV
Latin	Indo-European	CVV(C), CVC	CVV(C), CVC	s	none	n.a.	CVCC, CVVC
Laz	South Caucasian	q.i. (penult)	n.a.	n.a.	???	n.a.	???

Lillooet[e]	Salishan	Full V[60]	n.a.	ʕ̣, ʕ, ʕʷ	none	n.a.	(CVC)[61]
Lithuanian	Indo-European	n.a.	n.a.	n.a.	*CVVR	CVV(C), CVR	CVC
Loniu[c]	Austronesian	q.i. (phonemic)	n.a.	n.a.	none	n.a.	none
Luganda	Niger-Congo	n.a.	CVV(C), CVC	n.a.	*CVVC	CVV(C), CVC	none
Luiseño	Uto-Aztecan	CVV(C)	n.a.	n.a.	*CVVC	n.a.	CVC
Lushootseed[c]	Salishan	Full V	n.a.	n.a.	none	n.a.	(CVC)[62]
Macushi	Carib	CVV(C), CVC	n.a.	n.a.	OSVL	n.a.	???
Mai Brat[b]	West Papuan	q.i. (phonemic)	n.a.	n.a.	none	n.a.	none
Maidu	Penutian	CVV(C), CVC	n.a.	n.a.	OSVL	n.a.	none
Maithili[63]	Indo-European	CVV(C) > CVC> CV	n.a.	n.a.	none	n.a.	CVV
Malagasy[a]	Austronesian	CVV(C)	n.a.	n.a.	none	n.a.	CVV
Malay[c]	Austronesian	Red V in open syll light	n.a.	n.a.	none	n.a.	CVC
Malayalam	Dravidian	CVV(C)	CVV(C), CVC	n.a.	none	n.a.	CVC

(continued)

(*continued*)

Language	Macro-Phylum	Stress (heavy)	Metrics	Comp Length	Syll. Templ.	Tone	Minim. Word
Malecite Passamaquoddy	Algic	CVV(C)	n.a.	n.a.	none	n.a.	none
Malto	Dravidian	CVV(C)	n.a.	n.a.	none	n.a.	??
Mam	Mayan	CVV(C), CVʔ > CVC>CV	n.a.	n.a.	none	n.a.	CVC
Mandan	Siouan	q.i. (???)	n.a.	n.a.	none	n.a.	CVC??
Mandarin[b d]	Sino-Tibetan	q.i. (root)	n.a.	n.a.	none	none	none
Mangbetu	Nilo-Saharan	n.a.	n.a.	n.a.	none	none	CVC
Mari[b] (literary)	Uralic	Red V in open syll light	n.a.	n.a.	none	n.a.	none
Maricopa	Hokan	q.i. (final of root)	n.a.	none	n.a.	none	
Maru[b]	Sino-Tibetan	n.a.	n.a.	n.a.	*CVVC	CVV(C), CVR	CVfl
Marubu	Panoan	q.i (initial)	n.a.	n	none	n.a.	CVV
Maung[e]	Australian	CVV(C), CVC	n.a.	n.a.	none	n.a.	none
Mayo[b]	Sepik-Ramu	Low V	n.a.	n.a.	none	n.a.	none
Mazatec[a]	Oto-Manguean	q.i. (final)	n.a.	n.a.	none	none	none

Mbai[d]	Nilo-Saharan	n.a.	n.a.	n.a.	CVV(C), CVR	none
Mende[a]	Niger-Congo	n.a.	n.a.	none	none	none
Menomini	Algic	CVV(C)	n.a.	none	n.a.	CVVC
Miwok, Sierra	Penutian	CVV(C), CVC	n.a.	*CVVC	n.a.	CVC
Mixe, Coatlán	Mixe-Zoque	CVV(C), CVC[64]	n.a.	none	n.a.	??
Mixe, Totontepec	Mixe-Zoque	q.i. (initial of root)	n.a.	none	n.a.	CVC
Mixtec[a]	Oto-Manguean	n.a.	n.a.	none	none	none
Mocha	Afro-Asiatic	q.i. (phonemic)	n.a.	none	none	CVV
Moghol	Altaic	q.i. (final)	n.a.	none	n.a.	CVC
Mohawk	Iroquoian	q.i. (penult)	n.a.	OSVL	n.a.	CVCV
Mojave	Hokan	CVV(C)	n.a.	none	n.a.	none??
Mordvin[e]	Uralic	Full V	n.a.	none	n.a.	none
Moro[b]	Niger-Congo	CVC > Full V > Red V	n.a.	none	???	none
Movima[e]	unclassified	q.i. (penult)	n.a.	none	n.a.	none
Mulwi	Afro-Asiatic	n.a.	n.a.	*CVVC	none	none
Mumuye	Niger-Congo	n.a.	n.a.	none	CVV(C)[f]	none

(continued)

(continued)

Language	Macro-Phylum	Stress (heavy)	Metrics	Comp Length	Syll. Templ.	Tone	Minim. Word
Mundari[b]	Austro-Asiatic	Vʔ(C)	n.a.	n.a.	*CVVC	n.a.	none
Munsee	Algic	CVV(C), CVC	n.a.	n.a.	none	n.a.	???
Muong[b]	Austro-Asiatic	n.a.	n.a.	n.a.	none	CVV(C), CVR^n	none
Mura-Pirahã[a]	Mura	KVV > GVV > VV>KV > GV	n.a.	n.a.	none	CVV(C)	CVV
Murik	Trans New Guinea	CVV(C)	n.a.		none	n.a.	CVC
Murut	Austronesian	q.i. (penult and initial)	n.a.	n.a.	none	n.a.	CVV
Musey	Afro-Asiatic	n.a.	n.a.	r	*CVVC	CVV(C), CVC	none
Naga[b]	Creole	q.i. (initial)	n.a.	n.a.	none	n.a.	none
Nahuatl	Uto-Aztecan	q.i. (penult)	n.a.	n.a.	none	n.a.	CVC
Nama	Khoisan	q.i. (initial mora)	n.a.	n.a.	none	CVV(C), CVR	none
Nambiquara, N.	Nambiquaran	CVV(C), CVC	n.a.	n.a.	OSVL	???	none
Nambiquara, S.	Nambiquaran	???	n.a.	n.a.	*CVVC	???	???

Nandi	Nilo-Saharan	n.a.	n.a.	n.a.	none	none	none
Nankina[e]	Trans New Guinea	Full V, onset[65]	n.a.	n.a.	none	n.a.	none
Naro[d]	Khoisan	n.a.	n.a.	n.a.	???	CVV(C), CVR	CVR
Navajo[f]	Na Dene	n.a.	n.a.	n.a.	none	CVV(C)	none
Ndumbea[a]	Austronesian	n.a.	n.a.	n.a.	none	none	none
Ndyuka[d]	Creole	CVV(C), CVC	n.a.	none	none	CVV(C)	none
Nenets[e]	Uralic	q.i. (initial)	n.a.	n.a.	none	n.a.	none
Nez Perce	Penutian	CVV(C), CVC	n.a.	n.a.	none	n.a.	none
Nganasan	Uralic	CVV(C)	n.a.	n.a.	none	n.a.	none
Nocte[b]	Sino-Tibetan	n.a.	n.a.	n.a.	none	none	none
Nuuchahnulth	Wakashan	CVV(C), CVR	n.a.	n.a.	*CVVR	n.a.	none
Nubi	Creole	H tone	n.a.	n.a.	none	none[m]	none
Nung	Sino-Tibetan	n.a.	n.a.	n.a.	none	CVV(C), CVR[n]	CVC
Nyawaygi	Australian	CVV(C)	n.a.	ə[c]	none	n.a.	CVCV[g]
Ocaina[66]	Witotoan	n.a.	n.a.	n.a.	none	CVV(C)	CVCV[g]??
Ojibwa	Algic	CVV(C)	n.a.	n.a.	none	n.a.	CVV??

(continued)

(continued)

Language	Macro-Phylum	Stress (heavy)	Metrics	Comp Length	Syll. Templ.	Tone	Minim. Word
Oneida	Iroquoian	CVC (pitch accent)	n.a.	h	OSVL[67]	n.a.	CVCV
Onge[b]	Andamanese	???	n.a.	n.a.	none	n.a.	none
Onondaga	Iroquoian	q.i. (penult)	n.a.	n.a.	OSVL[68]	n.a.	CVCV
Orokolo[b]	Trans New Guinea	q.i. (penult)	n.a.	n.a.	none	n.a.	none
Oromo	Afro-Asiatic	pitch accent	n.a.	n.a.	none	n.a.	CVC
Orya	Trans New Guinea	CVR.R[69]	n.a.	n.a.	none	n.a.	none
Ostyak (Vach)[c]	Uralic	Full V[h]	n.a.	n.a.	none	n.a.	none
Otomi[a b]	Oto-Manguean	n.a.	n.a.	n.a.	n.a.	none	none
Pacoh[b]	Austro-Asiatic	q.i. (root)	n.a.	n.a.	*CFull VC, *CVVC[70]	none	none
Paez	Paezan	q.i. (penult)	n.a.	n.a.	n.a.	n.a.	none
Pagu[e]	West Papuan	q.i. . (penult)	n.a.	n.a.	n.a.	n.a.	CV.V
Paipai	Hokan	q.i. . (root)	n.a.	n.a.	none	n.a.	none
Paiwan[e]	Austronesian	q.i. (penult)	n.a.	n.a.	none	n.a.	CVC (<CV. VC)
Paraujano	Arawakan	q.i. (peninitial)	n.a.	n.a.	none	n.a.	none

		Full V			OSVL		
Patep	Austronesian	n.a.	n.a.	n.a.	none	n.a.	none
Pawnee	Caddoan	q.i. (initial-nouns, verbs-??)	n.a.	n.a.	none	n.a.	CVC??
Pemon[b]	Carib	q.i. (final)	n.a.	n.a.	n.a.	n.a.	none??
Persian	Indo-European	q.i. (final)	CVVC, CVCC > CVV, CVC > CV	n.a.	none	n.a.	none
Pomo, Eastern	Hokan	q.i. (initial)	n.a.	n[c]	none	n.a.	none
Pomo, Kashaya	Hokan	CVC (pitch accent)[71]	n.a.	l, n[c]	*CVVC[72]	n.a.	CVCV??
Quechua, Hual-laga	Quechan	CVV(C)	n.a.	q	*CVVC	n.a.	CVCV
Quechua, Inga[c]	Quechan	CVV(C), CVR[h]	n.a.	n.a.	none	n.a.	CVCV
Quechua, Junin-Huanca	Quechan	CVV(C)	n.a.	n.a.	*CVVC	n.a.	CVCV
Quicha	Quechan	q.i. (penult)	n.a.	n.a.	none	n.a.	CVCV
Quileute	Chimakuan	q.i. (penult)	n.a.	n.a.	OSVL	n.a.	none
Runga	Nilo-Saharan	n.a.	n.a.	n.a.	*CVVC	none[m]	none
Russian	Indo-European	q.i. (morph.)	n.a.	n.a.	none	n.a.	none

(continued)

(continued)

Language	Macro-Phylum	Stress (heavy)	Metrics	Comp Length	Syll. Templ.	Tone	Minim. Word
Saek	Daic	n.a.	n.a.	n.a.	none	CVV(C), CVR^n	none
Sahu	West Papuan	?:	n.a.	n.a.	none	n.a.	none
Sámi, Eastern	Uralic	q.i. (initial)	n.a.	n.a.	*CVVCC	n.a.	CVV
Sámi, Northern	Uralic	q.i. (initial)	n.a.	n.a.	*CVVCC	n.a.	CVV
Sango[a]	Creole	q.i. (initial)	n.a.	n.a.	none	none??	none
Santali	Austro-Asiatic	q.i. (initial)	n.a.	n.a.	none	n.a.	none
Sanuma[a e]	Yanomam	q.i. (penult and initial)	n.a.	n.a.	none	n.a.	none
Sapuan	Austro-Asiatic	q.i. (root)	n.a.	n.a.	none	n.a.	CVC
Sarangani Manobo[e]	Austronesian	Red V in open syll light	n.a.	n.a.	none	n.a.	CVC
Sarsi	Na Dene	n.a.	n.a.	n.a.	none	CVV(C)	none
Sawai[e]	Austronesian	/E/ light[73]	n.a.	n.a.	none	n.a.	none
Selknam	Chon	q.i. (penult)	n.a.	n.a.	none	CVV(C)	none
Selkup	Uralic	CVV(C)	n.a.	n.a.	OSVL	n.a.	none
Seneca	Iroquoian	(CVC)	n.a.	n.a.	none	n.a.	CVCV
Senoufo[a f]	Niger-Congo	q.i. (initial)	n.a.	n.a.	none	none	none
Sentani[e]	Trans New Guinea	Red V in open syll light	n.a.	n.a.	none	n.a.	none

Shan	Daic	n.a.	n.a.	n.a.	none	n.a.	CVV(C), CVR[n]	none
Shilluk	Nilo-Saharan	q.i. (root)	n.a.	n.a.	none	n.a.	CVV(C)[74]	CVC
Sierra Popoluca	Mixe-Zoque	q.i. (morph.)	n.a.	n.a.	none	n.a.	n.a.	CVC
Siona[a]	Tucanoan	q.i. (initial)	n.a.	n.a.	none	n.a.	n.a.	CVV
Siriano[a]	Tucanoan	q.i. (penult)	n.a.	n.a.	none	n.a.	n.a.	none
Siwa	Afro-Asiatic	q.i. (morph.)	n.a.	n.a.	none	n.a.	n.a.	???
Slavey	Na Dene	q.i. (root)	n.a.	n.a.	none	n.a.	none[m]	none
Somali	Afro-Asiatic	n.a.	n.a.	n.a.	none	n.a.	CVV(C)	CVC
Songai	Nilo-Saharan	???	n.a.	n.a.	???	n.a.	n.a.[75]	none
Sre	Austro-Asiatic	q.i. (root)	n.a.	n.a.	none	n.a.	n.a.	none
Stieng	Austro-Asiatic	q.i. (final of root)	n.a.	n.a.	none	n.a.	n.a.	none
Stoney Dakota[c][76]	Siouan	CVVC, CVCC	n.a.	n.a.	none	n.a.	n.a.	???
Sumbanese[a]	Austronesian	q.i. (initial)	n.a.	n.a.	none	n.a.	n.a.	CV.V
Tacana[a][c]	Tacanan	q.i. (penult)	n.a.	n.a.	none	n.a.	n.a.	none
Tai; Lung Ming	Daic	n.a.	n.a.	n.a.	none	n.a.	CVV(C), CVR[n]	none
Tamazight Berber[c]	Afro-Asiatic	q.i. (final)	CVC[77]	n.a.	none	n.a.	n.a.	none

(continued)

(continued)

Language	Macro-Phylum	Stress (heavy)	Metrics	Comp Length	Syll. Templ.	Tone	Minim. Word
Tamil	Dravidian	CVV(C) > CVC > CV	n.a.	n.a.	none	n.a.	CVC? CVCV[78]
Tangkhul[b]	Sino-Tibetan	n.a.	n.a.	n.a.	none	none??	none
Tangsa[b 79]	Sino-Tibetan	n.a.	n.a.	n.a.	none	none??	none
Taos (N.Tiwa)[b]	Kiowa-Tanoan	q.i. (phonemic)	n.a.	n.a.	none	none	none
Tatar[b]	Altaic	q.i. (final)	n.a.	n.a.	none	n.a.	none
Tauya[b]	Trans New Guinea	q.i. (final)[h]	n.a.	n.a.	none	n.a.	none
Tehit	West Papuan	??	n.a.	n.a.	none	n.a.	CCV, CVC
Telefol	Trans New Guinea	n.a.	n.a.	n.a.	none	CVV(C)	CVC
Telugu	Dravidian	CVV(C)	CVV(C), CVC	m	none	n.a.	CVC
Tepehuan	Uto-Aztecan	CVV(C), CVC	n.a.	n.a	none	n.a.	CVC
Ternate[e]	West Papuan	q.i. (penult??)	n.a.	n.a.	none	n.a.	CVC
Tetun[b]	Austronesian	q.i. (penult)	n.a.	n.a.	none	n.a.	none
Tewa[80]	Kiowa-Tanoan	q.i. (initial of stem)	n.a.	n.a.	none	CVV(C), CVR	none

Thai	Daic	q.i. (final of root)	CVV(C), CVC	k^c[81]	none	CVV(C), CVR	CVC[82]
Tibetan (Lhasa)	Sino-Tibetan	CVV(C)	n.a.	s^c, r, p, k	none	CVV(C), CVR	none
Tidore[b]	West Papuan	CVV(C)	n.a.	n.a.	none	n.a.	CVC??
Tigre[83]	Afro-Asiatic	n.a.	n.a.	n.a.	none	n.a.	none
Tiriyo[b]	Carib	q.i. (phonemic)	n.a.	n.a.	none	n.a.	CVV
Tiwi	Australian	q.i. (penult)	n.a.	n.a.	none	n.a.	CVV
Tlingit	Na Dene	n.a.	n.a.	n.a.	none	none[m]	none
Toda	Dravidian	??	n.a.	n.a.	none	n.a.	CVC??
Tol (Jicaque)[c]	isolate	CVV(C), CVC	n.a.	n.a.	none	n.a.	none
Tolojolabal[c]	Mayan	q.i. (penult)	n.a.	n.a.	none	n.a.	CVC
Tolowa	Na Dene	q.i. (final of root)	n.a.	n.a.	*CVVC	n.a.	none
Tonkawa	Coahuiltecan	q.i. . (penult)	n.a.	n.a.	none	n.a.	CVC
Torres Strait[b]	Creole	q.i. (follows source language)	n.a.	n.a.	none	n.a.	none
Totonac (Misantla)	Totonacan	CVV(C), CVC[84]	n.a.	n.a.	none	n.a.	CVC

(continued)

(*continued*)

Language	Macro-Phylum	Stress (heavy)	Metrics	Comp Length	Syll. Templ.	Tone	Minim. Word
Trique[85]	Oto-Manguean	n.a.	n.a.	n.a.	none	n.a.	none
Tsimshian	Penutian	q.i. (phonemic)	n.a.	n.a.	none	n.a.	none
Tsotsil	Mayan	q.i. (final)	n.a.	n.a.	none	n.a.	none
Tsou[a 86]	Austronesian	CVV(C)	n.a.	n.a.	none	n.a.	CVV
Tubatulabal	Uto-Aztecan	CVV(C)	n.a.	n.a.	none	n.a.	CVC
Tubu	Nilo-Saharan	n.a.	n.a.	n.a.	none	CVV(C)	none
Tunen	Niger-Congo	n.a.	n.a.	n.a.	none	none	none
Tunica[c]	Gulf??	q.i. (initial)	n.a.	n.a.	none	n.a.	none
Tura[d]	Niger-Congo	n.a.	n.a.	n.a.	*CVVC	CVV(C), CVR[87]	none
Turkana	Nilo-Saharan	n.a.	n.a.	n.a.	none	CVV(C), CVR[88]	none
Turkish	Altaic	CVV(C), CVC[89]	n.a.	v[90]	none	n.a.	CVC[91]
Tzutujil	Penutian	q.i. (final)	n.a.	n.a.	none	n.a.	CVC
Ubyx[92]	North Caucasian	q.i. (morph.)	n.a.	n.a.	none	n.a.	none
Urim[b 93]	Torricelli	Full V	n.a.	n.a.	none	n.a.	CVV[94]
Usan	Trans New Guinea	q.i. (penult)	n.a.	n.a.	none	n.a.	none

Uzbek	Altaic	q.i. (final)	n.a.	r[c], ?	none	n.a.	CVC
Vai[a]	Niger-Congo	n.a.	n.a.	n.a.	none	none[95]	none
Veps[b] [96]	Uralic	CVV(C), CVC	n.a.	l[c] [97]	none	n.a.	none
Vietnamese[b]	Austro-Asiatic	n.a.	n.a.	n.a.	none	CVV(C), CVR[98]	CVV?[99]
Votic	Uralic	CVV(C), CVC	n.a.	n.a.	none	n.a.	CVV
Waiwai	Carib	q.i. (final)	n.a.	n.a.	none	n.a.	none??
Wappo[b]	Yuki	q.i. (antepenult)	n.a.	n.a.	none	n.a.	none
Warao[a b]	isolate	q.i. (penult)	n.a.	n.a.	none	n.a.	CVV
Wardaman[e]	Australian	q.i. (penult)	n.a.	n.a.	none	n.a.	none
Warembori[d]	unclassified	q.i. (penult); onset[100]	n.a.	n.a.	none	n.a.	CVCV
Wari'[b]	Chapacura-Wanham	q.i. (final of phrase)	n.a.	n.a.	none	n.a.	CVC??
West Tarangan[e]	Austronesian	CVC	n.a.	n.a.	none	n.a.	none
Wichita	Caddoan	q.i. (phonemic)	n.a.	k[c], h	none	n.a.	none
Winnebago	Siouan	CVV(C)	n.a.	n.a.	none	n.a.	CVV
Wintu	Penutian	CVV(C)	n.a.	n.a.	none	n.a.	CVC

(continued)

(*continued*)

Language	Macro-Phylum	Stress (heavy)	Metrics	Comp Length	Syll. Templ.	Tone	Minim. Word
Wolof	Niger-Congo	CVV(C)	n.a.	n.a.	none	n.a.	CVC
Xavánte[101]	Macro-Ge	???	n.a.	n.a.	none	n.a.	none
Yagua[102]	Peba-Yaguan	q.i. (final) [103]	n.a.	n.a.	none	???	???
Yana	Hokan	CVV(C), CVC	n.a.	n.a.	*CVVC	n.a.	none
Yapese	Austronesian	CVV(C) > CVC > CV	n.a.	j, w	none	n.a.	(CVC)[104]
Yawelmani	Penutian	q.i. (penult-phrase)	n.a.	n.a.	*CVVC	n.a.	CVCV
Yele[a]	East Papuan	?:	n.a.	n.a.	none	n.a.	none
Yil[b] [105]	Torricelli	Full V	n.a.	n.a.	none	n.a.	none
Yimas	Sepik-Ramu	Low V	n.a.	n.a.	none	n.a.	none
Yonaguni	Japanese	n.a.	n.a.	n.a.	none	n.a.	none
Yucatecto	Mayan	n.a.	n.a.	n.a.	none	none	CVC
Yuchi[c]	isolate	q.i. (final)	n.a.	n.a.	none	n.a.	none
Yukaghir	Yukaghir	q.i. (morph.)	n.a.	n.a.	none	n.a.	CVC
Yulu	Nilo-Saharan	n.a.	n.a.	n.a.	none	none[m??]	none
Yupik, Central	Eskimo-Aleut	CVV(C); initial CVC	n.a.	n.a.	OSVL	n.a.	CVC

Yupik, Pacific Gulf	Eskimo-Aleut	CVV(C); initial CVC	n.a.	n.a.	OSVL	n.a.	CVC
Yupik, Sirenik[c]	Eskimo-Aleut	q.i. (peninitial)[h]	n.a.	n.a.	none	n.a.	CVC
Yurok	Algic	q.i. (initial)[106]	h[107]	n.a.	none	n.a.	CVC
Zapotec, Mitla[b]	Oto-Manguean	q.i. (final of root)	n.a.	n.a.	none	none	none
Zoque[c]	Mixe-Zoque	q.i. (penult)	n.a.	n.a.	none	n.a.	CVC??
Zuni	isolate	q.i. (initial and penult/antepenult)	n.a.	n.a.	*CVVCC	n.a.	none

Appendix Three

CORPORA FOR STUDY OF TONE AND SYLLABLE TEMPLATE RESTRICTIONS

Hausa		
Syllable Type	Word	Gloss
CV	**fà**sá:	
	sáfú:	row, line (also pronounced sáhú:)
CVO	**fàs**kí:	being very broad
	máskó:	large blacksmith's hammer
	râs:á:	branches
CVR	**ràn**dá:	large water pot
	mándá:	dark Bornu medicinal salt
	mântá:	forgot
CVV	**mà:**má:	breast
	rá:ná:	sun
	lâ:lá:	indolence

Cantonese		
Syllable Type	Word	Gloss
CV	mà	to curse
CVO	làp	to stand
CVR	sàm	very
CVVO	là:p	to cure meat
CVVR	là:m	to (use) indiscriminately

Navajo		
Syllable Type	Word	Gloss
CV	pìmàkí	his monkey
CVO	ʃàʃìkaìj	polar bear
CVR	pìyànkì	at his house
CVV	pìnà:níʃ	his work
CVVO	nà:ʃt'éʒí	Zuni
CVVR	pìkà:nkì	on his arm

Lithuanian	
bàndá	herd
gàlvá	head
ʒàrná	intestine
dàgné	
slàptá	in secret
lá:nda	hole
bá:ltas	white
má:rgas	colorful
sá:ptis	

Appendix Four

CORPUS OF WORDS FOR EXPERIMENTS ON
WEIGHT-SENSITIVE STRESS

(Stress on initial syllable unless otherwise noted; transcriptions are in IPA)

Bole		Chickasaw	
pòrɗi_____ láːʄi		_____ tʃikːoʔsi aːtʃi.	
Say _____ again please.		Say _____ quickly.	
pàtà	penis	pa'tʃiʔ	pigeon
pìtà		tʃi'liʔ	chili
pùtà		ʃaːtʃi	scrape
pàntà		tʃiːli	lay eggs
pìntà	fan	ʃan'tiʔ	rat
pùntà		sin'tiʔ	snake
pàːtà		im'pa	groceries
pìːtà	fan	ʃamba?	blind person
pùːtà	rest	al'biʔ	paint
zàmbà		il'bak	hand, arm
žìmbà	hit hard	al'ba¹	weed
pùmbà		taʃ'ki	lie down
pàltà		iʃ'kiʔ	mother
pìltà	hatch	paɬ'ki	go fast
pùltà	blow up (baloon)	piɬ'tʃi	sheep sorrel
tàrkà	get entangled	nak'siʔ	rib
tìrkà		tik'baʔ	crotch
tùrkà		nib'li	dismember
		tab'li	cut
		jaːk'niʔ	cave
		naːf'ka	dress
		iːs'taʔ	easter
		tiːb'li	reinjure

Farsi		Finnish	
dobari _____ beɣu.		sanon _____ kaksi kertaː.	
Say _____ again.		I say _____ two times.	
paˈʃe	mosquito	lakat	varnish nom.acc.pl.
piˈʃe	job	likat	dirt nom.acc.pl. (dialect)
puˈʃe	clothing	nukat	nap nom.acc.pl.
pamˈbe	cotton	naːkat	jackdaw nom.acc.pl.
pimˈbe		liːkat	surplus nom.acc.pl. (dialect)
pumˈbe		nuːkat	
panˈde		lampat	
pinˈde		limpat	
punˈde		lumpat	
palˈde		maltat	be patient 2psg.pres.
pilˈde		milkat	
pulˈde		multat	
parˈde	curtain	markat	Finnish mark (money) nom.acc.pl.
pirˈde		mirkat	
purˈde		murtat	break 2psg.pres. (dialect)
pafˈte		lastat	splint nom.acc.pl.
pifˈte		niskat	nape of neck nom.acc.pl.
pufˈte		mustat	black nom.acc.pl.
pasˈbe		matkat	journey nom.acc.pl.
pisˈbe		mitkat	
pusˈbe		mutkat	detour nom.acc.pl.
pazˈbe			
pizˈbe			
puzˈbe			
paʃˈte			
piʃˈte			
paʒˈbe			
piʒˈbe			
puʒˈbe			
taxˈte	wood		
tixˈte			
tuxˈte			
pakˈbe			
pikˈbe			
pukˈbe			
paɡˈbe			
piɡˈbe			
puɡˈbe			

French		Japanese	
ʒə di _____ dø fwɑ.		mou itʃido _____ to it:e.	
I say _____ two times.		Please say _____ again.	
paˈpe	father (dialect)	papa	papa
piˈpe	trick	pipa	
puˈpe	doll	pupa	
palˈpe	touch	paːpa	
pilˈpe		piːpa	
pulˈpe		puːpa	
paʁˈke	fold, enclose	pampa	
piʁˈke		pimpa	
puʁˈke		pumpa	
pasˈpe		panta	
pisˈpe		pinta	
pusˈpe		punta	

Javanese		Khalkha	
kandane _____ manɛh.		daxin xɛl _____.	
As its said _____ again.		Say again _____.	
ḍami	dried rice stalk	manax	keep vigil
ḍamu	to blow (on, out)	munax	become senile
gaḍu	club	maːnax	stupid
dəˈlap	covetous	muːrax	faint
badan	body	namtax	become lower
basin	foul odor	umbax	swim, ford
lamun	when, if	tsantax	be covered in frost
kaɲən	yearn for, miss	untax	sleep
babar	to proliferate	maltax	dig, excavate
ḍalir	stripes (on animal)	mulgax	be confused
balur	type of fish	martax	forget
marmər	marble	ursax	flow, stream
babat	tripe	naslax	age, grow old
babit	to swing at	nustax	get the flu
manut	according to	xaʃgar	shouting
padət	compact	muʃrax	
bagas	healthy looking	maxsax	crave meat
garis	fate	nuxlax	rub continuously
barus	chalk, udder	maktax	praise
gaməs	eat all one can get	uktax	welcome a visitor
		magnax	silk brocade
		uglax	insert

Russian	
skaʒi _____ .	
Say _____ .	
papa	papa
pipa	kid's term for vagina
pupa	

Telugu	
_____ kaːboːlu.	
Perhaps it is _____.	
para	foreign
pira	
pura	
paːra	spade
piːra	
puːra	
pampa	
pimpa	
pumpa	
palta	
pilta	
pulta	
parta	
pirta	
purta	
pasta	
pista	
pusta	
pakta	
pikta	
pukta	
paɡna	
piɡna	
puɡna	

Appendix Five

DISTINCTIONS BY ENERGY (IN ARBITRARY UNITS)

Distinctions in bold are phonological; shaded distinctions are complex

CHICKASAW	H	L	Diff	Norm	Wilkes λ	χ²	Sign
CVV(C) heavy	**140.4**	**69.9**	**70.5**	**80.6**	**0.603375**	**87.150**	**0.0000**
CVV(C), CVC heavy	**93.3**	**30.8**	**62.5**	**71.5**	**0.862489**	**25.518**	**0.0000**
CVV(C), V+R heavy	114.1	57.5	56.7	64.8	0.661233	71.354	0.0000
Low V heavy	95.3	79.8	15.5	17.7	0.974586	4.441	0.0351
Non-back V heavy	n.a.	n.a.	n.a.	n.a.	n.a.	n.a.	n.a.
Red V light	n.a.	n.a.	n.a.	n.a.	n.a.	n.a.	n.a.
Red V in open σ light	n.a.	n.a.	n.a.	n.a.	n.a.	n.a.	n.a.
CVVC, CVCC heavy	137.4	78.1	59.4	67.8	0.799441	38.613	0.0000
CVV(C), V+G heavy	105.9	56.6	49.3	56.3	0.760122	47.313	0.0000
CVV(C), V+S heavy	110.8	61.9	48.9	55.9	0.747150	50.282	0.0000
CVV(C), V-N heavy	95.4	67.6	27.8	31.7	0.934154	11.750	0.0006
CVV(C), V-T heavy	98.9	74.1	24.8	28.4	0.935120	11.571	0.0007
CVV(C), V-S heavy	97.5	70.4	27.0	30.9	0.928249	12.843	0.0003
CVV(C), V-R heavy	94.5	75.85	18.7	21.3	0.96557	6.044	0.0140
CVV(C), V-K heavy	98.9	38.9	60.0	68.6	0.766646	45.838	0.0000
CVV(C), V-B heavy	99.2	58.5	40.7	46.6	0.856505	26.719	0.0000
CVV(C), V-G heavy	100.7	72.7	28.0	32.0	0.917365	14.878	0.0001
CVV(C), V+T heavy	107.5	55.5	52.1	59.5	0.728644	54.608	0.0000
CVV(C), V+N heavy	116.8	64.6	52.2	59.7	0.715246	57.810	0.0000

CVV(C), V+K heavy	114.2	73.3	40.9	46.7	0.839106	30.260	0.0000
CVV(C), V+B heavy	110.4	69.3	41.1	47.0	0.823240	33.553	0.0000
CVV(C), CaC heavy	105.6	61.9	43.7	49.9	0.804409	37.544	0.0000
Short HiV in open σ light	90.2	32.3	57.9	66.2	0.938074	11.027	0.0009
CVV(C), a-G heavy	112.4	71.8	40.5	46.3	0.834539	31.201	0.0000
CVV(C), a-T heavy	115.2	69.2	46.1	52.7	0.784034	41.970	0.0000
CVV(C), a-S heavy	113.9	66.5	47.4	54.2	0.764725	46.271	0.0000
CVV(C), a-R heavy	106.8	72.5	34.3	39.2	0.877285	22.584	0.0000
CVV(C), a-N heavy	106.8	69.0	37.8	43.2	0.848862	28.266	0.0000
CVV(C), a-K heavy	109.8	61.2	48.7	55.6	0.750851	49.430	0.0000
CVV(C), a-B heavy	110.8	65.7	45.2	51.6	0.784228	41.927	0.0000
CVV(C), a+G heavy	116.4	64.4	52.0	59.4	0.716832	57.428	0.0000
CVV(C), a+T heavy	116.6	64.8	51.9	59.3	0.718884	56.935	0.0000
CVV(C), a+S heavy	118.4	67.6	50.8	58.1	0.738804	52.220	0.0000
CVV(C), a+R heavy	126.1	61.9	64.2	73.3	0.581391	93.552	0.0000
CVV(C), a+N heavy	128.9	65.5	63.4	72.5	0.612845	84.464	0.0000
CVV(C), a+K heavy	127.2	70.8	56.3	64.4	0.719131	56.875	0.0000
CVV(C), a+B heavy	123.1	68.1	54.9	62.8	0.707472	59.695	0.0000
CV, hiV-G light	97.8	54.1	43.8	50.0	0.854250	27.174	0.0000
CV, hiV-T light	100.8	44.5	56.2	64.3	0.759635	47.423	0.0000

(continued)

CHICKASAW—(*continued*)

	H	L	Diff	Norm	Wilkes λ	χ2	Sign
CV, hiV-S light	102.4	49.6	52.8	60.3	0.762186	46.845	0.0000
CV, hiV-R light	100.5	54.4	46.1	52.6	0.818834	34.478	0.0000
CV, hiV-N light	100.9	59.3	41.5	47.5	0.840982	29.874	0.0000
CV, hiV-K light	100.2	65.1	35.1	40.1	0.879571	22.135	0.0000
CV, hiV-B light	99.6	62.1	37.5	42.8	0.870430	23.937	0.0000
CV, hiV+G light	98.4	58.1	40.3	46.0	0.865065	25.004	0.0000
CV, hiV+T light	95.3	66.4	28.9	33.0	0.930488	12.428	0.0004
CV, hiV+S light	94.2	64.6	29.6	33.8	0.935674	11.469	0.0007
CV, hiV+R light	95.9	58.5	37.4	42.8	0.897251	18.702	0.0000
CV, hiV+N light	95.8	50.8	45.0	51.5	0.871636	23.699	0.0000
CV, hiV+K light	96.5	33.9	62.7	71.6	0.796293	39.293	0.0000
CV, hiV+B light	96.9	46.0	50.9	58.2	0.835881	30.924	0.0000
Ca, Cu: heavy	164.6	77.1	87.5	100.0	0.657425	72.351	0.0000
Cat, Ci: heavy	140.4	69.9	70.5	80.6	0.603375	87.150	0.0000
Ca: heavy	164.6	77.1	87.5	100.0	0.657425	72.351	0.0000
Ca, Cu heavy	95.3	79.8	15.5	17.7	0.974586	4.441	0.0351

Telugu	H	L	Diff	Norm	Willkes λ	χ2	Sign
CVV(C) heavy	**211.8**	**124.2**	**87.6**	**72.3**	**0.760039**	**36.356**	**0.0000**
CVV(C), CVC heavy	**148.7**	**52.4**	**96.3**	**79.5**	**0.709650**	**45.445**	**0.0000**
CVV(C), V+R heavy	162.6	105.4	57.1	47.1	0.780127	32.900	0.0000
Low V heavy	149.5	129.1	20.5	16.9	0.974847	3.375	0.0662
Non-back V heavy	148.5	111.5	37.0	30.5	0.916773	11.514	0.0007
Red V light	n.a.	n.a.	n.a.	n.a.	n.a.	n.a.	n.a.
Red V in open σ light	n.a.	n.a.	n.a.	n.a.	n.a.	n.a.	n.a.
CVCC, CVCC heavy	n.a.	n.a.	n.a.	n.a.	n.a.	n.a.	n.a.
CVV(C), V+G heavy	162.6	82.5	80.2	66.1	0.613276	64.785	0.0000
CVV(C), V+S heavy	157.0	112.5	44.5	36.7	0.866472	18.991	0.0000
CVV(C), V-N heavy	151.3	93.5	57.8	47.7	0.823348	25.755	0.0000
CVV(C), V-T heavy	157.3	116.6	40.8	33.6	0.887836	15.763	0.0001
CVV(C), V-S heavy	157.3	116.6	40.8	33.6	0.887836	15.763	0.0001
CVV(C), V-R heavy	151.0	122.7	28.3	23.3	0.946160	7.333	0.0068
CVV(C), V-K heavy	152.5	103.8	48.6	40.1	0.856137	20.581	0.0000
CVV(C), V-B heavy	151.3	93.5	57.8	47.7	0.823348	25.755	0.0000
CVV(C), V-G heavy	146.2	130.7	15.5	12.8	0.985616	1.920	0.1659
CVV(C), V+T heavy	157.0	112.5	44.5	36.7	0.866472	18.991	0.0000

(continued)

TELUGU—*(continued)*

	H	L	Diff	Norm	Wilkes λ	χ2	Sign
CVV(C), V+N heavy	173.2	122.3	50.9	42.0	0.862753	19.560	0.0000
CVV(C), V+K heavy	166.2	120.2	46.0	37.9	0.871466	18.229	0.0000
CVV(C), V+B heavy	173.2	122.3	50.9	42.0	0.862753	19.560	0.0000
CVV(C), CaC heavy	185.1	115.9	69.2	57.1	0.733673	41.034	0.0000
Short HiV in open σ light	145.1	41.6	103.5	85.4	0.764897	35.512	0.0000
CVV(C), a-G heavy	182.7	124.2	58.5	48.2	0.851945	21.231	0.0000
CVV(C), a-T heavy	183.4	120.5	62.8	51.8	0.802631	29.131	0.0000
CVV(C), a-S heavy	183.4	120.5	62.8	51.8	0.802631	29.131	0.0000
CVV(C), a-R heavy	180.6	121.4	59.2	48.8	0.824955	25.497	0.0000
CVV(C), a-N heavy	173.8	117.0	56.8	46.9	0.805666	28.631	0.0000
CVV(C), a-K heavy	173.0	119.2	53.8	44.4	0.831784	24.404	0.0000
CVV(C), a-B heavy	173.8	117.0	56.8	46.9	0.805666	28.631	0.0000
CVV(C), a+G heavy	179.6	116.2	63.4	52.3	0.766609	35.216	0.0000
CVV(C), a+T heavy	178.4	120.4	58.0	47.9	0.821869	25.993	0.0000
CVV(C), a+S heavy	178.4	120.4	58.0	47.9	0.821869	25.993	0.0000
CVV(C), a+R heavy	181.0	119.5	61.5	50.7	0.800008	29.565	0.0000
CVV(C), a+N heavy	193.9	123.4	70.6	58.2	0.802861	29.094	0.0000
CVV(C), a+K heavy	192.9	121.6	71.3	58.8	0.779827	32.951	0.0000
CVV(C), a+B heavy	193.9	123.4	70.6	58.2	0.802861	29.094	0.0000

CV, hiV-G light	159.2	72.0	87.2	71.9	0.597528	68.231	0.0000
CV, hiV-T light	155.6	101.3	54.4	44.9	0.814922	27.118	0.0000
CV, hiV-S light	155.6	101.3	54.4	44.9	0.814922	27.118	0.0000
CV, hiV-R light	159.2	93.6	65.6	54.1	0.733277	41.106	0.0000
CV, hiV-N light	162.6	112.5	50.1	41.3	0.830954	24.536	0.0000
CV, hiV-K light	158.6	111.5	47.1	38.8	0.850372	21.476	0.0000
CV, hiV-B light	162.6	112.5	50.1	41.3	0.830954	24.536	0.0000
CV, hiV+G light	149.4	121.8	27.6	22.8	0.948290	7.035	0.0080
CV, hiV+T light	154.6	106.9	47.7	39.4	0.852808	21.097	0.0000
CV, hiV+S light	154.6	106.9	47.7	39.4	0.852808	21.097	0.0000
CV, hiV+R light	150.8	113.6	37.2	30.7	0.909962	12.502	0.0004
CV, hiV+N light	150.7	84.2	66.5	54.9	0.793115	30.712	0.0000
CV, hiV+K light	152.7	91.3	61.4	50.6	0.797058	30.055	0.0000
CV, hiV+B light	150.7	84.2	66.5	54.9	0.793115	30.712	0.0000
Ca, Cu: heavy	190.9	130.5	60.3	49.8	0.920162	11.025	0.0009
Ca, Ci: heavy	246.3	125.1	121.2	100.0	0.677827	51.524	0.0000
Ca: heavy	239.0	131.1	107.9	89.0	0.866058	19.054	0.0000
Ca, Cu heavy	147.5	130.3	17.1	14.1	0.982521	2.336	0.1264

Khalkha	H	L	Diff	Norm	Wilkes λ	χ2	Sign
CVV(C) heavy	**266.9**	**160.1**	**106.7**	**89.7**	**0.832069**	**27.852**	**0.0000**
CVV(C), CVC heavy	175.4	118.1	57.3	48.1	0.948532	8.005	0.0047
CVV(C), V+R heavy	197.6	145.4	52.2	43.9	0.878960	19.546	0.0000
Low V heavy	176.7	162.6	14.1	11.9	0.991083	1.357	0.2441
Non-back V heavy	n.a.	n.a.	n.a.	n.a.	n.a.	n.a.	n.a.
Red V light	n.a.	n.a.	n.a.	n.a.	n.a.	n.a.	n.a.
Red V in open σ light	n.a.	n.a.	n.a.	n.a.	n.a.	n.a.	n.a.
CVVC, CVCC heavy	n.a.	n.a.	n.a.	n.a.	n.a.	n.a.	n.a.
CVV(C), V+G heavy	190.6	144.3	46.2	38.8	0.905707	15.004	0.0001
CVV(C), V+S heavy	177.0	160.5	16.5	13.9	0.988034	1.824	0.1769
CVV(C), V-N heavy	165.5	181.5	-16.0	-13.5	0.990921	1.382	0.2398
CVV(C), V-T heavy	182.3	160.0	22.3	18.8	0.978037	3.364	0.0666
CVV(C), V-S heavy	192.7	152.7	40.0	33.6	0.930093	10.979	0.0009
CVV(C), V-R heavy	171.5	168.0	3.4	2.9	0.999471	0.080	0.7770
CVV(C), V-K heavy	190.9	130.8	60.2	50.6	0.852856	24.113	0.0000
CVV(C), V-B heavy	169.4	171.5	-2.0	-1.7	0.999883	0.018	0.8939
CVV(C), V-G heavy	177.2	164.2	13.1	11.0	0.992500	1.141	0.2855
CVV(C), V+T heavy	185.0	151.2	33.8	28.4	0.949744	7.812	0.0052
CVV(C), V+N heavy	233.8	146.6	87.2	73.3	0.735041	46.636	0.0000

CVV(C), V+K heavy	270.3	169.6	100.7	84.6	0.999982	0.003	0.9580
CVV(C), V+B heavy	245.1	152.4	92.8	77.9	0.765396	40.505	0.0000
CVV(C), CaC heavy	192.2	147.5	44.7	37.5	0.910993	14.123	0.0002
Short HiV in open σ light	172.5	113.0	59.5	50.0	0.972591	4.210	0.0402
CVV(C), a-G heavy	192.9	161.2	31.7	26.6	0.964475	5.480	0.0192
CVV(C), a-T heavy	208.8	154.7	54.1	45.5	0.894868	16.828	0.0000
CVV(C), a-S heavy	222.7	150.7	72.0	60.5	0.819185	30.216	0.0000
CVV(C), a-R heavy	188.5	161.1	27.3	23.0	0.971100	4.443	0.0350
CVV(C), a-N heavy	176.5	165.1	11.5	9.6	0.994299	0.866	0.3520
CVV(C), a-K heavy	209.5	147.8	61.7	51.9	0.844022	25.691	0.0000
CVV(C), a-B heavy	183.3	158.7	24.6	20.7	0.973243	4.109	0.0427
CVV(C), a+G heavy	212.9	149.7	63.2	53.1	0.845571	25.413	0.0000
CVV(C), a+T heavy	199.0	156.6	42.4	35.6	0.931171	10.804	0.0010
CVV(C), a+S heavy	188.1	161.1	27.0	22.7	0.971512	4.379	0.0364
CVV(C), a+R heavy	221.4	150.5	70.9	59.6	0.822194	29.660	0.0000
CVV(C), a+N heavy	268.0	149.0	119.0	100.0	0.634865	68.833	0.0000
CVV(C), a+K heavy	194.7	162.2	32.5	27.3	0.966261	5.200	0.0226
CVV(C), a+B heavy	271.7	153.8	118.0	99.1	0.707726	52.373	0.0000
CV, hiV-G light	180.8	138.6	42.2	35.4	0.939030	9.530	0.0020
CV, hiV-T light	181.2	129.7	51.5	43.3	0.918691	12.848	0.0003

(continued)

KHALKHA—*(continued)*

	H	L	Diff	Norm	Wilkes λ	χ2	Sign
CV, hiV-S light	182.4	134.0	48.4	40.7	0.919558	12.705	0.0004
CV, hiV-R light	184.4	136.7	47.7	40.0	0.914103	13.607	0.0002
CV, hiV-N light	187.3	141.8	45.5	38.2	0.912863	13.812	0.0002
CV, hiV-K light	155.7	178.9	-23.1	-19.4	0.977306	3.478	0.0622
CV, hiV-B light	190.6	144.3	46.3	38.9	0.905333	15.067	0.0001
CV, hiV+G light	182.1	145.9	36.2	30.4	0.947688	8.140	0.0043
CV, hiV+T light	178.6	152.7	25.9	21.7	0.973281	4.103	0.0428
CV, hiV+S light	177.6	150.3	27.3	22.9	0.972861	4.168	0.0412
CV, hiV+R light	178.5	149.0	29.5	24.8	0.967904	4.942	0.0262
CV, hiV+N light	176.3	142.2	34.1	28.6	0.968376	4.868	0.0274
CV, hiV+K light	183.4	118.3	65.0	54.6	0.875825	20.087	0.0000
CV, hiV+B light	175.0	138.0	37.0	31.1	0.968332	4.875	0.0272
Ca, Cu: heavy	239.9	166.0	73.9	62.1	0.952007	7.451	0.0063
Ca; Ci: heavy	239.9	166.0	73.9	62.1	0.952007	7.451	0.0063
Ca: heavy	239.9	166.0	73.9	62.1	0.952007	7.451	0.0063
Ca, Cu heavy							

FINNISH	H	L	Diff	Norm	Wilkes λ	χ²	Sign
CVV(C) heavy	335.4	228.5	106.9	53.8	0.835684	29.708	0.0000
CVV(C), CVC heavy	**272.2**	**73.3**	**198.9**	**100.0**	**0.431361**	**139.154**	**0.0000**
CVV(C), V+R heavy	297.1	172.7	124.4	62.6	0.554805	97.502	0.0000
Low V heavy	245.2	243.1	2.2	1.1	0.999879	0.020	0.8872
Non-back V heavy	259.7	235.9	23.8	12.0	0.985190	2.469	0.1161
Red V light	n.a.	n.a.	n.a.	n.a.	n.a.	n.a.	n.a.
Red V in open σ light	n.a.	n.a.	n.a.	n.a.	n.a.	n.a.	n.a.
CVVC, CVCC heavy	n.a.	n.a.	n.a.	n.a.	n.a.	n.a.	n.a.
CVV(C), V+G heavy	297.1	172.7	124.4	62.6	0.554805	97.502	0.0000
CVV(C), V+S heavy	292.5	178.8	113.7	57.2	0.628306	76.913	0.0000
CVV(C), V-N heavy	273.8	168.8	105.1	52.8	0.735541	50.833	0.0000
CVV(C), V-T heavy	299.8	221.4	78.4	39.4	0.852665	26.379	0.0000
CVV(C), V-S heavy	266.2	227.0	39.2	19.7	0.95824	7.478	0.0062
CVV(C), V-R heavy	249.7	240.2	9.6	4.8	0.997459	0.421	0.5164
CVV(C), V-K heavy	272.2	73.3	198.9	100.0	0.431361	139.154	0.0000
CVV(C), V-B heavy	273.8	168.8	105.1	52.8	0.735541	50.833	0.0000
CVV(C), V-G heavy	249.7	240.2	9.6	4.8	0.997459	0.421	0.5164
CVV(C), V+T heavy	273.8	168.8	105.1	52.8	0.735541	50.833	0.0000

(continued)

Finnish— *(continued)*	H	L	Diff	Norm	Wilkes λ	χ2	Sign
CVV(C), V+N heavy	297.6	221.6	76.0	38.2	0.859856	24.989	0.0000
CVV(C), V+K heavy	335.4	228.5	106.9	53.8	0.835684	29.708	0.0000
CVV(C), V+B heavy	299.8	221.4	78.4	39.4	0.852665	26.379	0.0000
CVV(C), CaC heavy	286.2	217.7	68.5	34.4	0.870068	23.035	0.0000
Short HiV in open σ light	262.7	64.7	198.0	99.5	0.603583	83.556	0.0000
CVV(C), a-G heavy	289.3	229.6	59.7	30.0	0.924027	13.077	0.0003
CVV(C), a-T heavy	319.2	226.1	93.1	46.8	0.843001	28.265	0.0000
CVV(C), a-S heavy	295.2	227.7	67.5	33.9	0.903097	16.869	0.0000
CVV(C), a-R heavy	289.3	229.6	59.7	30.0	0.924027	13.077	0.0003
CVV(C), a-N heavy	288.5	221.5	67.0	33.7	0.882917	20.609	0.0000
CVV(C), a-K heavy	286.2	217.7	68.5	34.4	0.870068	23.035	0.0000
CVV(C), a-B heavy	288.5	221.5	67.0	33.7	0.882917	20.609	0.0000
CVV(C), a+G heavy	308.2	218.0	90.2	45.4	0.804984	35.902	0.0000
CVV(C), a+T heavy	288.5	221.5	67.0	33.7	0.882917	20.609	0.0000
CVV(C), a+S heavy	303.3	220.0	83.4	41.9	0.835480	30.132	0.0000
CVV(C), a+R heavy	308.2	218.0	90.2	45.4	0.804984	35.902	0.0000
CVV(C), a+N heavy	319.2	226.1	93.1	46.8	0.843001	28.265	0.0000
CVV(C), a+K heavy	335.4	228.5	106.9	53.8	0.835684	29.708	0.0000
CVV(C), a+B heavy	319.2	226.1	93.1	46.8	0.843001	28.265	0.0000

CV, hiV-G light	286.1	159.1	127.0	63.8	0.579346	90.339	0.0000
CV, hiV-T light	273.6	148.4	125.2	62.9	0.666238	67.211	0.0000
CV, hiV-S light	284.3	162.8	121.5	61.1	0.615140	80.417	0.0000
CV, hiV-R light	286.1	159.1	127.0	63.8	0.579346	90.339	0.0000
CV, hiV-N light	281.8	209.8	72.0	36.2	0.850884	26.725	0.0000
CV, hiV-K light	286.2	217.7	68.5	34.4	0.870068	23.035	0.0000
CV, hiV-B light	281.2	209.8	71.4	35.9	0.850884	26.725	0.0000
CV, hiV+G light	265.3	215.1	50.2	25.2	0.927577	12.442	0.0004
CV, hiV+T light	281.2	209.8	71.4	35.9	0.850884	26.725	0.0000
CV, hiV+S light	289.3	229.6	59.7	30.0	0.924027	13.077	0.0003
CV, hiV+R light	265.3	215.1	50.2	25.2	0.927577	12.442	0.0004
CV, hiV+N light	273.6	148.4	125.2	62.9	0.666238	67.211	0.0000
CV, hiV+K light	272.2	73.3	198.9	100.0	0.431361	139.154	0.0000
CV, hiV+B light	273.6	148.4	125.2	62.9	0.666238	67.211	0.0000
Ca, Cu heavy	335.0	234.2	100.9	50.7	0.897116	17.968	0.0000
Ca, Ci heavy	339.5	233.7	105.8	53.2	0.886856	19.872	0.0000
Ca: heavy	342.7	238.9	103.9	52.2	0.942539	9.794	0.0018
Ca, Cu heavy	235.9	259.7	-23.8	-12.0	0.985190	2.469	0.1161

JAPANESE

	H	L	Diff	Norm	Wilkes λ	χ2	Sign
CVV(C) heavy	222.1	185.7	36.4	17.5	0.982682	1.826	0.1767
CVV(C), CVC heavy	**247.3**	**39.7**	**207.6**	**100.0**	**0.435783**	**86.799**	**0.0000**
CVV(C), V+R heavy	247.3	39.7	207.6	100.0	0.435783	86.799	0.0000
Low V heavy	210.6	187.2	23.4	11.3	0.991636	0.878	0.3488
Non-back V heavy	198.7	187.0	11.7	5.6	0.997915	0.218	0.6405
Red V light	n.a.	n.a.	n.a.	n.a.	n.a.	n.a.	n.a.
Red V in open σ light	n.a.	n.a.	n.a.	n.a.	n.a.	n.a.	n.a.
CVVC, CVCC heavy	n.a.	n.a.	n.a.	n.a.	n.a.	n.a.	n.a.
CVV(C), V+G heavy	247.3	39.7	207.6	100.0	0.435783	86.799	0.0000
CVV(C), V+S heavy	222.1	185.7	36.4	17.5	0.982682	1.826	0.1767
CVV(C), V-N heavy	222.1	185.7	36.4	17.5	0.982682	1.826	0.1767
CVV(C), V-T heavy	238.8	150.2	88.6	42.7	0.863634	15.320	0.0001
CVV(C), V-S heavy	247.3	39.7	207.6	100.0	0.435783	86.799	0.0000
CVV(C), V-R heavy	222.1	185.7	36.4	17.5	0.982682	1.826	0.1767
CVV(C), V-K heavy	247.3	39.7	207.6	100.0	0.435783	86.799	0.0000
CVV(C), V-B heavy	243.1	147.6	95.4	46.0	0.841915	17.982	0.0000
CVV(C), V-G heavy	222.1	185.7	36.4	17.5	0.982682	1.826	0.1767
CVV(C), V+T heavy	243.1	147.6	95.4	46.0	0.841915	17.982	0.0000
CVV(C), V+N heavy	247.3	39.7	207.6	100.0	0.435783	86.799	0.0000

CVV(C), V+K heavy	222.1	185.7	36.4	17.5	0.982682	1.826	0.1767
CVV(C), V+B heavy	238.8	150.2	88.6	42.7	0.863634	15.320	0.0001
CVV(C), CaC heavy	237.7	163.8	73.9	35.6	0.907686	10.122	0.0015
Short HiV in open σ light	228.7	38.2	190.6	91.8	0.631846	47.977	0.0000
CVV(C), a-G heavy	222.1	185.7	36.4	17.5	0.982682	1.826	0.1767
CVV(C), a-T heavy	227.4	179.1	48.3	23.3	0.964406	3.787	0.0516
CVV(C), a-S heavy	237.7	163.8	73.9	35.6	0.907686	10.122	0.0015
CVV(C), a-R heavy	222.1	185.7	36.4	17.5	0.982682	1.826	0.1767
CVV(C), a-N heavy	222.1	185.7	36.4	17.5	0.982682	1.826	0.1767
CVV(C), a-K heavy	237.7	163.8	73.9	35.6	0.907686	10.122	0.0015
CVV(C), a-B heavy	233.0	176.4	56.7	27.3	0.950932	5.258	0.0219
CVV(C), a+G heavy	237.7	163.8	73.9	35.6	0.907686	10.122	0.0015
CVV(C), a+T heavy	233.0	176.4	56.7	27.3	0.950932	5.258	0.0219
CVV(C), a+S heavy	222.1	185.7	36.4	17.5	0.982682	1.826	0.1767
CVV(C), a+R heavy	237.7	163.8	73.9	35.6	0.907686	10.122	0.0015
CVV(C), a+N heavy	237.7	163.8	73.9	35.6	0.907686	10.122	0.0015
CVV(C), a+K heavy	222.1	185.7	36.4	17.5	0.982682	1.826	0.1767
CVV(C), a+B heavy	227.4	179.1	48.3	23.3	0.964406	3.787	0.0516
CV, hiV-G light	247.3	39.7	207.6	100.0	0.435783	86.799	0.0000
CV, hiV-T light	244.1	127.1	117.0	56.3	0.768535	27.512	0.0000

(continued)

JAPANESE—*(continued)*	H	L	Diff	Norm	Wilkes λ	χ2	Sign
CV, hiV-S light	237.7	163.8	73.9	35.6	0.907686	10.122	0.0015
CV, hiV-R light	247.3	39.7	207.6	100.0	0.435783	86.799	0.0000
CV, hiV-N light	247.3	39.7	207.6	100.0	0.435783	86.799	0.0000
CV, hiV-K light	237.7	163.8	73.9	35.6	0.907686	10.122	0.0015
CV, hiV-B light	243.6	125.2	118.4	57.0	0.764571	28.052	0.0000
CV, hiV+G light	237.7	163.8	73.9	35.6	0.907686	10.122	0.0015
CV, hiV+T light	243.6	125.2	118.4	57.0	0.764571	28.052	0.0000
CV, hiV+S light	247.3	39.7	207.6	100.0	0.435783	86.799	0.0000
CV, hiV+R light	237.7	163.8	73.9	35.6	0.907686	10.122	0.0015
CV, hiV+N light	237.7	163.8	73.9	35.6	0.907686	10.122	0.0015
CV, hiV+K light	247.3	39.7	207.6	100.0	0.435783	86.799	0.0000
CV, hiV+B light	244.1	127.1	117.0	56.3	0.768535	27.512	0.0000
Ca:, Cu: heavy	228.7	188.1	40.6	19.6	0.983977	1.688	0.1939
Ca:, Ci: heavy	233.6	187.1	46.6	22.4	0.978945	2.224	0.1359
Ca: heavy	258.3	189.1	69.3	33.4	0.974331	2.717	0.0993
Ca, Cu heavy	198.8	187.4	11.4	5.5	0.997960	0.213	0.6441

JAVANESE	H	L	Diff.	Norm	Wilkes λ	χ2	Sign.
CVV(C) heavy	n.a.	n.a.	n.a.	n.a.	n.a.	n.a.	n.a.
CVV(C), CVC heavy	119.9	77.5	42.4	53.3	0.864457	15.949	0.0001
CVV(C), V+R heavy	118.2	108.6	9.6	12.0	0.988028	1.319	0.2508
Low V heavy	98.9	127.6	-28.7	-36.1	0.890146	12.742	0.0004
Non-back V heavy	104.2	138.2	-33.9	-42.7	0.884289	13.465	0.0002
Red V light	**126.2**	**74.2**	**52.0**	**65.5**	**0.721594**	**35.729**	**0.0000**
Red V in open σ light	117.0	37.5	79.5	100.0	0.828389	20.616	0.0000
CVVC, CVCC heavy	n.a.	n.a.	n.a.	n.a.	n.a.	n.a.	n.a.
CVV(C), V+G heavy	118.2	108.6	9.6	12.0	0.988028	1.319	0.2508
CVV(C), V+S heavy	138.1	93.7	44.4	55.9	0.740907	32.837	0.0000
CVV(C), V-N heavy	126.4	90.8	35.6	44.8	0.839328	19.179	0.0000
CVV(C), V-T heavy	n.a.	n.a.	n.a.	n.a.	n.a.	n.a.	n.a.
CVV(C), V-S heavy	99.6	115.7	-16.2	-20.3	0.978710	2.356	0.1248
CVV(C), V-R heavy	121.8	106.7	15.1	19.0	0.970622	3.265	0.0708
CVV(C), V-K heavy	119.9	77.5	42.4	53.3	0.864457	15.949	0.0001
CVV(C), V-B heavy	119.9	77.5	42.4	53.3	0.864457	15.949	0.0001
CVV(C), V-G heavy	121.8	106.7	15.1	19.0	0.970622	3.265	0.0708
CVV(C), V+T heavy	119.9	77.5	42.4	53.3	0.864457	15.949	0.0001

(continued)

JAVANESE—*(continued)*

	H	L	Diff	Norm	Wilkes λ	χ2	Sign
CVV(C), V+N heavy	101.3	115.8	-14.6	-18.3	0.980861	2.116	0.1458
CVV(C), V+K heavy	n.a.	n.a.	n.a.	n.a.	n.a.	n.a.	n.a.
CVV(C), V+B heavy	n.a.	n.a.	n.a.	n.a.	n.a.	n.a.	n.a.
CVV(C), CaC heavy	123.5	109.8	13.7	17.2	0.983084	1.868	0.1717
Short HiV in open σ light	115.4	78.2	37.2	46.7	0.950932	5.509	0.0189
CVV(C), a-G heavy	122.1	111.6	10.5	13.3	0.994299	0.626	0.4288
CVV(C), a-T heavy	n.a.	n.a.	n.a.	n.a.	n.a.	n.a.	n.a.
CVV(C), a-S heavy	107.0	113.4	-6.4	-8.0	0.997927	0.227	0.6336
CVV(C), a-R heavy	122.1	111.6	10.5	13.3	0.994299	0.626	0.4288
CVV(C), a-N heavy	127.9	109.8	18.1	22.7	0.976457	2.609	0.1063
CVV(C), a-K heavy	123.5	109.8	13.7	17.2	0.983084	1.868	0.1717
CVV(C), a-B heavy	123.5	109.8	13.7	17.2	0.983084	1.868	0.1717
CVV(C), a+G heavy	124.8	111.3	13.6	17.1	0.990583	1.036	0.3087
CVV(C), a+T heavy	123.5	109.8	13.7	17.2	0.983084	1.868	0.1717
CVV(C), a+S heavy	139.9	109.5	30.5	38.3	0.952444	5.335	0.0209
CVV(C), a+R heavy	124.8	111.3	13.6	17.1	0.990583	1.036	0.3087
CVV(C), a+N heavy	110.3	112.9	-2.5	-3.2	0.999824	0.019	0.8896
CVV(C), a+K heavy	n.a.	n.a.	n.a.	n.a.	n.a.	n.a.	n.a.
CVV(C), a+B heavy	n.a.	n.a.	n.a.	n.a.	n.a.	n.a.	n.a.

CV, hiV-G light	106.6	126.2	-19.6	-24.7	0.955741	4.957	0.0260
CV, hiV-T light	119.9	77.5	42.4	53.3	0.864457	15.949	0.0001
CV, hiV-S light	117.8	101.6	16.2	20.3	0.969922	3.344	0.0674
CV, hiV-R light	106.6	126.2	-19.6	-24.7	0.955741	4.957	0.0260
CV, hiV-N light	97.9	133.2	-35.2	-44.3	0.838039	19.348	0.0000
CV, hiV-K light	123.5	109.8	13.7	17.2	0.983084	1.868	0.1717
CV, hiV-B light	123.5	109.8	13.7	17.2	0.983084	1.868	0.1717
CV, hiV+G light	110.4	117.3	-6.9	-8.7	0.994351	0.620	0.4309
CV, hiV+T light	123.5	109.8	13.7	17.2	0.983084	1.868	0.1717
CV, hiV+S light	99.0	140.6	-41.6	-52.4	0.794431	25.199	0.0000
CV, hiV+R light	110.4	117.3	-6.9	-8.7	0.994351	0.620	0.4309
CV, hiV+N light	116.4	100.0	16.4	20.6	0.975074	2.764	0.0964
CV, hiV+K light	119.9	77.5	42.4	53.3	0.864457	15.949	0.0001
CV, hiV+B light	119.9	77.5	42.4	53.3	0.864457	15.949	0.0001
Ca; Cu: heavy	n.a.	n.a.	n.a.	n.a.	n.a.	n.a.	n.a.
Ca; Ci: heavy	n.a.	n.a.	n.a.	n.a.	n.a.	n.a.	n.a.
Ca: heavy	n.a.	n.a.	n.a.	n.a.	n.a.	n.a.	n.a.
Ca, Cu heavy	130.8	94.0	36.8	46.3	0.818788	21.892	0.0000

BOLE	H	L	Diff	Norm	Wilkes λ	χ2	Sign
CVV(C) heavy	154.9	107.1	47.8	40.2	0.898783	14.140	0.0002
CVV(C), CVC heavy	128.6	50.4	78.2	65.8	0.728823	41.913	0.0000
CVV(C), V+R heavy	128.6	50.4	78.2	65.8	0.728823	41.913	0.0000
Low V heavy	134.1	106.2	27.9	23.5	0.946411	7.298	0.0069
Non-back V heavy	106.4	131.5	-25.1	-21.1	0.954628	6.152	0.0131
Red V light	n.a.	n.a.	n.a.	n.a.	n.a.	n.a.	n.a.
Red V in open σ light	n.a.	n.a.	n.a.	n.a.	n.a.	n.a.	n.a.
CVVC, CVCC heavy	n.a.	n.a.	n.a.	n.a.	n.a.	n.a.	n.a.
CVV(C), V+G heavy	128.6	50.4	78.2	65.8	0.728823	41.913	0.0000
CVV(C), V+S heavy	131.7	98.6	33.1	27.8	0.914060	11.906	0.0006
CVV(C), V-N heavy	131.7	98.6	33.1	27.8	0.914060	11.906	0.0006
CVV(C), V-T heavy	129.6	108.1	21.4	18.0	0.967984	4.311	0.0379
CVV(C), V-S heavy	134.5	96.4	38.1	32.1	0.886000	16.038	0.0001
CVV(C), V-R heavy	154.9	107.1	47.8	40.2	0.898783	14.140	0.0002
CVV(C), V-K heavy	128.6	50.4	78.2	65.8	0.728823	41.913	0.0000
CVV(C), V-B heavy	134.8	76.2	58.7	49.4	0.759792	36.399	0.0000
CVV(C), V-G heavy	154.9	107.1	47.8	40.2	0.898783	14.140	0.0002
CVV(C), V+T heavy	134.8	76.2	58.7	49.4	0.759792	36.399	0.0000
CVV(C), V+N heavy	134.5	96.4	38.1	32.1	0.886000	16.038	0.0001

CVV(C), V+K heavy	154.9	107.1	47.8	40.2	0.898783	14.140	0.0002
CVV(C), V+B heavy	129.6	108.1	21.4	18.0	0.967984	4.311	0.0379
CVV(C), CaC heavy	139.5	100.6	38.8	32.7	0.888596	15.650	0.0001
Short HiV in open σ light	124.5	41.8	82.7	69.6	0.788043	31.562	0.0000
CVV(C), a-G heavy	154.9	107.1	47.8	40.2	0.898783	14.140	0.0002
CVV(C), a-T heavy	141.6	107.8	33.8	28.4	0.938028	8.477	0.0036
CVV(C), a-S heavy	147.7	103.0	44.7	37.6	0.875070	17.682	0.0000
CVV(C), a-R heavy	154.9	107.1	47.8	40.2	0.898783	14.140	0.0002
CVV(C), a-N heavy	140.8	105.7	35.1	29.5	0.922996	10.617	0.0011
CVV(C), a-K heavy	139.5	100.6	38.8	32.7	0.888596	15.650	0.0001
CVV(C), a-B heavy	146.1	100.4	45.7	38.5	0.855884	20.620	0.0000
CVV(C), a+G heavy	139.5	100.6	38.8	32.7	0.888596	15.650	0.0001
CVV(C), a+T heavy	146.1	100.4	45.7	38.5	0.855884	20.620	0.0000
CVV(C), a+S heavy	140.8	105.7	35.1	29.5	0.922996	10.617	0.0011
CVV(C), a+R heavy	139.5	100.6	38.8	32.7	0.888596	15.650	0.0001
CVV(C), a+N heavy	146.1	100.4	45.7	38.5	0.855884	20.620	0.0000
CVV(C), a+K heavy	154.9	107.1	47.8	40.2	0.898783	14.140	0.0002
CVV(C), a+B heavy	141.6	107.8	33.8	28.4	0.938028	8.477	0.0036
CV, hiV-G light	128.6	50.4	78.2	65.8	0.728823	41.913	0.0000
CV, hiV-T light	132.2	72.2	60.0	50.5	0.771604	34.355	0.0000

(continued)

BOLE—(continued)

	H	L	Diff	Norm	Wilkes λ	χ^2	Sign
CV, hiV-S light	132.4	88.8	43.7	36.8	0.857064	20.437	0.0000
CV, hiV-R light	128.6	50.4	78.2	65.8	0.728823	41.913	0.0000
CV, hiV-N light	131.6	90.9	40.7	34.2	0.875323	17.644	0.0000
CV, hiV-K light	139.5	100.6	38.8	32.7	0.888596	15.650	0.0001
CV, hiV-B light	131.8	99.5	32.2	27.1	0.918533	11.260	0.0008
CV, hiV+G light	139.5	100.6	38.8	32.7	0.888596	15.650	0.0001
CV, hiV+T light	131.8	99.5	32.2	27.1	0.918533	11.260	0.0008
CV, hiV+S light	131.6	90.9	40.7	34.2	0.875323	17.644	0.0000
CV, hiV+R light	139.5	100.6	38.8	32.7	0.888596	15.650	0.0001
CV, hiV+N light	132.4	88.8	43.7	36.8	0.857064	20.437	0.0000
CV, hiV+K light	128.6	50.4	78.2	65.8	0.728823	41.913	0.0000
CV, hiV+B light	132.2	72.2	60.0	50.5	0.771604	34.355	0.0000
Ca, Cu: heavy	193.4	104.8	88.6	74.6	0.742370	39.473	0.0000
Ca, Ci: heavy	152.3	110.7	41.7	35.1	0.946139	7.336	0.0068
Ca: heavy	227.1	108.2	118.8	100.0	0.752831	37.619	0.0000
Ca, Cu heavy	132.7	78.0	54.7	46.1	0.795928	30.243	0.0000

Farsi	H	L	Diff	Norm	Wilkes λ	χ2	Sign
CVV(C) heavy	n.a.	n.a.	n.a.	n.a.	n.a.	n.a.	n.a.
CVV(C), CVC heavy	99.6	55.5	44.1	100.0	0.863679	40.815	0.0000
CVV(C), V+R heavy	104.4	92.6	11.9	27.0	0.971198	8.139	0.0043
Low V heavy	107.0	90.1	16.9	38.4	0.936202	18.360	0.0000
Non-back V heavy	97.8	92.0	5.8	13.1	0.993218	1.895	0.1686
Red V light	n.a.	n.a.	n.a.	n.a.	n.a.	n.a.	n.a.
Red V in open σ light	n.a.	n.a.	n.a.	n.a.	n.a.	n.a.	n.a.
CVVC, CVCC heavy	n.a.	n.a.	n.a.	n.a.	n.a.	n.a.	n.a.
CVV(C), V+G heavy	101.9	89.3	12.5	28.4	0.962062	10.771	0.0010
CVV(C), V+S heavy	109.5	73.6	36.0	81.5	0.705819	97.029	0.0000
CVV(C), V-N heavy	100.8	79.9	20.9	47.5	0.925919	21.436	0.0000
CVV(C), V-T heavy	80.9	105.5	-24.5	-55.6	0.862002	41.357	0.0000
CVV(C), V-S heavy	78.4	103.5	-25.2	-57.0	0.872014	38.141	0.0000
CVV(C), V-R heavy	97.2	94.3	2.9	6.6	0.998034	0.548	0.4591
CVV(C), V-K heavy	107.7	70.3	37.4	84.8	0.709590	95.545	0.0000
CVV(C), V-B heavy	101.5	77.9	23.6	53.6	0.904505	27.952	0.0000
CVV(C), V-G heavy	96.3	96.0	0.3	0.7	0.999981	0.005	0.9419
CVV(C), V+T heavy	112.7	76.6	36.1	81.9	0.685262	105.260	0.0000

(continued)

Farsi—*(continued)*

	H	L	Diff	Norm	Wilkes λ	χ2	Sign
CVV(C), V+N heavy	93.0	96.6	-3.7	-8.4	0.998352	0.459	0.4979
CVV(C), V+K heavy	75.31	102.36	-27.1	-61.3	0.873516	37.661	0.0000
CVV(C), V+B heavy	89.6	97.3	-7.7	-17.4	0.992722	2.034	0.1538
CVV(C), CaC heavy	110.9	88.8	22.1	50.2	0.894606	31.017	0.0000
Short HiV in open σ light	98.4	55.6	42.7	96.9	0.910235	26.194	0.0000
CVV(C), a-G heavy	113.2	93.4	19.7	44.7	0.955780	12.596	0.0004
CVV(C), a-T heavy	97.8	95.8	2.0	4.4	0.999565	0.121	0.7278
CVV(C), a-S heavy	90.9	96.7	-5.8	-13.1	0.996892	0.867	0.3518
CVV(C), a-R heavy	108.4	92.6	15.8	35.9	0.958119	11.915	0.0006
CVV(C), a-N heavy	112.7	89.9	22.8	51.8	0.899212	29.587	0.0000
CVV(C), a-K heavy	116.43	89.23	27.2	61.7	0.864171	40.657	0.0000
CVV(C), a-B heavy	112.3	89.0	23.3	52.8	0.903927	28.130	0.0000
CVV(C), a+G heavy	109.4	92.9	16.5	37.3	0.958473	11.812	0.0006
CVV(C), a+T heavy	120.0	90.3	29.7	67.3	0.865271	40.302	0.0000
CVV(C), a+S heavy	120.4	89.1	31.3	71.1	0.833884	50.593	0.0000
CVV(C), a+R heavy	115.8	93.7	22.2	50.3	0.953025	13.400	0.0003
CVV(C), a+N heavy	102.4	95.7	6.7	15.1	0.997678	0.647	0.4210
CVV(C), a+K heavy	93.1	96.4	-3.3	-7.4	0.999244	0.211	0.6463
CVV(C), a+B heavy	104.3	95.6	8.7	19.7	0.996075	1.095	0.2953

CV, hiV-G light	99.1	87.0	12.1	27.4	0.973708	7.420	0.0064
CV, hiV-T light	109.7	67.7	42.0	95.2	0.624625	131.063	0.0000
CV, hiV-S light	106.8	66.6	40.2	91.1	0.692784	102.220	0.0000
CV, hiV-R light	106.1	85.3	20.9	47.4	0.894140	31.162	0.0000
CV, hiV-N light	105.8	89.1	16.8	38.0	0.933506	19.163	0.0000
CV, hiV-K light	96.8	95.5	1.3	3.0	0.999585	0.116	0.7338
CV, hiV-B light	104.3	90.1	14.2	32.1	0.952375	13.590	0.0002
CV, hiV+G light	100.7	89.8	10.9	24.7	0.971801	7.966	0.0048
CV, hiV+T light	94.2	98.7	-4.6	-10.3	0.995054	1.381	0.2399
CV, hiV+S light	96.5	95.7	0.9	2.0	0.999816	0.051	0.8211
CV, hiV+R light	100.0	85.4	14.7	33.2	0.959161	11.612	0.0007
CV, hiV+N light	100.9	72.2	28.7	65.1	0.888394	32.958	0.0000
CV, hiV+K light	106.2	62.6	43.6	98.9	0.671280	111.002	0.0000
CV, hiV+B light	101.7	69.1	32.6	74.0	0.853362	44.162	0.0000
Ca, Cu heavy	n.a.	n.a.	n.a.	n.a.	n.a.	n.a.	n.a.
Ca, Ci heavy	n.a.	n.a.	n.a.	n.a.	n.a.	n.a.	n.a.
Ca heavy	n.a.	n.a.	n.a.	n.a.	n.a.	n.a.	n.a.
Ca, Cu heavy	100.2	88.4	11.8	26.7	0.969404	8.654	0.0033

French	H	L	Diff.	Norm	Wilkes λ	χ2	Sign.
CVV(C) heavy	n.a.	n.a.	n.a.	n.a.	n.a.	n.a.	n.a.
CVV(C), CVC heavy	96.6	57.0	39.7	39.3	0.896293	10.128	0.0015
CVV(C), V+R heavy	93.4	84.9	8.5	8.4	0.995096	0.455	0.5001
Low V heavy	146.4	56.9	89.5	88.7	0.357994	95.020	0.0000
Non-back V heavy	103.4	53.2	50.3	49.8	0.800531	20.579	0.0000
Red V light	n.a.	n.a.	n.a.	n.a.	n.a.	n.a.	n.a.
Red V in open σ light	n.a.	n.a.	n.a.	n.a.	n.a.	n.a.	n.a.
CVCC, CVCC heavy	n.a.	n.a.	n.a.	n.a.	n.a.	n.a.	n.a.
CVV(C), V+G heavy	98.0	75.9	22.1	21.9	0.956006	4.162	0.0413
CVV(C), V+S heavy	96.6	57.0	39.7	39.3	0.896293	10.128	0.0015
CVV(C), V-N heavy	96.6	57.0	39.7	39.3	0.896293	10.128	0.0015
CVV(C), V-T heavy	102.6	81.8	20.8	20.6	0.970651	2.755	0.0969
CVV(C), V-S heavy	n.a.	n.a.	n.a.	n.a.	n.a.	n.a.	n.a.
CVV(C), V-R heavy	98.3	75.6	22.7	22.5	0.953754	4.380	0.0364
CVV(C), V-K heavy	96.6	57.0	39.7	39.3	0.896293	10.128	0.0015
CVV(C), V-B heavy	96.6	57.0	39.7	39.3	0.896293	10.128	0.0015
CVV(C), V-G heavy	93.9	84.7	9.2	9.2	0.994205	0.538	0.4634
CVV(C), V+T heavy	93.7	80.3	13.4	13.3	0.983866	1.505	0.2200
CVV(C), V+N heavy	n.a.	n.a.	n.a.	n.a.	n.a.	n.a.	n.a.

CVV(C), V+K heavy	n.a.	n.a.	n.a.	n.a.	n.a.	n.a.	n.a.
CVV(C), V+B heavy	n.a.	n.a.	n.a.	n.a.	n.a.	n.a.	0.0000
CVV(C), CaC heavy	162.5	61.5	100.9	100.0	0.309496	108.485	0.0000
Short HiV in open σ light	96.8	35.1	61.7	61.2	0.817979	18.585	0.0000
CVV(C), a-G heavy	154.2	80.9	73.4	72.7	0.850898	14.935	0.0001
CVV(C), a-T heavy	165.8	79.8	86.1	85.3	0.794882	21.234	0.0000
CVV(C), a-S heavy	n.a.	n.a.	n.a.	n.a.	n.a.	n.a.	n.a.
CVV(C), a-R heavy	160.0	72.3	87.8	87.0	0.612364	45.365	0.0000
CVV(C), a-N heavy	162.5	61.5	100.9	100.0	0.309496	108.485	0.0000
CVV(C), a-K heavy	162.5	61.5	100.9	100.0	0.309496	108.485	0.0000
CVV(C), a-B heavy	162.5	61.5	100.9	100.0	0.309496	108.485	0.0000
CVV(C), a+G heavy	166.6	70.9	95.6	94.8	0.539931	57.009	0.0000
CVV(C), a+T heavy	160.8	72.1	88.7	87.9	0.604682	46.532	0.0000
CVV(C), a+S heavy	162.5	61.5	100.9	100.0	0.309496	108.485	0.0000
CVV(C), a+R heavy	167.3	79.7	87.6	86.8	0.787320	22.119	0.0000
CVV(C), a+N heavy	n.a.	n.a.	n.a.	n.a.	n.a.	n.a.	n.a.
CVV(C), a+K heavy	n.a.	n.a.	n.a.	n.a.	n.a.	n.a.	n.a.
CVV(C), a+B heavy	n.a.	n.a.	n.a.	n.a.	n.a.	n.a.	n.a.
CV, hiV-G light	106.0	59.8	46.3	45.8	0.814102	19.024	0.0000
CV, hiV-T light	104.0	62.7	41.3	40.9	0.851954	14.821	0.0001

(continued)

FRENCH—(*continued*)

	H	L	Diff.	Norm	Wilkes λ	χ2	Sign.
CV, hiV-S light	96.6	57.0	39.7	39.3	0.896293	10.128	0.0015
CV, hiV-R light	120.1	63.0	57.0	56.5	0.715318	30.990	0.0000
CV, hiV-N light	162.5	61.5	100.9	100.0	0.309496	108.485	0.0000
CV, hiV-K light	96.6	57.0	39.7	39.3	0.896293	10.128	0.0015
CV, hiV-B light	162.5	61.5	100.9	100.0	0.309496	108.485	0.0000
CV, hiV+G light	123.0	60.9	62.1	61.5	0.662290	38.115	0.0000
CV, hiV+T light	125.9	58.8	67.0	66.4	0.606431	46.265	0.0000
CV, hiV+S light	162.5	61.5	100.9	100.0	0.309496	108.485	0.0000
CV, hiV+R light	108.1	56.8	51.4	50.9	0.770650	24.098	0.0000
CV, hiV+N light	96.6	57.0	39.7	39.3	0.896293	10.128	0.0015
CV, hiV+K light	96.6	57.0	39.7	39.3	0.896293	10.128	0.0015
CV, hiV+B light	96.6	57.0	39.7	39.3	0.896293	10.128	0.0015
Ca, Cu: heavy	n.a.	n.a.	n.a.	n.a.	n.a.	n.a.	n.a.
Ca, Ci: heavy	n.a.	n.a.	n.a.	n.a.	n.a.	n.a.	n.a.
Ca: heavy	n.a.	n.a.	n.a.	n.a.	n.a.	n.a.	n.a.
Ca, Cu heavy	100.5	60.5	40.0	39.6	0.871699	12.701	0.0004

Russian	H	L	Diff	Norm	Wilkes λ	χ2	Sign
CVV(C) heavy	n.a.	n.a.	n.a.	n.a.	n.a.	n.a.	n.a.
CVV(C), CVC heavy	n.a.	n.a.	n.a.	n.a.	n.a.	n.a.	n.a.
CVV(C), V+R heavy	n.a.	n.a.	n.a.	n.a.	n.a.	n.a.	n.a.
Low V heavy	175.4	104.8	70.6	100.0	0.428184	13.147	0.0003
Non-back V heavy	129	127.1	1.9	2.7	0.999592	0.006	0.9366
Red V light	n.a.	n.a.	n.a.	n.a.	n.a.	n.a.	n.a.
Red V in open σ light	n.a.	n.a.	n.a.	n.a.	n.a.	n.a.	n.a.
CVVC, CVCC heavy	n.a.	n.a.	n.a.	n.a.	n.a.	n.a.	n.a.
CVV(C), V+G heavy	n.a.	n.a.	n.a.	n.a.	n.a.	n.a.	n.a.
CVV(C), V+S heavy	n.a.	n.a.	n.a.	n.a.	n.a.	n.a.	n.a.
CVV(C), V-N heavy	n.a.	n.a.	n.a.	n.a.	n.a.	n.a.	n.a.
CVV(C), V-T heavy	n.a.	n.a.	n.a.	n.a.	n.a.	n.a.	n.a.
CVV(C), V-S heavy	n.a.	n.a.	n.a.	n.a.	n.a.	n.a.	n.a.
CVV(C), V-R heavy	n.a.	n.a.	n.a.	n.a.	n.a.	n.a.	n.a.
CVV(C), V-K heavy	n.a.	n.a.	n.a.	n.a.	n.a.	n.a.	n.a.
CVV(C), V-B heavy	n.a.	n.a.	n.a.	n.a.	n.a.	n.a.	n.a.
CVV(C), V-G heavy	n.a.	n.a.	n.a.	n.a.	n.a.	n.a.	n.a.
CVV(C), V+T heavy	n.a.	n.a.	n.a.	n.a.	n.a.	n.a.	n.a.

(continued)

RUSSIAN—*(continued)*

	H	L	Diff	Norm	Wilkes λ	χ2	Sign
CVV(C), V+N heavy	n.a.	n.a.	n.a.	n.a.	n.a.	n.a.	n.a.
CVV(C), V+K heavy	n.a.	n.a.	n.a.	n.a.	n.a.	n.a.	n.a.
CVV(C), V+B heavy	n.a.	n.a.	n.a.	n.a.	n.a.	n.a.	n.a.
CVV(C), CaC heavy	n.a.	n.a.	n.a.	n.a.	n.a.	n.a.	n.a.
Short HiV in open σ light	n.a.	n.a.	n.a.	n.a.	n.a.	n.a.	n.a.
CVV(C), a-G heavy	n.a.	n.a.	n.a.	n.a.	n.a.	n.a.	n.a.
CVV(C), a-T heavy	n.a.	n.a.	n.a.	n.a.	n.a.	n.a.	n.a.
CVV(C), a-S heavy	n.a.	n.a.	n.a.	n.a.	n.a.	n.a.	n.a.
CVV(C), a-R heavy	n.a.	n.a.	n.a.	n.a.	n.a.	n.a.	n.a.
CVV(C), a-N heavy	n.a.	n.a.	n.a.	n.a.	n.a.	n.a.	n.a.
CVV(C), a-K heavy	n.a.	n.a.	n.a.	n.a.	n.a.	n.a.	n.a.
CVV(C), a-B heavy	n.a.	n.a.	n.a.	n.a.	n.a.	n.a.	n.a.
CVV(C), a+G heavy	n.a.	n.a.	n.a.	n.a.	n.a.	n.a.	n.a.
CVV(C), a+T heavy	n.a.	n.a.	n.a.	n.a.	n.a.	n.a.	n.a.
CVV(C), a+S heavy	n.a.	n.a.	n.a.	n.a.	n.a.	n.a.	n.a.
CVV(C), a+R heavy	n.a.	n.a.	n.a.	n.a.	n.a.	n.a.	n.a.
CVV(C), a+N heavy	n.a.	n.a.	n.a.	n.a.	n.a.	n.a.	n.a.
CVV(C), a+K heavy	n.a.	n.a.	n.a.	n.a.	n.a.	n.a.	n.a.
CVV(C), a+B heavy	n.a.	n.a.	n.a.	n.a.	n.a.	n.a.	n.a.

CV, hiV-G light	n.a.	n.a.	n.a.	n.a.	n.a.	n.a.	n.a.
CV, hiV-T light	n.a.	n.a.	n.a.	n.a.	n.a.	n.a.	n.a.
CV, hiV-S light	n.a.	n.a.	n.a.	n.a.	n.a.	n.a.	n.a.
CV, hiV-R light	n.a.	n.a.	n.a.	n.a.	n.a.	n.a.	n.a.
CV, hiV-N light	n.a.	n.a.	n.a.	n.a.	n.a.	n.a.	n.a.
CV, hiV-K light	n.a.	n.a.	n.a.	n.a.	n.a.	n.a.	n.a.
CV, hiV-B light	n.a.	n.a.	n.a.	n.a.	n.a.	n.a.	n.a.
CV, hiV+G light	n.a.	n.a.	n.a.	n.a.	n.a.	n.a.	n.a.
CV, hiV+T light	n.a.	n.a.	n.a.	n.a.	n.a.	n.a.	n.a.
CV, hiV+S light	n.a.	n.a.	n.a.	n.a.	n.a.	n.a.	n.a.
CV, hiV+R light	n.a.	n.a.	n.a.	n.a.	n.a.	n.a.	n.a.
CV, hiV+N light	n.a.	n.a.	n.a.	n.a.	n.a.	n.a.	n.a.
CV, hiV+K light	n.a.	n.a.	n.a.	n.a.	n.a.	n.a.	n.a.
CV, hiV+B light	n.a.	n.a.	n.a.	n.a.	n.a.	n.a.	n.a.
Ca, Cu heavy	n.a.	n.a.	n.a.	n.a.	n.a.	n.a.	n.a.
Ca, Ci heavy	n.a.	n.a.	n.a.	n.a.	n.a.	n.a.	n.a.
Ca heavy	n.a.	n.a.	n.a.	n.a.	n.a.	n.a.	n.a.
Ca, Cu heavy	151.2	82.57	68.7	97.3	0.458310	12.093	0.0005

Appendix Six

PHONOLOGICALLY SIMPLE DISTINCTIONS BY DURATION (IN MILLISECONDS)

Distinctions in bold are phonological.

Chickasaw

	H	L	Diff	Wilkes	χ^2	Sign	Rank
CVV(C) heavy	**161.4**	**147.0**	**14.4**	**0.975463**	**4.2850**	**0.0384**	**7**
CVV(C), CVC heavy	**159.8**	**58.7**	**101.2**	**0.466859**	**131.3980**	**0.0000**	**1**
CVV(C), V+R heavy	161.6	138.1	23.5	0.913970	15.5180	0.0001	6
Non-high V heavy	154.9	146.3	8.6	0.988497	1.9960	0.1577	8
Non-back V heavy	n.a.	n.a.	n.a.	n.a.	n.a.	n.a.	n.a.
Red V light	n.a.	n.a.	n.a.	n.a.	n.a.	n.a.	n.a.
Red V in open σ light	n.a.	n.a.	n.a.	n.a.	n.a.	n.a.	n.a.
CVVC, CVCC heavy	176.0	145.7	30.3	0.922670	13.8830	0.0002	4
CVV(C), V+G heavy	161.3	132.5	28.8	0.878344	22.3760	0.0000	5
CVV(C), V+S heavy	166.1	133.4	32.6	0.833595	31.3960	0.0000	3
CVV(C), V-N heavy	160.6	125.0	35.6	0.839960	30.0840	0.0000	2

TELUGU	H	L	Diff	Wilkes	χ^2	Sign	Rank
CVV(C) heavy	**132.5**	**119.4**	**13.1**	**0.972804**	**3.6530**	**0.0560**	**6**
CVV(C), CVC heavy	**130.0**	**63.4**	**66.5**	**0.301668**	**158.7920**	**0.0000**	**1**
CVV(C), V+R heavy	127.9	113.4	14.5	0.928512	9.8280	0.0017	4
Non-high V heavy	126.4	118.5	7.9	0.981127	2.5250	0.1121	8
Non-back V heavy	125.0	113.7	11.3	0.960681	5.3150	0.0211	7
Red V light	n.a.	n.a.	n.a.	n.a.	n.a.	n.a.	n.a.
Red V in open σ light	n.a.	n.a.	n.a.	n.a.	n.a.	n.a.	n.a.
CVVC, CVCC heavy	n.a.	n.a.	n.a.	n.a.	n.a.	n.a.	n.a.
CVV(C), V+G heavy	131.2	100.9	30.3	0.721997	43.1600	0.0000	3
CVV(C), V+S heavy	127.5	114.1	13.4	0.938757	8.3740	0.0038	5
CVV(C), V-N heavy	130.3	95.9	34.4	0.684134	50.2970	0.0000	2

Khalkha	H	L	Diff	Wilkes	$\chi2$	Sign	Rank
CVV(C) heavy	**141.3**	**139.0**	**2.3**	**0.999616**	**0.0580**	**0.8094**	**6**
CVV(C), CVC heavy	146.6	70.3	76.3	0.550702	90.3790	0.0000	1
CVV(C), V+R heavy	135.9	142.0	-6.1	0.991855	1.2390	0.2657	5
Non-high V heavy	138.6	139.8	-1.3	0.999653	0.0530	0.8186	7
Non-back V heavy	n.a.	n.a.	n.a.	n.a.	n.a.	n.a.	n.a.
Red V light	n.a.	n.a.	n.a.	n.a.	n.a.	n.a.	n.a.
Red V in open σ light	n.a.	n.a.	n.a.	n.a.	n.a.	n.a.	n.a.
CVVC, CVCC heavy	n.a.	n.a.	n.a.	n.a.	n.a.	n.a.	n.a.
CVV(C), V+G heavy	135.1	144.3	-9.2	0.981707	2.7970	0.0944	4
CVV(C), V+S heavy	150.7	124.3	26.3	0.850257	24.5760	0.0000	3
CVV(C), V-N heavy	148.3	114.9	33.4	0.805354	32.7960	0.0000	2

FINNISH	H	L	Diff	Wilkes	χ2	Sign	Rank
CVV(C) heavy	176.7	154.5	22.3	0.957281	7.2260	0.0072	6
CVV(C), CVC heavy	**171.3**	**75.8**	**95.5**	**0.215036**	**254.3650**	**0.0000**	**1**
CVV(C), V+R heavy	174.7	134.9	39.7	0.728271	52.4770	0.0000	4t
Non-high V heavy	164.3	154.3	10.0	0.984423	2.5980	0.1070	7
Non-back V heavy	158.5	157.2	1.3	0.999717	0.0470	0.8286	8
Red V light	n.a.	n.a.	n.a.	n.a.	n.a.	n.a.	n.a.
Red V in open σ light	n.a.	n.a.	n.a.	n.a.	n.a.	n.a.	n.a.
CVVC, CVCC heavy	n.a.	n.a.	n.a.	n.a.	n.a.	n.a.	n.a.
CVV(C), V+G heavy	174.7	134.9	39.7	0.728271	52.4770	0.0000	4t
CVV(C), V+S heavy	176.9	132.0	44.9	0.652818	70.5790	0.0000	3
CVV(C), V-N heavy	170.8	124.7	46.1	0.695429	60.1140	0.0000	2

JAPANESE

	H	L	Diff	Wilkes	$\chi 2$	Sign	Rank
CVV(C) heavy	108.4	99.3	9.1	0.994317	0.5960	0.4403	5t
CVV(C), CVC heavy	**122.2**	**40.7**	**81.5**	**0.544543**	**63.5160**	**0.0000**	**1t**
CVV(C), V+R heavy	122.2	40.7	81.5	0.544543	63.5160	0.0000	1t
Non-high V heavy	109.8	97.6	12.1	0.988190	1.2420	0.2652	4
Non-back V heavy	103.3	98.0	5.4	0.997703	0.2400	0.6240	8
Red V light	n.a.	n.a.	n.a.	n.a.	n.a.	n.a.	n.a.
Red V in open σ light	n.a.	n.a.	n.a.	n.a.	n.a.	n.a.	n.a.
CVVC, CVCC heavy	n.a.	n.a.	n.a.	n.a.	n.a.	n.a.	n.a.
CVV(C), V+G heavy	122.2	40.7	81.5	0.544543	63.5160	0.0000	1t
CVV(C), V+S heavy	108.4	99.3	9.1	0.982682	0.5960	0.4403	5t
CVV(C), V-N heavy	108.4	99.3	9.1	0.994317	0.5960	0.4403	5t

JAVANESE	H	L	Diff.	Wilkes	χ^2	Sign.	Rank
CVV(C) heavy	n.a.	n.a.	n.a.	n.a.	n.a.	n.a.	n.a.
CVV(C), CVC heavy	149.5	81.4	68.1	0.449306	87.6060	0.0000	2
CVV(C), V+R heavy	141.0	135.6	5.4	0.993946	0.6650	0.4148	11t
Non-high V heavy	129.9	146.6	-16.7	0.941003	6.6590	0.0099	7
Non-back V heavy	135.8	144.3	-8.5	0.988628	1.2520	0.2631	10
Red V light	**145.5**	**116.1**	**29.4**	**0.859949**	**16.5220**	**0.0000**	**4**
Red V in open σ light	143.8	34.0	109.8	0.483889	79.4860	0.0000	1
CVVC, CVCC heavy	n.a.	n.a.	n.a.	n.a.	n.a.	n.a.	n.a.
CVV(C), V+G heavy	141.0	135.6	5.4	0.993946	0.6650	0.4148	11t
CVV(C), V+S heavy	154.6	125.4	29.3	0.823063	21.3220	0.0000	5
CVV(C), V-N heavy	152.3	114.9	37.4	0.720056	35.9630	0.0000	3

(continued)

JAVANESE—*(continued)*

	H	L	Diff.	Wilkes	χ^2	Sign.	Rank
CVV(C), V-T heavy	n.a.	n.a.	n.a.	n.a.	n.a.	n.a.	n.a.
CVV(C), V-S heavy	147.0	135.8	11.1	0.984137	1.7510	0.1858	8t
CVV(C), V-R heavy	n.a.	n.a.	n.a.	n.a.	n.a.	n.a.	n.a.
CVV(C), V-K heavy	n.a.	n.a.	n.a.	n.a.	n.a.	n.a.	n.a.
CVV(C), V-B heavy	n.a.	n.a.	n.a.	n.a.	n.a.	n.a.	n.a.
CVV(C), V-G heavy	147.0	135.8	11.1	0.984137	1.7510	0.1858	8t
CVV(C), V+T heavy	n.a.	n.a.	n.a.	n.a.	n.a.	n.a.	n.a.
CVV(C), V+N heavy	141.3	137.0	4.3	0.997331	0.2930	0.5885	13
CVV(C), V+K heavy	n.a.	n.a.	n.a.	n.a.	n.a.	n.a.	n.a.
CVV(C), V+B heavy	n.a.	n.a.	n.a.	n.a.	n.a.	n.a.	n.a.
CVV(C), CaC heavy	151.3	134.3	17.0	0.959144	4.5680	0.0326	6

Bole	H	L	Diff	Wilkes	χ^2	Sign	Rank
CVV(C) heavy	117.7	114.9	2.8	0.999238	0.1010	0.7506	7
CVV(C), CVC heavy	128.9	49.3	79.6	0.400332	121.2990	0.0000	1t
CVV(C), V+R heavy	128.9	49.3	79.6	0.400332	121.2990	0.0000	1t
Non-high V heavy	128.8	108.9	20.0	0.941380	8.0040	0.0047	4
Non-back V heavy	116	114.3	1.8	0.999524	0.0630	0.8017	8
Red V light	n.a.	n.a.	n.a.	n.a.	n.a.	n.a.	n.a.
Red V in open σ light	n.a.	n.a.	n.a.	n.a.	n.a.	n.a.	n.a.
CVVC, CVCC heavy	n.a.	n.a.	n.a.	n.a.	n.a.	n.a.	n.a.
CVV(C), V+G heavy	128.9	49.3	79.6	0.400332	121.2990	0.0000	1t
CVV(C), V+S heavy	118.1	112.7	5.4	0.995088	0.6520	0.4193	5t
CVV(C), V-N heavy	118.1	112.7	5.4	0.995088	0.6520	0.4193	5t

FARSI	H	L	Diff	Wilkes	χ2	Sign	Rank
CVV(C) heavy	n.a.	n.a.	n.a.	n.a.	n.a.	n.a.	n.a.
CVV(C), CVC heavy	167.0	83.2	83.8	0.640529	124.0610	0.0000	1
CVV(C), V+R heavy	161.2	160.2	1.1	0.999832	0.0470	0.8287	18
Non-high V heavy	174.3	152.9	21.4	0.925612	21.5280	0.0000	11
Non-back V heavy	163.5	153.3	10.2	0.984679	4.3000	0.0381	14
Red V light	n.a.	n.a.	n.a.	n.a.	n.a.	n.a.	n.a.
Red V in open σ light	n.a.	n.a.	n.a.	n.a.	n.a.	n.a.	n.a.
CVVC, CVCC heavy	n.a.	n.a.	n.a.	n.a.	n.a.	n.a.	n.a.
CVV(C), V+G heavy	163.1	157.4	5.7	0.994214	1.6160	0.2037	16
CVV(C), V+S heavy	178.1	130.9	47.3	0.629240	129.0130	0.0000	2
CVV(C), V-N heavy	168.8	131.8	37.0	0.830988	51.5610	0.0000	4

CVV(C), V-T heavy	153.1	165.0	-11.9	0.976145	6.7240	0.0095	13
CVV(C), V-S heavy	143.5	167.6	-24.1	0.914353	24.9360	0.0000	9
CVV(C), V-R heavy	169.8	145.0	24.8	0.897571	30.0960	0.0000	8
CVV(C), V-K heavy	174.8	128.5	46.3	0.674650	109.6070	0.0000	3
CVV(C), V-B heavy	167.0	138.5	28.5	0.898815	29.7100	0.0000	7
CVV(C), V-G heavy	172.6	153.0	19.6	0.935673	18.5170	0.0000	12
CVV(C), V+T heavy	176.9	141.2	35.7	0.775605	70.7700	0.0000	5
CVV(C), V+N heavy	157.8	160.9	-3.1	0.999133	0.2420	0.6230	17
CVV(C), V+K heavy	143.82	165.5	-21.7	0.940737	17.0140	0.0000	10
CVV(C), V+B heavy	167.4	159.3	8.2	0.993984	1.6800	0.1949	15
CVV(C), CaC heavy	181.2	150.3	30.9	0.849973	45.2710	0.0000	6

FRENCH	H	L	Diff.	Wilkes	χ²	Sign.	Rank
CVV(C) heavy	n.a.	n.a.	n.a.	n.a.	n.a.	n.a.	n.a.
CVV(C), CVC heavy	139.3	69.5	69.8	0.388907	87.3580	0.0000	1t
CVV(C), V+R heavy	111.5	126.1	-14.5	0.972778	2.5530	0.1101	6
Non-high V heavy	139.2	113.9	25.3	0.902589	9.4800	0.0021	4
Non-back V heavy	126.2	114.5	11.8	0.979268	1.9380	0.1639	7
Red V light	n.a.	n.a.	n.a.	n.a.	n.a.	n.a.	n.a.
Red V in open σ light	n.a.	n.a.	n.a.	n.a.	n.a.	n.a.	n.a.
CVVC, CVCC heavy	n.a.	n.a.	n.a.	n.a.	n.a.	n.a.	n.a.
CVV(C), V+G heavy	130.3	114.3	16.0	0.956327	4.1310	0.0421	5
CVV(C), V+S heavy	139.3	69.5	69.8	0.388907	87.3580	0.0000	1t
CVV(C), V-N heavy	139.3	69.5	69.8	0.388907	87.3580	0.0000	1t

RUSSIAN	H	L	Diff	Wilkes	χ^2	Sign	Rank
CVV(C) heavy	n.a.	n.a.	n.a.	n.a.	n.a.	n.a.	n.a.
CVV(C), CVC heavy	n.a.	n.a.	n.a.	n.a.	n.a.	n.a.	n.a.
CVV(C), V+R heavy	n.a.	n.a.	n.a.	n.a.	n.a.	n.a.	n.a.
Non-high V heavy	112.7	72.8	39.9	0.219806	23.4830	0.0000	1
Non-back V heavy	91.5	75.167	16.3	0.869370	2.1700	0.1407	2
Red V light	n.a.	n.a.	n.a.	n.a.	n.a.	n.a.	n.a.
Red V in open σ light	n.a.	n.a.	n.a.	n.a.	n.a.	n.a.	n.a.
CVVC, CVCC heavy	n.a.	n.a.	n.a.	n.a.	n.a.	n.a.	n.a.
CVV(C), V+G heavy	n.a.	n.a.	n.a.	n.a.	n.a.	n.a.	n.a.
CVV(C), V+S heavy	n.a.	n.a.	n.a.	n.a.	n.a.	n.a.	n.a.
CVV(C), V-N heavy	n.a.	n.a.	n.a.	n.a.	n.a.	n.a.	n.a.

(continued)

RUSSIAN—*(continued)*

	H	L	Diff	Wilkes	χ^2	Sign	Rank
CVV(C), V-T heavy	n.a.	n.a.	n.a.	n.a.	n.a.	n.a.	n.a.
CVV(C), V-S heavy	n.a.	n.a.	n.a.	n.a.	n.a.	n.a.	n.a.
CVV(C), V-R heavy	n.a.	n.a.	n.a.	n.a.	n.a.	n.a.	n.a.
CVV(C), V-K heavy	n.a.	n.a.	n.a.	n.a.	n.a.	n.a.	n.a.
CVV(C), V-B heavy	n.a.	n.a.	n.a.	n.a.	n.a.	n.a.	n.a.
CVV(C), V-G heavy	n.a.	n.a.	n.a.	n.a.	n.a.	n.a.	n.a.
CVV(C), V+T heavy	n.a.	n.a.	n.a.	n.a.	n.a.	n.a.	n.a.
CVV(C), V+N heavy	n.a.	n.a.	n.a.	n.a.	n.a.	n.a.	n.a.
CVV(C), V+K heavy	n.a.	n.a.	n.a.	n.a.	n.a.	n.a.	n.a.
CVV(C), V+B heavy	n.a.	n.a.	n.a.	n.a.	n.a.	n.a.	n.a.
CVV(C), CaC heavy	n.a.	n.a.	n.a.	n.a.	n.a.	n.a.	n.a.

Notes

NOTES TO CHAPTER TWO

1. Tunica does not appear in Grimes and Grimes' classification, either as a member of the Gulf phylum, an isolate or an unclassified language. It is generally recognized as a Gulf language (cf. Haas 1951); hence, it is included in the Gulf phylum for purposes of this book.

2. An additional language whose accentual system observes a weight distinction, Amami, is a pitch accent language in which only certain words are pitch accented; Amami is not included in the figures presented below in the text.

3. Tiberian Hebrew, which is not included in the survey, also treats CVC as heavier than CVV (McCarthy 1979a).

4. Note that there are a small set of languages, e.g. Arabic and the variety of Estonian described by Hint (1973), in which CVCC is heavier than CVC but, unlike in Hindi, only in final position.

5. The weight distinction holds of nouns. In nouns, if the penult contains a long vowel, it is stressed. If not, stress falls on the last high-toned syllable, otherwise the first syllable.

6. Word-internal codas are permitted in Kawaiisu; these do not interact with stress.

7. CVV(C) is heavy in affixed forms.

8. Codas are found in non-final position in Tsou; these do not interact with stress.

9. The Hokkaido dialect has no long vowels.

10. The only long vowels in Apalaí are nasalized vowels; the weight distinction holds for secondary stress.

11. The weight distinction holds for secondary stress; primary stress falls on the initial syllable.

12. The weight distinction is for secondary stress.

13. Final CVC is not stressed in Cuna.
14. Final CVC is not stressed.
15. The weight distinction is for secondary stress.
16. This weight distinction is reported for secondary stress by Szinnyei (1912).
17. This weight distinction holds only of uninflected [unsuffixed] stems in which stress falls on a final CVC or CVV(C) syllable, otherwise on the penult. In inflected [suffixed] forms, stress falls on the final syllable of the stem regardless of weight.
18. Surface long vowels arise through a process of intervocalic glide deletion.
19. All heavy syllables attract at least secondary stress. Primary stress in verbs is final and, in nouns, on the ultima if heavy otherwise the penult, where heavy is CVV(C) and CVC closed by any consonant except a coronal obstruent.
20. The syllable weight distinction in Turkish manifests itself in place names and borrowings in Turkish (see Kaisse 1985, Barker 1989, and Kornfilt 1990 for discussion).
21. Long vowels occur in the southern dialects of Veps resulting from /l/ vocalization (Viitso 1997).
22. Only syllables closed by a sonorant preceding another sonorant are heavy in Orya.
23. There are also minimal pairs differentiated solely on the basis of stress, indicating that stress is phonemic as well as conditioned by weight.
24. Stress falls on the initial syllable unless it contains /i/, or if the first syllable is open and onsetless and the second syllable begins with a consonant cluster, in which case stress falls on the second syllable.
25. The vowel which is light is /ɛ/, which can be analyzed as a reduced vowel given its relatively central articulation; note though that /ɔ/ also occurs.
26. The only long vowel is long /aː/ in CVC words.
27. Diphthongs are phonetically short.
28. In certain grammatical forms, there are a small number of phonemic vowel length contrasts in the penultimate syllable, which is stressed unless it contains a reduced vowel.
29. The only permissible codas in Asheninca are nasals. Ci is the phonetic realization of phonemic /i/ in a syllable beginning with a coronal strident. Asheninca actually makes a weight distinction between Ca(C)and Ce(C), Co(C), CiC in stress clash environments: Ca(C) obligatorily wins a stress clash with an adjacent syllable, whereas Ce(C), Co(C), CiC win only optionally (see Payne 1990:194).
30. The only permissible codas are nasals.
31. The Hindi stress pattern is the subject of some debate; see Kelkar (1968) whose judgments form the basis of the data in the table and Ohala (1977).
32. The Irish weight contrast is found in Munster Irish. The distinction between Cax and CV is subject to some interesting restrictions (see Doherty 1991

for details). The velar fricative need not belong to the coda of the syllable containing /a/ to contribute weight.

33. See discussion of this weight distinction in Chapter Four.

34. Diphthongs are phonetically short.

35. Onset-sensitivity is reported for a fifth language, Warembori (Donohue 1999), but the data do not definitively establish the relevance of onsets for stress.

36. See Goedemans (1998) for some interesting work exploring the basis for onset insensitivity.

37. The conditions under which weight manifests itself in Acoma are complex; a contour tone (falling) occurs only on long vowels or short V followed by a short voweled high-toned syllable beginning with a sonorant.

38. The only coda is glottal stop.

39. Contours occur only on utterance final syllables.

40. The only coda is /m/ resulting from /mV/.

41. The only coda is glottal stop.

42. The restriction operates lexically.

43. The falling tone occurs only on long vowels or short V followed by a short voweled high-toned syllable beginning with a sonorant.

44. There is no vowel length contrast in open syllables in Cantonese; vowels in open syllables are phonetically long (see Chapter Three); syllables closed by an obstruent may not carry contour tones, whether they contain a long vowel or not.

45. The only sonorant codas are derived from loss of V2 in CVCV.

46. The weight distinction is found in the "minor" (unstressed, pre-root) syllables, which may themselves carry a tone only if they contain a sonorant.

47. Lhasa Tibetan has a four way tonal contrast in syllables containing a long vowel and syllables closed by a sonorant: high level, high fall, low rise, and low fall. Tibetan does not have phonemic long vowels in closed syllables. In short voweled open syllables and syllables closed by an obstruent, there is only a two-way contrast between a low tone, phonetically realized with a slight rise, and a high tone.

48. Tones on sonorant codas arise through intervocalic high vowel deletion and reassociation of the stranded tone originally on the vowel with the new sonorant coda. Tone does not reassociate with obstruent codas.

49. Syllables closed by an obstruent only contrast two tones compared to six tones in other syllable types. The two tones occurring in CVO syllables may be analyzed as high and low phonologically, though they are actually phonetically rising and falling. As in Cantonese, open syllables can carry all six tones in Vietnamese; there are two short centralized vowels that only occur in closed syllables, suggesting that vowels in open syllables may be longer than in closed syllables as in Cantonese.

50. Dawson (1980:16) describes one realization of the low falling tone as a complex tone consisting of a short rise followed by a longer fall.

51. Apropos Tibetan, it is also interesting to note that another variety of Tibetan, the Standard Refugee variety reported in Meredith (1990), differs from the Lhasa dialect in treating not just CVV but also CVC as heavy for stress.

52. Note that Figure 2.3 is simplified to include only those relations that are relevant for syllable weight. It does not include other phonological properties that may be phonetically motivated (see Flemming 1995, Steriade 1999, Kirchner 1998 among others for work on other phonetically motivated phenomena).

53. The reason why the feature [syllabic] is maintained here is because it offers a unified treatment between vowels and syllabic nasals, which, like vowels, are well suited to carrying contour tones (see section 2.3.2).

54. Hayes (1989) and Rialland (1993), however, discuss a few possible cases of compensatory lengthening triggered by loss of an onset consonant.

55. There are other types of compensatory lengthening. A vowel may be lost triggering lengthening of the preceding vowel: i.e. CVCV → CVː(C). Compensatory lengthening of this type appears to be fairly common cross-linguistically and is found, for example, in Hungarian and Korean (see Hock 1986 for discussion of these cases and others). Another type of compensatory lengthening arises when a high vowel following a consonant becomes a glide, triggering lengthening of the immediately following vowel: i.e. /CuV/ → /CwVː/ or /CiV/ → /CjVː/. This process of compensatory lengthening triggered by glide formation occurs, for example, in Ilokano (Hayes and Abad 1989) and Luganda (Hock 1986). Yet another process which also falls under the rubric of compensatory lengthening is the assimilation of one consonant to an adjacent consonant, typically a following one, i.e. $CVC_j.C_kV$ → $CVC_k.C_kV$ (see, Jun 1995, 1996 for cases of this sort).

56. It is also doubtful whether compensatory lengthening can diagnose weight distinctions based on vowel quality, since neither the absence nor occurrence of lengthening of a certain vowel quality necessarily establishes the weight of that vowel quality relative to others. For example, if only low vowels underwent compensatory lengthening triggered by vowel loss, this could simply be because low vowels make better long vowels. Conversely, the failure of low vowels to undergo compensatory lengthening could be attributed to an independent constraint (perhaps lowly prioritized in a given language) against long low vowels, possibly a manifestation of a syllable template restriction setting an upper weight limit per syllable (see Chapter Five).

57. Reduplication is similar to compensatory lengthening in being diagnostic for only a subset of weight criteria. If a language has a CVV template for the reduplicant and does not reduplicate CVC syllables, we cannot conclude

that codas are light in the language; it is plausible that the language simply wants to avoid closed syllables if possible, but that the requirement that underlying codas be preserved has priority over the avoidance of codas.

58. Collecting and interpreting data on minimal word requirements is more difficult than examining data on other weight sensitive processes, largely because most grammars do not explicitly provide information on minimal word requirements. Often the information must be collected by scanning dictionaries, word lists and grammars, a tedious process and one that is prone to error, since its involves diagnosis by exclusion. For example, if one finds no CV words, one concludes that there is a minimal word requirement. Similarly, if one finds neither CVC nor CV words, this implies that the minimal word requirement is CVV or CVCV. A further problem is that the corpus of words examined in a given language may not be large enough to conclude *definitively* that there is a minimal word requirement in effect. Many grammars contain a statement to the effect that most words or the majority of words conform to some minimal size. It is impossible to tell from such statements how great the dispreference for sub-minimal words is. Furthermore, some languages have minimal root requirements, as mentioned earlier, that are different from minimal word requirements.

59. It is important to note that a restriction against syllables closed by two consonants, i.e. CV(V)CC, is not a restriction on weight, if it applies symmetrically after both short and long vowels. Restrictions against doubly closed syllables, quite common in languages of the world, typically can be related to segmental properties or linear restrictions against three consecutive consonants or against certain combinations of three consecutive consonants.

60. This figures includes languages with other minimal word requirements, which treat codas as weighted segments (CVVC, CVCC heavy and CVVV, CVCCC heavy; see Chapter Five).

61. In order to allow for statistical comparison, weight criteria observed by no languages for either process considered in a pair wise comparison were omitted from the analysis.

62. The weight distinction is found in nouns. If the penult contains a long vowel, it is stressed. If not, stress falls on the last high-toned syllable, otherwise the first syllable.

63. Word-internal codas are permitted in Kawaiisu; these do not interact with stress.

64. CVV(C) is heavy in affixed forms.

65. Codas are found in non-final position in Tsou; these do not interact with stress.

66. The Hokkaido dialect has no long vowels.

67. The only long vowels in Apalaí are nasalized vowels; the weight distinction holds for secondary stress.

68. The weight distinction holds for secondary stress; primary stress falls on the initial syllable.
69. The weight distinction obtains for secondary stress.
70. Final CVC is not stressed.
71. The weight distinction is for secondary stress.
72. This weight distinction is reported for secondary stress by Szinnyei (1912).
73. This weight distinction holds only of uninflected [unsuffixed] stems in which stress falls on a final CVC or CVV(C) syllable, otherwise on the penult. In inflected [suffixed] forms, stress falls on the final syllable of the stem regardless of weight.
74. Surface long vowels arise through a process of intervocalic glide deletion.
75. The syllable weight distinction in Turkish manifests itself in place names and borrowings in Turkish (see Kaisse 1985, Barker 1989, and Kornfilt 1990 for discussion).
76. Long vowels occur in the southern dialects of Veps resulting from /l/ vocalization (Viitso 1997).
77. Only syllables closed by a sonorant preceding another sonorant are heavy in Orya.
78. There are also minimal pairs differentiated solely on the basis of stress, indicating that stress is also phonemic.
79. Stress falls on the initial syllable unless it contains /ɨ/ or the first syllable is open and onsetless and the second syllable begins with a consonant cluster, in which case stress falls on the second syllable.
80. The vowel which is light is /ɛ/, which can be analyzed as a reduced vowel given its relatively central articulation; note though that /ɔ/ also occurs.
81. The only long vowel is long /aː/ which occurs in CVC words.
82. Diphthongs are phonetically short.
83. In certain grammatical forms, there are a small number of phonemic vowel length contrasts in the penultimate syllable, which is stressed unless it contains a reduced vowel.
84. The only permissible codas in Asheninca are nasals. Cɨ is the phonetic realization of phonemic /i/ in a syllable beginning with a coronal strident. Asheninca actually makes a weight distinction between Ca(C) and Ce(C), Co(C), CiC in stress clash environments: Ca(C) obligatorily wins a stress clash with an adjacent syllable, whereas Ce(C), Co(C), CiC win only optionally (see Payne 1990:194).
85. The only permissible codas are nasals.
86. The Hindi stress pattern is the subject of some debate; see Kelkar (1968) whose judgments form the basis of the data in the table and Ohala (1977).
87. The Irish weight contrast is found in Munster Irish. The distinction between Cax and CV is subject to some interesting restrictions (see Doherty 1991

for details). The velar fricative need not belong to the coda of the syllable of the preceding /a/ to contribute weight.

88. See discussion of this weight distinction in Chapter Four.

89. Diphthongs are phonetically short.

90. Hindi makes a three-way distinction for metrics whereby CVCC and CVVC are treated as superheavy syllables.

91. In Chapter Five, we will address some non-accidental convergences in weight criteria between tone and syllable template restrictions.

92. Two of these cases are languages with a ternary weight distinction for stress, Hindi and Pulaar Fula.

93. The only coda is glottal stop.

94. Contours only occur on utterance final syllables.

95. The only coda is /m/ resulting from /mV/.

96. The only coda is glottal stop.

97. The weight distinction operates as a lexical restriction.

98. Falling tones occur only on long vowels or on short vowels followed by a short voweled high-toned syllable beginning with a sonorant.

99. There is no vowel length contrast in open syllables in Cantonese; vowels in open syllables are phonetically long (see Chapter Three); syllables closed by an obstruent may not carry contour tones, whether they contain a long vowel or not.

100. The only sonorant codas are derived from loss of V2 in CVCV.

101. The weight distinction is found in "minor" (unstressed, pre-root) syllables, which may themselves carry a tone only if they contain a sonorant.

102. Tibetan has a four way tonal contrast in syllables containing a long vowel and syllables closed by a sonorant: high level, high fall, low rise, and low fall. Tibetan does not have phonemic long vowels in closed syllables. In short voweled open syllables and syllables closed by an obstruent, there is only a two-way contrast between a low tone, phonetically realized as a slight rise, and high tone.

103. Tones on sonorant codas result from the reassociation of tones stranded by intervocalic high vowel deletion. Tone does not reassociate with obstruent codas.

104. Syllables closed by an obstruent only contrast two tones compared to six tones in other syllable types. The two tones occurring in CVO syllables may be analyzed as high and low phonologically, though they are actually phonetically rising and falling. As in Cantonese, open syllables can carry all six tones in Vietnamese; there are two short centralized vowels that only occur in closed syllables, suggesting that vowels in open syllables may perhaps be longer than in closed syllables as in Cantonese.

105. A fourth language (Crow) appears to display the same uniformity, although the minimal word requirement could not be determined with confidence.

NOTES TO CHAPTER THREE

1. I will not treat complex tones consisting of a rise followed by a fall or vice versa in the discussion that follows. The interested reader is referred to Yip (1995) for a summary of various formal analyses of complex tones proposed in the literature and Zhang (2002) for a phonetically-driven analysis of tonal weight that includes discussion of complex tones.

2. One language in this group, Cantonese, displays somewhat exceptional behavior and will be discussed in detail in section 3.2.2.

3. One language in the survey, Acoma, allows contours on short vowels, but only if followed by a short voweled high toned syllable with a sonorant in onset position. This distinction is unusual in that it not only is sensitive to an onset but that it is sensitive to both the vowel duration and the tone of the following syllable.

4. A voiceless segment does not inherently possess a fundamental frequency itself, although its laryngeal settings may influence the fundamental frequency of neighboring voiced segments, as demonstrated by the link between voiceless consonants and high tone in many languages. Influences of this sort are not strictly weight-sensitive and are thus not discussed here.

5. The same ANOVA also indicated that rime type had the most significant effect on vowel duration (F [2, 66]=867.747, p<.0001). This result is expected given the inclusion of both short and long voweled rimes in the analysis. Finally, tone type (contour vs. level) alone had the smallest effect on vowel duration (F [1, 66]=5.699, p=.0198). That the effect of tone type on vowel duration barely reached significance at all is attributed to the highly significant duration difference between level and contour tones in CVO.

6. A hypothesis worthy of investigation would be that in languages which allow contour tones on all syllable types, i.e. in languages without any weight-sensitive tone restrictions, not only would vowels in CVO syllables with contour tones be longer than vowels in CVO syllables with level tones, just as in Hausa, but also vowels in CV syllables with contour tones would be longer than vowels in CV syllables with level tones.

7. Contour tones can occur on syllables closed by an obstruent in certain morphologically derived forms and, more rarely, in certain reduplicated sandhi forms. These contour tones, which are members of the set of piːn jam, or 'changed tones,' are discussed at length in Bauer and Benedict (1997) and also in Yu (2003), who shows that they are associated with vowel lengthening. Their implications for the constraint system are discussed in section 3.6.4.

8. The measurements also indicate that vowels, both short and long, in syllables closed by a sonorant consonant are much longer than vowels in both

open syllables and syllables closed by an obstruent. This lengthening effect is limited to vowels before a tautosyllabic sonorant.

9. The scale of sonority for stress will be shown in Chapter Four to correspond to a phonetic measurement of energy.

10. The first variant of this form is not actually cited by Reh; it is assumed, on the basis of his description of vowel apocope and tonal restrictions.

11. Thanks to Russ Schuh for supplying me with these data.

12. Note that a constraint in Hausa against rising tones, not exemplified here, would also eliminate the third rival candidate in (43).

NOTES TO CHAPTER FOUR

1. Recall that reduced vowels in this context refers to underlying short central vowels and not to vowels which have undergone reduction in stressless syllables, as is common, e.g. in English.

2. The only permissible codas in Asheninca are nasals. Ci is the phonetic realization of phonemic /i/ in a syllable beginning with a coronal strident. Asheninca actually makes an additional weight distinction between low vowels and non-low vowels (i.e. Ca(C) vs. Ce(C), Co(C)) in stress clash environments: Ca(C) obligatorily wins a stress clash with an adjacent syllable, whereas Ce(C), Co(C), CiC win only optionally (see Payne 1990:194).

3. The only phonemic long vowel in Au is /aː/ which could plausibly be analyzed as an underlying /aʔa/ sequence in virtue of its phonetic realization in the central dialect (Scorza 1985: 219).

4. Based on the data that De Lacy presents, the Kara weight hierarchy could be reinterpreted in at least four ways. Three alternatives to the hierarchy in Table 4.1 are as follows: CVː > CaV, CaC > Ca > CV_iV_k , CNon-Low V(C) or CVː > CaV > Ca > CV_iV_k , CNon-LowC > CNon-Low V or, if one regards the data De Lacy considers exceptional as unexceptional, CVː > Ca > CNon-low VC > CNon-Low V(Non-Low V).

5. There are a small number of phonemic vowel length contrasts in certain morphologically complex forms in the penultimate syllable. Vowel length is not used to contrast lexical items, however.

6. In certain dialects of Mari, all closed syllables are also heavy (see Kenstowicz 1997).

7. I follow Davies (1980) transcription of one of the central vowels as /ə/ rather than Kenstowicz's transcription of /ö/.

8. It is conceivable that not only duration but also articulatory effort must be invoked in accounting for the failure of reduced vowels to receive a timing position under the proposed account. If, for example, it turned out that, in languages with a weight distinction between high and non-high vowels, the duration difference between the two vowel types were as great as the

duration difference between full and reduced vowels in languages which make a full vs. reduced vowel weight distinction, then it would be no more justified to assume that the full vs. reduced vowel weight distinction is represented as a difference between one and zero timing positions than to assume that the high vs. non-high vowel weight distinction is also represented as a difference between zero and one timing positions. It is plausible, however, that the duration difference between high and non-high vowels in languages in which the two differ in weight is smaller than the duration difference between full and reduced vowels. The reason for this becomes clearer when one considers that the intensity (one of the acoustic properties contributing to the measure of energy argued in this chapter to be responsible for weight-sensitive stress) of vowels is inversely proportional to their height; the higher the vowel, the lower the intensity. Because high vowels also have less intensity than non-high vowels, it is quite conceivable, indeed probable, that not only duration but also intensity is responsible for the high vs. non-high vowel weight distinction. Reduced vowels, on the other hand, would not necessarily be expected to have less intensity than full vowels, since reduced vowels like schwa are lower in height than the high vowels. This is an empirical issue which could be tested by examining duration differences between high and non-high vowels in a language in which the two differ in weight and comparing the results with the duration differences between full and reduced vowels in a language employing a full vs. reduced vowel weight distinction.

9. Recall that CVV stands for long vowels and diphthongs, while CVː stands for long vowels to the exclusion of diphthongs.

10. Note that vowel syncope is not instructive in diagnosing the phonetic duration of /i/ in closed syllables, since all closed syllables have a voiced coda which would not be expected to trigger syncope.

11. It is conceivable of course that other factors play a role in the assignment of stress, notably the ability of certain syllables to carry certain pitch (fundamental frequency) contours or peaks that could enhance the prominence of a syllable. Energy and duration, however, would appear to be on the whole more closely linked to "stress" as typically conceived, since there are certain weight distinctions that cannot easily be attributed to relative ability to carry pitch. For example, it is not clear why the class of closed syllables, including both obstruents and sonorants, would be better docking sites for a particular pitch contour than open syllables.

12. Due to gaps in the lexicon, the vowel in the second syllable could not always be held constant in Chickasaw. Where a different vowel was used, the energy of the second vowel was adjusted by an appropriate factor as determined by controlled comparisons (see Appendix Four).

13. Note that the French rhotic was voiceless in the data collected, presumably because it preceded a voiceless consonant in the words elicited.

14. In their study of Japanese, Dalby and Port (1981) also found that vowels in closed syllables were longer than vowels before single consonants (86 milliseconds to 68 milliseconds for /u/ and 106 milliseconds to 90 milliseconds for /a/). It should be pointed out, though, that the degree of lengthening found in the present study is greater than that observed by Dalby and Port. Part of this difference in results could be due to differences in the corpus set. Their study compared vowels before single and geminate /k/, whereas the present study examined vowels before nasals. Furthermore, in the present study, the vowels in open syllables appeared before /p/, whereas those in closed syllables occurred before nasals.

15. Anttila (1997) presents interesting data from Finnish demonstrating that not only stress but also vowel height plays a role in the choice of genitive morphology in Finnish nouns. Although the sensitivity to vowel sonority parallels distinctions made in stress systems in other languages, it is orthogonal to the stress system in Finnish; stress also interacts with genitive allomorphy. The interaction between sonority and genitive allomorphy is thus not strictly relevant for the present study.

16. Petrunicheva (1960:32) says that the third syllable is stressed in words containing more than three syllables all of which contain short vowels. This description does not accord with other descriptions of the stress system (e.g. Brown 1981); also, in the form he gives to illustrate this pattern, talaˈkaʈu 'cross,' the third syllable is the only one which is CVC, suggesting that non-final CVC is perhaps heavier than CV. I will not pursue this hypothesis here, though it is compatible with the weight hierarchy assumed in the text.

17. Ras (1982) reports an alternating stress pattern in longer words. However, all of his examples involve four syllable words with penultimate stress and a full vowel in the first syllable; he does not provide examples in which the alternating stress pattern would predict stress on a reduced vowel or words in which the last stress falls on the final syllable.

18. Horne (1974) reports that all sequences of two adjacent vowels are heterosyllabic in Javanese.

19. It is interesting to note that the differences in vowel duration between open and closed syllables in Finnish fall somewhere in between those reported in two other studies of Finnish duration. Lehtonen (1970) found slightly longer vowels in open than in closed syllables in his study of the variety of Finnish spoken around Helsinki. Leskinen and Lehtonen (1985), however, found substantial lengthening of vowels in closed syllables, greater than the differences found in the present study, in their study of southeastern varieties of Finnish. The speaker for the present study was from southwestern Finland.

20. /h/ also appears in coda position in Finnish; it is unclear whether it should be treated as a sonorant or an obstruent.

21. Davis (1988) discusses an additional case of onset sensitivity in Madimadi, which has subsequently been explained by Gahl (1996) in terms of morphological factors rather than onsets.

22. Gordon (2005) also discusses data from the historical phonology of Italian (Davis and Napoli 1994) that is potentially problematic for the account of onset-sensitive stress based on auditory recovery.

23. An alternative view is that evaluation of complexity is innate and that constraints referring to complex distinctions do not even exist in the grammar.

NOTES TO CHAPTER FIVE

1. Kavitskaya (2002) shows that compensatory lengthening is often triggered by sonorants, since sonorants characteristically have a lengthening effect on a preceding vowel.

2. Note that there are also languages, such as Germanic (e.g. θaŋxta > θaːxta English 'thought'), in which compensatory lengthening is triggered by loss of one coda consonant in a doubly closed syllable.

3. There are a small number of phonemic vowel length contrasts in certain grammatical forms in the penultimate syllable, which is stressed unless it contains a reduced vowel.

4. There is a match of weight criteria between compensatory lengthening and the pitch accent system.

5. Compensatory lengthening is found in Northern Thai dialects which have lost final /k/.

6. See Sezer (1986), Kornfilt (1990) and Inkelas and Orgun (1995) for discussion of compensatory lengthening in Turkish.

7. Long vowels occur in the southern dialects of Veps resulting from /l/ vocalization (Viitso 1997).

8. CVh becomes CVː before a voiced or glottalized consonant.

9. The Hindi stress pattern is the subject of some debate; see Kelkar (1968) whose judgments form the basis of the data in the table, and Ohala (1977).

10. Syllables closed by the first half of a geminate are light, whereas syllables closed by a consonant which is not the first half of a geminate and syllables containing a tautosyllabic geminate are heavy.

11. Codas are found in non-final position in Tsou.

12. Arabic almost falls into the category of languages with a CVVC or CVCC minimal word requirement; however, there are a small number of content words of the shape CVC at least in certain dialects (Harrell 1957).

13. CVC results from vowel apocope.

14. The Irish weight contrast is found in Munster Irish. The distinction between Cax and CV is subject to some interesting restrictions (see Doherty 1995 for details). The velar fricative need not belong to the same syllable as the preceding /a/ to contribute weight.

15. The weight distinction operates as a lexical restriction.
16. The CVC minimal word requirement holds of standard Tamil, while the colloquial variety employs a disyllabic minimal word requirement (Christdas 1996).
17. A syllable final glottal stop is inserted in word-final position in words ending in a short vowel. This glottal stop does not count as weight-bearing in the metrical system, however.
18. Compensatory lengthening is found in Northern Thai dialects which have lost final /k/.
19. Phonemic short vowels in open monosyllables phonetically lengthen. See Inkelas and Orgun (1995) for discussion of the minimal word and its complexities (some of which are speaker dependent) in Turkish.
20. The only coda is glottal stop.
21. The only coda is glottal stop.
22. Phonetically, the minimal word is CVV? due to a general phenomenon of glottal stop insertion after final vowels.
23. Word-internal codas are permitted in Kawaiisu.
24. Non-final codas are permitted in Maithili.
25. Tiwi lacks codas in the relevant position to determine the weight status of CVC syllables.
26. The only long vowel is long /a:/, which occurs in closed monsyllables.
27. The CVV minimal word is attributed to an underlying short vowel that is phonetically lengthened in an open final syllable.
28. This figure does not include another language, Tamil, which has a disyllabic minimal word requirement in the colloquial variety described by Christdas (1996) but a CVC minimal word in standard Tamil.
29. Estonian, though it has a minimal word requirement larger than CVC, is treated as a weight match between stress and minimal word requirements, since coda consonants contribute to the calculation of weight for both phenomena.
30. This figure does not include hearts and diamonds in parentheses or languages in which there is both a heart and a diamond in the stress column (corresponding to a complex weight hierarchy for stress).
31. The Hokkaido dialect has no long vowels.
32. The Ainu accent is a pitch accent.
33. This restriction only holds of syllables closed by the first half of a geminate.
34. The Hindi stress pattern is the subject of some debate; see Kelkar (1968) whose judgments form the basis of the data in the table, and, for another viewpoint, Ohala (1977).
35. CVC results from a final apocope rule.
36. Vowels in open penults lengthen, an historical process related to accent being on the penult.
37. Pretonic vowels in open but not closed syllables lengthen in Onondaga.

38. No full vowels or diphthongs occur in closed syllables.

39. Although exceptionless at one time in the history of the language, there are certain synchronic exceptions to Osthoff's law in Lithuanian, as discussed in Kenstowicz (1972) and Young (1991). There are some infinitival verb forms which contain a long vowel followed by a tautosyllabic sonorant coda, e.g. súːrti 'to grow salty' (Young 1991:9). Also CVVR surfaces in some nominal cases due to historical loss of the vowel in a final syllable, e.g. galvóːm(s) (<*galvóːmVs) 'head' dative plural (Young 10), as well as at compound boundaries, e.g. ʃóːnkaulis 'rib' (< ʃóːnas 'side' + káulas 'bone') (Young 9). In all of these exceptional cases we would expect shortening of the underlying long vowel before a tautosyllabic coda, as is the typical case in the language, as evidenced by the substantial number of forms which undergo alternations within a paradigm, e.g. dúːmeː: dúmti 'blow,' píːleː: pílti 'pour.' On the basis of the pervasiveness of these alternations, Kenstowicz (1972) posits a synchronic rule of vowel shortening affecting long vowels in syllables closed by a sonorant. My consultant also regarded hypothetical words containing long vowels in sonorant closed syllables as somewhat odd and unnatural, a judgment that is compatible with the view that Osthoff's law is productive synchronically. It is also interesting to note that my consultant failed to produce a quantitatively long vowel in the word súːrti 'to grow salty' (the only one of the exceptional infinitives elicited); rather she pronounced the vowel in question with the slightly more peripheral quality characteristic of long /u/ relative to short /u/. One other surface phonetic exception to Osthoff's law of a different nature is due to a general (but not exceptionless) process of vowel lengthening affecting /a/ and the lower front mid vowel /ɛ/ (there is no back counterpart to this vowel in the native vocabulary) when accented (Kenstowicz 1972); see the discussion of accented vowel lengthening in the text.

NOTES TO APPENDIX TWO

1. The only long vowel is /aː/.
2. The falling tone occurs only on long vowels or on short vowels followed by a short voweled high toned syllable beginning with a sonorant.
3. The Hokkaido dialect has no long vowels.
4. The Ainu accent is a pitch accent.
5. There are no diphthongs in Albanian.
6. CVV is historically derived from CVCV via intervocalic consonant loss.
7. In pitch accented nouns, the accent falls on the second mora if the first syllable is CV; otherwise it falls on a CVC or CVV first syllable.
8. The only long vowels are /ɛː/ and /ɔː/.
9. The only coda is glottal stop.

10. Contours are limited to utterance final syllables.
11. The only long vowels are nasalized vowels, which may only occur long; the weight distinction is for secondary stress. Main stress falls on the penult, with an optional secondary stress on the initial syllable as well.
12. Final CVC is not stressed.
13. /iː, uː/ may not occur in closed syllables.
14. The author suggests that this possibly might not be completely natural speech.
15. The only permissible codas in Asheninca are nasals. Cɨ is the phonetic realization of phonemic /i/ in a syllable beginning with a coronal strident. Asheninca actually makes a weight distinction between Ca(C)and Ce(C), Co(C), CiC in stress clash environments: Ca(C) obligatorily wins a stress clash with an adjacent syllable, whereas Ce(C), Co(C), CiC win only optionally (see Payne 1990:194).
16. The only permissible codas are nasals.
17. In disyllabic words, the first mora is stressed; in words with 3+ moras the 1st mora is stressed only if the first syllable has an onset.
18. A variety of stress and accentual patterns, ranging from peinitial to penultimate stress to pitch accent systems, are found in Basque, depending on the dialect; see Saltarelli (1988) for an overview and Elordieta (1997) for detailed analysis of Lekeitio Basque, a pitch accent variety of Basque.
19. The weight distinction is used for secondary stress.
20. There is no vowel length contrast in open syllables.
21. The only coda is glottal stop.
22. Syllables are either open or closed by a glottal stop. Syllables closed by a glottal stop carry a high tone, while other syllable types can carry either a high, a low tone, or another tone associated with creaky phonation.
23. There is no vowel length contrast in open syllables in Cantonese; vowels in open syllables are phonetically long (see Chapter Three); VV stands for phonetically lengthened vowels in open syllables and phonemic long vowels in closed syllables.
24. Vowels are phonetically long in open syllables; thus, the minimal word is either CVC or CVV (see Chapter Three).
25. The weight distinction is for secondary stress.
26. Vowels in open penults lengthen, an historical process related to accent being on the penult.
27. The only codas are /r/ and /b/ which occur only as the reduced forms of certain morphemes.
28. Penultimate stress is the dominant pattern, though Beeler (1970) does report that some words have final stress.
29. Final CVC is not stressed.
30. Final CVC is not stressed.
31. Contour tones (a falling tone) occur only on final syllables.

32. Vossen (1985:343) tentatively (subject to further research) suggests that verbs carry a stress in citation form.
33. High tones only occur on syllables containing a long vowel or a sonorant coda in Haida.
34. Galloway's (1993) description suggests that stress is gradient, i.e. there are differing levels of stress characterized by different tonal properties.
35. The Hindi stress pattern is the subject of some debate; see Kelkar (1968) whose judgments form the basis of the data in the table and Ohala (1977) for a different view.
36. Historically, the first half of geminates were lost and length was realized on the immediately preceding vowel.
37. This restriction only holds of syllables closed by the first half of a geminate.
38. CVC results from a final apocope rule.
39. This weight distinction is reported for secondary stress by Szinnyei (1912).
40. In nouns, if the penult contains a long vowel, it is stressed. If not, stress falls on the last high-toned syllable, otherwise the first syllable.
41. Closed syllables containing long vowels are exceedingly rare in Japanese and are limited to loans and morphologically complex words; Vance (1987:72) reports that long vowels often are shortened at conversational speech rates.
42. The only coda which occurs is the noun-suffix /ʃ/.
43. Stress falls on the final syllable unless it is onsetless.
44. See the discussion of this weight distinction in Chapter Five.
45. The only coda is glottal stop.
46. There are some surface CCV forms resulting from vowel loss.
47. Phonetically, the minimal word is CVV? due to a general phenomenon of glottal stop insertion after final vowels.
48. Word-internal codas are permitted in Kawaiisu.
49. The weight distinction is found in "minor" (unstressed, pre-root) syllables, which may carry a tone only if they contain a sonorant.
50. Combinations of vowels are disyllabic.
51. The only sonorant codas are derived from loss of V2 in CVCV.
52. Diphthongs are phonetically short.
53. Certain dialects have preserved long vowels.
54. Long vowels do not occur in syllables closed by the first half of a geminate.
55. CVV(C) is heavy in affixed forms.
56. The only coda is /m/ resulting from /mV/.
57. The only coda is glottals stop; only high and low tones may occur in syllables closed by a glottal stop; however, glottal stop is subject to reanalysis as a tonal feature of the preceding vowel.
58. There are a small number of phonemic vowel length contrasts in certain grammatical forms in the penultimate syllable, which is stressed unless it contains a reduced vowel.

59. Rising tones occur only in stressed syllables.

60. There are also minimal pairs differentiated solely on the basis of stress.

61. The CVC minimal word is due to a recstriction that all roots begin and end with a consonant.

62. Virtually all stems end in a consonant in Lushootseed.

63. Non-final codas are permitted in Maithili.

64. This weight distinction holds only of uninflected (unsuffixed) stems, in which stress falls on a final CVC or CVV(C) syllable, otherwise on the penult. In uninflected (suffixed) forms, stress falls on the final syllable of the stem regardless of weight.

65. Stress falls on the initial syllable unless it contains /i/, or if the first syllable is open and onsetless and the second syllable begins with a consonant cluster, in which case stress falls on the second syllable.

66. The only coda is glottal stop.

67. Vowels in open penults lengthen, an historical process related to accent being on the penult.

68. Pretonic vowels in open syllables lengthen in Onondaga.

69. Only syllables closed by a sonorant preceding another sonorant are heavy in Orya.

70. No full vowels or diphthongs occur in unstressed closed syllables.

71. The most prominent syllable in a word in Kashaya Pomo is realized with a pitch accent. CVV resists attracting the pitch accent but CVC does not (see Oswalt 1988 and Buckley 1994 for discussion).

72. Some word-final CVVC occur, however.

73. /ɛ/ is perhaps a central vowel; note, though, that /ɔ/ also occurs but is heavier than /ɛ/.

74. The syllable template restriction operates lexically.

75. Tone has a very low functional load in Songai.

76. Surface long vowels arise through a process of intervocalic glide deletion.

77. Syllables closed by the first half of a geminate are light, whereas syllables closed by a consonant which is not the first half of a geminate and syllables containing a tautosyllabic geminate are heavy.

78. The CVC minimal word requirement holds of standard Tamil, while the colloquial variety employs a bisyllabic minimal word requirement (Christdas 1996).

79. Some dialects have long vowels instead of diphthongs.

80. The only codas which occur in Tewa are glottal stop, /h/ and /n/.

81. Compensatory lengthening is found in Northern Thai dialects that have lost final /k/.

82. A syllable final glottal stop is inserted in word-final position in words ending in a short vowel. This glottal stop does not count as weight-bearing in the metrical system, however.

83. Final short vowels are rare, /aː/ is the only long vowel.

84. All heavy syllables attract at least secondary stress. Primary stress in verbs is final and, in nouns, on the ultima if heavy, otherwise the penult, where heavy is CVV(C) and CVC closed by any consonant except a coronal obstruent.

85. The only codas are glottal stop and /h/.

86. Codas are found in non-final position in Tsou.

87. The only permissible coda in Tura is /ŋ/, which can also be syllabic.

88. Tones on sonorant codas result from tone left over from intervocalic high vowel deletion. Tone does not reassociate with obstruent codas.

89. The syllable weight distinction in Turkish manifests itself in a set of words consisting of proper names and borrowings (Kaisse 1985, Barker 1986, Kornfilt 1990).

90. See Sezer (1986), Kornfilt (1990) and Inkelas and Orgun (1995) for discussion of compensatory lengthening in Turkish.

91. Phonemic short vowels in open monosyllables phonetically lengthen. See Inkelas and Orgun (1995) for discussion of the minimal word and its complexities (some of which are speaker dependent) in Turkish.

92. Long vowels can occur on the surface from underlying vowel plus glide sequence.

93. The only long vowel is long /aː/, which occurs in closed monosyllables.

94. Final CVV is an underlying short vowel that is phonetically lengthened in open final syllables.

95. Contours are rare, though, on short vowels in stems.

96. Long vowels occur in the southern dialects of Veps resulting from /l/ vocalization (Viitso 1997).

97. Compensatory lengthening is found in southern dialects.

98. Syllables closed by an obstruent only contrast two tones compared to six tones in other syllable types. The two tones occurring in CVO syllables may be analyzed as high and low phonologically, though they are phonetically rising and falling. As in Cantonese, open syllables can carry all six tones in Vietnamese; there are two short centralized vowels that only occur in closed syllables, suggesting that vowels in open syllables may be longer than in closed syllables as in Cantonese.

99. This minimal word requirement depends on whether vowels are phonetically long in open syllables.

100. Donohue (1999:7) reports that "heavy consonants" in onset position of a syllable attract stress to that syllable. He does not, however, offer a phonetic description of the heavy consonants, which he transcribes as "'b, 'd, 'n, 'm," in contrast to non-heavy "b, d, n, m." Furthermore, the examples given to illustrate the attraction of stress by these consonants conform to the general penultimate stress pattern of the language.

101. The only coda is the glide /j/.

102. The only coda is the glide /j/.

103. The intonation peak (perhaps signalling stress) falls on final syllables.
104. Virtually all native Yapese roots end in a consonant.
105. Diphthongs are phonetically short.
106. The vowel in the first syllable is longer than others suggesting perhaps that it is stressed.
107. CVh becomes CV: before a voiced or glottalized consonant.

NOTES TO APPENDIX FOUR

1. This word was compared to /albi?/ to calculate the difference in energy between /i/ and /a/ in the final syllable. This difference was then subtracted from /a/ in the second syllable of other words in the corpus, in order to allow for comparison of the first vowel in words containing /a/ in the second syllable with the first vowel in words containing /i/ in the second syllable.

References

Abaev, Vasilii Ivanovich. 1964. *A grammatical sketch of Ossetic*. Bloomington: Indiana University Center in Anthropology, Folklore and Linguistics.

Abbott, Miriam. 1991. Macushi. *Handbook of Amazonian languages*. Vol. 3, edited by Desmond Derbyshire & Geoffrey Pullum, 23–160. Berlin: Mouton de Gruyter.

Abbott, Stan. 1985. A tentative multilevel multiunit phonological analysis of the Murik language. *Papers in New Guinea Linguistics* 22, 339–73.

Abdel-Massih, Ernest. 1971. *A reference grammar of Tamazight: a comparative study of the Berber dialects of the Ayt Ayache and Ayt Seghrouchen*. Ann Arbor: Center for Near Eastern and North African Studies, University of Michigan.

Abitov, M. L., B. X. Balkarov, J. D. Desheriev, G. B. Rogava, X. U. El'berdov, B. M. Kardanov, T. X. Kuasheva. 1957. *Grammatika kabardino-cherkesskogo literaturnogo jazyka*. Moscow: Izdatel'stvo Akademii Nauk.

Abrahamson, Arne & Joyce Abrahamson. 1984. Os fonemas da língua Júma. *Estudos sobre línguas tupí do brasil* [*Série Lingüística* 11], edited by Robert Dooley, 157–74. Brasília: Summer Institute of Linguistics.

Adams, Karen & Linda Lauck. 1975. A tentative phonemic statement of Patep. *Phonologies of five Austronesian languages*. Ukarumpa, Papua New Guinea: Summer Institute of Linguistics.

Adisasmito-Smith, Niken & Abigail C. Cohn. 1996. Phonetic correlates of primary and secondary stress in Indonesian: A preliminary study. *Working Papers of the Cornell Phonetics Laboratory* 11, 1–16.

Agnew, Alene & Eunice Pike. 1957. Phonemes of Ocaina (Huitoto). *International Journal of American Linguistics* 23, 24–27.

Äimä, Frans. 1914. *Phonetik und Lautlehre des Inarilappischen*. Helsinki: Druckerei der Finnischen Literaturgesellschaft.

Ali, Mohammed. 1990. *Handbook of the Oromo language*. Wroclaw: Zaklad Narodowy im Ossolinskich.

Allen, W. Sidney. 1973. *Accent and rhythm*. Cambridge: Cambridge University Press.

Allen, W. Sidney. 1975. *Vox latina: A guide to the pronunciation of Classical Latin.* Cambridge: Cambridge University Press.

Anderson, Judi. 1989. *Comaltepec Chinantec syntax.* Arlington, Tex.: Summer Institute of Linguistics.

Anderson, Judi, Isaac Martinez & Wanda Pace. 1990. Comaltepec Chinantec tone. *Syllables, tone, and verb paradigms: studies in Chinantec Languages,* IV, edited by William Merrifield & Calvin Rensch, 3–20. Dallas: Summer Institute of Linguistics.

Andronov, M. S. 1989. *A grammar of modern and classical Tamil.* Madras: New Century Book House.

Angoujard, Jean-Pierre. 1990. *Metrical structure of Arabic* [*Publications in Language Sciences* 35]. Dordrecht: Foris.

d'Ans, Andre Marcel. 1968. *Le creole francais d'Haiti: Etude des unites d'articulation, d'expansion et de communication.* The Hague: Mouton.

Anttila, Arto. 1997. *Deriving variation from grammar: a study of Finnish genitives.* Ms. Stanford University. [Available on Rutgers Optimality Archive, ROA-63, http://ruccs.rutgers.edu/roa.html.]

Aoki, Haruo. 1970. *Nez Perce grammar.* Berkeley: University of California Press.

Aoki, Haruo. 1994. *Nez Perce dictionary.* Berkeley: University of California Press.

Archangeli, Diana. 1984. Extrametricality in Yawelmani. *The Linguistic Review* 4, 101–20.

Ariste, Paul. 1968. *A grammar of the Votic language.* Bloomington: Indiana University Press.

Armellada, Cesáreo. 1943. *Gramática y diccionario de la lengua pemón (arekuna, taurepán, kamarakoto) (familia Caribe).* Caracas: Artes gráficas.

Árnason, Kristján. 1980. *Quantity in historical phonology: Icelandic and related cases.* [*Cambridge Studies in Linguistics* 30]. Cambridge: Cambridge University Press.

Arokainathan, S. 1980. *Tangkhul Naga phonetic reader.* Mysore: Central Institute of Indian Languages.

Arokianathan, S. 1987. *Tangkhul Naga grammar.* Mysore: Central Institute of Indian Languages.

Aronson, Howard. 1991. *Georgian: a reading grammar.* Columbus, Ohio: Slavica.

Asher, R. E. & T. C. Kumari. 1997. *Malayalam.* New York: Routledge.

Ayala, José Valentin. 1996. *Gramática guaraní.* Buenos Aires: Ministerio de Educació ce la Nacion.

Bach, Emmon. 1975. Long vowels and stress in Kwakiutl. *Texas Linguistic Forum* 2, 9–19.

Bagemihl, Bruce. 1995. Language games and related areas. *Handbook of phonological theory,* edited by John Goldsmith, 697–712. Cambridge, Mass.: Blackwell.

Bailey, David. 1975. *Abau language phonology and grammar.* Ukarumpa, Papua New Guinea: Summer Institute of Linguistics.

Baitschura, Uzbek. 1976. Instrumental phonetische Beiträge zur Untersuchung der Sprachmelodie und des Wortakzentes im Tscheremissischen. *Études Finno-Ougriennes* XIII, 109–22.

Ballard, W. L. 1975. Aspects of Yuchi morphology. *Studies in southeastern Indian languages*, edited by James Crawford, 237–50. Athens, Ga.: University of Georgia Press.

Barker, Christopher. 1989. Extrameticality, the cycle, and Turkish word stress. *Phonology at Santa Cruz* 1, edited by Junko Ito and Jeff Runner, 1–33. Santa Cruz, Calif.: University of California, Santa Cruz, Syntax Research Center.

Barker, Muhammad Abd-al-Rahman. 1963. *Klamath dictionary*. Berkeley: University of California Press.

Barker, Muhammad Abd-al-Rahman. 1964. *Klamath grammar*. [*University of California Publications in Linguistics* 32]. Berkeley: University of California Press.

Batchelor, John. 1938. *An Ainu-English-Japanese dictionary*. Tokyo: Iwanami-Syoten.

Bauer, Winifred. 1993. *Maori*. New York: Routledge.

Bauer, Robert & Paul Benedict. 1997. *Modern Cantonese phonology*. New York: Mouton de Gruyter.

Bearth, Thomas. 1971. *L'Énoncé toura (Côte d'Ivoire)*. Norman, Okla.: Summer Institute of Linguistics.

Beasley, David & Kenneth Pike. 1957. Notes on Huambisa phonemics. *Lingua Posnaniensis* 6, 1–8.

Beaton, Arthur. 1968. *A grammar of the Fur language*. Khartoum: Research Unit, Faculty of Arts, University of Khartoum.

Beckman, Mary. 1986. *Stress and non-stress accent*. Dordrecht: Foris.

Beckman, Mary, Jan Edwards & Janet Fletcher. 1992. Prosodic structure and tempo in a sonority model of articulatory dynamics. *Papers in laboratory phonology* II: *Gesture, segment, prosody*, edited by G. Docherty & D. R. Ladd, 68–86. Cambridge: Cambridge University. Press.

Beeler, M. S. 1976. Barbareño Chumash: a farrago. *Hokan Studies: Papers from the 1st Conference on Hokan Languages held in San Diego, California April 23–25, 1970*, edited by Margaret Langdon & Shirley Silver, 251–70. The Hague: Mouton.

Bell, Alan. 1993. Jemez tones and stress. *Colorado Research in Linguistics* 12, 26–34. Boulder, Colo.: University of Colorado at Boulder.

Beller, Richard & Beller, Patricia. 1979. Huasteca Nahuatl. *Studies in Uto-Aztecan grammar, vol. 2, Modern Aztec grammatical sketches*, edited by Ronald Langacker, 199–306. Arlington, TX: Summer Institute of Linguistics.

Benzing, Johannes. 1955. *Lamutische Grammatik; mit Bibliographie, Sprachproben und Glossar*. Wiesbaden: F. Steiner.

Berchem, Jörg. 1993. *Referenzgrammatik des Somali*. Köln: Omimee.

Bergsland, Knut. 1994. *Aleut dictionary = Unangam tunudgusii: An unabridged lexicon of the Aleutian, Pribilof, and Cammander Islands Aleut language*. Anchorage, Alaska: Aang Angagin, Aleutian/Pribilof Islands Association.

Black, K. and Black. 1971. *The Moro language: grammar and dictionary*. Khartoum: Sudan Research Unit, Faculty of Arts.

Bladon, Anthony. 1986. Phonetics for hearers. *Language for hearers*, edited by G. McGregor, 1–24. Oxford: Pergamon Press

Bloomfield, Leonard. 1956. *Eastern Ojibwa: grammatical sketch, texts and word list.* Ann Arbor: University of Michigan Press.

Bloomfield, Leonard. 1962. *The Menomini language.* New Haven: Yale University Press.

Bloomfield, Leonard. 1975. *Menomini lexicon.* Milwaukee: Milwaukee Public Museum Press.

Boas, Franz. 1917. *Grammatical notes on the language of the Tlingit Indians.* Philadelphia: University Museum.

Boas, Franz. 1947. *Kwakiutl grammar with a glossary of the suffixes,* edited by Helene Boas Yampolsky & Zelig Harris. *Transactions of the American Philosophical Society* 37:3, 201–377.

Boas, Franz & Ella Deloria. 1933. Notes on the Dakota, Teton dialect. *International Journal of American Linguistics* 7,.97–121.

Boas, Franz & Ella Deloria. 1941. *Dakota grammar.* [*Memoirs of the National Academy of Sciences* 33]. Washington: United States Government Printing Office.

Boersma, Paul. 1998. *Functional phonology: Formalizing the interactions between articulatory and perceptual drives.* The Hague: Holland Academic Graphics.

Böhm, Gerhard. 1984. *Grammatik der Kunama-Sprache.* Wien: Institut für Afrikanistik.

Bondarko, L. V., L. P. Verbitskaya & L.P. Tscherbakova. 1973. Ob opredelenii mesta udareniya v slove. Izvestiya AN SSSR. [*Seriya OLYA* 2].

Borgman, Donald. 1989. Sanuma. *Handbook of Amazonian languages.* Vol. 2, edited by Desmond Derbyshire & Geoffrey Pullum, 15–248. New York: Mouton.

Borman, M. B. 1962. Cofan phonemes. *Studies in Ecuadorian Indian languages I,* edited by Benjamin Elson, 45–59. Norman, Okla.: Summer Institute of Linguistics.

Boruah, Bhimkanto. 1993. *Nagamese, the language of Nagaland.* New Delhi: Mittal.

Bosson, James E. 1964. *Modern Mongolian* [*Uralic and Altaic Series* 38]. Bloomington: Indiana University.

Boyeldieu, Pascal. 1987. *Les langues fer ("kara") et yulu du nord centrafricain: esquisses descriptives et lexiques.* Paris: Laboratoire de langues et civilisations à tradition orale.

Bradley, Charles Henry. 1970. *A linguistic sketch of Jicaltepec Mixtec.* Norman: Summer Institute of Linguistics.

Brainard, Sherri. 1994. *The phonology of Karao, the Philippines.* Canberra: Australian National University.

Bray, Denys. 1934. *The Brahui language.* Calcutta: Superintendent Government Printing.

Breeze, Mary. 1988. Phonological features of Gimira and Dizi. *Cushitic-Omotic papers from the international symposium on Cushitic and Omotic languages, Cologne, January 6–9, 1986,* edited by Marianne Bechhaus and Fritz Serzisko, 475–90. Hamburg: Helmut Buske Verlag.

Briggs, Elinor. 1961. *Mitla Zapotec grammar*. Mexico: Instituto Lingüístico de Verano.

Briggs, Lucy. 1976. *Dialectal variation in the Aymara language of Bolivia and Peru.*

Bright, Jane. 1964. The phonology of Smith River Athapaskan (Tolowa). *International Journal of American Linguistics* 30, 101–7.

Bright, William. 1957. *The Karok language*. Berkeley: University of California Press.

Bright, William. 1968. *A Luiseño dictionary*. Berkeley: University of California Press.

Broadbent, Sylvia. 1964. *The Southern Sierra Miwok language*. Berkeley: University of California Press.

Brockway, Earl. 1979. North Puebla Nahuatl. *Studies in Uto-Aztecan grammar, vol. 2, modern Aztec grammatical sketches*, edited by Ronald Langacker, 141–98. Arlington, Tex.: Summer Institute of Linguistics

Bromley, Myron. 1981. *A grammar of Lower Grand Valley Dani*. Canberra: Australian National University.

Broselow, Ellen, Susan Chen & Marie Huffman. 1997. Syllable weight: convergence of phonology and phonetics. *Phonology* 14(1), 47–82.

Brown, Charles P. 1981. *A grammar of the Telugu language*. New Delhi: Asian Educational Services.

Brown, Herbert. 1986. *A comparative dictionary of Orokolo, Gulf of Papua*. Canberra: Australian National University.

Brown, William. 1991. A quantitative phonology of Mai Brat. *Papers in Papuan Linguistics* 1, edited by Tom Dutton, 1–27. Canberra: Australian National University.

Bruce, Les. 1984. *The Alamblak language of Papua New Guinea (East Sepik)*. Canberra: Australian National University.

Bucca, Salvador & Alexander Lesser. 1969. Kitsai phonology and morphophonemics. *International Journal of American Linguistics* 35, 7–19.

Buckley, Eugene. 1994. *Theoretical aspects of Kashaya phonology and morphology*. Stanford: CSLI Publications.

Bunye, Maria & Elsa Yap. 1971. *Cebuano grammar notes*. Honolulu: University of Hawaii Press.

Burgess, Eunice and Patricia Ham. 1968. Multilevel conditioning of phoneme variants in Apinayé. *Linguistics: An International Review* 41, 5–18.

Burling, Robbins. 1967. *Proto Lolo-Burmese*. Bloomington: Indiana University Press.

Burtch, Shirley. 1983. *Diccionario huitoto murui*. Pucallpa, Peru: Ministerio de Educación: Instituto Lingüístico de Verano.

Callaghan, Catherine. 1987. *Northern Sierra Miwok dictionary*. Berkeley: University of California Press.

Camden, W. G. 1977. *A descriptive dictionary: Bislama to English*. Rosebery, Australia: Bridge Printery.

Capell, Arthur. 1970. *Maung grammar; texts and vocabulary*. The Hague: Mouton.

Cardona, George. 1965. *A Gujarati reference grammar*. Philadelphia: University of Pennsylvania Press.

Casad, Eugene. 1984. Cora.*Southern Uto-Aztecan grammatical sketches*, edited by Ronald Langacker. Dallas: Summer Institute of Linguistics.

Cerrón-Palomino, Rodolfo. 1976. *Gramática quechua, Junín-huanca*. Lima: Ministerio de Educacción.

Chadwick, Neil. 1975. *A descriptive study of the Djingili language*. Canberra: Australian National University.

Chafe, Wallace. 1970. *A semantically based sketch of Onondaga* [*Indiana University publications in anthropology and linguistics, memoir 25*]. Baltimore: Waverly Press (Indiana University).

Chafe, Wallace. 1976. *The Caddoan, Iroquoian, and Siouan languages* [*Trends in Linguistics, State of the Art Reports 3*]. The Hague: Paris.

Chafe, Wallace. 1977. Accent and related phenomena in the Five Nations Iroqouis languages. *Studies in stress and accent* [*Southern California Occasional Papers in Linguistics 4*], edited by Larry Hyman, 169–8.

Chafe, Wallace. 1996. Sketch of Seneca, an Iroquoian language. *Handbook of American Indian languages, vol. 17, languages*, edited by Ives Goddard (volume editor), 551–79. Washington: Smithsonian Institute.

Chafe, Wallace. 1998. *Morphological and discourse determinants of pitch in Seneca*. Paper presented at the annual SSILA meeting, New York City.

Chakrabarti, Byomkes. 1994. *A comparative study of Santali and Bengali*. Calcutta: KP Bagchit Company.

Chao, Yuen Ren. 1968. *A grammar of spoken Chinese*. Berkeley: University of California Press.

Charney, Jean. 1993. *A grammar of Comanche*. Lincoln: University of Nebraska Press.

Chéron, Georges. 1925. *Le dialect sénoufo du minianka (grammaire, textes et lexiques)*. Paris: Geuthner.

Childs, George Tucker. 1995. *A grammar of Kisi: a southern Atlantic language*. New York: Mouton de Gruyter.

Christdas, Prathima. 1996. *Syllable prominence and stress in Tamil*. Ms. University of Michigan, Ann Arbor.

Christensen, John. 1992. Kisar phonology. *Phonological studies in four languages of Maluku*, 33–66. Dallas: Summer Institute of Linguistics

Chung, Sandra. 1983. Transderivational relationships in Chamorro phonology. *Language* 59, 35–66.

Clements, George N. 1990. The role of the sonority cycle in core syllabification. *Papers in laboratory phonology I: Between the grammar and physics of speech*, edited by J. Kingston and M.Beckman, 283–333. Cambridge: Cambridge University. Press.

Clements, George N. 1991. Place of articulation in consonants and vowels: a unified theory. *Working Papers of the Cornell Phonetics Laboratory* 5, 77–123.

Clements, George N. & Samuel Jay Keyser. 1983. *CV Phonology: A generative theory of the syllable*. Cambridge, MA: MIT Press.

Clements, J. Clancy. 1996. *The genesis of a language : the formation and development of Korlai Portuguese*. Philadelphia : J. Benjamins Pub. Co.

Comrie, Bernard. 1990. Russian. *The world's major languages*, edited by Bernard Comrie, 329–47.New York: Oxford.

Conrad, Robert. 1991. *An outline of Bukiyip grammar*. Canberra: Australian National University.

Cook, Eung-Do. 1984. *A Sarcee grammar*. Vancouver: University of British Columbia Press.

Cook, William. 1979. *A grammar of North Carolina Cherokee*. Yale University Ph.D. dissertation.

Cooper, James & Nancy Cooper. 1966. Halang phonemes. *Mon Khmer Studies* II, 87–98.

Costa, Raquel. 2000. *Aspectos da fonologia Marubo (Pano): uma visão não-linear*. Ph.D. thesis, Universidade Federal do Rio de Janeiro.

Couro, Ted & Christina Hutcheson. 1973. *Dictionary of Mesa Grande Diegueño: 'Iipay Aa-English/English- 'Iipay Aa*. Banning, Calif.: Malki Museum Press.

Cowan, Hendrik. 1966. *Grammar of the Sentani language. With specimen texts and vocabulary*. 's Gravenhage: Martinus Nijhoff.

Crawford, James. 1973. Yuchi phonology. *International Journal of American Linguistics* 39, 173–9.

Crawford, John. 1963. *Totontepec Mixe phonotagmemics*. Norman, Okla.: Summer Institute of Linguistics.

Creider, Chet & Jane Creider. 1989. *A grammar of Nandi*. Hamburg: Helmut Buske Verlag.

Crook, Harold. 1999. *The phonology of Nez Perce*. UCLA Ph.D. dissertation.

Crosby, K. H. 1944. *An introduction to the study of Mende*. Cambridge: W. Heffer & Sons.

Crowhurst, Megan. 1991. Demorification in Tübatulabal: Evidence from initial reduplication and stress. *Proceedings of the Northeastern Linguistics Society* 21, 49–63.

Dabai, Ni. 1988. Yangfeng Mak of Libo County. *Comparative Kadai: Linguistics studies beyond Tai*, edited by Jerold Edmondson and David Solnit, 87–106. Arlington, Tex.: Summer Institute of Linguistics and The University of Texas at Arlington.

Dalby, J & R. Port. 1981. Temporal structures of Japanese: Segment, mora, and word. *Research in Phonetics* 2, 149–72. Bloomington: Indiana University, Department of Linguistics.

Das, Sisirkumar. 1973. *Structure of Malto*. Annamalainagar: Annamalai University.

Das Gupta, Kamalesh. 1971. *An introduction to the Nocte language*. Shillong: North-East Frontier Agency.

Das Gupta, Kamalesh. 1980. *The Tangsa language: a synopsis*. Shillong: Government of Arunachal Pradesh.

Dasgupta, Dipankar. 1982. *A handbook of Onge language*. Calcutta: Anthropological Survey of India.

Davies, H. J. 1980. *Kobon phonology* [*Pacific Linguistics Series B, No. 68*]. Canberra: Australian National University.

Davis, Stuart. 1988. Syllable onsets as factors in stress rules. *Phonology* 5, 1–19.

Davis, Stuart & Donna Jo Napoli. 1994. *A prosodic template in historical change: The passage of the Latin second conjugation in Romance*. Torino: Rosenberg and Sellier.

Dawson, Willa. 1980. *Tibetan phonology*. University of Washington Ph. D. dissertation.

Dayley, Jon. 1985. *Tzutujil grammar*. Berkeley: University of California Press.

De Chene, Brent & Stephen Andersen. 1979. Compensatory Lengthening. *Language* 55, 505–35.

De Jong, Kenneth. 1995. The supraglottal articulation of prominence in English: Linguistic stress as localized hyperarticulation. *Journal of the Acoustical Society of America* 97 (1), 491–504.

De Lacy, Paul. 1997. *Prosodic Categorization*. Ms. [Available on Rutgers Optimality Archive, ROA-236, http://ruccs.rutgers.edu/roa.html.]

De Lacy, Paul. 2002. The interaction of tone and stress in Optimality Theory. *Phonology* 19, 1–32.

de Goeje, Claudius Henricus. 1928. *The Arawak language of Guiana*. Amsterdam: Amsterdam Koninklijke Akademie van Wetenschappen.

Décsy, Gyula. 1966. *Yurak chrestomathy*. Bloomington: Indiana University Press.

Delattre, Pierre. 1966. *Les dix intonations de base du français. French Review* 40, 1–14.

Delgutte, B. 1982. Some correlates of phonetic distinctions at the level of the auditory nerve. *The representation of speech in the peripheral auditory system*, edited by R. Carlson & B. Granström, 131–50. Amsterdam: Elsevier.

Dell, Francois. 1997. *Morae in the versification of chleuh (tashlhiyt) Berber*. Colloquium talk given at UCLA.

Delord, J. 1976. *Le Kabiye*. Lomé: Institut National de la Recherche Scientifique.

Dempwolff, Otto. 1916–17. Wörter der Hatzasprache. *Beiträge zur Kenntnis der Sprachen in deutsch-Ostafrika* 12, *Zeitschrift für Kolonialsprachen* 7, 319–325.

Derbyshire, Desmond. 1985. *Hixkaryana and linguistic typology*. Dallas: Summer Institute of Linguistics.

Dez, Jacques. 1980. *Structures de la langue malgache: elements de grammaire a l'usage des francophones*. Paris: Publications orientalistes de France.

Dimmendaal, Gerrit. 1983. *The Turkana language*. Dordrecht: Foris.

Dixon, Robert. 1983. Nyawaygi. *Handbook of Austalian languages*, Vol. 3, edited by Robert Dixon & Barry Blake, 430–525. Amsterdam: J. Benjamins.

D'iachkov, M. V.1981. *Iazyk krio*. Moskva: Izdatelstvo Nauka.

Djawanai, Stephanus. 1983. *Ngadha text tradition: The collective mind of the Ngadha people, Flores* [*Pacific Linguistic Series D, No. 55*] Canberra: Australian National University.

Dobson, Rose. 1988. *Aspectos da língua kayabí*. Brasília: Summer Institute of Linguistics.

Doerfer, Gerhard. 1980. *Lamutisches Wörterbuch*. Wiesbaden: Otto Harrassowitz.

Doherty, Brian. 1993. *The acoustic-phonetic correlates of Cayuga word-stress*. Harvard University Ph.D. dissertation.

Doherty, Cathal. 1991. Munster Irish stress. *Phonology at Santa Cruz* 2, 19–32.

Donohue, Mark. 1999. *Warembori*. Munich: Lincom Europa.

Duanmu, San. 1994a. *Against contour tone units*. Linguistic Inquiry 25, .555–608.

Duanmu, San. 1994b. Syllabic weight and syllabic duration: A correlation between phonology and phonetics. *Phonology* 11, 1–24.

Dubert, Raymond & Marjorie Dubert. 1973. Biangai phonemes. *Phonologies of three languages of Papua New Guinea*, 5–36. Ukarumpa, Papua New Guinea: Summer Institute of Linguistics.5–36.

DuBois, Carl D. 1976. *Sarangani Manobo: An introductory guide* [*Philippine Journal of Linguistics Monograph* 6]. Manila: Linguistic Society of the Philippines.

Dugast, Idelette. 1967. *Lexique de la langue Tunen (parler des Banen du Sud-Ouest du Cameroun)*. Paris: Klincksieck.

Dugast, Idelette. 1971. *Grammaire du tùnen*. Paris: Klincksieck.

Dumézil, Georges. 1959. *Études oubykhs*. Paris: A. Maisonneuve.

Dunn, John. 1978. *A practical dictionary of the Coast Tsimshian language*. Ottawa: National Museums of Canada.

Dunn, John. 1979. *A reference grammar for the Coast Tsimshian language*. Ottawa: National Museums of Canada.

Eberhard, David. 1995. *Mamaindé stress: the need for strata*. Arlington, TX: Summer Institute of Linguistics and University of Texas at Arlington.

Echeverría, Max & Helen Contreras. 1965. Araucanian phonemics. *International Journal of American Linguistics* 31, 132–35.

Egerod, Søren. 1966. A statement on Atayal phonology. *Artibus Asiae Supplementum XXIII* (*Felicitation volume for the 75th birthday of Professor G. H. Luce*), 120–30.

Egerod, Søren. 1980. *Atayal-English dictionary*. London: Curzon Press.

Elenbaas, Nine. 1992. *Een vergelijking van twee ternaire analyses, getoest aan het Sentani*. University of Utrecht MA thesis.

Elenbaas, Nine. 1998. *A unified account of binary and ternary stress*. Utrecht: Netherlands Graduate School of Linguistics.

Elordieta, Gorka. 1997. Accent, tone, and intonation in Lekeitio Basque. *Issues in the Phonology and Morphology of the Major Iberian Languages*, edited by Fernando Martínez-Gil & Alfonso Morales-Front, 3–78. Washington, D.C.: Georgetown University Press.

Elwell-Sutton, L. P. 1976. *The Persian meters*. Cambridge: Cambridge University Press.

Elwell-Sutton, L. P. 1983. *Elementary Persian grammar*. Cambridge: Cambridge University Press.

Emeneau, M. B. 1955. *Kolami, a Dravidian language.* Berkeley: University of California Press.

Emeneau, M. B. 1984. *Toda grammar and texts.* Philadelphia: American Philosophical Society.

England, Nora. 1983. *A grammar of Mam, a Mayan language.* Austin: University of Texas Press.

Enrico, John. 1991. *The lexical phonology of Masset Haida.* Fairbanks, Alaska: Alaska Native Language Center.

Erdélyi, István. 1970. *Selkupisches Wörterverzeichnis: Tas-Dialekt.* Bloomington: Indiana University Press.

Erwin, Sean. 1996. Quantity and moras: an amicable separation. *The structure of Malagasy,* edited by Matthew Pearson & Ileana Paul, 2–30. Los Angeles: UCLA Department of Linguistics.2–30.

Evans, Nicholas. 1995. *A grammar of Kayardild : with historical-comparative notes on Tangkic.* New York: Mouton.

Everett, Daniel & Keren Everett. 1984. Syllable onsets and stress placement in Pirahã. *Proceedings of the West Coast Conference on Formal Linguistics* 3, 105–16.

Everett, Daniel. 1986. Pirahã. *Handbook of Amazonian languages,* Vol. 1, edited by Desmond Derbyshire & Geoffrey Pullum, 200–325. New York: Mouton.

Everett, Daniel. 1988. On metrical constituent structure in Pirahã. *Natural Language and Linguistic Theory* 6, 207–246.

Feeling, Durbin. 1975. *Cherokee-English dictionary.* Tahlequah, Okla.: Cherokee Nation of Oklahoma.

Ferrell, Raleigh. 1982. *Paiwan dictionary.* Canberra: Australian National University.

Field, Philip. 1991. A phonology of the Orya language. *Papers in Papuan Linguistics* 1, edited by Tom Dutton , 29–56. Canberra: Australian National University.

Finegan, Edward. 1990. English.*The world's major languages,* edited by Bernard Comrie, 77–109.New York: Oxford.

Flassy, Don & Stokhof, W. 1979. A note on Tehit (Bird's head-Irian Jaya). *Miscellaneous studies in Indonesian and languages of Indonesia,* edited by Amran Halim, 35–83. Jakarta: Badan Penyelenggara Seri Nusa.

Flemming, Edward. 1995. *Auditory Features in Phonology.* Ph.D. thesis, UCLA.

Foley, Lawrence. 1980. *Phonological variation in Western Cherokee.* New York: Garland.

Foley, William A. 1991. *The Yimas language of New Guinea.* Stanford: Stanford University Press.

Foreman, Velma. 1974. *Grammar of Yessan-Mayo.* Santa Ana, Calif.: Summer Institute of Linguistics.

Foreman, Velma & Helen Marten. 1973. Yessan-Mayo phonemes. *Phonologies of Three Languages of Papua New Guinea,* 79–108. Ukarumpa, Papua New Guinea: Summer Institute of Linguistics.

Fortescue, Michael. 1984. *West Greenlandic.* London: Croom Helm.

Fortier, Joseph. 1971. *Grammaire mbaye-moiessala (Tchad-groupe sara)*. Lyon: Afrique et langage.

Foster, Mary. 1948. *Sierra Popoluca speech*. Washington: Smithsonian Insitute.

Foster, Michael. 1982. Alternating weak and strong syllables in Cayuga words.*International Journal of American Linguistics* 48, 59–72.

Frantz, Donald. 1991. *Blackfoot grammar*. Toronto: University of Toronto Press.

Freeland, Lucy. 1951. *Language of the Sierra Miwok* [*International Journal of American Linguistics memoir* 6]. Bloomington: Indiana University Press.

Freudenberg, Allen & Marlene Freudenberg. 1974. Boiken phonemes. *Phonologies of four Papua New Guinea languages*. Ukarumpa, Papua New Guinea: Summer Institute of Linguistics.

Fry, D. B. 1955. Duration and intensity as physical correlates of linguistic stress. *Journal of the Acoustical Society of America* 27, 765–68.

Fry, D. B. 1958. Experiments in the perception of stress. *Language and Speech* 1, 120–52.

Furbee-Losee. 1976. *The correct language, Tojolabal: a grammar with ethnographic notes*. New York: Garland.

Gahl, Susanne. 1996. Syllable onsets as a factor in stress rules: The case of Mathimathi revisited. *Phonology* 13, 329–44.

Galloway, Brent. 1993. *A grammar of upriver Halkomelem*. Berkeley: University of California Press.

Gamble, David. 1990. *Gambian Wolof-English dicitionary*. Brisbane, CA.

Garrett, Edward. 1999. Minimal words aren't minimal feet. *UCLA Working Papers in Linguistics* 1 (*Papers in Phonology* 2), 68–105.

Gedney, William. 1991. *The Tai dialect of Lungming: glossary, texts, and translations*, edited by Thomas Hudak. Ann Arbor, Michigan: Center for South and Southeast Asian Studies.

Gilley, Leoma. 1992. *An autosegmental approach to Shilluk phonology*. Dallas: Summer Institute of Linguistics.

Glover, Warren. 1969. *Gurung phonemic summary*. Kirtipur, Nepal: Summer Institute of Linguistics.

Goddard, Ives. 1979. *Delaware verbal morphology*. New York: Garland.

Goddard, Ives. 1982. The historical phonology of Munsee. *International Journal of American Linguistics* 48, 16–48.

Goedemans, Rob. 1998. *Weightless segments*. The Hague: Holland Academic Graphics.

Golla, Victor. 1970. *Hupa grammar*. University of California, Berkeley Ph.D. dissertation.

Golla, Victor. 1996. Sketch of Hupa, an Athapaskan language. *Handbook of American Indian languages, vol. 17 Languages*, edited by Ives Goddard (volume editor), 364–89. Washington: Smithsonian Institute.

Gonzales, A. 1970. Acoustic correlates of accent, rhythm, and intonation in Tagalog. *Phonetica* 22, 11–44.

González, Benjamín Pérez. 1985. *El Chontal de Tucta.* Villahermosa, Tabasco, Mexico: Gobierno del Estado de Tabasco.

Gordon, E. V. 1927. *An introduction to Old Norse.* Oxford: Clarendon Press.

Gordon, Lynn. 1982. *Maricopa morphology and syntax.* Berkeley: University ofCalifornia Press.

Gordon, Matthew. 1999. Intonational structure of Chickasaw. *Proceedings of the XIVth international congress of phonetic sciences,* 1993–6.

Gordon, Matthew. 2001. A typology of contour tone restrictions. *Studies in Language* 25, 405–444.

Gordon, Matthew. 2002. Weight-by-positon adjunction and syllable structure. *Lingua* 112, 901–931.

Gordon, Matthew. 2005. A perceptually-driven account of onset-sensitive stress. *Natural Language and Linguistic Theory* 23, 595–653.

Gordon, Matthew, Pamela Munro & Peter Ladefoged. 1997. The phonetic structures of Chickasaw. *UCLA Working Papers in Phonetics* 95, 41–67.

Gorgoniyev, Y. A. 1966. *The Khmer language.* Moscow: Nauka.

Gralow, Frances. 1985. Coreguaje: tone, stress, and intonation. *From phonology to discourse: Studies in six Colombian languages,* edited by Ruth Brend, 3–11. Dallas: Summer Institute of Linguistics.

Greene, Laurie A.1999. *A grammar of Belizean Creole : compilations from two existing United States dialects.* New York: P. Lang.

Grimes, James Larry. 1972. *The phonological history of the Quichean languages.* Carbondale, IL: Southern Illinois University Museum.

Grimes, Joseph & Barbara Grimes. 1993. Ethnologue Language Family Index. Twelfth Edition. Dallas: Summer Institute of Linguistics.

Gruzov, Leonid Petrovich. 1960. *Sovremenyi mariiskii yazyk: fonetika.* Joshkar-ola: Mariiskoe Knizhnoe Izdatel'stvo.

Guédou, Georges A. G. 1985. *Xó et gbè langage et culture chez les Fon (Bénin).* Paris: SELAF.

Gulya, János. 1966. *Eastern Ostyak chrestomathy.* Bloomington: Indiana University Press.

Gwynn, J. P. L. 1991. *A Telugu-English dictionary.* New York: Oxford University Press.

Haas, Mary. 1946. A grammatical sketch of Tunica. *Linguistic structures of native America.* 337–66. New York: Viking Fund Publications in Anthropology.

Haas, Mary. 1951. The Proto-Gulf word for WATER. *International Journal of American Linguistics* 17, 71–79.

Hagege, Claude. 1981. *Le comox lhaamen de Colombie Britannique: presentation d'une langue amerindienne.* Paris: AEA.

Hagman, Roy. 1977. *Nama Hottentot grammar.* Bloomington: Research Center for Language and Semiotic Studies, University of Indiana.

Hale, Kenneth. 1985. A note on Winnebago metrical structure. *International Journal of American Linguistics* 51, 427–9.

Hale, Kenneth & Josie White Eagle. 1980. A preliminary metrical account of Winnebago accent. *International Journal of American Linguistics* 46, 117–32.

Hall, Robert. 1938. *An analytical grammar of the Hungarian language*. Baltimore: Linguistic Society of America.

Halle, Morris & Samuel Jay Keyser. 1971. *English stress: its form, its growth, and its role in verse*. New York: Harper and Row.

Halle, Morris & G.N. Clements. 1983. *Problem book in phonology*. Cambridge, Mass.: MIT Press.

Halle, Morris & Jean-Roger Vergnaud. 1987. *An essay on stress*. Cambridge: MIT press.

Hamel, Patricia. 1994. *A grammar and lexicon of Loniu, Papua New Guinea*. Canberra: Department of Linguistics, Research School of Pacific and Asian Studies, Australian National University.

Hangin, Gombojab. 1986. *A Modern Mongolian-English dictionary*. Bloomington: Indiana University, Research Center for Inner Asian Studies.

Hanson, Kristin & Paul Kiparsky. 1996. A parametric theory of poetic meter. *Language* 72, 287–335.

Hardman-de-Bautista, Martha James. 1966. *Jaqaru: outline of phonological and morphological structure*. The Hague: Mouton.

Harms, Robert. 1968. *Introduction to phonological theory*. Englewood Cliffs, N.J.: Prentice-Hall.

Harrell, Richard. 1957. *The phonology of colloquial Egyptian Arabic*. New York: American Council of Learned Societies.

Harrell, Richard. 1960. A linguistic analysis of Egyptian Radio Arabic. *Contributions to Arabic linguistics*, edited by Charles Ferguson, 3–77. Cambridge: Harvard University Press.

Harrington, John. 1910. A brief description of the Tewa language. *American Anthropologist* 12, 497–504.

Harris, Martin. 1990. French. The World's Major Languages, edited by Bernard Comrie, 210–35. New York: Oxford University Press.

Hartmann, Josef. 1980. *Amharische Grammatik*. Wiesbaden: Steiner.

Hawkins, W. Neil. 1950. Patterns of vowel loss in Macushi (Carib). *International Journal of American Linguistics* 16, 87–90.

Hawkins, W. Neill. 1952. *A fonologia da língua uáiuái*. São Paulo: Brazil Universidade.

Hayes, Bruce & May Abad. 1989. Reduplication and syllabification in Ilokano. *Lingua* 77, 331–74.

Hayes, Bruce. 1979. The rhythmic structure of Persian verse. *Edebiyat: The Journal of Middle Eastern Literatures* 4, 193–242.

Hayes, Bruce. 1988. Metrics and phonological theory. *Linguistics: The Cambridge Survey, vol. 2, Linguistic Theory: Extensions and Implications*, edited by F. Newmeyer. Cambridge: Cambridge University Press.

Hayes, Bruce. 1989. Compensatory lengthening in moraic phonology. *Linguistic Inquiry* 20, 253–306.

Hayes, Bruce. 1995. *Metrical stress theory: principles and case studies.* Chicago: University of Chicago Press.

Hayes, Bruce. 1999. Phonetically-driven phonology: the role of optimality theory and inductive grounding. *Proceedings of the 1996 Milwaukee Conference on Formalism and Functionalism in Linguistics, volume 1,* edited by M. Darnell, E. Moravscik, M. Noonan, F. Newmeyer, & K. Wheatley, 243–285. Amsterdam: Benjamins.

Healey, Alan. 1964. *Telefol phonology.* Canberra: Australian National University.

Healey, Phyllis. 1977. *Telefol dictionary.* Canberra: Australian National University.

Heasty, J. A. 1974. *English-Shilluk, Shilluk-English dictionary.* [reprint of 1937 edition published by the American Mission, Dolieb Hill, Anglo-Egyptian Sudan]

Heine, Bernd. 1983. *The Nubi language of Kibera: An Arabic creole.* Berlin: D. Reimer.

Heeschen, Volker. 1983. *Wörterbuch der Eipo-Sprache: eipo, deutsch, englisch.* Berlin: D. Reimer.

Henderson, James. 1995. *Phonology and grammar of Yele, Papua New Guinea.* Canberra: Australian National University.

Herrfurth, Hans. 1964. *Lehrbuch des modernen Djawanisch.* Leipzig: VEB Verlag.

Hess, Thomas. 1976. *Dictionary of Puget Salish.* Seattle: University of Washington Press.

Hess, Thomas. 1995. *Lushootseed reader with introductory grammar* [*University of Montana Occasional Papers in Linguistics* 11].

Hetzer, Armin. 1978. *Lehrbuch der vereinheitlichten albanischen Schriftsprache mit einem deutsch-albanischen Wörterbuch.* Hamburg: Helmut Buske Verlag.

Hewitt, B. G. 1989. *Abkhaz.* New York: Routledge.

Hint, Mati. 1973. *Eesti keele sõnafonoloogia I.* Tallinn: Eesti NSV Teaduste akadeemia.

Hinton, Leanne. 1984. *Havasupai songs : a linguistic perspective.* Tuebingen: G. Narr.

Hirayama, Teruo & Masatomo Nakamoto. 1964. *Ryuukyuu Yonaguni hoogen no kenkyuu.* Tokyo: Tokyoodoo.

Hock, Hans. 1986. Compensatory lengthening: In defense of the concept "Mora." *Folia Linguistica* 20, 431–60.

Hoff, B. J. 1968. *The Carib language. Phonology, morphonology, morphology, texts and word index.* The Hague: Martinus Nijhoff.

Hoijer, Harry. 1946a. Chiricahua Apache. *Linguistic structures of Native America.* New York: Viking Fund Publications in Anthropology.

Hoijer, Harry. 1946b. Tonkawa. *Linguistic structures of Native America.* New York: Viking Fund Publications in Anthropology.

Hoijer, Harry. 1949. *An analytical dictionary of the Tonkawa language.* Berkeley:University of California Press.

Hollenbach, Barbara. 1977. Phonetic vs. phonemic correspondence in two Trique dialects. *Studies in Otomanguean phonology,* edited by William Merrifield, 35–68. Arlington, Tex.: Summer Institute of Linguistics

Holmer, Nils. 1947. *Critical and comparative grammar of the Cuna language.* Göteborg: Etnografiska Museet.

Hoogshagen, Searle. 1984. Coatlán Mixe. *Supplement to handbook of Middle American Indians, vol. 2: Linguistics*, edited by Munro Edmonson, 3–19. Austin: University of Texas Press.

Horne, Elinor Clark. 1974. *Javanese-English dictionary*. New Haven: Yale University Press.

Holt, Dennis. 1999. *Tol (Jicaque)*. Munich: Lincom Europa.

House, David. 1990. *Tonal perception in speech*. Lund: Lund University Press.

Hualde, José Ignacio. 1991. *Basque phonology*. New York: Routledge.

Hudak, Thomas. 1990a. Thai. *The world's major languages*, edited by Bernard Comrie, 757–776. New York: Oxford.

Hudak, Thomas. 1990b. *The indigenization of Pali meters in Thai poetry*. Athens, Ohio: Ohio University Center for International Studies.

Huttar, George & Mary Huttar. 1994. *Ndyuka*. New York: Routledge.

Hyman, Larry M and Armindo Ngunga. 1994. On the non-universality of tonal association 'conventions': evidence from Ciyao. *Phonology* 11, 25–68.

Hyman, Larry. 1977. On the nature of linguistic stress. *Studies in stress and accent [Southern California Occasional Papers in Linguistics 4]*, edited by Larry Hyman, 37–82.

Hyman, Larry. 1985. *A theory of phonological weight*. Dordrecht: Foris.

Hyman, Larry. 1992. Moraic mismatches in Bantu. *Phonology* 9, 255–266.

Ingria, Robert. 1980. Compensatory lengthening as a metrical phenomenon. *Linguistic Inquiry* 11, 465–95.

Inkelas, Sharon & Cemil Orhan Orgun. 1995. Level ordering and economy in the lexical phonology of Turkish. *Language* 71, 763–93.

Innes, Gordon. 1962. *A Mende grammar*. London: Macmillan.

Innes, Gordon. 1969. *A Mende-English dictionary*. London: Cambridge University Press.

Itkonen, Erkki. 1955. Über die Betonungsverhältnisse in den finnisch-ugrischen Sprachen. *Acta Linguistica Academiae Scientiarum Hungaricae* 5, 21–34.

Itkonen, Erkki. 1986. *Inarilappisches Wörterbuch*. Helsinki: Suomalais-ugrilainen seura.

Ittmann, Johannes. 1978. *Grammaire du duala*. Douala: Collége Libermann.

Ivanov, I. G. & G. M. Tuzharov. 1970. *Severo-zapadnoje narechije marijskogo jazyka*. Joshkar-ola.

Jacobson, Steven. 1984. *Yup'ik Eskimo dictionary*. Fairbanks, Alaska: Alaska Native Language Center, University of Alaska.

Jacobson, Steven. 1985. Siberian Yupik and Central Yupik prosody. *Yupik Eskimo prosodic systems: descriptive and comparative studies*, edited by Michael Krauss, 25–46. Fairbanks: Alaska Native Language Center.

Jacq, Pascale & Paul Sidwell. 1999. *Sapuan (S'puar)*. Munich: Lincom Europa.

Jakobson, Roman. 1931. Die Betonung und ihre Rolle in der Wort- und Syntagma-Phonologie. *Roman Jakobson, Selected Writings* I, 117–136. The Hague: Mouton.

Jakobson, Roman. 1962. Contributions to the study of Czech accent. *Roman Jakobson, Selected Writings* I, 614–25. The Hague: Mouton.

Jamieson, Allan. 1977a. Chiquihuitlan Mazatec phonology. *Studies in Otomanguean phonology*, edited by William Merrifield, 93–106. Arlington, Tex.: Summer Institute of Linguistics. .

Jamieson, Allan. 1977b. Chiquihuitlan Mazatec tone. *Studies in Otomanguean phonology*, edited by William Merrifield, 107–36. Arlington, Tex.: Summer Institute of Linguistics.107–136.

Jassem, W., J. Morton & M. Steffen-Batóg. 1968. The perception of stress in synthetic speech-like stimuli by Polish listeners. *Speech Analysis and Synthesis* I, 289–308.

Jeanne, Laverne. 1982. Some phonological rules of Hopi. *International Journal of American Linguistics* 48, 245–70.

Jensen, John. 1977.*Yapese reference grammar*. Honolulu: University of Hawaii Press.

Jha, Subhadra. 1940–4. Maithili phonetics. *Indian Linguistics* 8, 435–59.

Jha, Subhadra. 1958. *The formation of the Maithili language*. London: Luzac.

Joel, Dina Judith. 1966. *Paipai phonology and morphology*. UCLA Ph.D. dissertation.

Jones, Robert. 1961. *Karen linguistic studies: description, comparison, and texts*. Berkeley: University of California Press.

Joseph, Brian. 1990. Greek. *The world's major languages*, edited by Bernard Comrie, 410–39. New York: Oxford.

Judy, Roberto. 1962. *Fonemas del movima; con atención escpecial a la serie glottal*. Cochabamba: Instituto Lingüístico de Verano.

Jun, Jongho. 1995. *Perceptual and articulatory factors in place assimilation: An Optimality-theoretic approach*. UCLA PhD dissertation.

Jun, Jongho. 1996. Place assimilation as the result of conflicting perceptual and articulatory constraints, *West Coast Conference on Formal Linguistics* 14, 221–38. Palo Alto: CSLI.

Ka, Omar. 1987. *Wolof phonology and morphology: A non-linear approach*. University of Illinois at Urbana-Champaign Ph.D. dissertation.

Kager, René. 1990. Dutch schwa in moraic phonology. *Chicago Linguistics Society* 26 *Parasession on the syllable in phonetics and phonology*, 241–56.

Kaisse, Ellen. 1985. Some theoretical consequences of stress rules in Turkish. *Chicago Linguistics Society* 21, 199–209.

Kaisse, Ellen. 1986. Towards a lexical phonology of Turkish. *A festschrift for Sol Saporta*, edited by Michael Brame, Helen Contreras, & Frederick Newmeyer, 231–9. Seattle: Noit Amrofer.

Kao, Dianna. 1971. *Structure of the syllable in Cantonese*. The Hague: Mouton.

Kaplan, Lawrence. 1981. *Phonological issues in North Alaskan Inupiaq*. Fairbanks: Alaska Native Language Center.

Kaschube, Dorothea. 1967. *Structural elements of the language of the Crow Indians of Montana*. Boulder: University of Colorado Press.

Kavitskaya, Darya. 2002. *Compensatory lengthening: phonetics, phonology, diachrony*. New York: Routledge.

Kaye, Jonathan. 1973. Odawa stress and related phenomena. *Odawa language project: second report.* Centre for Linguistic Studies, edited by Glyne Piggott & Jonathan Kaye, 42–50.

Kelkar, Ashok R. 1968. *Studies in Hindi-Urdu I: introduction and word phonology.* Poona: Deccan College.

Keller, Charles. 1976. *A grammatical sketch of Brao, a Mon-Khmer language.* Grand Forks: Summer Institute of Linguistics.

Kennard, Edward. 1936. Mandan grammar. *International Journal of American Linguistics* 9, 1–43.

Kensinger, Kenneth. 1963. The phonological hierarchy of Cashinahua (Pano). *Studies in Peruvian Indian Languages* I, edited by Benjamin Elson, 207–18. Norman, OK: Summer Institute of Linguistics.

Kenstowicz, Michael. 1972. Lithuanian phonology. *Studies in the Linguistic Sciences* 2, 1–85.

Kenstowicz, Michael. 1994b. *Phonology in generative grammar.* Blackwell: Oxford.

Kenstowicz, Michael. 1997. Quality-sensitive stress. *Rivista di Linguistica* 9, 157–188.

Kerek, Andrew. 1971. *Hungarian metrics: some linguistic aspects of iambic verse* [*Indiana University Publications, Uralic and Altaic Series* 117]. The Hague: Mouton.

Key, Harold. 1961. Phonotactics of Cayuvava. *International Journal of American Linguistics* 27, 143–50.

Key, Harold. 1967. *Morphology of Cayuvava.* Janua Linguarum. The Hague: Mouton

Key, Mary. 1968. *Comparative Tacanan phonology with Cavineña phonology and notes on Pano-Tacanan relationship.* The Hague: Mouton.

Kimball, Geoffrey. 1991. *Koasati grammar.* Lincoln: University of Nebraska Press.

Kimball, Geoffrey. 1994. *Koasati dictionary.* Lincoln: University of Nebraska Press.

Kiparsky, Paul. 1968. Metrics and morphonemics in the Kalevala. *Studies presented to Roman Jakobson by his students*, edited by C.E. Gribble, 137–48. Cambridge, MA: Slavica Publishers.

Kiparsky, Paul. 1975. Stress, syntax, and meter. *Language* 51, 576–616.

Kiparsky, Paul. 1977. The rhythmic structure of English verse. *Linguistic Inquiry* 8, 189–247.

Kiparsky, Paul. 1989. Sprung rhythm. *Rhythm and meter*, edited by P. Kiparsky & G. Youmans. San Diego: Academic Press.

Kirchner, Robert. 1998. *An effort-based approach to consonant lenition.* Ph.D. thesis, UCLA.

Klamer, Margaretha. 1994. *Kambera: a language of Eastern Indonesia.* The Hague: Holland Academic Graphics.

Kleinschmidt, Samuel. 1968. *Grammatik der grönländischen Sprache; mit teilweisem Einschluss des Labradordialekts.* Hildesheim: G. Olms.

Knudson, Lyle. 1975. A natural phonology and morphophonemics of Chimalapa Zoque. *Papers in Linguistics* 8, 283–346.

Kodzasov, S. & I. Muravyova. 1978. Stress in the Alutor language. *Estonian Papers in Phonetics 1978*, 47–8.

Koehn, Edward & Sally Koehn. 1986. Apalai. *Handbook of Amazonian languages*, Vol. 1, edited by Desmond Derbyshire & Geoffrey Pullum, 33–127. New York: Mouton.

Konstantinova, Olga. 1964. *Evenskiiskii iazyk: fonetika, morfologiia*. Leningrad: Nauka.

Kornfilt, Jaklin. 1990. Turkish and the Turkic languages. *The world's major languages*, edited by Bernard Comrie, 619–44. New York: Oxford.

Kouwenberg, Silvia. 1994. *A grammar of Berbice Dutch Creole*. New York: Mouton de Gruyter.

Krauss, Michael. 1985a. Sirenikski and Naukanski. *Yupik Eskimo prosodic systems: descriptive and comparative studies*, edited by Michael Krauss, 175–90. Fairbanks: Alaska Native Language Center.

Krauss, Michael. 1985b. Supplementary notes on central Alaskan Yupik. *Yupik Eskimo prosodic systems: descriptive and comparative studies*, edited by Michael Krauss, 47–50. Fairbanks: Alaska Native Language Center.

Kreinovich, E. A. 1982. *Issledovaniia i materialy po iukagirskomu iazyku*. Leningrad: Nauka.

Krishnamurti, Bhadriraju & J. P. L. Gwynn .1985. *A grammar of modern Telugu*. New York: Oxford University Press

Kroeber, Alfred Louis & Grace, William. 1960. *The Sparkman grammar of Luiseño*. Berkeley: University of California Press.

Krueger, John Richard. 1961. *Chuvash manual [Uralic and Altaic series 7]*. Bloomington: Indiana University Press.

Kucera, Henry. 1961. *The phonology of Czech*. 's-Gravenhage: Mouton.

Ladefoged, Peter, Jenny Ladefoged & Daniel, Everett 1997. Phonetic structures of Banawá, an endangered language. *Phonetica* 54(2), 94–111.

Laidig, Carol. 1992. Kisar phonology. *Phonological studies in four languages of Maluku*, 67–126. Dallas: Summer Institute of Linguistics.

Landaburu, Jon. 1979. *La langue des Andoke (Amazonie Colombienne): grammaire*. Paris: Société d'études linguistiques et anthropologiques de France.

Langdon, Margaret. 1970. *A grammar of Diegueño: The Mesa Grande dialect*. Berkeley: University of California Press.

Langdon, Margaret. 1977. Stress, length, and pitch in Yuman languages. *Studies in stress and accent [Southern California Occasional Papers in Linguistics 4]*, edited by Larry Hyman, 239–59.

Larochette, J. 1958. *Grammaire des dialectes mangbetu et medje, suivie d'un manuel de conversation et d'un lexique*. Tervuren, Belgium: Annales du Musee royal du Congo belge.

Larsen, Raymond and Pike, Eunice. 1949. Huasteco intonations and phonemes. *Language* 25, 268–77.

Lawrence, Erma. 1977. *Haida dictionary*. Society for the Preservation of Haida Language and Literature.

Laycock, Donald C. 1965. *The Ndu language family (Sepik district, New Guinea)*. Canberra: Australian National University.

Le Bris, Pierre. 1981. *Dictionnaire bobo-français: précédé dúne introduction grammaticale, et suivi d'un lexique français-bobo*. Paris: SELAF.

Leer, Jeff. 1985a. Prosody in Alutiiq. *Yupik Eskimo prosodic systems: descriptive and comparative studies*, edited by Michael Krauss, 77–134. Fairbanks: Alaska Native Language Center.

Leer, Jeff. 1985b. Evolution of prosody in the Yupik languages. *Yupik Eskimo prosodic systems: descriptive and comparative studies*, edited by Michael Krauss, 135–158. Fairbanks: Alaska Native Language Center.

Leer, Jeff. 1985c. Toward a metrical interpretation of Yupik prosody. *Yupik Eskimo prosodic systems: descriptive and comparative studies*, edited by Michael Krauss, 159–173. Fairbanks: Alaska Native Language Center.

Lehiste, Ilse. 1970. *Suprasegmentals*. Cambridge, MA: MIT dissertation.

Lehiste, Ilse. 1978. The syllable as a structural unit in Estonian. *Syllables and segments*, edited by Alan Bell & Joan Hooper. New York: North-Holland Publishing Company.

Lehtonen, Jaakko. 1970. *Aspects of quantity in standard Finnish*. Jyväskylä: K.J. Gummerus Osakeyhtiön Kirjapaino.

Leidenfrost, Theodore. 1973. *Kpelle-English dictionary*. Totota: Kpelle Literacy Center, Lutheran Church in Liberia.

Leskinen, Heikki & Jaakko Lehtonen. 1985. Zur wortphonologische Quantität in den Südostdialekten des Finnischen. *Studia Fennica* 28, 49–83.

Leslau, Wolf. 1959. *A dictionary of Moca (southwestern Ethiopia) [University of California Publications in Linguistics* 18]. Berkeley: University of California Press.

Leslau, Wolf. 1992. Outline of Gurage phonology. *Gurage studies: collected articles*, edited by Wolf Leslau, 1–116. Wiesbaden: Otto Harrassowitz.

LeSourd, Philip. 1984. *Kolusuwakonol: peskotomuhkati-wolastoquewi naka ikolisomani latuwewakon/ English and Passamaquoddy-Maliseet dictionary*. Frederiction, New Brunswick: Micmac-Maliseet Institute, University of New Brunswick.

LeSourd, Philip. 1993. *Accent and syllable structure in Passamaquoddy*. New York: Garland.

Levin, Juliette. 1985. *A metrical theory of syllabicity*. MIT PhD dissertation.

Levin, Norman. 1964. *The Assiniboine language*. Bloomington: Indiana University Press.

Levinsohn, Stephen H. 1976. *The Inga Language*. The Hague: Mouton.

Lewis, Henry & Holger Pedersen. 1937. *A concise comparative Celtic grammar*. Göttingen: Vandenhoeck and Ruprecht.

Li, Paul Jen-Kuei. 1982. Kavalan phonology. *GAVA, Studies in Austronesian languages and cultures*, edited by Rainer Carle, Martina Heinschke, Peter Pink, Christel Rost & Karen Stadtlander, 479–96. Berlin: Dietrich Reimer.

Lichtenberk, Frantisek. 1983. *A grammar of Manam [Oceanic Linguistics Special Publications* 18]. Honolulu: University of Hawaii Press.

Liljencrants, Johan & Björn Lindblom. 1972. Numerical simulation of vowel quality systems: the role of perceptual contrast. *Language* 48, 839–62.

Lin, Shi & Cui Jianxin. 1988. An investigation of the Ai-Cham Language. *Comparative Kadai: Linguistics studies beyond Tai*, edited by Jerold Edmondson & David Solnit, 59–86. Arlington, Tex.: Summer Institute of Linguistics & The University of Texas at Arlington.

Lin, Y-H. 1993. Degenerate affixes and templatic constraints. *Language* 69, 649–82.

Lindblom, Björn. 1986. Phonetic universals in vowel systems. *Experimental phonology*, edited by J. Ohala & J. Jaeger, 13–44. New York: Academic Press.

Lindblom, Björn & Karin Rapp. 1973. *Some temporal regularities of spoken Swedish* [*Publication* 21]. Institute of Linguistics. University of Stockholm.

Lindskoog, John & Ruth Brend. 1962. Cayapa phonemics. *Studies in Ecuadorian Indian Languages* I, editedby Benjamin Elson, 31–44 . Norman, Okla.: Summer Institute of Linguistics.

Lipkind, William. 1945. *Winnebago grammar*. New York: King's Crown Press.

Loos, Eugene Emil. 1969. *The phonology of Capanahua and its grammatical basis*. Norman: Summer Institute of Linguistics.

Lukas, Johannes. 1953. *Die Sprache der Tubu in der zentralen Sahara*. Berlin: Akademie-Verlag.

Lukas, Johannes. 1969. Tonpermeable und tonimpermeable Konsonanten im Bolanci Nordnigerien. *Ethonological and Linguistic Studies* 52, 133–138.

Luoma, Pirkko. 1985. Tentative phonemic statement of Urim. *Five phonological studies*, 101–22. Ukarumpa, Papua New Guinea: Summer Institute of Linguistics.

Lyman, Thomas. 1979. *Grammar of Mong Njua (Green Miao): a descriptive linguistic study*.

Lytkin, V. I. 1961. *Komi-Yaz'vinckii dialekt*. Moscow: Akademii Nauk.

MacDonald, Lorna. 1990. *A grammar of Tauya*. New York: Mouton de Gruyter.

MacEachern, Margaret, Barbara Kern, & Peter Ladefoged. 1997. Wari' phonetic structures. *The Journal of Amazonian Languages* 1, 5–30.

MacKay, Carolyn. 1999. *A grammar of Misantla Totonac*. Salt Lake City: University of Utah Press.

Maddieson, Ian. 1984. *Patterns of sounds*. Cambridge: Cambridge University Press.

Maddieson, Ian. 1985. Phonetic cues to syllabification. *Phonetic linguistics: Essays in honor of Peter Ladefoged*, edited by V. Fromkin, 203–21. Orlando: Academic Press.

Majewicz, Alfred & Majewicz, Elzbieta. 1986. *An Ainu-English index-dictionary to B. Pilsudski's materials for the study of the Ainu language and folklore of 1912*. Poznan: Adam Mickiewicz University Press.

Maldonado Andrés, Juan, Juan Ordoñez Domingo & Juan Ortiz Domingo. 1986. *Diccianario mam*. Guatemala City: Talleres gráficos del Centro de Reproducciones de la Universidad Rafael Landívar.

Manley, Timothy. 1972. *Outline of Sre structure*. Honolulu: University of Hawaii Press.

Manoharan, S. 1989. *A descriptive and comparative study of Andamanese language.* Calcutta: Anthropological Survey of India.

Manuel, Victor. 1955. *Elementos de gramática otomí.* Mexico: Patrimonio Indígena del Valle del Mezquital.

Marr, Nikolai Iakovlevich. 1910. *Grammatika chanskago (lazskago) iazyka, s khrestomatieiu i slovarem.* Saint Petersburg: Tipografiia Imperatorskoi Akademii Nauk.

Martens, Mary & Salme Tuominen. 1977. A tentative phonemic statement in Yil in West Sepik district. *Phonologies of five Papua New Guinea languages,* 29–48. Ukarumpa, Papua New Guinea.

Martin, Samuel. 1970. Shodon: A dialect of the northern Ryukyus. *Journal of the American Oriental Society* 90–1, 97–139.

Martin, Samuel. 1992. *A reference grammar of Korean: a complete guide to the grammar and history of the Korean language.* Rutland, Vermont: C. E. Tuttle.

Matisoff, James. 1973. *The grammar of Lahu.* Berkeley: University of California Press.

Matisoff, James. 1988. *The dictionary of Lahu.* Berkeley: University of California Press.

Mazaudon, Martine & Boyd Michailovsky. 1988. Lost syllables and tone contour in Dzongkha (Bhutan). *Prosodic Analysis and Asian Linguistics: to honour R.K. Spriggs [Pacific Linguistics* C-104], edited by David Bradley, Eugénie Henderson & Martine Mazaudon. Canberra: Australian National University.

McArthur, Henry & Lucille McArthur. 1956. Aguacatec Mayan phonemes in the stress group. *International Journal of American Linguistics* 22, 72–76.

McCarthy, John. 1979a. *Formal problems in Semitic phonology and morphology.* MIT Ph. D. dissertation.

McCarthy, John. 1979b. On stress and syllabification. *Linguistic Inquiry* 10, 443–65.

McCarthy, John & Alan Prince. 1986. *Prosodic morphology.* ms. University of Massachusetts & Brandeis University.

McCarthy, John & Alan Prince. 1990. Foot and word in prosodic morphology: The Arabic broken plural. *Natural Language and Linguistic Theory* 8, 209–83.

McCarthy, John & Alan Prince. 1993. Generalized alignment. ms. University of Massachusetts & Rutgers University. [Available on Rutgers Optimality Archive, ROA-7, http://ruccs.rutgers.edu/roa.html.]

McCarthy, John & Alan Prince. 1995a. Prosodic morphology. *Handbook of phonological theory,* edited by J. Goldsmith, 318–66. Cambridge, Mass.: Blackwell.

McCarthy, John & Alan Prince. 1995b. Faithfulness and reduplicative identity. *University of Massachusetts Occasional Papers in Linguistics* 18: *Papers in Optimality Theory,* edited by J. Beckman, S. Urbanczyk & L. Walsh, 249–384. Graduate Linguistics Student Association, University of Massachusetts, Amherst.

McGregor, Ronald Stuart. 1993. *The Oxford Hindi-English dictionary.* New York: Oxford University Press.

McLendon, Sally. 1975. *A grammar of Eastern Pomo*. Berkeley: University of California Press.

McLeod, Ruth & Valerie Mitchell. 1977. *Aspectos da língua xavánte*. Brasília: Summer Institute of Linguistics.

McMahon, Ambrose. 1967. Phonemes and phonemic units of Cora (Mexico). *International Journal of American linguistics* 33, 128–34.

Meiklejohn, Percy & Kathleen Meiklejohn. 1958. Accentuation in Sarangani Manobo. *Studies in Philippine linguistics*[*Oceania Linguistic Monographs* 3], 1–3. Sydney: University of Sydney.

Menovshchikov, G. A. 1962. *Grammatika iazyka aziatskikh eskimosov*. Leningrad: Izdatelstvo Akademii Nauk SSR.

Menovshchikov, G. A. 1975. *Iazyk naukanskikh eskimosov*. Leningrad: Nauka.

Meredith, Scott. 1990. *Issues in the phonology of prominence*. MIT Ph.D. Dissertation.

Merlan, Francesca. 1994. *A grammar of Wardaman: a language of the Northern Territory of Australia*. New York: Mouton de Gruyter.

Mester, Armin. 1994. The quantitative trochee in Latin. *Natural Language and Linguistic Theory* 12, 1–61.

Michelson, Gunther. 1973. *A thousand words of Mohawk*. Ottowa: National Museum of Man.

Michelson, Karin. 1988. *A comparative study of Lake-Iroquoian accent*. Dordrecht: Kluwer.

Migliazza, Ernest. 1965. *Notas fonológicas de língua Tiriyó* [*Nova Série Antropologia* 29].Belém: Boletim do Museo Paraense Emílio Goeldi

Miller, Vera Grace. 1976. *An overview of Stiêng grammar*. Grand Forks: Summer Institute of Linguistics.

Miller, Wick. 1965. *Acoma grammar and texts*. Berkeley: University of California Press.

Miller-Ockhuizen, Amanda. 1998. Towards a unified decompositional analysis of Khoisan lexical tone. *Languages, identity, and conceptualization among the Khoisan*, edited by Mathias Schladt, 217–43 . Köln: Rüdiger Köppe Verlag.

Mills, Eêlizabeth. 1984. *Senoufo phonology, discourse to syllable (a prosodic approach)*. Dallas: Summer Institute of Linguistics.

Miner, Kenneth. 1979. Dorsey's Law in Winnebago-Chiwere and Winnebago accent. *International Journal of American Linguistics* 45, 25–33.

Miner, Kenneth. 1989. Winnebago accent: the rest of the data. *Anthropological Linguistics* 31, 148–72.

Minor, Eugene & Dorothy Minor. 1976. *Fonologia del huitoto*. Bogota: Ministerio de Gobierno.

Mitchell, T.F. 1960. Prominence and syllabification in Arabic. *Bulletin of Oriental and African Studies* 23, 369–89. [Reprinted in Mitchell, T.F. 1975. *Principles of Firthian Linguistics*. London: Longmans]

Mixco, Mauricio. 2000. *Kiliwa*. Munich: Lincom Europa.

Miyaoko, Osahito. 1985. Accentuation in Central Alaskan Yupik. *Yupik Eskimo prosodic systems: descriptive and comparative studies*, edited by Michael Krauss, 51–76. Fairbanks: Alaska Native Language Center.

Miyaoka, Osahito. 1996. Sketch of Central Alaskan Yupik, an Eskimoan Language. *Handbook of American Indian lLanguages, vol. 17 Languages*, edited by Ives Goddard (volume editor), 325–63. Washington: Smithsonian Institute.

Mohanan, K. P. 1986. *The theory of lexical phonology*. Dordrecht: Reidel.

Moore, Brian. 1995. *An Introduction to the Psychology of Hearing*. San Diego: Academic Press.

Morén, Bruce. 2000. The puzzle of Kashmiri stress: implications for weight theory. *Phonology* 17, 365–396.

Morev, L. N. 1983. *Shanskii iazyk*. Moskva: Izdatelstvo Nauka.

Morev, L. N. 1988. *Iazyk Sek*. Moskva: Nauka.

Morev, L. N.; A. A. Moskalev & Y. Y. Plam. 1979. *The Lao language*. Moskva: Izdatelstvo Nauka.

Morris, Cliff. 1984. *Tetun-English dictionary*. Canberra: Australian National University.

Morrison, Heather. 1994. *Morphological influences on Winnebago accent*. UCLA MA thesis.

Mous, Maarten. 1993. *A grammar of Iraqw*. Hamburg: Helmut Buske Verlag.

Munro, Pamela. 1976. *Mojave syntax*. New York: Garland.

Munro, Pamela. 1996a. Cherokee papers from UCLA: an introduction. *Cherokee Papers from UCLA*. Los Angeles: UCLA Department of Linguistics.3–8.

Munro, Pamela. 1996b. *The Chickasaw sound system*. ms. UCLA.

Munro, Pamela. 2005. Chickasaw. *Native languages of the southeastern United States*, edited by Heather Hardy & Janine Scancarelli, 114–156. Lincoln: University of Nebraska Press.

Munro, Pamela & Peter Benson. 1973. Reduplication and rule ordering in Luiseño. *International Journal of American Linguistics* 39,.15–21.

Munro, Pamela, Nellie Brown & Crawford, Judith. 1992. *A Mojave dictionary* [*UCLA Occasional Papers in Linguistics* 10]. Los Angeles: UCLA Department of Linguistics.

Munro, Pamela & Dieynaba Gaye. 1991. *Ay baati Wolof : a Wolof dictionary* [*UCLA Occasional Papers in Linguistics* 9]. Los Angeles: UCLA Department of Linguistics.

Munro, Pamela & Charles Ulrich. 1984. Structure-preservation and Western Muskogean rhythmic lengthening. *West Coast Conference on Formal Linguistics* 3, 191–202.

Munro, Pamela & Catherine Willmond. 1994. *Chickasaw: An analytical dictionary*. Norman: University of Oklahoma Press.

Nagaraja, K. S. 1985. *Khasi, a descriptive analysis*. Pune: Deccan College Post-Graduate and Research Institute.

Naish, Constance & Gillian Story. 1963. *English-Tlingit dictionary: nouns*. Fairbanks: Summer Institute of Linguistics.

Najlis, Elena. 1973. *Lengua selknam*. Buenos Aires: Universidad del Salvador.

Nanni, Debbie 1977. Stressing words in -Ative. *Linguistic Inquiry* 8, 752–62.

Newman, Paul. 1972. Syllable weight as a phonological variable. *Studies in African Linguistics* 3, 301–324.

Newman, Paul. 1990. Hausa and the Chadic languages. *The world's major languages*, edited by Bernard Comrie, 705–24. New York: Oxford University Press.

Newman, Stanley. 1944. *Yokuts language of California*. New York: Johnson Reprint Corporation.

Newman, Stanley. 1958. *Zuni dictionary*. Bloomington: Indiana University Research Center in Anthropology, Folklore and Linguistics.

Newman, Stanley. 1965. *Zuni grammar*. Albuquerque: University of New Mexico Press.

Nguyen Dang Liem. 1969. *Vietnamese pronounciation*. Honolulu: University of Hawaii Press.

Nguyen, Dinh-hoa. 1990. Vietnamese. *The world's major languages*, edited by Bernard Comrie, 777–796. New York: Oxford.

Niang, Mamadou. 1995. Syllable "sonority" hierarchy and Pulaar stress: A metrical approach. *Kansas Working Papers in Linguistics* 20, 53–68.

Nielsen, Konrad. 1926. *Lærebok i Lappisk*. Oslo: A. W. Brøggers.

Nielsen, Konrad. 1932. *Lappisk ordbok, grunnet på dialektene i Polmak, Karasjok og Kautokeino*. Cambridge, MA: Harvard University Press.

Nivens, Richard. 1992. A lexical phonology of West Tarangan. *Phonological studies in four languages of Maluku*, edited by Donald Burquest & Wyn Laidig, 127–227. Arlington, Tex.: Summer Institute of Linguistics.

Noonan, Michael. 1992. *A grammar of Lango*. New York: Mouton de Gruyter.

Noss, Richard B. 1964. *Thai: reference grammar*. Washington: Foreign Service Institute, Department of State.

Nougayrol, Pierre. 1990. *La langue des Aiki dits rounga: Tschad, République centrafricaine: esquisse descriptive et lexique*. Paris: Laboratoire de langues et civilisations a tradition orale, Départment "Langues et parole en Afrique centrale."

Ó Siadhail, Mícheál. 1989. *Modern Irish: grammatical structure and dialect variation*. New York: Oxford University Press.

Odden, David. 1979. Principles of stress assignment: A cross-linguistic view. *Studies in the Linguistic Sciences* 9, 157–75.

Odden, David. 1983. Aspects of Didinga phonology and morphology. *Nilo-Saharan language studies*, edited by In Lionel Bender, 148–176. East Lansing: African Studies Center, Michigan State University. .

Ohala, Manjari. 1977. Stress in Hindi. *Studies in stress and accent [Southern California Occasional Papers in Linguistics* 4], edited by Larry Hyman, 327–338.

Ohala, Manjari. 1983. *Aspects of Hindi phonology*. Delhi: Motilal Banarsidass.

Okell, John. 1969. *A reference grammar of colloquial Burmese*. London: Oxford University Press.

Orr, Carolyn. 1962. Ecuador Quicha phonology. *Studies in Ecuadorian Indian Languages* I, edited by Benjamin Elson, 60–77. Norman, Okla.: Summer Institute of Linguistics.

Osborn, Henry. 1948. Amahuaca phonemes. *International Journal of American Linguistics* 14, 188–90.

Osborn, Henry. 1966. Warao I: phonology and morphophonemics. *International Journal of American Linguistics* 32, 108–23.

Osborne, C. R. 1974. *The Tiwi language: grammar, myths and dictionary of the Tiwi language spoken on Melville and Bathurst Islands, Northern Australia.* Canberra: Australian Institute of Aboriginal Studies.

Oswalt, Robert. 1961. *A Kashaya grammar (Southwestern Pomo).* University of California, Berkeley Ph. D. dissertation.

Oswalt, Robert. 1988. The floating accent of Kashaya. *In Honor of Mary Haas,* edited by William Shipley, 611–22. Berlin: Mouton.

Owens, Jonathan. 1984. *A short reference grammar of Eastern Libyan Arabic.* Wiesbaden: Otto Harrassowitz.

Paasonen, Heikki. 1990–6. *H. Paasonens Mordwinishes Wörterbuch.* Helsinki: Suomalais-ugrilainen seura.

Paita, Yvonne & Tadahiko L. A. Shintani. 1983. *Esquisse de la Langue de Paita (Nouvelle-Calédonie).* SETOM, Nouméa.

Panfilov, Vladimir Zinovevich. 1962. *Grammatika nivkhskogo iazyka.* Moskva: Izdatelstvo Akademii Nauk SSSR.

Parks, Douglas. 1976. *A grammar of Pawnee.* New York: Garland.

Patte, Marie France. 1989. *Estudio descriptivo de la lengua añún (o "paraujano).* San Cristobal: Universidad Católica del Táchira.

Paula, Ruth Wallace de Garcia. 1980. *Língua Kaxuyána: fonologia segmental e afixos nominais.* Rio de Janeiro: Museo Nacional.

Payne, David. 1981. *The phonology and morphology of Axininca Campa.* Arlington, Tex.: Summer Institute of Linguistics.

Payne, David, Judith Payne & Jorge Sanchez Santos. 1982. *Morphologia, fonologia y fonetica del asheninca del Apurucayali* [*Serie Lingüística Peruana* 18]. Pucallpa, Peru: Instituto Lingüístico de Verano.

Payne, Doris & Thomas Payne. 1990. Yagua. *Handbook of Amazonian languages,* Vol.2, edited by Desmond Derbyshire & Geoffrey Pullum, 249–474. New York: Mouton.

Payne, Judith. 1990. Asheninca stress patterns. *Amazonian linguistics,* edited by Doris Payne, 185–212. Austin: University of Texas Press.

Petrunicheva, Z. N. 1960. *Iazyk Telugu.* Moskva: Izdatel'stvo Vostochnoi Literaturi.

Piggott, Glyne. 1980. *Aspects of Odawa morphonemics.* New York: Garland.

Piggott, G. L. & A. Grafstein. 1983. *An Ojibwa lexicon.* Ottawa: National Museums of Canada.

Pike, Kenneth & Eunice Pike. 1947. Immediate constituents of Mazateco syllables. *International Journal of American Linguistics* 13, 78–91.

Pikkert, Joost & Cheryl Pikkert. 1995. A first look at Tidore phonology. *Descriptive studies in languages of Maluku*, edited by Wyn Laiding, 43–70. Jakarta: Badan Penyelenggara Seri Nusa, Universitas Katolik Indonesia Atma Java.

Pitkin, Harvey. 1984. *Wintu grammar*. Berkeley: University of California Press.

Pitkin, Harvey. 1985. *Wintu dictionary*. Berkeley: University of California Press.

Polotsky, Hans Jakob. 1951. *Notes on Gurage grammar*. Jerusalem: Israel Oriental Society.

Popjes, Jack & Jo Popjes. 1986. Canela-Krahô. *Handbook of Amazonian languages*, Vol. 1, edited by Desmond Derbyshire & Geoffrey Pullum, 128–99. New York: Mouton.

Popova. I. N. 1978. *Nenetsko-russkii slovar: lesnoe narechie*. Szeged: Universitatis Szegediensis de Attila József Nominata.

Poppe, Nicholas. 1951. *Khalkha-Mongolische Grammatik, mit Bibliographie, Sprachproben und Glossar*. Wiesbaden: F. Steiner.

Poppe, Nicholas. 1960. *Buriat grammar*. Bloomington: Indiana University Press.

Poppe, Nicholas. 1962. *Uzbek newspaper reader, with glossary*. Bloomington: Indiana University Press.

Poppe, Nicholas. 1963. *Tatar manual: descriptive grammar and texts with a Tatar-English glossary*. Bloomington: Indiana University Press.

Poppe, Nicholas. 1964. *Bashkir manual: descriptive grammar and texts with a Bashkir-English glossary*. Bloomington: Indiana University Press.

Posti, Lauri. 1980. *Vatjan kielen Kukkosin murteen sanakirja*. Helsinki: Suomalais-ugrilainen seura.

Powell, J. V & Fred Woodruff. 1976. *Quileute dictionary*. Moscow: University of Idaho.

Prabodhachandran Nayar, V. R. 1973. *Malayalam, a linguistic description*. Kazhakuttam: National Research Publishing Company.

Prentice, D. J. 1971. *The Murut languages of Sabah*. Canberra: The Australian National University.

Prentice, D. J. 1990. Malay (Indonesian and Malaysian). *The world's major languages*, edited by Bernard Comrie, 913–35. New York: Oxford.

Price, P. D. 1976. Southern Nambiquara phonology. *International Journal of American Linguistics* 42, 338–48.

Price, P. J. 1980. Sonority and syllabicity: acoustic correlates of perception. *Phonetica* 37, 327–343.

Priest, Perry. 1968. Phonemes of the Sirionó language. *Linguistics: An International Review* 41, 102–108.

Prince, Alan 1983. Relating to the grid. *Linguistic Inquiry* 14, 19–100.

Prince, Alan & Paul Smolensky.2004. *Optimality theory: constraint interaction in generative grammar*.Malden, Mass.: Blackwell Publishers.

Prost, André. 1956. *La langue sonay et ses dialectes*. Dakar: IFAN.

Prost, Gilbert. 1960. *Fonemas de la lengua Chacobo*. La Paz: Publicaciones del Instituto Lingüístico de Verano en colaboración con el Ministerio de Asuntos Campesinos.

Prunet, J. F. & C. Tellier. 1984. Interaction des niveaux en phonologie: l'abregement vocalic en Pulaar. *McGill Working Papers in Linguistics* 2, 65–90.

Pulte, William & Durbin Feeling. 1975. *Outline of Cherokee grammar*. Tahlequah, Okla.: Cherokee Nation of Oklahoma.

Qani, Abdi-Asis Muhumed. 1993. *OMIMEE's English-Somali dictionary*. Cologne: OMIMEE Intercultural Publishers.

Queixalós, Francisco. 1985. *Fonología sikuani*. Bogota: Instituto Caro y Cuervo.

Radin, Paul. 1929. *A grammar of the Wappo language*. Berkeley: University of California Press.

Ras, J. J. 1982. *Inleiding tot het modern Javaans*. 'S-Gravenhage: Martinus Nijhoff.

Raz, Shlomo. 1983. *Tigre grammar and texts*. Malibu, CA: Undena Publications.

Redden, James. 1966. Walapai I: Phonology. *International Journal of American Linguistics* 32, 1–16.

Reed, Irene, Osahito Miyaoka, Steven Jacobson, Paschal Afcan & Michael Krauss. 1977. *Yup'ik Eskimo grammar*. Fairbanks: Alaska Native Language Center.

Reesink, Ger. 1987. *Structures and their functions in Usan: a Papuan language of Papua New Guinea*. Philadelphia: Benjamins.

Refsing, Kirsten. 1986. *The Ainu language: the morphology and syntax of the Shizunai dialect*. Århus, Denmark: Aarhus University Press.

Reh, Mechthild. 1985. *Die Krongo-Sprache (Nìinò-mó-dì): Beschreibung, Texte, Wörterverzeichnis*. Berlin: D. Reimer.

Rialland, Annie. 1993. L'allongement compensatoire: nature et modèles. *Architecture des représentations phonologiques*, edited by Bernard Laks & Annie Rialland, 59–92. Paris: CNRS Editions.

Rice, Keren. 1989. *A grammar of Slave*. New York: Mouton de Gruyter.

Rich, Furne. 1963. Arabela phonemes and high-level phonology. *Studies in Peruvian Indian Languages* I, edited by In Benjamin Elson, 193–206.

Rickard, David. 1970. *Kru grammar*. Monrovia, Liberia: Department of Literacy Work and Literature Production of the United Methodist Church.

Rigault, André. 1962. Rôle de la fréquence, de l'intensité et de la durée vocaliques dans la perception de l'accent en francais. *Proceedings of the Fourth International Congress of Phonetic Sciences, Helsinki*, 735–48.

Rischel, Jørgen. 1974. *Topics in West Greenlandic phonology: Regularities underlying the phonetic appearance of wordforms in a polysynthetic language*. Kopenhagen: Akademisk Forlag.

Rivierre, Jean-Claude. 1973. *Phonologie comparée des dialectes de l'extrême-sud de la Nouvelle Calédonie*. SELAF, Paris.

Robbins, Scarlett. 1991. Lexicalized metrical foot structure in Maidu. *Phonology at Santa Cruz* 2, 95–116.

Roberts, John. 1987. *Amele*. New York: Croom Helm.

Robins, Robert Henry. 1958. *The Yurok language: grammar, texts, lexicon* [*University of California Publications in Linguistics* 15]. Berkeley: University of California Press.

Robinson, Lila. 1990. *Comanche dictionary and grammar*. Dallas: Summer Institute of Linguistics.

Robinson, Orrin. 1992. *Old English and its closest relatives: a survey of the earliest Germanic languages*. Stanford: Stanford University Press.

Rood, David. 1976. *Wichita grammar*. New York: Garland.

Rosato, Michele. 1980. *Didinga grammar and dictionary (Sudan-Equatorial)*. Rome.

Rose, Françoise. 2002. Le problème de la nasalité dans l'inventaire phonologique de l'émérillon. *Amerindia* 26/27, 147–72.

Rozelle, Lorna. 1997. The effect of stress on vowel length in Aleut. *UCLA Working Papers in Phonetics* 95, 91–101.

Ruiz de Bravo Ahuja, Gloria. 1983. *Huave de San Mateo del Mar, Oaxaca*. Mexico D. F.: El Colegio de Mexico.

Saagpakk, Paul. 1982. *Eesti-inglise sõnaraamat/Estonian-English dictionary*. New Haven: Yale University Press.

Sadeniemi, Matti. 1949. *Metriikkamme perusteet*. Helsinki: SKST.

Saeed, John. 1993. *Somali reference grammar*. Kensington, MD: Dunwoody Press.

Saelzer, Meinke. 1976. Fonologia provisória da língua Kamayurá.*Série Lingüística* 5, 131–70.

Sakthivel, S. 1976. *Phonology of the Toda language with vocabular*. Annamalainagar: Annamalai University.

Saltarelli, Mario. 1988. *Basque*. New York: Croom Helm.

Samarin, William J. 1967. *A grammar of Sango*. The Hague: Mouton.

Samely, Ursula. 1991. *Kedang, (Eastern Indonesia), some aspects of its grammar*. Hamburg: Helmut Buske Verlag.

Santandrea, Stefano. 1970. *Brief grammar outlines of the Yulu and Kara languages*. Bologna: Editrice Nigrizia.

Sapir, David. 1965. *A grammar of Diola-Fogny: a language spoken in the Basse-Casamance region of Senegal*. Cambridge: Cambridge University Press.

Sapir, Edward & Harry Hoijer. 1967. *The phonology and morphology of the Navaho language*. Berkeley: University of California Press.

Sapir, Edward & Morris Swadesh. 1939. *Nootka texts, tales and ethnological narratives, with grammatical notes and lexical materials*. Philadelphia: Linguistic Society of America.

Sapir, Edward & Morris Swadesh. 1960. *Yana dictionary* [*University of California Publications in Linguistics* 22]. Berkeley: University of California Press.

Saul, Janice. 1980. *Nùng grammar*. Dallas: Summer Institute of Linguistics.

Scancarelli, Janine. 1987. *Grammatical relations and verb agreement in Cherokee*. UCLA Ph.D. dissertation.

Schermair, Anselmo. 1949. *Gramática de la lengua Sirionó*. La Paz.

Schiefer, Lieselotte. 1975. *Phonematik und phonotaktik des Vach-Ostjakischen*. Munich: Finnisch-Ugrisches Seminar an der Universität München.

Schuh, Russell. 1996. Metrics of Arabic and Hausa poetry. *Proceedings of the 1996 Annual Conference on African Linguistics*. University of Florida.

Schütz, Albert. 1985. *The Fijian language*. Honolulu: University of Hawaii Press.

Shnukal, Anna. 1988. *Broken : an introduction to the Creole language of Torres Strait*. Canberra: Australian National University.

Scorza, David. 1985. A sketch of Au morphology and syntax [*Pacific Linguistics* A63]. Canberra: Australian National University. .

Seaman, P. David. 1985. *Hopi dictionary: Hopi-English, English-Hopi, grammatical appendix*. Flagstaff: Department of Anthropology, Northern Arizona University.

Sebeok, Thomas & Francis Ingemann. 1961. *An Eastern Cheremis manual* [*Uralic and Altaic Series* 5]. Bloomington: Indiana University Press.

Segert, Stanislaw. 1983. *Altaramäische Grammatik mit Bibliographie, Chrestomathie und Glossar*. Leipzig: Verlag Enzyklopädie.

Seiler, Hansjakob. 1965. Accent and morphophonemics in Cahuilla and Uto-Aztecan. *International Journal of American Linguistics* 31, 50–9.

Selkirk, Elisabeth. 1984. *Phonology and syntax: The relation between sound and structure*. Cambridge, Mass.: MIT Press.

Senft, Gunter. 1986. *Kilivila: the language of the Trobriand Islanders*. New York: Mouton de Gruyter.

Senn, Alfred. 1957–66. *Handbuch der litauischen Sprache*. Heidelberg: C. Winter.

Serebrennikov, B. A. 1956. *Mariisko-ruskii slovar*. Moskva: Gosudarstvennie Izdatelstvo inostrannykh i natsionalnykh slovarei.

Severn, John. 1995. The phonemic syllable in Sahu: a computer-aided phonological analysis. *Descriptive studies in languages of Maluku*, edited by Wyn Laiding, 71–87. Jakarta: Badan Penyelenggara Seri Nusa, Universitas Katolik Indonesia Atma Java.

Sezer, Engin. 1986. An autosegmental analysis of compensatory lengthening in Turkish. *Studies in compensatory lengthening*, edited by L. Wetzels & E. Sezer. Dordrecht: Foris.227–50.

Shackle, C. 1976. *The Siraiki language of central Pakistan: A reference grammar*. London: University of London.

Sharpe, Margaret. 1972. *Alawa phonology and grammar*. Canberra: Australian National University.

Shaw, Patricia. 1980. *Theoretical issues in Dakota phonology and morphology*. New York: Garland.

Shaw, Patricia. 1985. Coexistent and competing stress rules in Stoney (Dakota). *International Journal of American Linguistics* 51(1), 1–18.

Shibatani, Masayoshi. 1990. *The languages of Japan*. Cambridge: Cambridge University Press.

Shimizu, Kiyoshi. 1980. *A Jukun grammar*. Wien: Veröffenlichungen der Institute für Afrikanistik und Ägyptologie der Universität Wien.

Shimizu, Kiyoshi. 1983. *The Zing dialect of Mumuye: A descriptive grammar with a Mumuye-English dictionary and an English-Mumuye index*. Hamburg: Helmut Buske Verlag.

Shipley, William. 1963. *Maidu texts and dictionary.* Berkeley: University of California Press.

Shipley, William. 1964. *Maidu grammar.* Berkeley: University of California Press.

Shryock, Aaron. 1993. A metrical analysis of stress in Cebuano. *Lingua* 91, 103–48.

Shryock, Aaron. 1995. *Investigating laryngeal contrasts: an acoustic study of the consonants of Musey.* UCLA PhD dissertation [*UCLA Working Papers in Phonetics 89*].

Silbajoris, Rimvydas. 1968. *Russian versification.* New York: Columbia University Press.

Silverman, Daniel. 1995. *Phrasing and recoverability.* UCLA PhD dissertation. [Published by Garland Press in 1997]

Silverman, Daniel. 1997. Laryngeal complexity in Otomanguean vowels. *Phonology* 14, 235–62.

Singh, U. Nissor. 1983. *Khasi-English dictionary.* Delhi: Cultural Publishing House.

Sinha, N. K. 1975. *Mundari grammar.* Mysore: Central Institute of Indian Languages.

Sischo, William. 1979. Michoacán Nahual. Studies in Uto-Aztecan Grammar, vol. 2, Modern Aztec Grammatical Sketches, edited by Ronald Langacker, 307–80. Arlington, Tex.: Summer Institute of Linguistics.

Sitapati, G. V. 1936. Accent in Telugu speech and verse. *Indian Linguistics* 6, 201–11.

Skorik, Petr. 1961. *Grammatika chukotskogo iazyka.* Moskva. Izdatelstvo Akademii Nauk.

Slocum, Marianna. 1985. *Gramática Páez.* Lomalinda, Colombia: Editorial Townsend.

Sluijter, A. M. C. & V. J. van Heuven. 1996. Spectral balance as an acoustic correlate of linguistic stress. *Journal of the Acoustical Society of America* 100, 2471–2485.

Smith, Richard & Connie Smith. 1971. Southern Barasano phonemics. *Linguistics: An International Review* 75, 80–85.

Snoxall, R. A. 1967. *Luganda-English dictionary.* London: Oxford University Press.

Snyman, Jannie Winston. 1975. *Zǔ\'Hõasi fonologie & woordeboek.* Rotterdam: A. A. Balkema.

Solntsev, V. M., Khoang Tue, et al. 1987. *Iazyk myong: materialy Sovetsko-vetnamskoi lingvisticheskoi ekspeditsii 1979 goda.* Moskva: Izdatelstvo Nauka.

Sovijärvi, Antti. 1956. *Über die phonetischen Hauptzüge der finnischen und der ungarischen Hochsprache.* Wiesbaden: Otto Harrassowitz.

Spaulding, Craig & Pat Spaulding. 1994. Phonology and grammar of Nankina [*Data papers on Papua New Guinea languages*, vol. 41]. Ukarumpa, New Guinea: Summer Institute of Linguistics.

Speirs, Randall. 1966. *Some aspects of the structure of Rio Grande Tewa.* SUNY Buffalo Ph.D. dissertation.

Sreedhar, M. V. 1985. *Standardized grammar of Naga Pidgin.* Mysore: Central Institute of Indian Languages.

Sroufkova, Miloslava, Rostislav Plesky & Marta Vencovská. 1987. *Rusko-Cesky a Cesko-Rusky slovnik.* Praha: Státní Pedagogické Nakladatelstvi Praha.

Stanford, Ronald & Lynn Stanford. 1970. *Collected field reports on the phonology and grammar of Chakosi*. University of Ghana.

Steever, Sanford. 1998. Gondi. *The Dravidian languages*, edited by Sanford Steever, 270–300. New York: Routledge.

Steriade, Donca. 1982. *Greek prosodies and the nature of syllabification*. MIT Ph.D. dissertation.

Steriade, Donca. 1991. Moras and other slots. *Proceedings of the Formal Linguistics Society of the Midamerica* 1, 254–80.

Steriade, Donca. 1999. Licensing laryngeal features. *UCLA Working Papers in Phonology* 3, 25–146.

Stevens, Kenneth & Samuel Jay Keyser. 1989. Primary features and their enhancement in consonants. *Language* 65, 81–106.

Stevenson, R. C. 1969. *Bagirmi grammar*. Khartoum: University of Khartoum.

Stolte, Joel & Nance Stolte. 1971. A description of Northern Barasano phonology. *Linguistics: An International Review* 75, 86–92.

Stonham, John. 1990. *Current issues in morphological theory*. Stanford Ph.D. dissertation.

Story, Gillian & Constance Naish. 1973. *Tlingit verb dictionary: part 1 English-Tlingit, part 2 Tlingit-English*.

Stout, Mickey & Ruth Thomson. 1974. Fonêmica Txukuhamei (Kayapó). *Série Lingüística* 3, 153–76. Brasília: Summer Institute of Linguistics.

Straight, Henry Stephen. 1976. *The acquisition of Maya phonology: variation in Yucatec child language*. New York: Garland.

Sulkala, Helena & Merja Karjalainen. 1992. *Finnish*. New York: Routledge.

Susman, Amelia. 1943. *The accentual system of Winnebago*. Columbia University Ph.D. dissertation.

Suvageot, Serge. 1965. *Description synchronique d'un dialecte Wolof: le parler du Pyolof*. Dakar: Ifan.

Svantesson, Jan-Olaf. 1983. *Kammu phonology and morphology*. Lund: CWK Gleerup.

Swadesh, Morris. 1946. Chitimacha. *Linguistic structures of Native America*, edited by Cornelius Osgood, 312–336. New York: Viking Fund Publications in Anthropology.

Swanton, John. 1921. The Tunica language. *International Journal of American Linguistics* 2, 1–39.

Swanton, John. 1929. A sketch of the Atakapa language. *International Journal of American Linguistics* 5, 121–49.

Szabó, László. 1967. *Selkup texts with phonetic introduction and vocabulary*. Bloomington: Indiana University Press.

Szinnyei, Josef. 1912. *Ungarische Sprachlehre*. Berlin: Göschen.

Teeter, Karl & Philip LeSourd. 1983. Vowel length in Malecite. *Actes du quatorzième congrès des algonquinistes*, edited by William Cowan, 245–8. Ottawa: Carleton University.

Teeter, Karl. 1971. The main features of Malecite-Passamaquoddy grammar. *Studies in American Indian languages*, edited by Jesse Sawyer. Berkeley: University of California Press.

Tereshchenko, N. M. 1979. *Nganasankii iazyk.* Leningrad: Nauka.

Thalbitzer, William. 1976. *A phonetical study of the Eskimo language: based on observations made on a journey in north Greenland, 1900–1901.* New York: AMS Press.

Thalmann, Peter. 1980. *Phonologie du kroumen.* Abidjan, Ivory Coast: Université d'Abidjan, Institut de linguistique appliquée.

Thompson, E. David. 1983. *Kunama: phonology and noun phrase.* Nilo-Saharan language studies, edited by Lionel Bender, 281–322. East Lansing: African Studies Center, Michigan State University.

Thurston, William. 1982. *A comparative study in Anem and Lusi.* Canberra: Australian National University.

Tiffou, Etienne. 1982. *Contes du Yasin: introduction au bourochaski du Yasin avec grammaire et dictionnaire analytique.* Paris: Peeters/SELAF.

Topping, Donald. 1973. *Chamorro reference grammar.* Honolulu: University of Hawaii Press.

Tourneux, Henry. 1978. *Le mulwi ou vulum de Mogroum, Tchad: language du groupe musgu, famille tschadique: phonologie, éléments de grammaire.* Paris: SELAF.

Trager, Felicia. 1971. The phonology of Picuris. *International Journal of American Linguistics* 37, 29–33.

Trager, George. 1946. An outline of Taos grammar. *Linguistic structures of Native America*, 184–221. New York: Viking Fund Publications in Anthropology.

Traill, Anthony. 1985. *Phonetic and phonological studies of !Xōo Bushman.* Hamburg: Helmut Buske Verlag.

Trubetzkoy, N.S. 1939/1958. *Grundzüge der Phonologie.* Göttingen: Vandenhoeck and Ruprecht.

Tsygankina, D. V. 1980. *Grammatika mordovskikh iazykov: fonetika, grafika, orfografiia, morfologiia: uchebnik dlia natsionalnykh otdelenii vuzov.* Saransk: Moskva Gosudarstvennii Universitet.

Tucker, Archibald Norman. 1962. *The syllable in Luganda: a prosodic approach.* London.

Tuggy, David. 1979. Tetelcingo Nahuatl. *Studies in Uto-Aztecan grammar, vol. 2, modern Aztec grammatical sketches*, edited by Ronald Langacker, 1–140. Arlington, TX: Summer Institute of Linguistics. .

Tung, T'ung-ho. 1964. *A descriptive study of the Tsou language, Formosa.* Taipei: Institute of History and Philology, Academia Sinica.

Tyler, Stephen. 1969. *Koya: an outline grammar*, Gommu dialect. Berkeley: University of California Publications in Linguistics.

Vall, M. N. & I. A. Kanakin. 1990. *Ocherk fonologii i grammatiki ketskogo iazyka.* Novosibirsk: Nauka.

van Driem, George. 1993. *A grammar of Dumi.* New York: Mouton de Gruyter.

van Eijk, Jan. 1997. *The Lillooet language: Phonology, morphology, syntax.* Vancouver: University of British Columbia Press.

Van-Chinh, Truong. 1970. *Structure de la langue vietnamienne.* Paris: Imprimerie Nationale.

Vance, Timothy. 1987. *An introduction to Japanese phonology.* Albany: State University of New York Press.

Vansina, Jan. 1959. *Esquisse de grammaire bushong.* Tervuren: Musée royal du Congo belge.

Viitso, Tiit-Rein. 1997. The prosodic system of Estonian in the Finnic space. *Estonian prosody: Papers from a symposium,* edited by Ilse Lehiste & Jaan Ross, 222–34. Tallinn: Institute of Estonian Language.

Voegelin, Charles. 1935. *Tübatulabal grammar.* Berkeley: University of California Press.

Vogt, Hans. 1940. *The Kalispel language, an outline of the grammar with text, translations and dictionary.* Oslo: J. Dybwad.

Vollrath, Paul. 1985. Hewa phonemes: a tentative statement. *Five phonological studies,* 51–84. Ukarumpa, Papua New Guinea: Summer Institute of Linguistics.

Volodin, A. P. 1976. *Itel'menskii iazyk.* Leningrad: Izdatel'stvo Nauka.

Vossen, Rainer. 1986. Zur Phonologie des //Ani. *Contemporary studies on Khoisan in honour of Oswin Köhler on the occasion of his 75th Birthday,* edited by Rainer Vossen & Klaus Keuthmann, 321–46. Hamburg: Helmut Buske Verlag.

Vossen, Rainer. 1997. *Die Khoe-Sprachen [Quellen zur Khoisan—Forschung 12].* Köln: Rüdiger Köppe Verlag.

Walker, Rachel. 1995. Mongolian stress: Typological implications for Nonfinality in unbounded systems. *Phonology at Santa Cruz* 4, 85–102.

Walker, Rachel. 1996. *Prominence-driven stress.* ms. University of California, Santa Cruz. [Available on Rutgers Optimality Archive, ROA-172, http://ruccs.rutgers.edu/roa.html.]

Walker, W. Seymour. 1921. *The Siwi language; a short grammar of the Siwi language, with a map and ten appendices, including a brief account of the customs, etc. of the Siwani, together with a description of the oasis of Siwa.* London: K. Paul, Trench, Trubner and Company, Ltd.

Warren, R. M. 1970. Elimination of biases in loudness judgements for pure tones. *Journal of the Acoustical Society of America* 48, 1397–1413.

Watkins, Laurel. 1984. *A grammar of Kiowa.* Lincoln: University of Nebraska Press.

Watson, Richard. 1966. *Reduplication in Pacoh [Hartford studies in linguistics 21].* Hartford: Watson.

Watuseke, F. S. 1991. The Ternate language. *Papers in Papuan linguistics* 1, edited by Tom Dutton, 223–44. Canberra: Australian National University.

Weathers, Nadine. 1947. Tsotsil phonemes with special reference to allophones of B. *International Journal of American Linguistics* 13, 108–111.

Weber, David. 1989. *A grammar of Huallaga (Huánanco) Quechua.* Berkeley: University of California Press.

Weidert, Alfons. 1977. *Tai-Khamti phonology and vocabulary*. Wiesbaden: Steiner.

Weiers, Michael. 1972. *Die Sprache der Moghol der Provinz Herat in Afghanistan*. Opladen: Westdeutscher Verlag.

Welmers, William. 1962. *The phonology of Kpelle*. Journal of African Languages 1, 69–93.

Welmers, William. 1976. *A grammar of Vai*. Berkeley: University of California Press.

Werle, Johannes-Martin. 1976. *Phonologie and morphonologie du bété de la région de Guiberoua*. Abidjan: Université d'Abidjan, Institut de linguistique appliquée.

Westbury, John & Keating, Patricia. 1980. Central representation of vowel duration. *Journal of the Acoustical Society of America* 67, S37 A.

Westermann, Diedrich. 1930. *The Kpelle language in Liberia: grammatical outline, colloquial sentences, and vocabulary*. Berlin: D. Reimer.

Wheatley, Julian. 1990. Burmese. *The world's major languages*, edited by Bernard Comrie, 834–854. New York: Oxford.

Wheeler, Alva & Margaret. 1962. *Studies in Ecuadorian Indian Languages* I, edited by Benjamin Elson, 96–113. Norman: OK: Summer Institute of Linguistics.

Wheeler, Marcus. 1984. *Oxford Russian-English Dictionary*. New York: Oxford University Press.

Whisler, Ronald. 1992. *Phonological studies in four languages of Maluku*, edited by Donald Burquest & Wyn Laidig, 7–32. Arlington, Tex.: Summer Institute of Linguistics.

Whorf, Benjamin. 1946. The Hopi language, Toreva dialect. *Linguistic structures of Native America*, edited by Cornelius Osgood, 158–83. New York: Viking Fund Publications in Anthropology.

Wiedemann, F. J. 1964. *Syrjänisch-deutsches Wörterbuch, nebst einem wotjakisch-deutschen im Anhange und einem deutschen Register*. The Hague: Mouton.

Wiesemann, Ursula. 1972. *Die phonologische und grammatische Struktur der Kaingáng Sprache*. The Hague: Mouton.

Wightman, C.W., S. Shattuck-Hufnagel, M. Ostendorf & P.J. Price. 1992. Segmental durations in the vicinity of prosodic phrase boundaries. *Journal of the Acoustical Society of America* 92, 1707–17.

Willett, Thomas. 1991. *A reference grammar of Southeastern Tepehuan*. Dallas: Summer Institute of Linguistics.

Williamson, Kay. 1965. *A grammar of the Kolokuma dialect of Ijo*. Cambridge: Cambridge University Press.

Wilson, Peter. 1992. *Una descripción preliminar de la gramática del achagua (arawak)*. Bogotá: Asociación Instituto Lingüístico de Verano.

Wilson, Stephen. 1986. Metrical structure in Wakashan phonology. *Proceedings of the 12th Meeting of the Berkeley Linguistics Society*, 283–291.

Wimbish, Sandra. 1992. Pagu phonology. *Descriptive studies in languages of Maluku*, Vol. 34, edited by Donald Burquest & Wyn Laidig, 69–90. Jakarta: Badan Penyelenggara Seri Nusa, Universitas Katolik Indonesia Atma Java.

Windfuhr, Gernott. 1990. Persian. *The world's major languages*, edited by Bernard Comrie, 523–46. New York: Oxford.

Winfield, W.W. 1928. *A grammar of the Kui language*. Calcutta: Asiatic Society of Bengal.

Winstedt, Richard O. 1927. *Malay grammar*. Oxford: Oxford University Press.

Wolff, Ekkehard. 1983. *A grammar of the Lamang language*. Glückstadt: Verlag J.J. Augustin.

Wolff, Ekkehard. 1993. *Referenzgrammatik des Hausa: zur Begleitung des Fremdsprachenunterrichts und zur Einführung in das Selbststudium*. Munster: LIT.

Wolgemuth, Carl. 1981. *Gramática náhuatl de Mecayapan*. Verano: Instituto Lingüístico de Verano.

Wonderly, William. 1951. Zoque II: Phonemes and morphophonemes. *International Journal of American Linguistics* 17(2), 105–23.

Woo, Nancy. 1969. *Prosody and phonology*. MIT Ph.D. dissertation.

Woodbury, Anthony. 1981. *Study of the Chevak dialect of Central Alaskan Yupik*. UC Berkeley PhD. dissertation.

Woodbury, Anthony. 1985. Graded syllable weight in Central Alaskan Yupik Eskimo (Hooper Bay-Chevak). *International Journal of American Linguistics* 51, 620–3.

Woodbury, Anthony. 1987. Meaningful phonological processes: a consideration of Central Alaskan Yupik Eskimo prosody. *Language* 63, 685–740.

Woodbury, Anthony. 1989. Phrasing and intonational tonology in Central Alaskan Yupik Eskimo: some implications for linguistics in the field. *1988 Mid-America Linguistics Conference Papers*, 3–40.

Woollams, Geoff. 1966. *A grammar of Karo Batak, Sumatra*. Canberra: Australian National University.

Worth, Dean. 1969. *Dictionary of Western Kamchadal*. Berkeley: University of California Press.

Wright, Richard. 1996. Tone and accent in Oklahoma Cherokee. *Cherokee papers from UCLA*, 11–22. Los Angles: UCLA Department of Linguistics.

Wright, Richard & Peter Ladefoged. 1997. A phonetic study of Tsou. *Bulletin of the Institute of History and Philology* 68(4), 987–1028.

Wright, W. 1971. *A grammar of the Arabic language*. Cambridge: Cambridge University Press.

Wuolle, Aino. 1962. *Finnish-English dictionary*. Helsinki: Werner Söderström Osakeyhtiö.

Yadav, Ramawatar. 1984. *Maithili phonetics and phonology*. Mainz: Selden and Tamm.

Yip, Moira. 1995. Tone in East Asian languages. *Handbook of phonological theory*, edited by J. Goldsmith. Cambridge, Mass.: Blackwell.

Young, Linda Wai Ling. 1985. *Shan chrestomathy: an introduction to Tai Mau language and literature*. Lanham, MD: University Press of America.

Young, Robert & William Morgan. 1992. *Analytical lexicon of Navajo*. Albuquerque: University of New Mexico Press.

Young, Steven. 1991. *The prosodic structure of Lithuanian*. New York: University Press of America.

Yu, Alan. 2003. Some methodological issues in phonetic typology research: Cantonese contour tone revisited. *Berkeley Linguistics Society* 29, 623–634.

Zaitseva, Mariia Ivanova. 1972. *Slovar vepsskogo iazyka*. Leningrad: Nauka.

Zaitseva, Mariia Ivanova. 1981. *Grammatika vepsskogo iazyka: fonetika i morfologiia*. Leningrad: Nauka.

Zec, Draga. 1988. *Sonority constraints on prosodic structure*. Palo Alto, CA: Stanford University PhD dissertation. [Published by Garland 1994]

Zhang, Jie. 2002. *The effects of duration and sonority on contour tone distribution: typological survey and formal analysis*. New York: Routledge.

Zhgenti, Sergi. 1964. The Problem of Rhythmical Stress and Intonation Structure of the Georgian Language. *Zeitschrift fur Phonetik, Sprachwissenschaft und Kommunikationsforschung* 17, 357–368.

Zhirkov, L. I. 1955. *Lakskii iazyk: fonetika i morfologiia*. Moskva: Izdatelstvo Akademii Nauk.

Zhukova, A. N. 1967. *Russko-koriakskii slovar*. Moskva: Sovetskia entsikopediia.

Zhukova, A. N. 1972. *Grammatika koriakskogo iazyka: fonetika, morfologiia*. Leningrad: Izdatelstvo Nauka.

Zigmond, Maurice, Curtis Booth & Pamela Munro. 1991. *Kawaiisu: a grammar and dictionary with texts*. Berkeley: University of California Press.

Zoll, Cheryl. 1997. Conflicting directionality. *Phonology* 14(2), 263–286.

Index

Language Index